Issues in Green Criminology

Confronting harms against environments, humanity and other animals

Edited by

Piers Beirne and Nigel South

WILLAN
PUBLISHING

Published by

Willan Publishing
Culmcott House
Mill Street, Uffculme
Cullompton, Devon
EX15 3AT, UK
Tel: +44(0)1884 840337
Fax: +44(0)1884 840251
e-mail: info@willanpublishing.co.uk
website: www.willanpublishing.co.uk

Published simultaneously in the USA and Canada by

Willan Publishing
c/o ISBS, 920 NE 58th Ave, Suite 300,
Portland, Oregon 97213-3786, USA
Tel: +001(0)503 287 3093
Fax: +001(0)503 280 8832
e-mail: info@isbs.com
website: www.isbs.com

First published 2007

Reprinted 2009

Hardback
ISBN-13: 978-1-84392-220-9

Paperback
ISBN-13: 978-1-84392-219-3

British Library Cataloguing-in-Publication Data

A catalogue record for this book is available from the British Library

This book is printed on 100% recycled, acid-free paper

FSC

Mixed Sources
Product group from well-managed
forests and other controlled sources

Cert no. SGS-COC-2482
www.fsc.org
© 1996 Forest Stewardship Council

Typeset by GCS, Leighton Buzzard, Bedfordshire
Project managed by Deer Park Productions, Tavistock, Devon
Printed and bound by TJI Digital, Padstow, Cornwall

Contents

Preface and acknowledgements   *vii*
Contributors   *ix*

Introduction: approaching green criminology   *xiii*
Piers Beirne and Nigel South

Part I   Introduction to green criminology

1   Ecology, community and justice: the meaning of green   3
     Ted Benton

2   Green criminology and the pursuit of social and
     ecological justice   32
     Rob White

3   Animal rights, animal abuse and green criminology   55
     Piers Beirne

Part II Animal rights and animal abuse

4   Labelling animals: non-speciesist criminology
     and techniques to identify other animals   87
     Geertrui Cazaux

5   Vivisection: the case for abolition   114
     Tom Regan

6   Debating 'animal rights' online:
the movement–countermovement dialectic revisited   140
Roger Yates

Part III Ecological systems and environmental harms

7   'At risk': climate change and its bearing on
women's vulnerability to male violence   161
Sandra Wachholz

8   Crime, regulation and radioactive waste in the
United Kingdom   186
Reece Walters

9   Food crime   206
Hazel Croall

10   The 'corporate colonisation of nature': bio-prospecting,
bio-piracy and the development of green criminology   230
Nigel South

11   Green criminology in the United States   248
Michael J. Lynch and *Paul Stretesky*

12   Non-compliance in small-scale fisheries: a threat
to security?   270
Maria Hauck

Webliography   *290*
Index   *301*

Preface and acknowledgements

Issues in Criminology: confronting harms against environments, humanity and other animals is a book of original essays. Its authors originate from and/or are based in Australia, Belgium, England, New Zealand, Scotland, South Africa, the United States and Wales. Its 12 chapters explore the myriad ways in which governments, transnational corporations, military apparatuses and ordinary people going about their everyday lives routinely harm environments, humanity and other animals. We hope that the book will have a broad audience not only in colleges and universities but also among activists in the environmental and animal rights movements. It is, we believe, long overdue.

We are indebted, first and foremost, to the colleagues and comrades who appear with us as green authors between these covers. In every case their work, either in the academic community or in day-to-day struggles for environmental justice and animal rights or both, has been a constant source of inspiration. Each of the authors responded in timely fashion and more or less cheerfully to our begging invitations to write and contribute a specific chapter on their area of expertise. Working with them through to the completion of their chapters has been a genuine source of pleasure for both of us.

During the past decade all of the contributors to this book – or nearly so – have read each other's work, especially in the pages of the journals *Theoretical Criminology* and *Society & Animals*. In the last two or three years most of us have presented papers on the same green panels at professional academic conferences. Given this good fellowship, if we as editors continue to insist on not seeing the wood for the trees, so to speak, it is not our colleagues' fault but ours alone.

Many others also helped us along the way. Steve Tombs and two anonymous reviewers wrote challenging yet helpfully flattering comments about our book proposal to our would-be publisher. Brian Willan, our main contact at Willan Publishing, has been a model of patience. At every twist and turn he has offered encouragement, not least with his generous commitment to produce this book on 100 per cent, acid-free recycled paper. Many thanks, too, to Michelle Antrobus, our production editor at Willan, for her care and thoroughness. Ken Shapiro, Ray Michalowski, Chris Powell, Rosemary Miller and Rebecca Grotton managed, in quite different ways and at usually just the right moments, to steer us away from some rocky hazards. Ed Friedman, Kathleen McGee, Jason Ditton, Furzana Khan and, especially, Gerry and Simon very gracefully offered their friendship and advice when it seemed to be needed (and sometimes when it didn't), as also did Livvy, Bozz, Daisy-the-good-listener and Lydia. Jules Pretty and Colin Samson have been influential in ways they may not realise, while Alison and Daniel know very well how important their support and advice have been. Thanks to one and all!

While we're at it, finally, we may as well acknowledge and thank each other. Roughly 10 years after our initial contact, after sustained correspondence and after jointly editing three collections of green criminology, we met face to face and hand to glass for the first time in July, 2006. The Spanish Tapas Bar, the Red Lion, the Wivenhoe riverside and a country walk all therefore deserve a special mention.

Piers Beirne and Nigel South
December, 2006

Contributors

PIERS BEIRNE is Professor of Sociology and Legal Studies in the Department of Criminology, University of Southern Maine. He is the founding co-editor (with Colin Sumner) of the journal *Theoretical Criminology* and author of *Inventing Criminology: Essays on the Rise of 'Homo Criminalis'*. If he is not working on his book *Confronting Animal Abuse*, it might be because he is still trying, unsuccessfully, to play traditional Irish music on his fiddle.

TED BENTON is Professor of Sociology at the University of Essex. He is the author of numerous books and articles on sociological theory and ecological issues, most notably *Natural Relations* and *The Greening of Marxism (Democracy and Ecology)*. He is actively involved in the process of bringing together groupings on the green left in the UK.

GEERTRUI CAZAUX received her Ph.D. in Criminology from the University of Ghent (Belgium 2002) on *Anthropocentrism and Speciesism in Contemporary Criminology*. She edited *Mensen en Andere Dieren* (Garant 2001), the first Flemish-based reader on relations between humans and other animals. She currently works in youth welfare work and takes care of donkeys and other animals at home.

HAZEL CROALL is Professor of Criminology at Glasgow Caledonian University, where she has been responsible for developing an undergraduate programme in criminology. She has authored and co-authored texts on criminal justice and criminology and has published widely in the area of white-collar and corporate crime, including *Understanding White-Collar Crime* for Open University Press.

MARIA HAUCK is a senior researcher at the Environmental Evaluation Unit, University of Cape Town, South Africa. She has spent the past decade researching fisheries compliance and governance in South Africa. She has co-edited two publications: *Waves of Change: Coastal and Fisheries Co-management in South Africa* (2003) and *Fisheries Reform in South Africa 1994–2004* (*Marine Policy* special issue, 2006).

MICHAEL J. LYNCH is Professor of Criminology at the University of South Florida with research interests in environmental law, crime and justice; racial bias in the criminal justice process; and radical criminology. His recent books include *Primer in Radical Criminology* (4th edition 2006, with R. J. Michalowski), and *Environmental Crime: A Sourcebook* (2004, with R.G. Burns).

TOM REGAN is Emeritus Professor of Philosophy, North Carolina State University, where he received the William Quarles Holloday Medal, the highest honour the university can bestow on one of its faculty. Among his more than 20 books are *The Case for Animal Rights* (1983) and *Empty Cages: Facing the Challenge of Animal Rights* (2004).

NIGEL SOUTH is Professor in the Department of Sociology, University of Essex. He has teaching and research interests in criminology, drug use, and health and environmental issues and is currently a Pro-Vice Chancellor (Academic Development) at the University of Essex and a member of the Royal Society of Arts' *Commission of Inquiry into Illegal Drugs, Communities and Public Policy*.

PAUL STRETESKY is an Associate Professor of Sociology at Colorado State University – Fort Collins. His research on environmental crime and justice has appeared in journals in several disciplines. He has recently completed a two-year grant provided by the U.S. Environmental Protection Agency on self-policing environmental compliance policies.

SANDRA WACHHOLZ received her Ph.D. from the Criminal Justice Center at Sam Houston State University in Huntsville, Texas. She teaches criminology at the University of Southern Maine. Her research focuses on barriers to justice for abused immigrant women, hate crimes against the homeless, and climate change. She complements her academic work with involvement in social justice organisations.

REECE WALTERS is a Professor in Criminology at the Open University in England. He has also worked at universities in Scotland, Australia and New Zealand. He has published three books, including *Deviant Knowledge: Politics, Policy and Practice* and will soon publish his fourth book on *Eco-Crime, Political Economy and Genetically Modified Food*. He has also published widely on crimes of the powerful and juvenile justice. His current research focuses on eco-crime with specific reference to crimes involving food and waste.

ROB WHITE is Professor of Sociology at the University of Tasmania. He has research, scholarly and practical interests in areas such as juvenile justice, crime prevention, youth studies, corrections, and green criminology. Recent books include *Crime and Society; Crime and Social Control; Juvenile Justice: Youth and Crime in Australia; Crime and Criminology;* and *Youth and Society* (all with Oxford University Press) and *Controversies in Environmental Sociology* (with Cambridge University Press). He has written about environmental trends and regulation from the viewpoints of political economy, eco-philosophy, theoretical frameworks and legal issues.

ROGER YATES completed his doctoral thesis on human–nonhuman relations in 2004, following more than a decade working in the animal protection movement. He teaches undergraduate courses on social movements and protest, critical theory and the sociology of humour at the University of Wales, Bangor. He is currently examining the relationship between theoreticians as producers of ideas and social movement activists as producers of action.

Introduction: approaching green criminology

Piers Beirne and Nigel South

[T]he addiction to beef that is characteristic of people in the industrialized countries is not only a moral atrocity for animals but also causes health problems for consumers, reduces grain supplies for the poor, precipitates social divisions in developing countries, contributes to climate change, leads to the conversion of forests to pasture lands, is a causal factor in overgrazing, and is implicated in the destruction of native plants and animals.

Dale Jamieson (2002: 46) *Morality's Progress*

Though the movements in green environmentalism and in animal rights arose at about the same time, in the early to mid-1960s, only quite recently have they explicitly started to forge a common agenda.[1] This book reflects such convergence and its contents represent a major step in the direction of a green criminology.

What do we mean by the term 'green criminology'? At its most abstract level, green criminology refers to the study of those harms against humanity, against the environment (including space) and against non-human animals committed both by powerful institutions (e.g. governments, transnational corporations, military apparatuses) and also by ordinary people. Like most abstractions, of course, this one invites more questions than it was designed to answer. For example, it is often analytically difficult to disentangle environmental harms from the abuse of non-human animals (henceforth, 'animals'). Animals of course live in environments, and their own well-being

– physical, emotional, psychological – is absolutely and intimately linked to the health and good standing of their environments.

The forms of these 'green harms' are numerous and their financial costs alone are staggeringly large.[2] They range from the everyday to the exceptional. Green harms include the abuse and exploitation of ecological systems, including animal life; corporate disregard for damage to land, air and water quality; profiteering from trades and practices that destroy lives and which leave a legacy of damage for subsequent generations; military actions in war that adversely affect the environment and animals; new challenges to international treaties and to the emerging field of bio-ethics, such as bio-piracy; illicit markets in nuclear materials; and legal monopolisation of natural resources (e.g. privatisation of water, patenting of natural products, etc.) leading to divisions between the resource rich and the resource impoverished and the prospects of new forms of conflict, harm, injury, damage and crime. They include, also, individual acts of cruelty to animals and the institutional, socially-acceptable human domination of animals in agribusiness, in slaughterhouses and abattoirs, in so-called scientific experimentation and, in less obviously direct ways, in sports, colleges and schools, zoos, aquaria and circuses.

Although the term conceals numerous general and local problems, we believe that, expressed this simply as a harm-based discourse, green criminology will be seen as a welcome addition to existing critical, democratic and left-oriented perspectives on crime and social harm. Like these allied criminologies, green criminology begins by problematising the nature of crime: how is it defined, by whom and with what purpose(s) and effects? Which harms are defined as crimes? Which are not? Which harms are defined as both harmful and criminal? Which are defined as neither? As such, our view is that green criminology should be a harm-based discourse that addresses violations of what some have variously termed environmental morality, environmental ethics, and animal rights. It will try to uncover relevant sources and forms of power, including the state's willingness or reluctance to construct certain forms of harm as crimes, as well as social inequalities and their ill effects. The authors in this volume make significant contributions to the development of this relatively new field by generating theory and debate and offering important and informative case studies that will help to build up the agenda for future work.

The 12 chapters of the book are organised in three *Parts*, as follows.

Part I Introduction to green criminology

In combination the first three chapters in *Part I* provide a broad introduction to a green criminology. In essence, they introduce discussions about the meaning of green and green politics, concepts of environmental and ecological justice and animal rights and speciesism. In its own way each chapter confronts, too, some of the cumbersome baggage associated with these concepts.

In Chapter 1 ('Ecology, community and justice: the meaning of green') Ted Benton provides us with a careful analysis of four features of social and political thought associated with the green movement, including consideration of animal rights and welfare movements. Of course, he reminds us, these differing directions of green thought pose several problems in formulating proposals about justice and contemporary green movements. At the same time, Benton argues, considerations of justice also pose a challenge to at least some versions of green social and political thought.

Benton's chapter may be read in a number of ways and from a variety of vantage points. It may be seen, for example, as an introduction to and/or as an overview of the numerous green issues that are displayed more-or-less consciously and with differing degrees of assurance in all the other chapters. In this respect, it also operates as a yardstick of sorts. As a concluding agenda for his own essay – and an agenda for this collection as a whole – Benton offers a provisional 'list of conditions' that global society would have to meet in order to make any progress towards what he terms 'green justice'.

In Chapter 2 ('Green criminology and the pursuit of social and ecological justice') Rob White argues that those environmental and ecological harms that are criminalised, by and large, reflect an anthropocentric (or human-centred) perspective. White considers the complexities and conflicts associated with efforts to develop notions of ecological citizenship and eco-human rights that include consideration of both human and ecological systems. A key thematic concern of the chapter is the problematic nature of how best to move from abstract pro-environment principles to making concrete decisions about matters that involve conflicts over rights.

Explicit rights talk is, of course not – or *not yet* – the normal discourse of pro-environmental groups but of those of the animal protection community (but see Revkin 2004). In Chapter 3 ('Animal rights, animal abuse and green criminology'), therefore, Piers Beirne offers an overview of the intersection of animal rights theory with existing green criminology. Suggesting that some of the major concerns of the one can illuminate and extend those of the other, the chapter tries to develop a space within green criminology for the rights of non-human animals. Behind Beirne's chapter lurks a number of thorny questions. How do animals differ from humans? Are the interests of animals in avoiding pain of the same sort as those of humans? Are the grounds for not abusing animals the same as those for not abusing humans?

Part II   Animal rights and animal abuse
Each of the three chapters in *Part II* subscribes to a strong version of animal rights theory. Though that theory is not necessarily explicit on every page of these chapters, it is employed throughout by the authors in their respective studies of how humans abuse animals through their techniques of identifying them, in the various forms of vivisection, and in the harmful images of them that are circulated online.

In Chapter 4 ('Labelling animals: non-speciesist criminology and techniques to identify other animals'), Geertrui Cazaux identifies certain techniques that are employed to identify or label animals, such as branding, tattooing, ear tagging, radio collaring, amputating toes and using transponders. In so doing, in a creative and original way, she examines the impact of these techniques on animal welfare and explores parallels between them and the identification of humans and their relevance to concepts such as unnecessary suffering and colonisation.

Like the authors of the other chapters in *Issues in Green Criminology*, Cazaux also has her mind set firmly on the likely development of green criminology. In an assessment rich with insight she writes that

> it is imperative that we see the body of green criminology as more than just a topic-widening to include 'greenish' issues. Direct or indirect human victimisation through pollution, fragmentation or other infringements of the environment should not be the assembling smithery of a green criminology. If green criminology fails to integrate the impacts of such processes beyond the human-centred criterion of victimisation, it will be no more than just another horizontal broadening. Although we humans cannot escape epistemological anthropocentrism in the way we look at the world and describe others and our surroundings, the growing body of both animal ethics and environmental ethics has given us ample incentives to break through and transcend a normative anthropocentrism. In this way, green criminology can truly turn out to be a vertical breakthrough in criminological research (this volume: 88).

In Chapter 5 Tom Regan defends and explains his longstanding opposition to vivisection ('Vivisection: the case for abolition'). A moral philosopher whose ideas about animal rights exert unparalleled influence in the anglophone world and beyond, Regan limits his discussion of vivisection to harmful, non-therapeutic experimentation using non-human animals. Though his discussion is largely illustrated with types of vivisection in the United States, there is no good reason to think, he says, that the culture of vivisection is much different anywhere else.

With the relentless logic to be expected from the author of *The Case for Animal Rights*, Regan methodically dismantles the misleading views of vivisection's defenders and upsets the scales of those who seek a rational balance between the supposed costs and benefits of vivisection. He argues, too, that the evil that vivisection represents is quite beyond regulation or reform. The only adequate moral response to vivisection, he therefore concludes, is its complete abolition.

In Chapter 6 ('Debating "animal rights" online: The movement–countermovement dialectic') Roger Yates examines the antagonistic dynamics of the public marketplace of competing images of human–animal relationships. He begins with the commanding role of animal-user industries. How do those industries' harmful images of animals and of human–animal interaction tend to hold sway? To the point, why does this happen, given the committed opposition of the pro-animal movement to harms against animals?

With this question in mind, Yates then explores the extent to which the general public, pet owners, dog show advocates, and other 'pro-use' interests, learn and recycle countermovement message(s) about the theories of change and their advocates. Do the arguments laid out by countermovements act as 'scripts' to aid those who oppose the ideas of the pro-animal movement? Using the avenue of social constructionism, Yates investigates the movement–countermovement dialectic with data he gathered from the public on-line forum 'Animal Rights Debate'.

Part III   Ecological systems and environmental harms
The six chapters in *Part III* each maintain the concern with a harm-based approach. Each aims to explore not only the obvious and primary issues at stake in their area of interest but also the hidden and neglected but no less important matters. The concerns of these chapters range from the global, for example, under-examined social consequences of climate change and transnational trade in genetic resources, to the national and local, for example, cases of environmental injustices in the U.S. and in South Africa.

Although criminologists have examined correlations between weather patterns and opportunity crime, for example, the wider significance of both weather events and natural disasters as sources of influence and stress regarding violence and other crimes has been neglected. In Chapter 7 ('At risk: climate change and its bearing on women's vulnerability to male violence') Sandra Wachholz reviews various studies and agency reports that examine levels of violence against women after slow and sudden-onset climate-related natural disasters. She argues that the predicted rise in natural disasters tied to climate change is likely to be correlated with increases in violence against women within the regions that experience extreme weather events. In doing so, Wachholz emphasises why the gender-differentiated impacts of climate change should be included within the emerging discourses in green criminology.

In Chapter 8 ('Crime, regulation and radioactive waste in the United Kingdom') Reece Walters provides a critique of the relationship between science, policy and law in the formulation of strategies for the long-term management of radioactive waste in the UK. In so doing he revisits the question 'What do criminology and criminologists do to decrease the chances of the extinction of mankind and the destruction of the planet?' (Harding 1983: 82). As a result, this chapter aims to shift the criminological debate to include harms of ecological and global significance. Walters argues that emerging discourses in eco-crime and green criminology that contribute to what could be termed 'global criminology' provide useful pathways into the identification and critique of actions that adversely affect nature and humanity.

Walters also alerts us to issues of topical importance regarding future choices about energy policy. We are dependent on complex energy production systems that carry inevitable environmental consequences and raise vital questions. The same applies to our dependence on equally complex bio-social production systems and, in the next two chapters, Hazel Croall and then Nigel South focus on case examples.

In Chapter 9 ('Food crime') Hazel Croall reports on how crimes including fraud, adulteration and misrepresenting the contents, origins or quality of food products are present throughout the food chain. They can be part of global and transnational criminal or legitimate industries with perpetrators ranging from multinational food-producing corporations, supermarkets and organised criminal enterprises, to small shopkeepers, farmers, restaurateurs and market traders selling the products of local cottage industries. Consumer victims can suffer food poisoning, ill health or injury as a result of food consumption and can be cheated and misled about its contents. Food production also involves harms to workers, non-human animals and the environment. Although the subject of recurrent 'food scandals' (for example, BSE, E.coli and, more recently, Sudan1), crimes involving food have received little attention within criminology, raising a number of questions. Should there be a category of 'food crime'? What might such a category consist of? How is it regulated? Is it to be considered as a form of organised or corporate crime? Can its analysis be furthered by the growth of a 'green criminology'?

In Chapter 10 ('The "corporate colonisation of nature": bio-prospecting, bio-piracy and the development of green criminology') Nigel South addresses how green criminology can be brought to bear on injustices and controversies that arise from the chain of discovery, exploitation and production of various goods that – as in the case of Croall's food chain – end up on the shelves of supermarkets. In the case of both pharmaceutical and bio-agricultural multinational corporations, the questions of the origins and ownership of profitable products derived from plant, animal or human life in the developing world are increasingly contested with accusations of bio-piracy levelled at them. Both the rise of intellectual property rights and the modern mobilities of ideas, knowledge, people and objects across global economies play key roles here.

In Chapter 11 ('Green criminology in the United States') Michael Lynch and Paul Stretesky argue that traditional criminology fails to take the environmentally destructive behaviour of corporations seriously. The authors provide an overview of green criminology in the U.S. that complements other chapters in this volume, exploring eco-critical criminology and the environmental justice approach. It is particularly valuable that these authors also apply their methodical approach to scientific data in exposing the widespread and damaging but underreported nature of toxic crimes and crimes against non-human animals. Linking the levels of political economy and the life chances of the individual, the authors show how the health of the economy will be favoured over healthy environmental conditions.

Much green criminological work has so far focused on Europe, North America and Australia. The next chapter provides a case study from South Africa. In Chapter 12 ('Non-compliance in small-scale fisheries: a threat to security?'), Maria Hauck develops work based on a fruitful interdisciplinary engagement between criminology and marine biology. Hauck explores the nature and complexity of small-scale fisheries' non-compliance with environmental law and regulations in South Africa. In this context, adopting a 'green criminology' perspective has meant the bridging of disciplines to understand how law is defined and by whom, and the exploration of the intricacies between the social, political, economic and institutional dynamics of the defined environmental 'crime'. At the heart of her research is Hauck's recognition of the need to move beyond a traditional understanding of what is considered 'illegal' and beyond traditional approaches to regulating the environment.

In combination the chapters in this book aim to provide, if not a manifesto, then at least a significant resource for thinking about green criminology. It offers a set of introductions and a variety of current and new directions, wide-ranging in scope and international in terms of coverage and contributors. Almost needless to say, we do not see the collection of essays in *Issues in Green Criminology* as a definitive work. They are, instead, focused discussions of current and cutting-edge issues that will influence the emergence of a coherent perspective on green issues.

We expect that green criminology will continue to investigate the generation and control of the many dimensions of harm to environments, ecological systems and animal species. We expect, too, that it will prove capable of identifying and investigating an expanding agenda of harms whose new forms will doubtless include, though not be limited to, exploitation, modes of discrimination and disempowerment, degradation, abuse, exclusion, pain, injury, loss and suffering. Straddling and intersecting these many forms of harm are key concepts for a green criminology such as gender inequalities, racism, dominionism and speciesism, classism, the north/south divide, the accountability of science, and the ethics of global capitalist expansion. Green criminology has the potential to provide not only a different way of examining and making sense of various forms of crime and control responses (some well known, others less so) but can also make explicable much wider connections that are not generally well understood. As all societies face up to the need to confront harms against environments, humanity and other animals, criminology will have a major role to play.

Notes

1   Some of the key theoretical landmarks and the relevant pathways in the split between the respective ethics and goals of the environmental movement and animal rights can be found in Callicott (1980, 1985, 1989), Regan (1981) and Jamieson (1998, 2002). For a satisfying recent synthesis, especially relevant to our concerns here as it addresses the numerous intersecting sites of environmental histories and the emerging interdisciplinary field of human–animal studies, see also Ritvo (2004).

2   While not implying on our part any necessary priority in the logic and type of measurement, the findings of a recent editorial in *Environmental Health Perspectives* (Editorial 2004) deserve mention. This estimates that (*ibid*: A80):

> As far as we know, the total value of the major forms of international environmental crime – illegal logging and fishing, illegal trade in wildlife and in ozone-depleting substances, and illegal dumping in hazardous waste – may be on the order of $20–40 billion a year, about 5–10 per cent of the size of the global drug trade. Compared to the 'war on drugs' however, the resources and political will that are being devoted to tackling the problems of international environmental crime are derisory; yet, also unlike the drug trade, they threaten every citizen of the world.

References

Callicott, J.B. (1980, 1989) 'Animal Liberation: A Triangular Affair', reprinted in pp. 15–8 of Callicott *In Defense of the Land Ethic: Essays in Environmental Philosophy*. Albany, NY: State University of New York Press.

Callicott, J.B. (1985) 'Review of Tom Regan, *The Case for Animal Rights*', *Environmental Ethics*, 7: 365–72.

Callicott, J.B. (1989) 'Animal Liberation and Environmental Ethics: Back Together Again', pp. 49–59 in Callicott, *In Defense of the Land Ethic: Essays in Environmental Philosophy*. Albany, NY: State University of New York Press.

Editorial (2004) *Environmental Health Perspectives*, p. A80.

Harding, R. (1983) 'Nuclear Energy and the Destiny of Mankind – Some Criminological Perspectives', *Australian and New Zealand Journal of Criminology*, 16: 81–92.

Jamieson, D. (1998) 'Animal Liberation is an Environmental Ethic', *Environmental Values*, 7 November: 41–57.

Jamieson, D. (2002) *Morality's Progress: Essays on Humans, Other Animals, and the Rest of Nature*. Oxford: Clarendon Press.

Regan, T. (1981) 'The Nature and Possibility of an Environmental Ethic', *Environmental Ethics*, 3: 19–34.

Regan, T. (1983) *The Case for Animal Rights*. Berkeley, CA: University of California Press.

Revkin, A. (2004) 'Eskimos Seek to Recast Global Warming as a Rights Issue', *New York Times*, 15 December: pp. A3–A4.

Ritvo, H. (2004) 'Animal Planet', *Environmental History*, 9(2): 204–220.

Part I

Introduction to green criminology

Chapter I

Ecology, community and justice: the meaning of green

Ted Benton

The focus of this chapter is on the implications of the new green agenda for one concept in particular albeit a very broad one: that of social justice. Historically, of course, the idea of justice is a contested one, and this contest itself is one field of contemporary political dispute. Because my aim is a wide and programmatic one, I shall not engage in detailed analytical treatment of rival philosophical positions on justice. Instead I will draw upon and comment upon several views of justice, both as they have been articulated in political philosophy, and as they exist in 'common sense' political thought and institutional politics. One important 'broad brush' contrast I shall draw upon is that between formal theories of justice, generally derived from 'first principles' (often associated with liberalism, but sometimes yielding unmistakably socialist implications), and 'communitarian' views of justice which at least claim the status of articulations of the normative commitments of actual moral communities. The work of the American political theorist John Rawls (Rawls 1971) has been astonishingly influential in academic discussion of the concept of justice for more than three decades. So, where names are mentioned, Rawls will be the exemplar of formal theories of justice.

I will begin with four features of the social and political thought which have arisen in association with the green movement. For my purposes in this context, it makes sense to include the thinking of the animal rights and welfare movements as integral to the 'green challenge', though in other respects these movements are quite distinct from each other. I then go on to explore how each of these four features of green thought poses problems for ways of thinking about justice developed (largely) independently of and prior to the rise of contemporary green movements. The main drift of the argument in each case will be that green issues do pose deep and serious questions for established views of justice. However, it will also be noted that considerations of justice also pose a challenge to at least some versions of green social and political thought.

The green challenge

There are four aspects of the social thought associated with the green and animal liberation movements which are especially challenging to pre-existing conceptions of justice. These include both cognitive claims and innovative value-orientations. They are:

1 *Natural limits*. Humans are held to be dependent on ecological 'life-support systems' which impose outer limits on the scope and scale of human activity in relation to the rest of nature. This is often supplemented by a second claim: that extrapolation of current growth trends (in population and/or resource use, pollution, CO_2 emissions, etc.) into the future predicts exceeding natural limits, and consequent catastrophic collapse. The urgency of tackling these growth trends may override other deeply held moral or practical considerations.

2 *Human/animal continuity*. Since Darwin, this has been the ruling orthodoxy in the life-sciences. The claim is that our species evolved from some ape-like ancestor as a result of the operation of broadly similar mechanisms to those which gave rise to other species. It follows that other animal species are our more-or-less distant kin. This basic evolutionary claim can be complemented by subsequent ecological and ethological research to yield two further, but more scientifically contentious, general claims:

a that (many) other animal species have a range of capacities for social interaction, emotional expression, communication, and puzzle-solving, and are vulnerable to associated sources of suffering in ways which differ from but are comparable with those experienced by humans; and
b that the first claim under 1 above is but a special case of the ecological 'embedding' of all animal species.

3 *Non-anthropocentric values.* Greens proclaim an innovation in values which marks a qualitative break from all previous Western thought. This innovation is expressed through a variety of different polarities (ecologism/environmentalism; ecocentrism/technocentrism; deep/ shallow; biocentrism/anthropocentrism and others), but the core claim is that the non-human world, or parts of it, have value in themselves, independently of their capacity to serve some human purpose. Green thinkers also sometimes claim that substantive normative principles can be derived from nature, or from ecological characterisations of it. A separate but related move is made by animal liberationists who use human/animal continuity to justify extending the scope of received anthropocentric moral theories (mainly rights theory and utilitarianism) beyond the boundaries of the human species.

4 *Ecotopia.* Distinctively green visions of the 'good life' are rarely spelled out in terms of detailed institutional forms, but from such speculations as exist, from attempts at actual communal living inspired by green ideas, and from the various 'platforms' and statements of principles issued by radical ecologists we can reconstruct a cluster of widely shared themes and preferences. The green society would be one in which:

a humans would live in ways which minimally disrupt the rest of nature;
b decision-making would be decentralised to small, self-sufficient and self-governing communities;
c self-government would take the form of active, or participatory democracy;
d either as a separate principle, or as a consequence of the above, these self-governing communities would be radically egalitarian, or 'non-hierarchical';
e the purposes of individual and collective life would give priority to aesthetic, spiritual and convivial sources of fulfilment, as against the 'materialist' pursuit of material acquisition and competitive advantage; and
f work to meet basic physical needs would be intrinsically fulfilling, and employ tools appropriate to small-scale egalitarian communities and to ecologically sustainable production and consumption.

Social justice and the green challenge

I now explore some of the implications of these features of green thinking for views of justice which have been for the most part developed independently of, and prior to, green thought in its present form.

Natural limits and social justice

Taken together, the claims that there are natural limits and that current growth trends are carrying us beyond them towards catastrophe can be used to justify 'going beyond' – or displacing – concern with social justice in two distinct ways. One argument is that urgent action to secure human (and natural) survival overrides other values. Implicit in this is a widely shared notion of a hierarchy of needs or values, in which survival is the first priority, followed by emotional security, and then 'higher' considerations of aesthetics and 'self-actualisation'. On the 'survivalist' view, it may be necessary to assign authoritarian powers to governments to secure reductions in population growth, or restrict the ecologically significant uses of certain private as well as common property and open-access resources in order to protect the environment.

A powerful objection to this way of thinking is to ask why survival is accorded such a high priority. Clearly, there are widely praised and widely condemned acts of self-sacrifice in which war heroes or terrorists willingly die for values or purposes which they presumably set higher than their own survival. It may be retorted that such cases are in one way or another exceptional, and inappropriate to set standards for the rest of humanity, for whom survival is the overriding consideration. However, it still seems relevant to ask what, for the great majority of us not given to ultimate acts of supererogation, is the point of 'bare' survival? Survival, I submit, is of value to us solely in virtue of the purposes and experiences it makes possible. Mere survival under increasingly authoritarian rule, deprived of access to meaningful engagement with the rest of nature, let alone to basic material conditions of healthy life, presents a severe limit to those valued purposes and experiences. So, to override all other values in order to secure survival would be perverse. It would be to destroy, or severely limit, whatever made survival a valued aim in the first place.

The second line of argument derives from the 'catastrophist' prediction. This is the 'delayed gratification' argument. It relies on the same hierarchy of values and needs as does the first survivalist argument, but the urgency of the ecological crisis is held to be such that if we fail to address it now, we will lose the opportunity to realise other values. This was the core of Rudolph Bahro's early (1982) call for socialists to give priority to the ecological question: there could be no prospect for socialism unless urgent action were taken to secure survival! Although, in Bahro's case, there was a convenient complementary argument to the effect that the objectives of the greens could only be met by the overthrow of capitalism (which Bahro at that time took to be equivalent to a transition to socialism), there remained a certain echo of earlier postponements until 'after the revolution'.

Another example is that of the influential environmentalist James Lovelock (2006) who has argued strongly for a turn to nuclear energy in response to the urgency of the prospect of catastrophic climate change. His argument is no simple 'survivalist' one: indeed, he denounces 'ecofascism' and warns that we 'may be unable to prevent a global decline into a chaotic world ruled by brutal warlords on a devastated earth' (2006: 154). His alternative is to retreat into a defensive strategy based on the nation state, and aimed at the preservation of 'civilisation':

> In several ways we are at war with Gaia, and to survive with our civilization intact we urgently need to make a just peace with Gaia ... Can the present-day democracies, with their noisy media and special interest lobbies, act fast enough for an effective defence against Gaia? We may need restrictions, rationing and the call to service that were familiar in wartime and in addition suffer for a while loss of freedom. We will need a small permanent group of strategists who, as in wartime, will try to out-think our Earthly enemy and be ready for the surprises bound to come. (*ibid:* 153)

There is no direct answer to the question whether our 'present-day democracies' will be able to act fast enough, but what follows strongly suggests not: restrictions, loss of freedom, and a 'permanent' group of strategists. The authoritarian drift is evident elsewhere, as in this comment on fellow environmentalists:

> My feelings about modern environmentalism are more parallel with those that might pass through the mind of the head-mistress of an inner-city school or the colonel of a newly formed

7

> regiment of licentious and naturally disobedient young men:
> how the hell can these unruly charges be disciplined and made
> effective? (*ibid:* 140)

Lovelock's concept of 'Gaia' refers to the immensely complex
web of physical, chemical and biological interactions that sustains
life on planet earth. Though the idea has scientific pretensions,
Lovelock concedes that the concept works as metaphor. In his more
freely metaphorical uses of the term, it represents the planetary system
as a nurturing mother, upon whom we are all wholly dependent,
but also as a fragile and vulnerable friend whom we are at risk
of destroying, and, yet again, as a sternly disciplining father, who
becomes a deadly enemy when abused. It is the last of these that is
foremost in the quotation above.

Lovelock's argument poses a serious challenge: if the threat posed
by escalating demands on the natural world is as dire as current
evidence suggests, are there not strong grounds for abandoning, at
least temporarily, cherished social and political values in the effort
to offset impending catastrophe? The parallels between this style
of argument and current arguments for restriction of civil liberties
in the face of a new kind of terrorist threat are noteworthy. One
key reason for resisting them is that the forms of power relation
which are tolerated to address what is seen as an emergency have
a habit of persisting as a long-term obstacle to the realisation of the
promised values. This is commonly acknowledged as an objection
to 'vanguardist' strategies on the left, but it applies equally well to
a certain style of ecological alarmist politics, which is prepared to
countenance extensions of state power without serious consideration
of the consequences for other social and political values.

A second reason for, at least, healthy scepticism about such
arguments is that they are very convenient for already powerful
institutions that seek to enhance their power and limit the capacity of
popular movements to mount effective resistance. It is arguable that
Western rulers have 'talked up' the threat of global terrorism both in
a bid to secure public legitimacy for aggressive foreign policies, and
to justify erosion of democratic and civil liberties. Could the same
be said of current alarmism in official circles about the ecological
threat – most notably global climate change? It seems to me that
here the analogy breaks down. The growing international scientific
consensus about the link between greenhouse gas emissions and
climate change is in many respects a deeply uncomfortable one
for Western governments and economic élites. The restraints on

environmentally significant production and consumption that would be called for in any serious attempt to deal with the issue would not only be deeply unpopular with electorates, but would also cut against the interests of key business sectors with powerful political lobbies.

I have argued elsewhere (Benton 1989) that ecological limits are a function of the specific articulation of socio-economic forms with their ecological conditions and media. If this argument is right, we cannot establish 'limits' in abstraction from social relations and processes. It follows from this that the kinds of 'physicalist' modelling that have been the main basis for the 'limits to growth' argument are inappropriate. It is at least theoretically possible that new technologies and forms of social organisation, some of which may be in principle unpredictable, may enable continued growth in agricultural production, industrialisation, population and so on without global catastrophe. This sort of counter-argument to the strong 'limits' position is the basis for more moderate forms of environmentalism which go by such names as 'sustainable development' and 'environmental modernisation'.

However, it does not follow that such positions are either coherent or practically feasible. The argument that 'limits' should be theorised in ways which take account of the relationship of social practices to their material conditions and consequences does not do away with the concept of ecological limits as such – it rather relativises them to specific socio-economic and technical relations and dynamics. Whether currently prevailing power relations and economic structures are capable of being reformed to render them ecologically 'sustainable', and what would be the consequences of such reforms for other values and purposes, remains very much open to question. A strong tradition of ecological Marxist and radical political economy maintains that capitalism has an intrinsic growth dynamic that renders it inherently unsustainable (for example, see O'Connor 1994). By contrast, 'ecological contrarians', 'ecological modernisers' and former radical greens hold that modern capitalism either has a long-term tendency to cleaner technology or can be rendered sustainable by appropriate political action (see Lomborg 2001; Mol and Sonnenfeld 2000; Porritt 2005).

Nevertheless, the notion of sustainable development, in almost all its versions, is sharply opposed to 'survivalism'. Considerations of social justice, especially, are integral to virtually all influential definitions. There are two reasons for this. First, an empirical case can be made out that distributional inequalities are *causally responsible* for a great deal

9

of environmental degradation. Reducing inequalities, especially by empowering women and reducing rural poverty in the 'third world' is often held to be a necessary *means* of achieving sustainability. Second, most advocates of sustainable development include socio-political objectives in their view of 'development' – it is held to mean more than mere continued or accelerated economic growth. So justice is a part of the *content* of 'sustainable development' as a social, economic and political strategy: both justice as between rich and poor in the present, and as between present and future generations.

However, giving weight to considerations of justice in the context of sustainability poses a significant challenge to established ways of thinking in several respects. The first is the practical challenge that the global context in which the concept of sustainable development has emerged is one in which the agencies charged with developing strategies for implementing it generally lack either the will or the power and resources to do so. The current dominance of neo-liberal ideology and its associated institutional framework for regulating international trade and investment runs directly counter to the imposition of normative restraints on economic activity.

But also at the level of national government policy, the objectives of sustainable development are radically at odds with established ways of legitimating economic inequalities. Economic growth – albeit unevenly distributed in both time and space – is intrinsic to capitalist forms of economic organisation. There is also now a widespread acknowledgement that unrestrained capitalist growth tends to widen the gap between rich and poor. However, inequalities as such are not necessarily incompatible with justice according to the widely influential account given by Rawls. According to his 'difference principle', inequalities can be justified if the state of affairs in which they occur is one in which those who are least well off are still better off than they would be under any other arrangement. According to the 'trickle down' model associated with the New Right, unrestrained economic growth produces just this outcome: the gap between rich and poor may be widened, but the poor are still made better off in absolute terms by the success of the rich. In fact, there is empirical evidence that the effects of economic deregulation bring about a reverse redistribution away from the poorest and in favour of the richest. This is especially clear if essential public services and environmental conditions of life are included in the measure in addition to simple money income. However, the point here is that sustainable development requires reregulation of capitalist growth, so that both the rate and the character of economic development

...ight back within the sphere of economic planning (even if ...done indirectly through fiscal policies). The presumed link ... unrestrained growth and rising absolute standards of the ... can no longer be deployed even as ideology, if sustainability ... seriously as an objective of economic policy, since support ...strained growth is itself inconsistent with sustainability.

.... other way in which the difference principle can be used to reconcile capitalist growth with justice is the social democratic project of promoting economic growth so as to enhance the tax base for redistributive public provision. Again, how far the poorest actually gain from these redistributive activities is open to empirical question, but, again, for us the point is that sustainable development calls into question the centrality of growth as such as the central purpose of economic policy. In general terms, drawing on some version of the 'difference principle' to justify the inequalities that characterise capitalist societies requires economic policies which run up against sustainability. The current institutional order *might* be able to deliver Rawlsian justice, *or* sustainability, but not both together. This consideration does not, of course, tell against the difference principle itself. However, what it does suggest is that to combine together the requirements of Rawlsian justice and those of sustainability will call for much more profound social change than might have been expected. If we can countenance only economic growth which does not undermine the ecological conditions for the well-being of future generations, questions of distributive justice arise as fundamental questions about the *mode of wealth creation itself*, rather than as add-on optional extras. Since capitalist growth is notoriously generative of distributional inequalities, the 'capitalist growth with redistribution' package which might otherwise be defended in terms of the Rawlsian 'difference principle' becomes much more suspect. The least well off in this and future generations might well be benefited by a more egalitarian and less dynamic but sustainable economy than by a high-growth, inegalitarian, unsustainable one.

Yet another challenge posed for established thinking about justice by the requirement of sustainability is a consequence of economic (and ecological) globalisation. Economic forces redistribute materials, manufactured products, foodstuffs, cultural symbols, money, populations, toxic wastes, weaponry, political power and information across the globe in ways which not only fail to correspond with the boundaries of moral and political communities, but which also actually disrupt, fragment and dislocate them. This presents difficulties for theories of justice such as those advanced by 'communitarians' that attempt to ground themselves in normative beliefs held by geographically localised moral communities. Do communities with the requisite moral consensus and cultural integrity (any longer) exist? Even if this problem can be overcome, the dislocation between the global processes of distribution of goods and bads and the intra-cultural normative order poses other, more intractable ones. How do we think about questions of justice *between* communities, and *across* cultures? This is a particularly acute problem when a 'good' (e.g. energy use) which comes up for distribution in one community imposes harms (e.g. acidification, fuel shortages, climate change, etc.) on others. In these cases there are questions about distributive justice within the community, but also questions of distributive justice between communities which cannot be settled by appeal to the local normative order of either. To the extent that such global distributions are subject to any normative order at all, it is to the procedural order of international trading agreements such as GATT, and NAFTA, which may be more appropriately understood as forms of institutionalisation of radically unequal economic and diplomatic power relations. Of course, these arrangements are morally contested in terms of their injustice, not only by coalitions of social movement organisations and NGOs, but increasingly by national government representatives from poorer countries. However, in terms of the available views of justice, such contestations must either base themselves on the emergence of some form of global moral community or on an appeal to universalistic moral principles that are authoritative independently of their positive adoption by some actual moral community. In relation to the former basis, it is true that the new communications media have significantly increased the capacity of social movements to coordinate resistance internationally, and to form an embryonic global civil society. Immensely important as this development is, it does not resolve the issue, since a feature of civil society, whether at national or international level, is its openness to a wide diversity of voices in mutual contention and dialogue. Global civil society does not entail global 'community' in the required sense.

This leaves us with the need for a view of justice, such as the Rawlsian, one which allows for the critical appraisal of basic social and economic structures in terms of independently grounded moral principles. However, since the distributions which require regulation are global, the social structures at stake are, likewise, global in reach. In Rawlsian terms, a just global economic order would be one which benefited the least well off in the world more than any alternative, so long as it was consistent with basic liberties and equality of opportunity. If we include access to and enjoyment of basic environmental and socio-cultural conditions of life in our concept of well-being, rather than mere money income, again, Rawlsian justice, in the context of sustainability, has very radical implications, in this case for the global economic order.

The final issue posed for our thinking about justice by 'sustainability' has been the most widely discussed – the question of distribution across generations. At first sight a communitarian approach might seem well suited to address this issue, since communities are the paradigm repositories of tradition through which moral standards are passed from generation to generation. Strong and stable communities might be expected to have respect for the past, and concern for the future. However, again, the conditions under which 'sustainability' is sought are precisely ones under which the requisite characteristics of communities are undermined. Handing on valued goods to one's descendants is a priority which can be given little sense when one's descendants may live out their lives on a different continent, and may themselves have quite radically different values and concerns to one's own. The rapidity and unpredictability of cultural change is a particularly difficult problem for any concept of justice concerned with distributions of goods over time. Not so long ago the arable monocultures not far from where I live were orchid-rich downland. Could the farmers who carried out the change of land use have predicted that a future generation might come to value the unproductive flower-rich grassland more than food surpluses generated by their destruction? For communitarians, what are to count as 'goods', as well as the appropriate norms for distributing them, are given by local cultural practices. Radical cultural change must undermine the conditions of possibility of rules of justice governing allocations over time-spans within which significant cultural change can occur.

It seems that only a universalistic view of justice, in which goods could be identified and 'weighed' independently of local cultural norms could provide decision procedures for cross-generational justice. But how might this be possible? In the Rawlsian account, the imaginary choice between possible alternative institutional orders has to be made behind a 'veil of ignorance' – ignorance of where one might be in the imagined order, and of one's specific attributes. The standard objection to this construct is the extreme abstraction it requires. How can we even conceptualise desirable or undesirable possibilities in abstraction from a more substantive sense of self, place and time? In practice, the risk is that the 'choice' of a just institutional order will express unreflective prejudices associated with currently dominant cultural values, gender and ethnic identities and so on. One possible response is to render the 'veil of ignorance' less opaque, and fill in at least some of the substantive conditions that would have to be presupposed in any social order for questions of justice to arise at all. Rawls's account already does this to some extent: protection of basic liberties and equality of opportunity are necessary frameworks within which questions of just distribution are settled. The consideration of 'sustainability' would require us to at least add to this framework the proviso that environmental conditions of life were also protected, whatever system for distribution were adopted. But the concept of environmental sustainability is itself essentially contested. Incorporation of the concept into neo-classical economics has yielded weaker versions, allowing significant depletion of environmental goods so long as at least 'total capital' wealth can be passed on to future generations. Such accounts lose the sense of the psychological, social and cultural importance that our relation to the rest of nature has for us. Also lost is the connected recognition that non-human nature may have value in itself, independently of its relevance to specific human needs or desires. So, if this route to an ecologically informed view of justice is to be taken, then a 'strong' view of sustainability has to be taken: one that preserves as much of the non-human context and conditions for human life as possible. This must allow not just for cultural diversity in what is valued now, but also for the likelihood that future generations may find value in aspects of nature currently unknown or unvalued by us (see Dobson's seminal 1998, 2000 for further discussion).

Animals and social justice

I want to start with some reflection on the ontological claims associated with the animal liberation movement. Broadly speaking, animal welfare approaches are linked with an emphasis on sentience as the key 'qualifying condition' for moral standing, whereas the 'rights tradition' is more stringent. Quite complex psychological capacities and vulnerabilities, such that the individual may be considered 'subject of a life' are required to ground rights. Animal rights advocates extend these characteristics to (some) non-human animals on grounds of common-sense experience and usage, as well as evolutionary theory. They are our kin, so why should we suppose that attributes such as consciousness and subjectivity are unique to us?

It is reasonable to believe that individuals of other animal species are the subjects of more or less complex psychological and emotional lives. But evolutionary kinship implies more than this. Organic embodiment, with its associated needs and vulnerabilities, sexuality, mortality, liability to disease, capacities and needs for social relations, and complex ecological dependencies are the shared conditions of both human and non-human animal life. More than this, humans and other animals are interdependent in several respects. Most obviously the majority of human populations directly depend on a small number of other species as sources of food, and often shelter and clothing. Where land is managed for forestry products, or arable agriculture, populations of other animal species are treated as competitors and eliminated. Urban development destroys habitat for other species of animals and plants on an ever-growing scale. At the same time, areas are deliberately excluded from development as 'reserves', and some animal species are kept as domesticated companions, guards, guides and servants. Finally, other animals have a significant symbolic significance in most cultures: as sources of entertainment, as means of thought (including thought about our own nature), as objects of worship and superstition, and so on.

This list could be amplified, but should be sufficient to at least ground the plausibility of the following propositions:

a The ecological, social and cultural *relations* between humans and other animals are bound up with central features of the lives of both. These relations are neither marginal nor incidental. This is true across cultures (though, of course, the nature of the relations concerned varies enormously).

b Hitherto-dominant Western ontologies which divide material beings into 'things' and 'persons' are challenged by contemporary knowledge about other animals. Neither the anthropomorphic assimilation of animals (except possibly a few primates and marine mammals) to personhood, nor their Cartesian reification can be reasonably sustained.

c At least some non-human animals have enough *in common* with humans to render the refusal to extend moral standing beyond the boundaries of the human species unreasonable.

The broad perspective I sketch here (and see Benton 1993, 1998) I call 'human/animal continuism'. It follows from it that *if* humans are proper subjects of moral concern in their own right, then so are (many) non-human animals. If we also accept that at least one test of the adequacy of any moral theory is that it provides us with means of distinguishing right and wrong in the conduct of central dimensions of our personal and social lives, it further follows that no moral theory which fails to offer such guidance in the sphere of our relations with other species can be adequate. Animals are not only proper subjects of moral concern, but they are also an important test of the adequacy of any moral theory.

Of course, justice is just one moral concept. It may be that animals are morally considerable, but it does not follow that every moral consideration applies to them. Even the most ardent advocate of animal rights will not include freedom of religious confession among their rights. So what about justice? Is the owner of two dogs morally required to treat them fairly? The question is not *obviously* absurd, so why not ask it in the broader context of evaluating rival possible institutionalisations of our relations with other animals? Can we meaningfully extend the veil of ignorance in the original position to cover even the species membership of the hypothetical chooser of appropriate principles of justice? We can, certainly, as humans, imagine what it might be like to be a veal calf, or a chimp undergoing vivisection, and, indeed, think that institutions which routinise such treatments must be unjust. However, Rawls's method requires us to imagine principles of justice as objects of possible choice by an occupant of the 'original position'. Could a being of indeterminate species occupy such a position? Since the unencumbered self of the original position is at least required to be motivated to the rational pursuit of a life plan, and, indeed, to be able to choose on a rational basis between possible contexts for the living of such a life, we must conclude that animals stand outside the terms of any just settlement. It seems that on a Rawlsian view of justice, animals cannot be victims of injustice.

A communitarian approach might at first seem more inclusive of animals. After all, there have been historical societies in which animals could be charged with criminal offences, were entitled to legal representation and so on. Many of the regulations governing our contemporary treatment of laboratory and farm animals, too, could be represented as attempts to apply minimal standards of justice to them. However, this could be used as an argument against the communitarian position in so far as such regulations have their origins not in appeals to existing values of the respective communities, but in moral campaigns to change them. More fundamentally, however, there is a problem about how 'communities' are defined.

For Walzer (1983), norms of just distribution are intrinsic to the kinds of goods under consideration, a thesis which depends on more or less consensual cultural valuations of what is to count as a 'good'. Animals do not participate in the symbolic and normative practices through which these goods are identified and valued as such, so it is hard to see how a culture's norms of justice could apply to them.

Both of these negative outcomes are to some degree unsatisfactory or paradoxical. Animals are present in the interstices of human societies and they participate in a wide range of social practices, generally through asymmetrical power relations, but often as active contributors, nonetheless. Much the same could be said of subordinate castes, classes or genders, within humankind, to whom considerations of justice certainly are due. Similarly with Rawlsian justice. Animals can suffer a range of harms or benefits as a result of different possible 'basic social structures', no less than can humans. It is true that some basic liberties and socio-economic goods could not be appreciated by animals, but there seems to be no good reason why considerations of justice should not apply to animals over that range of goods which they *can* appreciate – such as freedom from torture. On the contrary, 'reflective intuition' suggests that they should.

One possible diagnosis of these difficulties – favoured by the perspective of human/animal continuism – is that both liberal and communitarian traditions for thinking about justice arbitrarily privilege certain attributes, either in defining the conditions of admission into moral communities, or in characterising the appropriate conditions for deciding moral principles. These attributes include a rather narrow concept of rational autonomy and capacities for participating in the symbolic and normative practices of a human community. These capacities are (probably) uniquely human, and have certainly been widely presupposed in Western cultures as definitive of the human/animal boundary. However, the case for human/animal continuity establishes a dissociation between, on the one hand, those attributes which are required for the exercise of full moral agency and, on the other, those which make their bearers proper objects of moral concern – 'moral patients', as Tom Regan (1988, 2001) calls them. Now, if non-human animals are proper objects of moral concern, despite not possessing full moral agency, then the main conditions for the appropriateness to them of considerations of justice seem to be satisfied. The pursuit of human purposes is liable to cause harm to non-human animals, either directly or indirectly (e.g. through habitat destruction), so that the condition of scarcity sets their interests in opposition to one another, at least across a range of their mutual interactions. Manifestly, complete benevolence on the part of humans cannot be relied upon in the resolution of these conflicts of interest, and neither can adequate knowledge of the interests of animals be relied upon even where benevolence is forthcoming. *Prima facie*, these considerations seem to call for a view of justice which recognises that non-human animals can benefit from just, or suffer from unjust treatment, whilst acknowledging that they do not belong to the class of beings capable of establishing or living by the principles in terms of which that treatment is *judged* just or unjust.

Attempting to press some notion of justice beyond species boundaries seems to be supported by strong moral and factual considerations. However, it has some deeply problematic consequences. The *de facto* inability of practically all non-human animals to participate as moral agents in human moral communities implies an element of irreducible vicariousness, or 'paternalism' in any institutionalisation of dispensing justice to them. The interests of non-human animals would, in any such attempt to institutionalise cross-species justice, have to be represented indirectly, by human advocates or 'proxies'. For this to be possible, in turn, human cultures would need to be enlarged by non-anthropocenric understandings of the conditions for flourishing and the vulnerabilities of non-human animals. If the matter of the cultural relativity of 'goods' is a problem for justice across human communities, how much more serious does this diversity become across the boundaries of species?

Another cluster of problems centres on the association (particularly on the political left) of the concept of justice with egalitarianism. In the animal rights debate, strongly egalitarian positions at the level of abstract principle tend to be softened in the direction of inegalitarian intuitions by the application of secondary principles in actual cases (see Benton 1993: 86–7). To accept that there are strong reasons for regarding non-human animals as morally considerable is not necessarily to accept that they are *equally* morally considerable. In the absence of strong arguments in favour of giving equal consideration to the interests of humans and non-human animals, we may be tempted to follow widely shared moral intuitions which recognise the moral standing of non-human animals, but assign a lower priority to it in cases of conflict with human interests (see Hayward 1995). There is at least one strong argument for doing this. It is that to render a position of cross-species moral egalitarianism at all plausible, one must restrict the scope of moral concern for non-humans to a rather narrow circle of species with the requisite similarity to humans in their psychological complexity and vulnerability to suffering. Allowing for some differentiation in the sources and degrees of appropriate moral concern across the species barrier allows us to bring into the sphere of moral considerability a far wider range of species and forms of social relationship to them.

In their rather different ways, Peter Singer (1976) and Arne Naess (1990) argue for equality of moral concern as between humans and non-humans. If successful, their arguments would tell against my proposal of a view of justice across the species boundary which assigns moral standing to non-human beings, but not necessarily equal moral standing. Peter Singer recognises that there are empirical differences of abilities of various sorts between individuals. He seeks to preserve the value of moral entitlement to equal consideration by dissociating it from the empirical characteristics of individuals. Two people of very different levels of ability, for example, should still be given equal consideration as persons. The point can be extended for differences of kind (as distinct from differences of degree, such as ability). So, for example, we might follow Marx in recognising that an egalitarian distribution would take into account differences of need. People like myself who have myopic vision need glasses to move around safely; people with normal sight do not. In this sort of case, being able to judge what counts as 'giving equal consideration' to two beings with different characteristics depends on being able to bring to bear background assumptions of the kinds of things both individuals might need or legitimately want to do, and the abilities/resources they would need to do them. That is to say, some notion of a shared 'form of life' is presupposed in judgements as to what counts as 'giving equal consideration'. To the extent that, within the human species, there are commonalities associated with our universal human nature, then equality of consideration can be given a determinate meaning. However, organic, behavioural and ecological diversity across the species boundary must render the conditions under which the phrase 'equal consideration' can be given a determinate meaning very problematic. The point here is not so much that it may be right to treat humans and non-humans unequally, but more that there may be no clear way of deciding what is or is not equal treatment (though it may still be clear what counts as exploitative, abusive or cruel treatment).

A second attempt to defend cross-species egalitarianism is offered by the 'platform' of deep ecology (Naess 1990: 28 ff.). Naess calls his principle 'biospherical egalitarianism'. He concedes that some 'killing, exploitation, and suppression' is necessary, and it is not entirely clear whether he thinks that this constitutes a limit to the practical applicability of his principle, or whether it is included in its meaning. In some ways the latter offers a more promising reading. It might be taken to recognise as a right on the part of humans what is *de facto* the case for other species: to meet their needs by preying upon or otherwise using or consuming members of other species of animals and plants. The reciprocal of this right would be the non-right of humans to impose harms on other species in excess of what was necessary to meet their needs (or 'vital needs' as Naess expresses it). However, it is clear from the context of Naess's discussion that the distributive justice involved here is one which operates at the level of populations, or species. What humans have no right to do is excessively reduce 'richness' (i.e. population size) or 'diversity' (numbers of species). But in the absence of any independent criteria of what count as 'vital needs' in the human case, or of the appropriate human population size, the principle seems to generate no clear decision procedures even at the level of populations. The question of criteria of just treatment as between *individuals* of different species is simply not posed at all.

There are strong moral and logical considerations which favour the extension of a notion of justice across the boundaries of species. There are also some strong reasons for thinking that an egalitarian conception of justice across species lapses into undecidability the further we depart from comparability with the human case. One possible response to this tension might be to abandon the link between justice and egalitarianism. This might be done across the whole scope of the concept of justice, including its use for adjudicating the rival claims of individuals and groups of humans. This would entail a retreat from the whole range of emancipatory uses of the aspiration to justice in modern times, and clearly falls out of consideration in the context of the project outlined at the beginning of this chapter. A less drastic option might be to retain an egalitarian conception of justice among humans, but to drop the requirement of equal consideration as between human and non-human individuals and populations. This strategy could be rendered less *ad hoc* than it might at first seem. We might define an inclusive concept (or 'category') of justice which comes into play whenever there is a situation of 'scarcity', competing interests, and lack of mutual benevolence and knowledge between individuals or groups which each have moral standing (irrespective of species). This general category of justice imposes a requirement upon all moral agents in such situations to exercise self-restraint in satisfying their wants in consideration of the needs and preferences of competing moral patients. In some contexts this might amount to leaving for them what is their due, in other contexts the more open-ended concepts of diversity and richness as used in the tradition of deep ecology might be more appropriate. In situations where relations between individual or groups of (generally human) moral agents are concerned, then equality of consideration would be the appropriate principle of justice.

Though I think that such a multilayered view of justice might be rendered logically and morally coherent, there remains a danger that the partial abandonment of the tight linkage between justice and egalitarianism might lead to some backsliding on equality among human groups. Pragmatically, it might be preferable to retain the common-sense restriction of the term 'justice' to human relations with one another, and invent or adapt another vocabulary (such as 'respect for' or 'responsibility to' the 'other') to express the broader requirement for self-restraint in our relations with other species. Either way, to acknowledge the moral requirement for such restraint is to accept some constraints on legitimate strategies for bringing about justice among humans. These constraints are in addition to those mentioned above as implications of the requirement of 'sustainability', and the above arguments for them are an indication of the limitations of prevailing conceptions of sustainability as a response to green moral sensibilities.

Non-anthropocentric justice?

Ecocentric writers commonly commit themselves to one or other of two sorts of innovative moral claim. The first is that the non-human world (or some parts of it) has value in itself, independently of human purposes. The second is that authoritative norms for human conduct can be grounded in or derived from nature (or from ecological characterisations of it).

This second type of moral claim is the one which looks most threatening to the concept of justice. This is partly because of the substantive moral positions that are commonly advocated by ecocentrics. These invariably assign moral priority to preserving or restoring system properties, such as (e.g. Leopold 1968) 'integrity, stability and beauty', or diversity, interdependence, cooperation and symbiosis. Now, it is true that justice may also be a property of a system, but it is morally important as a system property only because the properties of systems have consequences for the well-being of members. The moral focus of the concern for justice, at least as it applies to human relations, is the individual subject, whereas the moral focus of the concern for the stability of the 'biotic community' is the biotic community. The moral (as distinct from ontological) holism of most ecocentric moral thinking sets it in opposition to the moralities of rights, justice, and liberty which have been at the centre of Western emancipatory thought in modern times. The interesting exceptions here are anarchist green theorists who work with a 'mutualist' interpretation of ecological relationships, emphasising symbiotic and egalitarian features of relations in nature, as against the Darwinian picture of nature 'red in tooth and claw'.

Of course, it is quite easy to show that the characterisations of nature from which these normative conclusions are drawn are highly contentious and selective ways of reading into nature the very values which are subsequently read out again. However, it is still worth pausing to consider how well or badly grounded the rival descriptions are. Such features of ecosystems as diversity, stability, and the interdependence of the populations of the different species which make them up are system-level properties which both form the context of and are reproduced outcomes of micro-level processes. These micro-level processes – comprising the interactions between individuals of the same and other species within the localised populations which comprise ecosystems – are often 'hierarchical', predatory, competitive, and the lives of individual organisms caught up in them often 'nasty, brutish and short'. Predator–prey relationships, for example, much studied by ecologists, may be quite stable, conducive to diversity, even beautiful, according to taste, when considered at the level of interacting populations, but hardly attractive models for human conduct viewed at the individual level.

It seems, then, that the moral holism of this strand of ecocentric value-theory is not merely a contingent feature. Anarchist green theorists – such as Bookchin – who see themselves as belonging to the broad stream of progressive politics can do this plausibly only on the basis of a selective refusal to include the micro-level interactions underlying system properties in nature in the grounding of his prescriptions for human conduct. For more conservative and reactionary thinkers these micro-level mechanisms may well be endorsed, and even advocated as means to desirable ecosystem ends.

These considerations can, of course, be by-passed by a reassertion of ethical anti-naturalism. Whatever agreement we might come to about how ecological relations in nature are properly characterised, it would not follow that such a description was in any way normative for human conduct. The logical force of this argument is complemented by the sheer diversity of often contradictory 'oughts' which ecocentric ethical naturalists derive from their various accounts of what 'is'. However, it is important to keep in mind what ethical anti-naturalism does *not* demonstrate. First, whilst it may show that ecocentric moral claims cannot be logically grounded in factual statements about nature, it does not show that those moral claims may not be supported on other grounds. Stability, interdependence, cooperation and so on may still be *desirable* features of social, as well as *actual* features of ecological systems, without the latter being a reason for believing the former. Second, and more importantly for my argument here, ethical anti-naturalism does not rule out the possibility that factual claims may be *relevant* to moral questions in a variety of ways. Indeed, any approach to moral theory which seeks to give some place to ethical reasoning, but which acknowledges the force of ethical anti-naturalism, has as its central task consideration of how factual matters may be *relevant to* without strictly logically implying moral conclusions.

A view on this, which I have already drawn upon without explicitly stating it, is that a range of factual claims about features of human (and non-human) existence may serve to impose requirements on moral theories, or tests of their adequacy. If all objects of desire were available at no cost and in unlimited abundance, for example, we would have no need for institutions to regulate their distribution, nor principles to guide them, nor moral theories to adjudicate between rival principles. Scarcity relative to the desires of a plurality of individuals establishes the possibility of conflict and competition. Resolution by way of authoritative norms of distributive justice stands as the principal, if not the only alternative to the Hobbesian options of violent conflict and coercive imposition from above. One requirement, I am suggesting, for any moral theory is that it pass this test: it is a plausible candidate to provide authoritative normative regulation in those areas of social life which require it. My provisional account of what it is for a feature of social life to require normative regulation is that it would otherwise be characterised by violence and coercion. This will certainly do as a first approximation in the case of theories of justice. My claim is not that certain facts about the human condition imply that any particular distribution is just, nor that any particular theory of justice is true. Rather, it is that these factual claims, if true, serve to define the tasks that any moral theory – including theory of justice – is required to address.

Where does this leave us on the matter of ecocentric values? If we reject, as I do, the view that moral norms can be logically derived from factual claims about nature or about ecosystems, we are left with the more open question: does what we know about the ecological predicament of humankind define tasks for moral theory which 'mainstream' moral theories have failed to address because of their (relative) lack of ecological awareness? Is, for example, the unencumbered self in Rawls's 'original position' unencumbered in just those respects which need to be included if we are to have a defensible view of the problems a theory of justice has to solve?

To begin to answer this question I will turn to the first sort of innovative ecocentric moral claim that I mentioned at the beginning of this section. This is that non-human nature (or some parts of it) is valuable independently of its relation to any human purpose. This is sometimes expressed as the 'intrinsic value' of nature, or natural objects. From the secular point of view which I adopt it is hard to make sense of what it could mean for something to have value independently of the human cultural practices through which value is assigned. However, this is not to say that value is a merely subjective matter. Cultural traditions provide rules and resources for the learning, transmission and creation of individual capacities for valuing.

But this intersubjective 'sociologising' of what is independent of individual subjectivity in the making of value judgements does not go quite far enough in at least two respects. The first, and most controversial, is that there may be some cultural universals in what we value as members of the species. Less controversial, perhaps, is that any serious analysis of cultural traditions of valuing must recognise that they indispensibly involve practical engagement with the objects of valuation. Learning how to appreciate music involves listening to it, being taught what to listen for, comparing different performances, trying out different interpretations on different occasions of listening and so on. None of this would make any sense unless what we valued was *already there* in the music.

My suggestion is that something of this is also true of our valuation of natural objects. In fact the two types of case (art objects and natural objects) are not so easy to separate as it might seem. Most of what we value as 'landscape', for example, is the outcome (both intended and unintended) of past generations of human interaction with the biological and physical environment. Symmetrically, artistic traditions necessarily depend upon and work with the pre-given properties of their materials.

But ecocentrics tend to reserve their deepest regard for nature as untouched by human activity. For them the highest priority must go not to the 'cultured' lansdcape, but to the ancient forest, or the arctic 'wilderness'. Here, the cultural resources through which we appreciate 'wild' nature have no counterpart in the cultural resources through which the object of our appreciation is produced, as in the case of art objects. Nevertheless, these cultural traditions are like those involved in artistic appreciation in that they, too, necessarily require active attention and practical engagement with the object. Gardeners, hunters, anglers, farmers, landscape painters, ecologists, naturalists, ramblers, astronomers, ornithologists, climbers and others come to their different understandings and valuations of the world they engage with through activity and reflection upon it. The ways in which they value the non-human world are certainly products of culture, but what makes that culture possible is that the world has the properties that make these practices possible, and which they both discover and represent in their different ways.

The position I am approaching here is a secular reworking of what seems to me true and important in ecocentric value theory. In the course of practical engagement with, or of intellectual reflection on the world we inhabit, we encounter its autonomy *vis-à-vis* human purposes, and its awesome transcendence of our cognitive powers. These recognitions can bring us up against deeper questions about the nature of our own lives in the wider context of our presence in a universe of unimaginable complexity and vastness. The proper attitudes of awe and wonder in the face of all this amount to a valuing of the world for what it is, as distinct from valuing it merely as a means to human ends, or as a bundle of resources for economic exploitation.

Some ecocentrics will object to this secular reworking on the grounds that the activity of metaphysical contemplation of our place in nature with which I replace the notion of intrinsic values in nature is itself a human purpose – albeit a very worthy one. This is still a case of valuing nature for some human purpose, and so belongs within the spectrum of anthropocentric positions, they might argue. My response is to distinguish between an environmental ethic which advocates preservation of nature because it is necessary to enable humans to engage in metaphysical contemplation, and the activity of metaphysical contemplation itself. The former certainly is advocating the protection of nature for a human purpose. However, that human purpose itself necessarily involves a non-instrumental orientation to the non-human world. It is an example of what Max Weber would have called 'value-rational', as distinct from 'instrumentally rational' action. This suggests that the logical relations between anthropocentrism and ecocentrism are more complex than they are generally taken to be. A certain kind of anthropocentric case is required to secure the conditions for the flourishing of an ecocentric orientation to the world. Reciprocally, the anthropocentric case depends on recognising and valuing the ecocentric orientation to the world as a human purpose.

So, what is the bearing of all this on the concept of social justice? The above reworking of the anthropocentric/ecocentric opposition suggests that there are two dimensions of the problem. First, if we value nature for its own sake, then this implies that protection of nature may set constraints on the ways in which we seek to achieve justice among humans. This might be conceptualised in terms of doing justice as between humans and nature, or we might think of it in terms of the independent value of nature having implications for the ways in which we try to achieve social justice conceived more narrowly as a relation between humans. Either way, there is a second dimension to the problem if we accept that the opportunity to benefit from a non-instrumental (metaphysical, aesthetic, cognitive, etc.) relation to nature is an important good for humans. This second dimension is the matter of how this opportunity is distributed among humans (in this or future generations). This second dimension integrates the requirements for protection of nature and concern for social justice, but it does so in a way which deepens the nature-protection requirement beyond what is usual in the more widely diffused concepts of 'sustainability'. So far as the first dimension is concerned, we have to consider further the options of a broader conceptual integration of considerations of justice and the protection of nature, on the one hand, as against continuing to think of nature-protection as an independent value which might in principle compete with, override or be overridden by considerations of justice among humans.

Our current situation is shaped by the practical consequences of the second option. Unrestrained growth has been advocated as necessary for the resolution of distributional issues. It has been pursued at the expense of non-human nature. At least in their rhetorical strategies, some third world leaders have insisted on their right to destroy their own ecological heritage in pursuit of living standards comparable to those enjoyed by Westerners. In many local communities in Western countries, blighted by de-industrialisation and high levels of unemployment and social disintegration, the demand for development overrides the desire for environmental quality. Opinion surveys show clear evidence of a shift away from environmental priorities in periods of recession. But there are also situations in which powerful minorities are able to impose (non-utilitarian) environmental preservation at the cost of social justice. Colonial powers in Africa, for example, have secured the preservation of huge areas of land for their exclusive use as game reserves, excluding indigenous people both from direct use and from any possibility of development. Comparable ecological 'enclosures' have been established in the name of biodiversity preservation in recent times, with associated exclusion of indigenous peoples. In Western countries, too, some on the left have argued that pressure groups for rural preservation seek to impose a privileged value system and lifestyle at the expense of the rural poor.

These historical examples suggest that élite pursuit of environmental preservation at the expense of social justice is counterproductive. If struggles for social justice are experienced as struggles against the privileges of the defenders of the environment, then the environmental case is delegitimated, as in much of post-colonial Africa. Similarly, pursuit of social justice without concern for the ecological consequences is also liable to be self-defeating. This is partly because of the ecological requirements for sustainability, discussed above, but, more centrally to my argument here, also because it involves a disastrous impoverishment of the content of justice itself.

This brings us to the second option mentioned above: to consider some form of conceptual integration of social justice and environmental value. One way of doing this might be revise a Rawlsian approach by building into the 'original position' a constraint on the selection of principles of justice such that the outcome should be consistent with environmental protection. Indeed, the case for this is conclusive if Rawlsian justice is to be rendered compatible with sustainability. In this case, cross-generational justice requires preservation of those features of the non-human environment which are either goods in themselves, or are necessary to the continued provision of other goods.

But does this take us far enough? The requirement of sustainability is an injunction to preserve whatever is necessary for future generations to enjoy the goods we enjoy. However, it says nothing about what goods they might be. We have already seen that Rawlsian justice faces difficulties in offering principles to deal with justice between cultures which value 'goods' differently, and in dealing with comparable issues arising from cultural change across generations. My reworked version of the ecocentric notion of intrinsic value in nature adds some further difficulties. It is not at all clear that the opportunity for the sort of non-instrumental appreciation of nature I tried to describe figures in Rawls's list of primary goods. The socio-economic goods of wealth, income, power and authority may certainly be dependent on environmental integrity in ways which the sustainability requirement might secure, but they are quite consistent with the 'bundle of resources' view of nature. The basic liberties which comprise Rawls's other category of primary goods do include liberty of conscience, which seems to come close. However, much depends on whether we think of this as a 'negative' liberty, as the non-right of others to persecute us for our beliefs, and so on, or as a positive liberty. If we are to think of it as the latter, then the opportunity for a non-instrumental orientation to nature, as a component of human well-being, has some very extensive conditions attached to its realisation. It must include freedom from the constraint of material poverty which drives people to destroy their environments out of desperation, and freedom from the cultural poverty which excludes from public discourse visions of well-being other than what can be promised by the commodity system. It must also include the opportunity to participate in shaping the primary institutional forms through which needs are met and the allocation of resources is decided. In other words, it implies the democratisation of both economic and cultural life.

But already in this line of thinking there has arisen a further difficulty for Rawlsian justice. This difficulty is posed when we ask the question, having accepted that the opportunity for a non-instrumental appreciation of nature is to be included as a 'good', what would count as a just distribution of it? If it is included as a basic liberty, then justice is satisfied only by arrangements which give the most extensive opportunity for it consistent with equal opportunity for all. Part of the problem here is that the opportunity for a non-instrumental appreciation of nature is a collective good. The need for it could not be satisfied by dividing up nature into parcels and allocating them to individuals according to a principle of justice. In this respect it is a radically different kind of good from either income or the right to personal property. It is a collective good not just because, as an object of non-instrumental valuing, the non-human world cannot be disaggregated, but also because the opportunity for such an orientation also requires access to cultural resources. The integrity of human cultures and their non-human environments and sustaining conditions are, on this view, goods in themselves. Justice with respect to them requires both their continuity (though not necessarily unchanged) through time, and equality of participation in and access to them (as distinct from shares in their distribution).

Green Utopia

This discussion, of course, poses more questions than it answers. There is certainly too little here to ground any firm specification of the institutional framework which might give practical effect to a green view of justice. However, perhaps enough has been done to demonstrate that the considerations posed for political theory by the emergent green challenge by no means displace the central significance of questions of justice. If anything, the green challenge requires us to give still more urgent attention to questions of justice, as well as providing new work for the concept and principles of justice to do. At the same time, I have suggested that the green challenge renders both communitarian and Rawlsian accounts of justice still more problematic than they would otherwise be. The requirement to conceptualise justice across species boundaries is perhaps the most testing of all. So far as the political left, and the more broadly 'progressive' current in modern politics is concerned, this latter challenge seems to require a partial abandonment of the tight conceptual linkage of justice and equality. The more 'anthropocentric' concern for sustainability also constitutes a challenge to the 'growth plus redistribution' strategy for distributive justice which has become widely accepted on the reformist left.

The above argumentation has also begun to sketch out some of the ways in which inherited notions of justice might be rethought and revised in the face of the green challenge. In a provisional way this discussion yields the following list of conditions which any 'green Utopia' might have to satisfy in order to be consistent with a 'strong programme' of green justice:

1 Universal freedom from material poverty.

2 Cultural traditions offering resources for respecting and valuing the non-human world, and equal access to those resources.

3 Acquisition of normative control over those economic and technical forces which distribute human life chances, and mediate human impacts on the non-human world.

4 Democratic participation in the shaping of cultural and economic life.

5 Open access to valued human environments for non-destructive activity and contemplation.

6 Preservation of sufficient environmental space in relation to human populations for open access to be compatible with the purposes of appreciation and contemplation of the non-human world.

7 In association with 3 above, procedures for including consideration of the interests of non-human beings in decisions affecting their well-being in accordance with culturally formed notions of cross-species justice, or an ethic of responsibility for the 'other'.

8 Enough long-run continuity and integrity of human cultures to give coherence to the notion of justice across generations.

It is my contention that such a view of justice has a recognisable continuity with the political thought of the socialist left, especially its 'utopian' strands. However, the green challenge, and the associated changes in moral sensibilities towards the non-human world, do demand a radical reworking of that socialist heritage. It is, of course, a further and much more intractable question how such a vision might take root in the broader political culture, and be eventually institutionalised in a realisable 'ecotopia'.

References

Bahro, R. (1982) *Socialism and Survival*. London: Heretic.

Benton, T. (1989) 'Marxism and Natural Limits: An Ecological Critique and Reconstruction', *New Left Review*, 178: 51–86.

Benton, T. (1993) *Natural Relations: Ecology, Animal Rights and Social Justice.* London: Verso.

Benton, T. (1998) 'Rights and Justice on a Shared Planet', *Theoretical Criminology*, 2 (1): 149–175.

Dobson, A. (1994) 'Ecologism and the Relegitimation of Socialism', *Radical Philosophy*, 67: 13–19.

Dobson, A. (1998) *Justice and the Environment*. Oxford: Oxford University Press.

Dobson, A. (2000) *Green Political Thought*. London: Routledge.

Hayward, T. (1995) *Ecological Thought: An Introduction*. Cambridge: Polity.

Leopold, A. (1968) *A Sand County Almanac*. Oxford: Oxford University Press.

Lomborg, B. (2001) *The Sceptical Environmentalist*. Cambridge: Cambridge University Press.

Lovelock, J. (2006) *The Revenge of Gaia*. London: Allen Lane.

Mol, A. J. P. and Sonnenfeld, D. A. (eds) (2000) *Ecological Modernisation Around the World*. Special issue of *Environmental Politics*, 9 (1).

Naess, A. (1990) *Ecology, Community and Lifestyle*. Cambridge: Cambridge University Press.

O'Connor, M. (ed.) (1994) *Is Capitalism Sustainable?* New York: Guilford.

Porritt, J. (2005) *Capitalism as if the World Matters.* London: Earthscan.

Rawls, J. (1971) *A Theory of Justice.* Oxford: Oxford University Press.

Regan, T. (1988) *The Case for Animal Rights.* London: Routledge.

Regan, T. (2001) *Defending Animal Rights.* Urbana, Illinois: University of Illinois Press.

Singer, P. (1976) *Animal Liberation.* London: Cape.

Walzer, M. (1983) *Spheres of Justice.* Oxford: Blackwell.

Chapter 2

Green criminology and the pursuit of social and ecological justice

Rob White

Introduction

Green criminology often incorporates consideration of two broad strands of analytical thought and activist energy. *Environmental justice* tends to be concerned with issues of social inequality, while *ecological justice* tends to be concerned with issues of conservation of specific environments, animal rights and preservation of the biosphere generally. In the first instance, environmental harm is constructed around notions of harm to humans; the latter extends the concept to include the non-human. In either case, what actually gets criminalised generally reflects an anthropocentric (or human-centred) perspective on the nature of the harm in question. This chapter considers the complexities and conflicts associated with efforts to develop notions of ecological citizenship and eco-human rights that take into account consideration of both human and ecological systems. The strategic role and dynamics of human intervention, within a green criminological framework, will be discussed.

The chapter begins by describing the differences between environmental and ecological justice approaches. While not necessarily mutually exclusive, an emphasis on one or the other of these approaches does lead to substantively different kinds of analysis and intervention focus. Whether and how these perspectives or approaches can be integrated is one of the underlying themes of the paper. So, too, how environmental harm itself is constructed and responded to becomes highly contingent upon which approach is adopted in understanding environment issues. A key thematic concern of the chapter, therefore, is the problematic nature of how best to move from abstract pro-environment principles to making concrete decisions about matters that involve conflicts over rights in sometimes very complicated situations.

Green criminology and ecological thought

A distinctive, critical 'green criminology' has emerged in recent years, a criminology that takes as its focus issues relating to the environment (in the widest sense possible) and social harm (as defined in ecological as well as strictly legal terms). Much of this work has been directed at exposing different instances of substantive environmental injustice and ecological injustice. It has also involved critique of the actions of nation-states and transnational capital for fostering particular types of harm, and for failing to adequately address or regulate harmful activity. Drawing upon a wide range of ideas and empirical materials, recent work dealing with environmental issues has ventured across many different areas of concern:

- it has documented the existence of law-breaking with respect to pollution, disposal of toxic waste and misuse of environmental resources (Pearce and Tombs 1998);

- it has raised questions relating to the destruction of specific environments and resources, in ways which are 'legal' but ecologically very harmful to plants, animals and humans (Halsey 1997a);

- it has challenged corporate definitions of good environmental practice and emphasised the claims of non-human nature to ecological justice (Lynch and Stretesky 2003);

- it has emphasised the dynamic links between distribution of environmental 'risk' and distinct communities, and particularly how poor and minority populations experience disproportionate exposure to environmental harm (Bullard 1994);

- it has investigated the specific place of animals in relation to issues of 'rights' and human–non-human relationships on a shared planet (Benton 1998; Beirne 1999; see also essays by Beirne, Benton, Regan, this volume);

- it has criticised the inadequacies of environmental regulation in both philosophical and practical terms (Low and Gleeson 1998; Halsey and White 1998);

- it has exposed corporate attempts to stifle environmental critique and dissent through the use of public relations propaganda and strategic lawsuits against public participation (White 2005a; Walters 2003);

- it has reconsidered the nature of victimisation in relation to environmental changes and events, including social and governmental responses to this victimisation (Williams 1996; Hauck, this volume);

- it has explored the ways in which law enforcement officials – particularly the police but also including environmental protection authorities – have intervened with regard to regulation of fisheries, prosecution of polluters and conservation of specific environs and species (Tomkins 2005).

Given the pressing nature of many environmental issues it is not surprising that many criminologists are now seeing environmental crime and environmental victimisation as areas for concerted analytical and practical attention – as areas of work that require much more conceptual development, empirical attention and international networking (see South 1998; White 2005b).

Within the broad green criminological literature, however, there are varied emphases in terms of how 'the problem' might best be framed. How we understand the relationship between humans and the environment is crucial to defining and responding to environmental issues. Different perspectives or eco-philosophies include, for example: anthropocentric (or human-centred); biocentric (or species-centred); and ecocentric (socio-ecological-centred). These perspectives can be assessed on the basis of how they conceive environmental problems, how they depict the role of humans in the production of such problems and how they approach the issue of environmental regulation (see Halsey and White 1998). Such a conceptualisation of eco-philosophy is itself also subject to challenge by those who wish to offer alternative 'fluid' descriptors of the human–environment interface (Halsey 2004).

For many of those working on environmental issues, the question of broad philosophy translates into specific concerns with the idea of eco-human rights or ecological citizenship (see for example, Halsey

1997b; Smith 1998). In practice, this means that present generations ought to act in ways that do not jeopardise the existence and quality of life of future generations. It also means that we ought to extend the moral community to include non-human nature. By doing so, we enter a new politics of obligation:

> In ecological thought, human beings have obligations to animals, trees, mountains, oceans, and other members of the biotic community. This means that human beings have to exercise extreme caution before embarking upon any project which is likely to have the possibility of adverse effects upon the ecosystems concerned. (Smith 1998: 99)

This particular notion of ecological citizenship thus centres on human obligations to all living things and obliges us to carefully assess the impacts of human activity across the human and non-human domains.

However, such considerations are not without their problems. Thus, the conceptualisation of 'rights' is itself contentious when extended to the non-human (see Christoff 2000). For example, should environmental rights be seen as an extension of human or social rights (e.g. related to the quality of human life, such as provision of clean water), or should human rights be seen as merely one component of complex ecosystems that should be preserved for their own sake (i.e. as in the notion of the rights of the environment)? While increasingly acknowledged in international law, the environmental connection with human rights continues to be somewhat ambiguous and subject to diverse practical interpretations (Thornton and Tromans 1999). Nevertheless, such ambiguities and tensions over 'rights' are essential parts of criminological debates that mark the shift from eco-philosophy to conceptions of environmental crime.

Environmental justice and ecological justice

Within criminology there are significant issues surrounding scale, activities and legalities as these pertain to environmental harm. A strict legalist approach tends to focus on the central place of criminal law in the definition of criminality (see del Frate and Norberry 1993; Situ and Emmons 2000). Thus, as Situ and Emmons (2000: 3) see it: 'An environmental crime is an unauthorised act or omission that violates the law and is therefore subject to criminal prosecution and criminal sanctions.' Here we see a strictly legal interpretation of 'harm', one that intrinsically relies upon and reflects state definitions of environmental crime, regardless of ecological processes and outcomes.

However, other writers argue that, as with criminology in general, the concept of 'harm' ought to encapsulate those activities that may be legal and 'legitimate' but which nevertheless negatively impact on people and environments (Lynch and Stretesky 2003). Harm, in this conception, is about deviance rather than legality as such. This broader conceptualisation of crime or harm is deemed to be essential in evaluating the systemic, as well as particularistic, nature of environmental harm. To put it differently, it is important to distinguish (and make the connection between) specific instances of harm arising from imperfect operation (such as pollution spills), and systemic harm which is created by normatively sanctioned forms of activity (clear-felling of Tasmanian forests). The first is deemed to be 'criminal' or 'harmful', and thus subject to social control. The second is not. The overall consequence of this is that global environmental problems will become more serious and severe in the very midst of the proliferation of a greater range of regulatory mechanisms, agencies and laws. This is something of a paradox but partly ingrained in the way in which environmental risk is compartmentalised: specific events or incidents attract sanction, while wider legislative frameworks may set parameters on, but nevertheless still allow, other ecologically harmful practices to continue.

The state nevertheless has a formal role and commitment to protect citizens from the worst excesses or worst instances of environmental victimisation. Hence, the introduction of extensive legislation and regulatory procedures designed to give the appearance of active intervention, and the implication that laws exist which actually do deter such harms. The existence of such laws may be encouraging in that they reflect historical and ongoing struggles over certain types of capitalist activity. However, how or whether they are used once again begs the questions of the relationship between the state and the corporate sector, and the capacity of business to defend its interests through legal and extra-legal means. Much of the critical environmental criminology attempts to expose the class-based, gendered and racialised origins and effects of environmental harms, and thereby to illustrate the circuits of power that lie behind the harms that occur (see for examples, Chunn et al. 2000).

The responses of the state to environmental harm (however defined) are guided by a concern with environmental protection. This is generally framed in terms of ensuring future resource exploitation and dealing with specific instances of victimisation that have been socially defined as a problem. Risk management in this case is directed at preventing or minimising certain destructive or injurious practices into the future, based upon analysis and responses to harms identified in the present.

Criminological analysis of environmental issues proceeds on the basis that someone or something is indeed being harmed. *Environmental justice* refers to the distribution of environments among peoples in terms of access to and use of specific natural resources in defined geographical areas, and the impacts of particular social practices and environmental hazards on specific populations (e.g. as defined on the basis of class, occupation, gender, age, and ethnicity). In other words, the concern is with humans as the centre of analysis. The focus of analysis therefore is on human health and well-being and how these are affected by particular types of production and consumption. Here we can distinguish between environmental issues that affect everyone, and those that disproportionately affect specific individuals and groups (see Williams 1996; Low and Gleeson 1998). In some instances, there may be a basic 'equality of victims', in that some environmental problems threaten everyone in the same way, as in the case for example of ozone depletion, global warming, air pollution and acid rain (Beck 1996).

As extensive work on specific incidents and patterns of victimisation demonstrates, however, it is also the case that some people are more likely to be disadvantaged by environmental problems than others. For instance, American studies have identified disparities involving many different types of environmental hazards that adversely affect people of colour throughout the United States (Bullard 1994). Other work in Canada and Australia has focused on the struggles of indigenous people to either prevent the environmental degradation of their lands, or to institute their own methods of environmental protection (see Rush 2002; Langton 1998). The specificity of those placed at greater or disproportionate risk from environmental harm is reflected in literature that acknowledges the importance of class, occupation, gender, and more recently, age, in the construction of special environmental interest groups (Stephens 1996; Chunn *et al*. 2002; Williams 1996). There are thus patterns of 'differential victimisation' that are evident with respect to the siting of toxic waste dumps, extreme air pollution, access to safe, clean drinking water and so on. Another dimension of differential victimisation relates to the subjective disposition and consciousness of .the people involved. The specific groups who experience environmental problems may not always describe or see the issues in strictly environmental terms. This may be related to knowledge of the environmental harm, explanations for calamity and socio-economic pressures to 'accept' environmental risk (see Julian 2004). The environmental justice discourse challenges the dominant discourses by placing *inequalities* in the distribution of environmental quality at the top of the environmental agenda (Julian 2004; Harvey 1996).

By way of contrast, *ecological justice* refers to the relationship of human beings generally to the rest of the natural world, and includes concerns relating to the health of the biosphere, and more specifically plants and creatures that also inhabit the biosphere (Benton 1998; Franklin 1999; Beirne 1999). The main concern is with the quality of the planetary environment (that is frequently seen to possess its own intrinsic value) and the rights of other species (particularly animals) to life free from torture, abuse and destruction of habitat. Specific practices and choices in how humans interact with particular environments present immediate and potential risks to everything within them. For example, the practice of clear-felling old-growth forests directly affects many animal species by destroying their homes. Similarly, local natural environments and non-human inhabitants of both so-called wilderness and built environments are negatively impacted by human practices that destroy, rechannel or pollute existing fresh water systems. If we pollute our rivers, our streams and our waterways, we are affecting not simply humans but also living creatures such as the platypus. When we destroy the habitat of the platypus, we simultaneously destroy the biosphere.

In specific instances, concepts such as speciesism may be invoked (Beirne 1999). This refers to the practice of discriminating against non-human animals because they are perceived as inferior to the human species in much the same way that sexism and racism involve prejudice and discrimination against women and people of different colour (Munro 2004). However, it is important to recognise that the environmental justice discourse is critical of many mainstream environmental groups precisely because of the latter's 'focus on the fate of "nature" rather than humans' (Harvey 1996: 386). To put it differently, taking action on environmental issues involves choices and priorities. Thus, many communities who suffer from the 'hard end' of environmental harm feel that their well-being ought to take priority over 'natural environments' or specific plants and animals as such.

The differences between human-centred and nonhuman-centred notions of rights and justice are summarised in Table 2.1. In the first instance, environmental rights are seen as an extension of human or social rights, because the goal is one of enhancing the quality of human life (e.g. access to clean air, water, space, and a sustainable supply of natural resources valued in relation to human health and amenity). This is reflected, for example, in the 1972 Stockholm Declaration on the Human Environment (see Thornton and Tromans 1999):

Principle 1:
Man has a fundamental right to freedom, equality and adequate conditions of life, in an environment of a quality that permits a life of dignity and well-being, and he bears a solemn responsibility to protect and improve the environment for present and future generations.

This principle encapsulates two key obligations: first, intergenerational responsibility – such that present generations do not act in ways which jeopardise the existence of future generations (intergenerational equity); and secondly, environmental justice in the here and now –

Table 2.1 Green constructions of justice

	Notions of rights	Key concepts	Notion of harm
Environmental justice	Environmental rights as an extension of human or social rights so as to enhance the quality of human life	*Intergenerational responsibility* – equity and future generations *Environmental Justice* – equity for present generations	Environmental harm is constructed in relation to human-centred notions of good and bad
Ecological justice	Ecological rights acknowledge that human beings are merely one component of complex ecosystems that should be preserved for their own sake via the notion of the rights of the environment	*Global transboundary* – issues of scale and interconnectedness *Ecological justice* – quality of biosphere and rights of non-human species	Environmental harm is constructed in relation to notions of ecological harm and destructive techniques of human intervention

such that access to and use of specific natural resources in defined geographical areas, and the impacts of particular social practices and environmental hazards, are 'shared out' on an equal rather than discriminatory basis (social equity). Environmental harm is thereby constructed in relation to perceptions of 'value' that place humans at the core.

Environmental issues are examined in terms of effects on human populations, including the ramifications of certain practices on competing industries (e.g. negative impact of clear-fell logging on tourism). The use of pesticides, to take another example, may have dramatic impacts on animal species (e.g. these seem to have coincided with the spread of a tumour disease amongst the Tasmanian devil population in recent years) and on specific environments (the pollution of coastal waters in north-eastern Tasmania). But the damage is often framed in terms of human loss (of a Tasmanian tourism icon; of the destruction of oyster farms) rather than impact on the biosphere or non-human animals *per se*. Not surprisingly, then, environmental justice movements are largely focused on redressing the unequal distribution of environmental disadvantage and, in particular, with preventing environmental hazards being located in their local area. However, if the notion of environmental justice is simply confined to this 'Not In My Back Yard' (NIMBY) approach, then issues of justice to the wider, non-human environment can, and will, be largely ignored.

By contrast, ecological notions of rights and justice see humans as but one component of complex ecosystems that should be preserved for their own sake, as supported by the notion of the rights of the environment. As Smith (1998: 99) puts it:

> By extending the moral community we are attributing intrinsic value to creatures and other natural things, as ends in themselves rather than the means to some set of human ends ... In ethical terms, any set of moral rules should consider these duties toward non-human animals, the land, forests and woodland, the oceans, mountains and the biosphere.

Translated into the language of rights, it has been argued by Berry (in Cullinan 2003: 115) that every component of the Earth Community has three rights: 'The right to be, the right to habitat, and the right to fulfil its role in the ever-renewing processes of the Earth Community'. What this actually means in practice is difficult to determine, however, since any decision about a particular environmental issue very much depends upon situational factors, community norms and values, and available technologies and techniques.

Nevertheless, even given the ambiguities of practice, what necessarily follows from this particular ecological perspective are notions of interconnectedness and human obligations to the non-human world around them. All living things are bound together, and environmental matters are intrinsically global and transboundary in nature (as witnessed, for example, by the spread of the bird flu virus worldwide, across national borders). Ecological justice demands that how humans interact with their environment be evaluated in relation to potential harms and risks to specific creatures and specific locales as well as the biosphere generally. Clear-felling of old-growth forests, accompanied by the laying of poison baits to kill animals and the burning of remnants, is inherently wrong and deviant from this perspective.

Human intervention and ecological citizenship

When it comes to environmental harm, what actually gets criminalised by and large reflects an anthropocentric perspective on the nature of the harm in question. In part this stems from the ways in which 'environmental rights' have been framed in law, particularly in relation to broader developments *vis-à-vis* human rights legislation (see Thornton and Tromans 1999). It also relates to the strategic interests of industries and indeed humanity as a whole to protect and preserve particular environments and/or species for the 'greater good'. Part of the dilemma for green criminologists is how to sensibly move the debate beyond standard anthropocentric approaches to environmental crime, and how to shift policy and practice in ways that are more effective than conventional forms of environmental regulation.

Perhaps the answer lies in a form of *ecological citizenship* that incorporates the key concerns of both environmental justice and ecological justice. Arguably, however, there still has to be a point at which human interests become privileged in determining the nature of the relationship between 'nature' and 'society'. This is so for several reasons.

Ecological justice could be viewed as an end in itself. However, the problem then is twofold: first, humans are responsible for much of the destruction of ecological systems and, as such, are the key agents of environmental change in the contemporary time period. There may well be a tango between humans and their environments but the dance tends to strongly reflect how humans as a whole transform their immediate environments for their own purposes. The net result is to the detriment of both human and non-human, but the causal force for environmental degradation is ultimately human. This is not to deny post-human observations on the powerful shaping of human society by 'nature' and natural phenomena (such as river systems, burning forests and so on). But at a gross, historical level it is what humans do *en masse* that reshapes landscapes, pollutes air, water and soil, leads to species decline among plants and animals, and changes the content of the atmosphere and the level of the seas. The moral responsibility for this lies with us humans.

Secondly, the construction of moral egalitarianism across species and systems is both illogical and impractical (Low and Gleeson 1998). At what point do we let the mosquito live and the human die? Do harmful bacteria automatically have a right to life? A biocentric perspective can lead to a misanthropic perspective that belittles the differences between species and which sees the human species as intrinsically and innately destructive to the environment. Thus, AIDS or famine may be seen as nature's way of controlling population growth and this is viewed as good for the planet as a whole (White 1994). Such views quickly lead to racism, élitism and anti-human policies. They are morally repugnant and politically suspect.

The key questions are: how do we engender a system of regulation and human intervention that will provide the best outcome for human and non-human, and what criteria do we use to conceptualise the nature of environmental harm arising from human actions? To answer these, we need to appreciate why it is that human societies simultaneously respect and protect certain creatures (especially animal companions such as dogs and cats) while allowing and even condoning the utterly dreadful treatment of others (as in the case of factory farming of battery hens to produce eggs) (Beirne 2004). We need to know why it is that we strive to preserve some environments (via creation of national parks), while at the same time ensuring the devastation of particular ecosystems (such as clear-felling of old-growth forests). In exploring these kinds of social processes, it becomes clear very quickly that political economy is at the heart of the exploitation of animals and environments – that capitalism, in particular, demands profitable use of such as a means to assign value (White 2002).

By contrast, an ecocentric perspective does not reduce people from social beings to simple species (as may occur in biocentric perspectives), but explores the dialectical relationship between the human and the non-human. An ecocentric or social ecology perspective emphasises humanity and the ability of humans to change themselves and the natural world. It looks to the human causes of environmental destruction but in so doing attempts to specify which particular categories of humans are responsible for this destruction and which social systems lead inexorably to ecological disaster. It is a perspective grounded in recognition of different social interests, different forms and types of social power, and clear distinctions being drawn between exploiter and exploited, oppressor and oppressed.

The notion of 'universal human interests' is useful here in contradistinction to sectoral human interests. Interestingly, appealing to universal human interests as part of a social reform process is precisely what President Gorbachev of the former Soviet Union did in the mid-1980s. During this time Gobachev started to rethink the nature of his particular regime and society, and he came up with the ideas of 'perestroika' (meaning restructuring) and 'glasnost' (meaning openness). As part of his reform agenda for communism and what was a totalitarian society, he began to speak about how humans are at the stage in their history where we now have to go beyond simple class interests as such and start to talk about universal human interests. The context of this was the threat of nuclear annihilation due to a clash of ideologies and ambitions between the two world superpowers. The other example of potential global catastrophe was the environmental crisis. According to Gorbachev, unless we deal with the environmental crisis as a universal problem then we risk humanity as a whole (Gorbachev 1987).

Humanity has common interests – universal human interests – namely, the survival of the human race in the face of things like nuclear holocaust or ecological degradation. There are thus common human interests that need to take priority over any other kind of interests if we are, as a species, to survive. However, while everybody on the planet has a common interest in the survival of the human race, the specific class interests of business, of transnational companies, of corporations, mean that they are not willing to implement or enact strategies and policies that would, in fact, further the common human interest. In other words the reason why we are not fixing up the planet, even though it is to the advantage of all that we work together in our common interest, is that specific class interests intrude upon the process whereby planetary well-being might be prioritised (see Athanasiou 1996).

From an ecocentric point of view the relationship between the human and non-human is largely informed by the notion of the *enlightened self-interest* of humans. This is, in one sense, a human-centred or anthropocentric viewpoint. But what makes it different from the dominant anthropocentric perspective is the sensitivity to the dialectical nature of change, including those constant changes in the relationship between humans and nature over time. A dynamic concept of 'nature' is complemented by a notion of 'totality' and interconnectedness. Thus, the relationship between humans and the so-called natural environment is seen as one that includes consideration of the impact of humans on particular environments beyond the physical boundaries of human settlement (e.g. pollution in cities affecting forests via acid rain). Respect for nature is integral to the well-being of humans.

Environmental harm and conflicts over rights

What constitutes an environmental harm or environmental crime is partly a matter of visibility of the issues, partly a matter of public policy. What can be identified via personal experiences, expert representation or sectional interest group as being worthy of attention is that which is most likely to gain recognition as a public issue (Hannigan 1995). Meanwhile, governments have laws across a wide range of issues, relating to air, water, toxic waste, use of public lands, endangered species and the list goes on. The relationship between public policy and government strategic action is also shaped by contingency – specific events, situations and disasters tend to shake things up rapidly and with immediate effect.

The precise nature of an environmental issue is in itself linked to specific group interests and consciousness of harm. For example, environmental issues have been categorised according to three different types of harm (Crook and Pakulski 1995; Tranter 2004; see also Curson and Clark 2004). These are set out in Table 2.2. *Brown* issues tend to be defined in terms of urban life and pollution, *green* issues mainly relate to wilderness areas and conservation matters, and *white* issues refer to science laboratories and the impact of new technologies. Conceptualising environmental issues in this way helps to demonstrate the link between environmental action (usually involving distinct types of community and environmental groups), and particular sites (such as urban centres, wilderness areas or sea-coast regions). Some issues tend to resonate more with members

Table 2.2 Colouring environmental issues

'Brown' issues	'Green' issues	'White' issues
air pollution	acid rain	genetically modified organisms
pollution of urban storm water	habitat destruction	food irradiation
pollution of beaches	loss of wildlife	*in vitro* processes
pesticides	logging of forests	cloning of human tissue
oil spills	depletion of ozone layer	genetic discrimination
pollution of water catchments	toxic algae	environmentally related communicable diseases
disposal of toxic/ hazardous waste	invasive species via human transport water pollution	pathological indoor environments

Source: White (2005b)

of the public than others; other issues generally only emerge if an accident or disaster brings them to the fore.

The mobilisation of opinion is crucial to determination of what is or is not considered a 'crime' (or 'harm'), and how the state will in the end respond to the phenomenon in question. The complex relationship between human and non-human 'rights' is thus played out in practice through the importance of 'place' in the lives of diverse communities. This inevitably leads to conflicts over purposes, as each place or site is subject to competing demands – jobs (via logging), recreation (via tourism), sustenance (via settlement), aesthetics (via photography) and so on. Disputes over value and use are settled using the full range of political, ideological, legal, coercive and persuasive means available to stakeholder parties. The complexities of conflict over rights is well captured by Christoff (2000: 204):

Claims relating to environmental rights potentially conflict with social and economic rights. Consider, for instance, the struggle over the fate of Australia's old growth forests. On the one hand, timber companies want to harvest 'their' logs (property rights), while timber workers want to preserve their jobs and resource managers want to be able to manage the forests for products such as timber and water for immediate human use (social rights to employment, culture, and development). On the other hand, environmentalists want to preserve forests for their wilderness values (reflecting social rights to meet 'abstract' aesthetic and spiritual needs) and biodiversity (reflecting environmental rights protecting an unquantifiable asset benefiting present and future humans, and intrinsic values relating to the existence of species and ecosystems). It is the presence of such – at their most fundamental – irreconcilable value conflicts which makes the relationship between social, environmental and ecological rights (and citizens) so problematic in practice.

There is, of course, an array of conflicts and confusions regarding environmental and ecological rights (see for examples, Goldman 1998; Low and Gleeson 1998; Cullinan 2003; Munro 2004), including:

- jobs versus environment (where a social right to livelihood conflicts with ecological imperatives to sustain species and environments);

- intrinsic values (constructing 'value' and drawing lines around speciesism, so that we can identify to what and to whom rights apply in specific circumstances);

- perils of non-intervention (acknowledging the practicalities of human need *vis-à-vis* food, shelter, clothing, and the potential problems that arise if management of seal numbers, or deer herds, or kangaroo populations does not occur);

- individual versus collective notions of rights (the ongoing tensions between bourgeois notions of private property and public interest notions of property);

- prioritising actions on rights (in specific cases, putting an emphasis on homeless humans rather than loss of bird habitat);

- constructing the global commons (corporate definitions of what is 'best' for local peoples and transnational interference from afar versus grassroots organising and input into decision-making).

Philosophically, a framework of ecological citizenship orients us towards a positive and healthy relationship between human endeavour and the non-human world around us, but it does not provide a blueprint for how to resolve practical problems and conflicts of rights. Nor should it. After all, 'nature' by definition is complex, uncertain, interconnected and ever-changing. What is apparently a benign policy prescription one day may lead to disaster the next. For example, one alternative to clear-felling of old-growth forests has been greater reliance on pine forest plantations. However, while some of the old-growth forests may have been protected, the planting of one species of tree lends itself to greater susceptibility to disease and diminution of biodiversity. Only a flexible approach to logging and forestry will allow change in perspective and practices over time, as we better understand the nuances and dangers of solutions that at the time seem to make sense.

Deliberative democracy

The foregoing discussion highlights the need to deliberate extensively on environmental issues, due to their complexity and due to the various conflicts that arise in any given situation. The dialogue must be continuous and extensive. For this deliberation to occur, there is a need to expand democratic space, and to broaden the base of expertise and understanding of environments and environmental issues, often against those who wish to restrict discursive spaces.

A starting point for deliberation, from the point of view of ecological citizenship, is the concept that human laws and human rights have to be tempered by the acknowledgement that human interests are intimately bound up with the well-being of the planet as a whole. Human intervention, of any kind, needs to be considered in the light of this. Hence, the importance of the precautionary principle in gauging potential and real impacts arising from human activity cannot be overstated. Moreover, the concern in many cases is not with the protection of specific individuals or consideration of particular human rights. Rather, when we plan on the basis of intergenerational equity or biosphere integrity we do so with the collectivity in mind, not the individual *per se*.

Taking precautions is not only about risk assessment. It is about marshalling requisite expertise in order to best understand the specific problem at hand. Science can and must be a major tool in deliberations over human interventions and human impacts. But this is only one sort of knowledge. Expertise is also very much developed from the ground up, not simply on the basis of experiment and scientific method. Farmers on the land, and fishers of the sea, for example, have generations of expertise built up over time and under varying environmental conditions. Indigenous peoples frequently have knowledge and understandings of their environments that go back to time immemorial (South, this volume). The fact that some indigenous people have survived and thrived for thousands of years in extremely hostile environments (the frozen lands of the north, the deserts of the dry continents) is testimony to human practices that are connected, positively, to immediate environs (Robyn 2002). A public participatory process of deliberation needs to incorporate all of these kinds of voices and be able to challenge the 'wisdom' and 'truth' of each, without prejudice or fear.

The mobilisation of different kinds of expertise, and confrontations over different values, is an essential part of the deliberation. Certain types of logging practice, for example, are invariably accompanied by clashes of values and by conflicts relating to impact. Clear-felling old-growth forest raises issues of the aesthetics of wilderness, about the importance of other species being able to live within old-growth forests, about the impact on tourism, and so on. From a technical point of view, the cutting of trees in certain locations can also affect watersheds, and ultimately the quality and quantity of drinking water. On the other hand, consider the circumstances of the logging community. In places like Tasmania, a fairly small number of people work in the forestry industry, usually on a sub-contracted basis and usually involving hard work for relatively little pay. In many cases, the same family has been involved in the industry over many generations. Logging is the lifeblood of their close-knit community, and the rituals, legends and habits associated with it are essential parts of the cultural tradition of those families. It is all they have ever known. Will they easily accept the transition to other kinds of work (serving coffee in a restaurant?) or the demise of centuries of tradition (based upon hard physical labour, certain roles for menfolk and womenfolk, pride in doing dangerous jobs well)? The issue here is not simply 'jobs' versus 'environment' – it pertains to whole ways of life. And without dialogue around these issues, as well as about the nature, problems and contributions of specific kinds of logging, conflict will inevitably ensue. The division between workers and environmentalists can be further exacerbated when legal action is taken by one side against the other (McCulloch 2005). This, too, reduces the space for discussion of shared interests (and shared enemies) and potential common ground.

In 1990 the United Nations Commission on Human Rights adopted a first resolution on human rights and the environment, which affirmed the relationship between the preservation of the environment and the protection of human rights. By 1998 there had been developed an Environmental Rights Convention – the Convention on Access to

Information, Public Participation and Decision Making and Access to Justice in Environmental Matters. What that convention expresses is that everyone should have access to information about the environment and that we collectively should have rights to participate in decisions about the environment (see Thornton and Tromans 1999). For this to happen there is a need for transparency and the 'right to know' what governments, community groups and corporations are doing in relation to the environment.

Among the challenges to deliberative democracy are the 'silences' that permeate environmental planning and particular types of human intervention. These silences may be bolstered by appeal to commercial confidentiality clauses in government contracts and by inadequate corporate reporting mechanisms. They may be reinforced by concerted attempts to greenwash issues (this pulp mill will be the most environmentally friendly ever built, claimed a prominent Tasmania-based company, which then proceeded to whittle away each safeguard that was central to the initial claim) and companies (we do everything in a sustainable and environmentally friendly way, says the same company). Greenwashing is basically about public relations and is today a huge part of any corporate image-making (see Beder 1998; Athanasiou 1996; Hager and Burton 1999). Assessing environmental harm, from either an environmental justice or an ecological justice perspective, is difficult if the issues are clouded and obscured from the beginning.

When environmental harm is contested – conceptually and evidentially – and there are major specific social interests at play (governments, companies, workers, consumers, environmentalists, residents), then those with the power tend to shape public debate in ways that often diminish participation and deliberation. This diminishment and distortion may take the form of out-and-out propaganda wars. For instance, the forest debates in Tasmania are shaped by the fact that political power is closely tied up with the industry and that the media is basically looking for sensationalism (in those instances when it is not reliant upon industry advertising and thus already 'compliant' to industry perspectives). As a consequence, the debate is presented as highly polarised, and each side engages in what might be seen as a propaganda, rather than deliberative, process.

The green criminologist must also be cognisant of how litigation can be used to silence critics and curtail public debate. A lawsuit filed against 20 environmental activists (including Green politicians, as well as the Wilderness Society and others) by the largest logging company in Australia in December 2004 was precisely intended to shut down alternative voices in the forestry debate (see White 2005a). The use of Strategic Lawsuits Against Public Participation (SLAPPs) is not new but it can be highly effective in shutting down opposition to specific projects and developments (Walters 2003). Or, as in the Gunns20 case, it may generate fierce resistance and broader public consternation about the practices of large companies (White 2005a). The criminalisation of environmental dissent, whether it be through SLAPPs or through particular types of policing of environmental protests and activism, is a topic warranting close scrutiny. This is especially so if we acknowledge the centrality of public participation in decision-making processes involving environmental issues.

Conclusion

I started this chapter by observing that green criminology is an emergent but already very diverse area of research and activism. It covers a wide range of issues and incorporates a spectrum of ideological and philosophical perspectives. Broadly speaking, these distil down to two key approaches or bundles of concern: environmental justice, with a special focus on human rights and social equity; and ecological justice, with a special focus on the biosphere generally and the rights of the non-human as well as human. Bridging these two approaches is the notion of ecological citizenship, the idea that as central actors in shaping environments, humans must act in accordance with their universal human interests and govern their actions so as to ensure the well-being of the ecosystem as a whole.

Acknowledgement of basic principles allows us to identify differences in values and perspective. It also provides the connection between apparently incompatible approaches. A major argument of this chapter is that there is no one 'right answer' when it comes to evaluation of ecological systems and environmental harm. Which human interventions and activities ought to be criminalised, which forms of social regulation would be most appropriate, how best to respond to pressing issues of species and environmental protection – these are open-ended matters. More often than not there are competing social interests that must be taken into account, and this requires sensitivity to the expression of different voices, different beliefs and different expertise. Furthermore, the dynamics of animal life and of local ecosystems means that any action taken must be subject to ongoing review. Life is ever-changing and dealing with unintended consequences is one of its perennial challenges.

The essence of contemporary green criminology, therefore, must be to defend and expand the democratic impulse. This means being willing and able to expose environmental harms and social injustices, very often by engaging in counterhegemonic struggle against the powerful institutions of late capitalism and of nation-states that perpetuate much of the degradation of humans and non-humans alike. It means opening up discussion about the complexity of environmental obligations and the need for information, diverse expertise and constant dialogue with regard to the human–environment interface. It means taking a planetary view, one that recognises the global and local nature of environmental interests, and the need for positive action at different levels to deal with matters such as climate change or inappropriate fishing practices. It means challenging those who wish to diminish public participation, whether through lawsuits, media misinformation campaigns, trade agreements or outright thuggery.

Ultimately green criminology ought to be about public accountability in regard to how specific populations of people live their lives and how humans, generally, relate to the biosphere and non-human world. Accountability is about being responsible for ourselves and for the world around us. Ecological citizenship means taking environmental harm seriously, both as an object of study and as an agenda for action. It is time for a green 'perestroika'. This, too, demands an environmental 'glasnost' – one that is participatory, positive and constant if planetary well-being is truly the goal.

References

Athanasiou, T. (1996) *Divided Planet: The Ecology of Rich and Poor*. Boston: Little, Brown.

Beck, U. (1996) 'World Risk Society as Cosmopolitan Society? Ecological Questions in a Framework of Manufactured Uncertainties', *Theory, Culture, Society*, 13 (4): 1–32.

Beirne, P. (1999) 'For a Nonspeciesist Criminology: Animal Abuse as an Object of Study', *Criminology*, 37 (1): 117–148.

Beirne, P. (2004) 'From Animal Abuse to Interhuman Violence? A Critical Review of the Progression Thesis', *Society and Animals*, 12 (1): 39–65.

Benton, T. (1998) 'Rights and Justice on a Shared Planet: more rights or new relations?', *Theoretical Criminology*, 2 (2): 149–175.

Bullard, R. (1994) *Unequal Protection: Environmental Justice and Communities of Color*. San Francisco: Sierra Club Books.

Christoff, P. (2000) 'Environmental Citizenship', in W. Hudson and J. Kane (eds) *Rethinking Australian Citizenship*. Melbourne: Cambridge University Press.

Chunn, D., Boyd, S. and Menzies, R. (2002) '"We all live in Bhopal": Criminology Discovers Environmental Crime', in Boyd, Chunn and Menzies (eds) *Toxic Criminology: Environment, Law and the State in Canada*. Halifax: Fernwood Publishing.

Crook, S. and Pakulski, J. (1995) 'Shades of Green: Public Opinion on Environmental Issues in Australia', *Australian Journal of Political Science*, 30: 39–55.

Cullinan, C. (2003) *Wild Law: A Manifesto for Earth Justice*. London: Green Books in association with The Gaia Foundation.

Curson, P. and Clark, L. (2004) 'Pathological Environments', in R. White (ed.) *Controversies in Environmental Sociology*. Melbourne: Cambridge University Press.

del Frate, A. and Norberry, J. (eds) (1993) *Environmental Crime: Sanctioning Strategies and Sustainable Development*. Rome: UNICRI /Sydney: Australian Institute of Criminology.

Franklin, A. (1999) *Animals and Modern Cultures: A Sociology of Human–Animal Relations in Modernity*. London: Sage.

Goldman, M. (1998) 'Inventing the Commons: Theories and Practices of the Commons' Professional', in M. Goldman (ed.) *Privatizing Nature: Political Struggles for the Global Commons*. London: Pluto Press in association with Transnational Institute.

Gorbachev, M. (1987) *Perestroika: New Thinking for Our Country and the World*. London: Collins.

Hager, N. and Burton, B. (1999) *Secrets and Lies: The Anatomy of an Anti-Environmental PR Campaign*. New Zealand: Craig Potton Publishing.

Halsey, M. (1997a) 'The Wood for the Paper: Old-Growth Forest, Hemp and Environmental Harm', *Australian and New Zealand Journal of Criminology*, 30 (2): 121–148.

Halsey, M. (1997b) 'Environmental Crime: Towards an Eco-Human Rights Approach', *Current Issues in Criminal Justice*, 8 (3): 217–242.

Halsey, M. (2004) 'Against "Green" Criminology', *British Journal of Criminology*, 44 (6): 833–853.

Halsey, M. and White, R. (1998) 'Crime, Ecophilosophy and Environmental Harm', *Theoretical Criminology*, 2 (3): 345–371.

Hannigan, J. (1995) *Environmental Sociology: A Social Constructionist Perspective*. London: Routledge.

Harvey, D. (1996) *Justice, Nature and the Geography of Difference*. Oxford: Blackwell.

Julian, R. (2004) 'Inequality, Social Differences and Environmental Resources', in R. White (ed.) *Controversies in Environmental Sociology*. Cambridge: Cambridge University Press.

Langton, M. (1998) *Burning Questions: Emerging Environmental Issues for Indigenous Peoples in Northern Australia*. Darwin: Centre for Indigenous Natural and Cultural Resource Management.

Low, N. and Gleeson, B. (1998) *Justice, Society and Nature: An Exploration of Political Ecology*. London: Routledge.

Lynch, M. and Stretesky, P. (2003) 'The Meaning of Green: Contrasting Criminological Perspectives', *Theoretical Criminology*, 7 (2): 217–238.

McCulloch, J. (2005) 'Loggerheads over Old Growth Forests: Growing Civil Society Against State Crime and the Timber Wedge', *Current Issues in Criminal Justice*, 16 (3): 351–367.

Munro, L. (2004) 'Animals, "Nature" and Human Interests', in R. White (ed.) *Controversies in Environmental Sociology*. Melbourne: Cambridge University Press.

Pearce, F. and Tombs, S. (1998) *Toxic Capitalism: Corporate Crime and the Chemical Industry*. Aldershot: Dartmouth.

Robyn, L. (2002) 'Indigenous Knowledge and Technology', *American Indian Quarterly*, 26(2): 198–220.

Rush, S. (2002) 'Aboriginal Resistance to the Abuse of their Natural Resources: The Struggle for Trees and Water', in S. Boyd, D. Chunn and R. Menzies (eds) *Toxic Criminology: Environment, Law and the State in Canada*. Halifax: Fernwood Publishing.

Situ, Y. and Emmons, D. (2000) *Environmental Crime: The Criminal Justice System's Role in Protecting the Environment*. Thousand Oaks: Sage.

Smith, M. (1998) *Ecologism: Towards Ecological Citizenship*. Minneapolis: University of Minnesota Press.

South, N. (1998) 'A Green Field for Criminology', *Theoretical Criminology*, 2 (2): 211–234.

Stevens, S. (1996) 'Reflections on Environmental Justice: Children as Victims and Actors', *Social Justice*, 23 (4): 62–86.

Thornton, J. and Tromans, S. (1999) 'Human Rights and Environmental Wrongs: Incorporating the European Convention on Human Rights: Some Thoughts on the Consequences for UK Environmental Law', *Journal of Environmental Law*, 11 (1): 35–57.

Tomkins, K. (2005) 'Police, Law Enforcement and the Environment', *Current Issues in Criminal Justice*, 16 (3): 294–306.

Tranter, B. (2004) 'The Environmental Movement: Where To From Here?', in R. White (ed.) *Controversies in Environmental Sociology*. Cambridge: Cambridge University Press.

Walters, B. (2003) *Slapping on the Writs: Defamation, Developers and Community Activism*. Sydney: UNSW Press.

White, R. (1994) 'Green Politics and the Question of Population', *Journal of Australian Studies*, 40: 27–43.

White, R. (2002) 'Environmental Harm and the Political Economy of Consumption', *Social Justice*, 29 (1–2): 82–102.

White, R. (2003) 'Environmental Issues and the Criminological Imagination', *Theoretical Criminology*, 7 (4): 483–506.

White, R. (2005a) 'Stifling Environmental Dissent: On SLAPPS and GUNNS', *Alternative Law Journal*, 30 (6): 268–273.

White, R. (2005b) 'Environmental Crime in Global Context: Exploring the Theoretical and Empirical Complexities', *Current Issues in Criminal Justice*, 16 (3): 271–285.

Williams, C. (1996) 'An Environmental Victimology', *Social Justice*, 23 (4): 16–40.

Chapter 3

Animal rights, animal abuse and green criminology

Piers Beirne[1]

This chapter offers an overview of the intersection of animal rights theory with existing green criminology. As a sociologist and as someone who regularly inhabits both sides of this intersection, I believe that some of the major concerns of the one can illuminate and extend those of the other. My particular focus here is to develop a space within green criminology for the rights of non-human animals (hereinafter, 'animals').

By the term 'animal abuse' I mean those diverse human actions that contribute to the pain, suffering or death of animals or that otherwise adversely affect their welfare. Animal abuse may be physical, psychological or emotional. It may involve active maltreatment or passive neglect, and may be direct or indirect (and see Cazaux and Beirne 2001). Sometimes, of course, animals are harmed when their environments are degraded through the sheer chaos wrought by natural disasters such as earthquakes, hurricanes and tsunamis, or through human-induced causes like wars, climate change, oil spills and road construction. From the outset I must stress, too, that the sources of animal abuse lie not only in the personal biographies of those humans who abuse animals in one-on-one situations of cruelty and neglect, but also in various institutionalised social practices where animal abuse is seen as socially acceptable.

There is a certain obviousness about how to forge some common ground between the animal-centred discourse of animal rights and the environmentalist-based discourse of green criminology. They already have much in common, for example. Each has been nurtured within a much larger social movement – respectively, the animal protection community and various environmentalism(s). These larger movements originated at roughly the same time and under similar circumstances, namely, the turbulence, iconoclasm and leftist political activism of the early- to mid-1960s ('*For* Social Justice!' '*For* Environmental Justice!' '*Save* the Animals!'). Moreover, in terms of their ethical perspectives and much of their theoretical assumptions, both movements have an underlying concern with relations of power and inequality and with the elimination of their undesirable effects. These latter include harm, exclusion, injury and suffering. Each in its own way is more or less consciously anti-statist and anti-authoritarian. Each embraces participatory democracy. Adherents of one movement often travel seamlessly to the other, and they often support the causes of both, including buying locally and buying less, reusing and recycling, using public transportation, and vegetarianism.

However, the task of finding in the area of animal abuse common ground between an environmentally- (or ecologically-) based green criminology and an animal-centred animal rights theory, worthwhile as it might be, is not altogether a straightforward one. This is so not only because most of us are normally in a state of denial about animal rights issues, as some sociologists have pointed out (Agnew 1997; Cohen 2001: 205, 289; and see Yates 2004: 394–395). Several other obstacles confront this task, moreover, some of them matters of convenience and definition, still others without clear resolution. What follows here, therefore, is introductory, provisional and argumentative.

Images of non-human animals in criminology

Though animal abuse is not a well-developed category in criminology, various images of animals' capacities are nevertheless present in its discourse. These include animals as (A) property; (B) prototypes of criminality in humans; (C) abused signifiers of interhuman violence; and as (D) the apparent bearers of rights in the emerging literature of green criminology.

(A) **Animals as property** Animals' role as human property has always been the master status assigned them. This is so in anti-cruelty statutes, for example, and in other dividing practices, where a human community's moral standards are invoked to support legalistic norms about acceptable and unacceptable treatment of animals (Francione 1995). Animals typically enter criminology as objects whose property identity has been stolen, poached, damaged, held as ransom, rustled or otherwise misappropriated or spoiled. As property, too, animals appear at different points in the food chain of carnivorous societies (Adams 1999). In this guise they appear, for example, in studies of class, gender, cultural and other practices to do with the appropriation of animals from the 'wild'; of the utility of law, of gamekeepers and of ecological police set against the desired health and size of animal populations; and of the meat and poultry industries, when their quantity or quality as commodities may variously signify theft, fraud, deceptive advertising, and unhealthy or dangerous practices (see Croall, this volume chapter 9).

Clinard's (1952) *The Black Market* is a classic example of just this. Clinard's focus here was white-collar crimes associated with the slaughter and distribution of meat in the context of the system of meat rationing that existed in the US during the 1939–45 war. The animals in his analysis appear only as commodities that arrive in supermarkets and butchers as neatly-wrapped packages of flesh and which can be had for tickets in coupon books. Nowhere did Clinard consider whether, before the rationed carcasses of these animals were distributed, white-collar executives or slaughterhouse workers had participated in cruel practices against them (or what those practices might be).[2]

Consider also David Simon's (2006: 137) lament in *Elite Deviance* for the ingredients of the 'hot dog'.

> The hot dog ... by law can contain 69 per cent water, salt, spices, corn syrup and cereal and 15 per cent chicken; that still leaves a little room for goat meat, pigs' ears, eyes, stomachs, snouts, udders, bladders and esophagus – all legally okay. There is no more all-American way to take a break at the old ball game than to have water and pigs' snouts on bun, but you might prefer to go heavier on the mustard from now on.

The surface message here is that the deceptive practices of 'meatpackers' can result in 'dangerous nutrition' and in 'adulterated products'. This happens, Simon suggests, because profit-conscious meatpackers know better than to label hot dog packages with a full list of ingredients for squeamish consumers. But nothing is said about how, precisely, chickens, goats and pigs are raised, fed, and slaughtered for consumption as hot dogs by humans. Moreover, one must assume that no sarcastic complaint about the need for extra mustard would have been made if, instead of using eyes, ears and other organs, hot dog producers used the less visually challenging and more palatable flesh of breasts, legs and wings.

(B) **Animals as prototypes of criminality in humans** This role has largely appeared in three movements in criminology.

(i) *Lombrosian criminal anthropology* Atavism, 'the wild' and the 'primitive' lie close to the positivist centre of Lombrosian anthropology, which wielded intellectual and social power in Europe from the mid-1870s to approximately the beginning of the 1914–1918 war (and into the 1930s in the United States). In his foundational text *Criminal Man* Lombroso (1876) invented his notion of the 'born criminal', who exhibited a constellation of ape-like attributes – known as atavism – dependent on a demarcation of the 'normal' and 'law-abiding citizenry' from the criminal type. Lombroso claimed that criminals were 'survivals of primitive man and of carnivorous animals' and that, in order to uncover the origins of criminality, one might have to go 'as far back' as various insectivorous plants.

(ii) *The Chicago school of sociology/social ecology* Animals and plants appeared in many works of the Chicago school between 1914 and 1945. Fleetingly and behind the empirical stage, they are lodged in Park and Burgess's (1921) *Introduction to the Science of Sociology* (at that time termed 'the Green Bible'), for example, in the ecological notions of competition, conflict, accommodation and assimilation, where competition in the plant and non-human animal communities is a thinly disguised veneer of normalcy for the normalisation of competition in the capitalist, *laissez-faire* economy. Animal behaviour (e.g. of bees swarming) was also used as an homology to describe delinquent or deviant or criminal behaviour, such as that of boys' gangs (Thrasher 1927) and of homeless migratory men (Anderson 1923).

(iii) *Biocriminology* Animals were again assigned importance in criminology in the 1980s, this time reflecting a coincidence in the respective domain concerns of, first, those natural scientists wishing to apply ethological and ecological principles to the study of human societies and, second, some sociologists who wished to abandon Durkheim's imperialistic dictum in *The Rules* that the social and cultural realms are autonomous from the biological.

Animals have been assigned at least two distinct roles in biocriminology. In the one, especially in lines of reasoning that claim causal relationships between human nature and crime, animal behaviour tends implicitly to be posited as an expression of the unproblematic negation of human morality, as the dark underbelly of human life (e.g. Wilson and Herrnstein 1985: 508–529; and see

Rowe 2002). In the other, animals appear when generalisations about their social behaviour comprise sites of extrapolation for inferences about the criminal behaviour of humans. To Daly and Wilson (1988), for example, much can be learned from the actions of usually timid small mammals, who become fiercewhen they have pups to defend – because the properties of all organisms are adaptively constructed as a result of natural selection, all animal behaviour (including that of humans) is organised to serve narrow self-interest.

(C) **Animals as abused signifiers of interhuman violence** The claim that there is a significant relationship between animal abuse and interhuman violence is nowadays disseminated in the mantra-like catchphrase 'The Link'. This has two related, if analytically separable, directions: respectively, family violence and 'the progression thesis'.

(i) *Family violence* It is well established that different forms of family violence tend to coexist. If a male is battering his spouse, for example, then it is more likely that children in that household are also being abused or neglected there. Households where men abuse women, and vice versa, are more likely to have not only children who are being abused but also one child who is abusing another.

Existing data, sparse as they are, suggest that in situations of intrafamilial conflict humans often use animals as instruments of psychological and physical terror. Precisely because the several forms of family violence tend to cluster and because companion animals – or as Geertrui Cazaux (this volume, p. 92) rightly identifies them, animals appointed as companions – are usually regarded as family members, we should expect to find that in families where any given form of family violence exists, animal abuse is also more likely to exist there.

Empirical evidence does indeed indicate that companion animal abuse often occurs disproportionately in quite diverse situations of family violence, including heterosexual partner abuse; lesbian partner abuse; child physical abuse; child sexual abuse; and sibling abuse (Agnew 1997; Arluke, Levin, Luke and Ascione 1999; Flynn 2000; Ascione 2001; Baldry 2003). One of the undoubted strengths of this generalisation is the diversity of its data sources. These latter derive from both structured interviews with battered women and abused children and also from reports of animal abuse to veterinarians, animal control officers, animal shelters, women's shelters and police.

(ii) *The 'progression thesis'* When it first appeared in sociological research of the 1960s and 1970s, the term 'the progression thesis' was used to refer to apparent cause-and-effect relationships in the non-medical use of drugs and alcohol. In human–animal studies, it has appeared in a rather focused way only in the last decade. At root, it claims that there is an escalating causal relationship between animal abuse and interhuman violence.

Before it can confidently be said that a pattern of progression from animal abuse to interhuman violence really exists – and, if so, then of what sort(s) – several quite thorny evidentiary problems must first be explored.[3] Operating almost mechanically as a point of entry into an inevitable upward spiral in which violence is alleged to move from lower to higher degrees of seriousness – finding its apex in the acts of multiple murderers (i.e. serial- and mass-) – the thesis, as it is currently articulated, is quite unconvincing (Beirne 2004). Moreover, especially in popular discourse, the lack of subtlety with which the complex relationship between animal abuse and interhuman violence is sometimes asserted makes it appear, however well intentioned, more the brittle product of sloganeering than of hard evidence and logic.

(D) **Animal rights in green criminology** While not seeing animals as 'living artifacts' – in the rights-denying sense of Callicott (1989) – existing green criminology has not yet properly problematised terms like 'animal', 'animal rights' and 'animal abuse'. My complaint about this can be illustrated by the focal concerns of two recent 'environmentalist-based' projects.[4] One champions green criminology, the other strongly opposes it.

Consider, first, a chapter entitled 'The Greening of Criminology' in a popular British criminology text (Carrabine, Iganski, Lee, Plummer and South 2004). Though green criminology is defined there as the study of 'crimes against the environment' (*ibid.*: 313), there is much discussion of crimes and other harms to animals, including the poisoning of cattle during the 1984 Bhopal disaster in India; the illegal trawling for salmon and other fish in seas off Alaska; crimes of species decline; and the resurgence in Britain of 'animal spectacles', including dog fights and badger baiting, for entertainment purposes (p. 317).

A discussion of these harms to animals is most welcome indeed. While these actions are regarded as one of several 'primary green crimes' under the general rubric 'crimes of species decline and animal rights' (*ibid.*), insufficient attention is paid to the content of animal rights, which particular animal species fall within its scope and why.

Consider, second, Mark Halsey's (2004) stinging post-structuralist rebuke to reformist environmentalism. Halsey's chief intention here is to nip green criminology firmly in the bud. As such, he attacks the very possibility of green criminology – depicting it as a conservative, uncritical tendency, ostensibly because its environmentalist aims derive from anthropocentric and statist definitions of social harm. 'Perhaps the most worrying trend emerging from recent criminological work on environmental issues', Halsey complains,

> is that such efforts have generally been of an *un*critical kind. By this I mean that such studies support and adhere to the tenets associated with ... a liberal ecological outlook – an outlook imbued by *anthropocentric* principles and practices. (pp. 835–836, emphases in original)

I learned a great deal about environmentalism from Halsey's comments. But his argument seems deliberately obscure and more nihilist than constructive. In particular, I am puzzled by his charge that an as-yet-unformed green criminology is an outlook 'imbued by *anthropocentric* principles and practices'.

I agree that there is often too much 'anthro' in various 'ologies' and 'isms'. But perhaps by 'anthropocentrism' Halsey means something other than 'human-centred'? Assuming that he is unable definitively to answer Thomas Nagel's (1974) famous question 'What Is It Like To Be a Bat?', Halsey's reasoning is hoist with its own petard. Put bluntly, his argument is a thoroughly anthropocentric way of looking at non-human animals and their exploitation by humans. Indeed, humans are the only animals who inhabit the pages of Halsey's environmentalist discourse!

To be fair, Halsey does rightly mention the general lack of criminological concern with such 'disturbing trends' as overfishing and species decline (p. 834). He also volunteers that he is 'deeply troubled by' statistics about the illicit trade in wildlife. But is he aware that 'wildlife' and 'fisheries' are anthropocentric categories with no objective ontological reality? Halsey briefly refers, too, to the need 'to view "others" as having to include non-human as well as human bodies' (p. 849)[5] – but in his view the bodies of these "others" might as well be Cartesian automata.

What, then, does criminology teach us about animals and, in particular, about animal abuse? The short answer is: not very much at all.

When animals appear in criminology they are almost always passive, insentient objects acted upon by humans. Discursively, as objects of human agency, animals reflect or are drawn into some aspect of the complex web of human relationships that is deemed problematic or undesirable. In research on family violence, for example, investigators admit the discursive relevance of animal abuse but tend not to perceive the physical, psychological or emotional abuse of animals as objects of study in their own right. In the literature on rapists and serial murderers, as another example, animals acquire significance only as pre-assaultive or pre-homicidal signs of interhuman conflict. Animal abuse has little or no significance *sui generis* presumably because it is not seen as 'real' crime but, rather, as a minor offence against property.

In particular, there has been almost no critical discussion of the employment and constitution of core concepts such as 'animal abuse' and 'animal cruelty', let alone of 'rights' and 'harms'. Yet, among the basic tasks of a non- (or less-) speciesist or green criminology is surely to understand the 'hows', the 'whys' and the 'whens' of animal abuse and how to confront it. Moving in that direction now, I do so with a note on speciesist language.

Speciesism and the power of language

The distinction between *Homo sapiens* and 'non-human animals' carries with it a cumbersome cultural baggage. Implicitly, it tends to be voiced as if humans were somehow not animals and as if all other animals were insapient ('dumb animals'). At root, the distinction assumes that non-human animals are necessarily the Other, among whose undesirable traits are uncleanliness, irrationality, untrustworthiness, lust, greed and the potential for sudden violence.

We humans routinely discriminate against non-human animals with our everyday usage of 'speciesist language', namely, utterances that express a prejudice or attitude towards one species – usually, one's own – and against those members of other species.[6] The Latin words *anima* (spirit, or breath) and *animal* probably entered old English as *'beste'* or 'beast' from the French *'bête'* which, in turn, likely derived from the Sanskrit 'that which is to be feared' (and see Collard 1989: 24).

The often-violent images and metaphors of speciesist language are saturated with implicit declarations about the differences between worthwhile lives and ones with little or no intrinsic value. For example, we refer without hesitation to humans as 'human *beings*' – a symbolic term of personhood that denotes volitional and sentient forms of life with self-consciousness and with bundles of rights and obligations that are worthy of respect. But we rarely, if ever, refer to non-human animals as 'animal beings'. Rather, they are named simply as 'animals' – the Other – an implicitly derogatory term synonymous with the notion that they are altogether different from humans and, *as such*, necessarily less than human.

Moreover, humans tend to be understood as complex creatures whose gender is an important item in forms of address. We refer to Jane Smith as 'Ms X', for example, or to Jack Jones as 'Mr Y', and to 'she who ...' or to 'he who ...' Except for animals appointed as companions ('pets'), however, non-human animals are seen as undifferentiated objects each of whom is normally identified not as a 'she' or a 'he' but an 'it' (it *'which'* ...).

Speciesism and sexism clearly operate together and in tandem, with women and non-human animals depicted as objects to be controlled, manipulated and exploited. Thus, when men describe women as 'cows', 'bitches', '(dumb) bunnies', 'birds', 'chicks', 'foxes', 'fresh meat', and their genitalia as other species, they use derogatory language to position both women and animals to an inferior status of 'less than human'.

Some forms of speciesist language are seemingly more subtle. These often hinge on animals' master status as the property of humans. 'Fisheries', for example, refers to no objective ontological reality but to diverse species that are acted upon as objects of commodification by humans and, as such, trapped or otherwise 'harvested', killed and consumed. The same sort of egregious misdescription appears in many other categories as well, including 'laboratory animals' (see Tom Regan, this volume, chapter 5), 'pets', 'circus animals' and 'racehorses'. The latter, to offer another example, misdescribes horses that are *used* by humans to race against each other over tracks and on courses. In fact, they are horses *used* as racehorses.[7]

Clearly, radical revision of speciesist nomenclature is long overdue. In some cases new descriptions altogether are needed – for example, 'misothery' for hatred of and contempt for animals (Mason 1993: 163–168); 'animal sexual assault' for bestiality (Beirne 2000); and, I suggest, 'theriocide' for the killing of non-human animals by humans.

But the central juxtaposition, namely, between 'humans' and 'non-human animals', seems quite hard to avoid. Several attempts have been made to overcome it, including that of 'non-human animals', a term that is in vogue among members of the animal protection community. Other candidates include the rather cumbersome 'animals other than humans' (the preferred usage in the journal *Society & Animals*) and, derivative of this, Geertrui Cazaux's (2003: 119–145;

and this volume) clever, if obscure, acronym 'aothas' (animals other than human animals).

However, set against the obvious errors embedded in the dichotomous phrase 'human/animal', none of its three erstwhile alternatives quite escapes the clutches of speciesism either. In a sort of Wittgensteinian vicious circle, all three fail for precisely the same reason. Consider the phrase 'non-human animals'. While the term 'non-human animals' is a welcome reminder that the terrain of human/animal relations is marked by speciesist language, to speak of *non-human* animals' is ironically to privilege humans for it defines all animals other than *Homo sapiens* as lacking in certain qualities that allegedly inhere only in humans. Put another way, 'non-human animals' involves rather the same error as if we were to speak of (human) women as non-male humans (and see Cazaux 1998).

So, what is to be done? My own practice – unsatisfactory though it is – is initially to juxtapose 'humans' with 'non-human animals' and then, at a suitably proximate point, to attach '('hereinafter, 'animals')' after the term 'non-human animals'. This might look like a lot of effort to arrive at a point no further than the one of departure, but I think that the jarring effects of the journey are well worth it – especially if our fellow creatures are thereby accorded more respect.

The movement in human–animal studies

Though the concept of 'Other' rarely includes non-human animals, there has been considerable growth in the last decade in the new animal-centred field of 'human–animal studies'.

The development of 'human–animal studies' has been accompanied by a small flurry of ongoing institutional activity, including dedicated book series and revised reading lists for scholars and would-be student- and scholar-activists; new animal-centred journals, such as *Anthrozoös* and *Society & Animals* and the on-line *Between the Species*; new or repackaged undergraduate courses, some postgraduate dissertations and, even, a small handful of new interdisciplinary degree programmes (or streams within such programmes).[8]

Evidence of this apparent shift in scholarly attention can be found in small pockets in the US, the UK and many other European societies, and in Canada, Australia, New Zealand and elsewhere. While its disciplinary antecedents might be identified as moral philosophy, feminism, law and biology, its adherents are also drawn from animal sciences, anthropology, economics, environmental studies, geography, history, literary studies, political science, humane education, psychology and sociology.

Various sociological perspectives on human–animal interaction have played an at first precarious, but now increasingly prominent, role in the development and maintenance of human–animal studies. They seem to have begun with the application of social theory to the history and aims of the animal rights movement (e.g. Tester 1991; Jasper and Nelkin 1992; Benton 1993; Silverstein 1996; Nibert 2002), though they now include, but are by no means limited to, intellectual history, social constructivism, ethnography and ethnomethodology. Sociologists have contributed frequently, for example, to the journal *Society & Animals*, which celebrates its 15th anniversary in 2007. Moreover, exceeding the requisite minimum of 300 signatories, 'Animals and Society' has recently achieved full section status within the American Sociological Association.

The increased visibility of non-human animals in sociology reflects a number of factors. The most important of these is the animal rights movement which, for our purposes, is notable for the central role it attaches to advancement through theoretical debate. However, though the several strands and objects of animal rights theory lie squarely within their intellectual and moral compass, criminologists seem either unaware of them or else indifferent. In what follows, therefore, I have in mind chiefly an introductory placement of animal rights within green criminology.

Towards animal rights

Since the mid-1960s support for animal rights has grown into a large-scale, well-publicised and theoretically informed social movement. In some parts of the more developed world the movement's gains seem to have been extraordinary. In some societies among its achievements might be counted the movement's contribution to state regulation of the production, transport and slaughter of cattle and poultry; a gradual decline in the consumption of meat, and a concomitant rise in consumption of grains, fruit and vegetables; stricter controls on animal shelters, zoos, circuses and aquaria; greater restrictions on the use of vivisection in scientific and commercial laboratories and in schools; a drastic reduction in sales of animal skin and fur; and the protection of endangered species, especially exotica such as whales, wolves, and raptors.

The pro-animal movement actually has little by way of an agreed-upon theoretical core. Rather, it comprises numerous and often internally conflicting theoretical assumptions and tendencies. Depending on how these are characterised, by whom and with what intent, they are variously known as 'animal rights', 'animal liberation', 'animal welfare,' 'animal defence' and 'animal protection'. Behind these several pro-animal labels lie very real political, ethical and moral differences about the obligations of humans towards animals and of the latter's rights. What to some are legislative victories are moral defeats to others.

The key theoretical perspectives within the pro-animal movement emerged from the writings of a small group of moral philosophers (e.g. Godlovich, Godlovitch and Harris 1974; Singer 1975; Clark 1977; Regan 1983; and see Armstrong and Botzler 2003). Their chief goals have been, first, to end the practices and ideologies of speciesism and, second, largely through the vehicles of utilitarianism and rights theory, to create a non-speciesist discourse for the just governance of our relationships with animals. Alongside these founding statements are pioneering feminist contributions (e.g. Donovan 1990; Adams 1994, 1999; Adams and Donovan 1995a, 1995b; Noske 1997; Dunayer 2004).

The large and very real differences among these three pro-animal perspectives are motivated as much by genuine concern for animals as by perennial puzzles about the nature of the good society and of a responsible citizenry. How do animals and humans differ? Are animals' interests in avoiding pain of the same sort as those of humans? Are the grounds for not abusing animals the same as those for not abusing humans?

(i) *Utilitarianism; on suffering and equal consideration* In its modern form, the utilitarian argument against animal abuse derives from the conjunction of two eighteenth-century Enlightenment traditions. Of these one rejected the Cartesian view that animals are the moral equivalent of machines, the other accepted the doctrine of utility established both by the Italian and French *philosophes* and by the Scottish civic tradition. To the *philosophes* the key ethical principle was that righteous actions are those which maximise happiness and pleasure and which minimise suffering and pain; an ethical society is one which tries to minimise pain and suffering wherever and however they occur.

In claiming that humans should not be allowed to torment animals or to be cruel to them, Jeremy Bentham was one of the first to extend utilitarianism to human–animal interaction. Attacking the degradation of animals into 'the class of *things*', he famously declared that '[t]he day *may* come when the rest of the animal creation may acquire those rights which never could have been withholden from them but by the hand of tyranny' (1789: 283). However, 'the question is not', Bentham insisted, '[c]an they *reason*? Can they *talk*? But, Can they suffer?' (*ibid*.) Because for Bentham animals are sentient beings who can suffer and feel pain, it follows that they have an interest in avoiding pain and that, given the principle of utility, humans are obliged not to inflict it on them.

Such utilitarian strictures against our infliction of pain on animals have become the theoretical focus of the reformist tendency in the animal protection community known as 'welfarism'. This tendency has been nurtured by Peter Singer's (1975) widely-read *Animal Liberation*, a book of consequentialist moral theory applied to animal suffering. Singer begins by pointing out that the basis of Bentham's argument about animal rights is not that animals have rights but that, in respect of their avoidance of pain and their seeking of pleasure, they should be allowed the same consideration as humans. Just as some males attach greater weight to the interests of their own gender at the expense of females (sexism), and just as there are others who give preference to their own race at the expense of other races (racism) so, Singer continues, some humans give greater consideration to the interests of their own species than to those of animals (speciesism).

In supporting the extension of utilitarianism to animals, Singer elevates the capacity to suffer above all other capacities, like those for language or mathematics. This he does because he holds that the capacity to suffer is the *sine qua non* of having interests at all. As such, neither vegetables nor trees nor clods of earth enter his calculus because they are not sentient beings capable of feeling pain or happiness. Rather, as insentient objects they are without interests.

For Singer the capacity for suffering is thus the essential precondition for having interests. Both because humans and animals have an equal interest in avoiding suffering, and because utilitarianism entails equality of consideration for all animals, moral actions are those that uphold those interests. To his cardinal rule of equal consideration, Singer attaches the qualification that equal consideration does not mean that all animals should be treated identically. Animals of different species have different interests and to treat them the same ('equally') would thus amount to mistreatment. Singer's position that one law for the lion and the ox is oppression allows him to admit to obvious differences between humans and animals while retaining the principle of equal consideration for all animals. Singer thus enjoins us to avoid the infliction of pain and suffering on humans and animals alike. We should make our lives as free from cruelty as possible and we must refuse to buy the products of modern animal farming. We must become vegetarian. We must expose and condemn the suffering involved in hunting, trapping, rodeos, zoos, circuses and in the buying and selling of animals.

Despite its great influence, Singer's act-utilitarianism does not really position animals' liberation from suffering very securely.[9] If an action's rightness or wrongness is calculated only by its consequences for maximising pleasure and minimising suffering, then particular acts of suffering may well be justified if they serve to increase the collective good. In fact, Singer's utilitarianism does not condemn animal experimentation absolutely, and actually supports particular cases of it if they are believed to lead to a scientific cure for illness and disease *in humans*. In principle, there is nothing in his utilitarianism that would preclude any form of torture or suffering inflicted on a minority if it reduced the suffering of the majority. Indeed, one wonders if there are scenarios which would allow Singer to support experimentation on humans if so doing might lead to good health in sick animals.

(ii) *Animals as subjects of rights* Some of the difficulties associated with Singer's utilitarianism provide an opening into the non-consequentialist, deontological theory of animal rights offered by Tom Regan (1983; and see Regan 2001a, 2001b: 191–222).

To simplify greatly, in his book *The Case for Animal Rights* Regan first distinguishes legal rights from moral rights. Legal rights, on the one hand, are those which particular laws happen to classify as rights. As such, their existence and facticity depend on the society in which they are enacted. The degree of respect accorded them varies by such factors as race, class, gender and religion. Moral rights, on the other hand, are universal rights. They apply equally to all their holders and do not flow from the creative or capricious acts of individuals (e.g. despots) or groups (e.g. legislatures). Moral rights are not acquired rights but basic ones, and everyone is obliged to uphold them. Of all moral rights the most basic is the right to respectful treatment.

Second, Regan identifies the sort of individuals who are the bearers of rights, namely, those with a variety of sophisticated abilities whom he terms 'moral agents'. He objects that utilitarianism views individuals as 'mere receptacles' for value. To put this another way, on the utilitarian or receptacle view of value it is what goes into the cup, rather than the cup itself, that has value. On Regan's postulate of inherent value, it is the cup itself that has value – a value that is reducible neither to what goes into it nor to others' evaluations of it. Inherent value resides in those individuals who are moral agents, and it resides in them equally – if it did not, then it would lead to an unacceptable 'perfectionist' theory of justice that would allow differential treatment of individuals according to the quantity and quality of various virtues that they exhibited. Because moral agents have equal inherent value, all are equally valuable: thus, '[a] criminal is no less inherently valuable than a saint' (1983: 237).

Who is a moral agent? To be a moral agent is to be more than alive and merely conscious, though it may also be less than an autonomous agent in the Kantian sense. A moral agent is a 'subject-of-a-life'.

> [I]ndividuals are subjects-of-a-life if they have beliefs and desires, perceptions, memory and a sense of the future, including their own future; an emotional life together with feelings of pleasure and pain; preference- and welfare-interests; the ability to initiate action in pursuit of their desires and goals; a psychophysical identity over time; and an individual welfare in the sense that their experiential life fares well or ill for them. (*ibid*.: 243)

Regan argues that the moral community consists of both moral agents and also all those to whom moral agents owe duties, i.e. both other moral agents and also 'moral patients'. Moral patients are those who lack the prerequisites that would enable them to control their behaviour in ways that would make them morally accountable. Moral patients include human infants, young children, the mentally ill and the enfeebled of all ages. Even though they have the ability to harm others, moral patients can do neither right nor wrong. They are always innocent. Since moral patients are subjects-of-a-life, they have inherent value and we must respect them no less than we respect moral agents. To respect moral patients means not only to revere their lives but also to defend them from harm; not to respect them would be arbitrary and unjust.

Regan claims, third, that among the leading attributes of the mental life of many animals – especially normal mammals aged one or more – are perception, memory, desire, belief, self-consciousness, intention and a sense of the future. Because such animals satisfy the criterion of a subject-of-a-life they have inherent value. They therefore have the same basic rights as human moral patients, including the right to respectful treatment and the right not to be harmed.[10] Indeed, to treat animals with respect is to treat them not with kindness but with justice.

Finally, and with special relevance for my aim here, Regan identifies two ways in which animals can be harmed, namely, through inflictions and deprivations. While disdaining its utilitarian framework, Regan applauds Bentham's focus on the ability of animals to suffer because it is suffering that is the paradigm of a harm understood as an infliction. It is a form of prolonged pain of considerable intensity that diminishes the victims' satisfaction of their needs and/or interests, their quality of life and their physiological and emotional welfare. Harms as inflictions would therefore seem to constitute cruelty writ large. Harms as deprivations are those harms that do not necessarily involve pain and suffering and about whose existence the harmed individual might not even be aware.

> That harms can take the form of deprivations, independent of considerations about suffering, and that animals can be the subjects of such harm, is readily seen if we recall that many animals have needs and attendant desires over and above the basic biological ones for food, water, rest, and the like. Humans are, we say, social animals, but we are not the only ones. The more we learn about animals, both domesticated and wild, the more we must be impressed with the social needs and arrangements that characterize their lives ... To place animals with such desires in situations in which these desires cannot be fulfilled – as is done by caging wolves in, say, roadside zoos – is to cause them *prima facie* harm, whether they suffer or not, because it is to deny them the opportunity to satisfy their desires for companionship or physical freedom of movement. (p. 98)

Though deprivations need not involve pain and suffering, sometimes they do, as when a caged wolf is drugged into a stupor. Conversely, suffering can itself lead to deprivation, as in the case of an intensively-raised farm animal who thereby suffers ulcers that diminish her ability to fulfil a variety of her natural desires. Because the loss of life forecloses all possibilities of the satisfaction of desires, the ultimate form of deprivation – and of suffering, if it involves pain – is death.

To summarise, Regan provides a powerful framework for the assignment of roughly the same sort of *prima facie* rights to animals as are assigned to humans under the banner of human rights. Yet, it has been actively opposed by a handful of philosophers who raise different sorts of difficulty for his theory of animal rights, and with varying degrees of importance. Some claim, for example, that not all animals, including humans, have equal inherent worth. Others assert that the concept of animal rights devalues the notion of human rights. Still others take issue with the apparently low level of consciousness attributed by Regan to non-mammals and, therefore, with the overly narrow range of animals that might have rights.

Surprisingly, and to a degree unfairly, among the most vociferous of Regan's (and Singer's) critics have been (eco-) feminists.

(iii) *Feminism, animals and an ethic of care* Some feminists within the animal rights community have argued that Singer's utilitarianism and Regan's animal-rights theory share a common failure, namely, their alleged masculinist adherence to scientific rationalism. This, they charge, inevitably entails a politics of exclusion and a sneering dismissal of sentimentalism.

Undeniably, both Singer[11] and Regan[12] have distanced themselves from a purely sentimentalist or emotional attachment to animals. But feminists retort that this distancing is a classic exemplar of epistemological dualism – it effectively equates 'sentimental' and 'emotional' with 'irrational' and all three traits with 'less than male' and 'female' (e.g. Donovan 1990; Adams 1995; Noske 1997; and see Regan 2001: 62–64). For this reason they have derided Regan's epistemology as a masculinist rationalism which rejects the importance of emotions and sentiments both in life and in understanding. Instead, feminists have developed what Josephine Donovan describes as 'more of a sense of emotional bonding with animals as the basis for their theory than is evident in the male literature' (1990: 351). Indeed, since for theologians, philosophers and statesmen a clinical and unemotional rationalism has been one of the key criteria for admission to the moral community, there is, she asserts, an almost inevitable commonality of interests among all disenfranchised minorities.

This commonality of interests is chiefly evident as the 'feminist ethic of care' and 'good fellowship'. These seek to identify the myriad ways in which patriarchal societies oppress women and how women's oppression stems from and parallels the same sources as the dominionistic treatment of all Others. Feminism must therefore uncover how patriarchal ideologies create categories of despised and disenfranchised bodies and how they aid men in their subjugation of women, slaves, persons of colour, non-dominant men and animals. As Adams and Donovan stress, the recognition of these ideologies is crucial because they provide 'the context for women's oppression and the relationship it has with other forms of oppression' (1995b: 2). It would therefore be beneficial for women to seek common fellowship, for example, with those indigenous peoples who make no

71

conceptual distinction between humans and other animals and who tend to equate all living beings, plants, earth and water. According to Adams and Donovan (p. 3),

> feminist theory must engage itself with the status and treatment of the other animals ... We believe that feminism is a transformative philosophy that embraces the amelioration of life on earth for all life-forms, for all natural entities ... [A]ll oppressions are interconnected: no one creature will be free until all are free – from abuse, degradation, exploitation, pollution and commercialization.

One key strategy has been broadly pursued to realise this holistic vision, namely, the development of a feminist ethic of care. This ethic has been approached through the evolving debates on the 'morality of responsibility and caring' notably displayed in Carol Gilligan's (1993) *In a Different Voice*. Crucially, Gilligan rejects the emphasis of utilitarianism and rights theory on abstract rules, procedural consistency and justice. Instead, she embraces the particular, the connection among all beings and an ethic of responsible caring.

The three main theoretical perspectives described above clearly entail quite different routes to rather different goals. Indeed, the respective adherents of utilitarianism, rights-based theory and feminism often seem to be engaged in the sort of internecine warfare typical of movements that have splintered into irreconcilable camps: passionate disagreement over tactics and strategy and charges and counter-charges of selling out, of reformism and of idealism.

With such antagonisms in mind, let me now briefly identify some principled differences between the animal rights and environmental movements. This I do as a prelude to identifying some common ground not only between them but also, finally, between the pro-animal and pro-environment emphases within an emerging green criminology.

Animal rights, environmentalism(s) and green criminology: principled differences, common ground

The animal protection and environmental movements seem to have diverged sharply in their respective aims, philosophies and theoretical assumptions from the moment of their emergence in the 1960s. As a result, the movements often think and act at best in parallel and, at worst, in vehement opposition to each other.

A description of the main source of this disengagement and/ or conflict can be traced to an essay on environmental ethics by J. Baird Callicott (1980). Developing the biological holism of Aldo Leopold's (1949) *A Sand County Almanac*, Callicott argued that environmental ethics and animal liberation are, he argued, in key respects philosophically quite opposed to each other. Thus, whereas environmental ethicists focus broadly on the health of the biotic community as a whole, animal liberationists focus on the narrower criteria of the bases of moral standing and rights holders.

> [A]llied to this difference are many others. One of the more conspicuous is that in environmental ethics, plants are included within the parameters of the ethical theory as well as animals. Indeed, inanimate entities such as oceans and lakes, mountains, forest, and wetlands are assigned a greater value than individual animals and in a way quite different from systems which accord them moral considerability through a further multiplication of competing individual loci of value and holders of rights. (Callicott 1980: 37)

Callicott thus drove a wedge firmly between the ecologism/ holism of the environmental movement and the liberation/rights of the animal protection community. Soon afterwards, however, he said he regretted this divisiveness and instead suggested that the movements actually have common ground. In a review of Regan's *The Case for Animal Rights*, for example, Callicott (1985: 47; and see Regan 1981; Shepard 1996: chapter 23; Jamieson 1998: 41–46) indicated that they could be placed on a common footing, if only the animal rights movement would refrain from a concern with wild animals and restrict itself to domestic, farm and laboratory animals – 'which, most unfortunately, sometimes include animals stolen from the wild'!

To some extent, this sort of principled conflict is already present in green criminology in notions such as 'fisheries' and 'conservation' (supra: 60–62). However, within the evolving discourse of green criminology, let me now chart constructively and with enthusiasm three areas of likely common ground between an animal-centred rights perspective and green environmentalism.

Human–animal relationships and environmental politics In countless ways human–animal relationships have traditionally been an inextricable part of humans' domination of one another, of the environment and of nature. Our understanding of the awesome scale and depth of these relationships continues to be enriched by the several branches of the human–animal studies movement.

Environmental historians, for example, have shown how in prehistoric and preliterate hunting and gathering societies, in agricultural societies and later during urbanisation and industrialisation, humans have exploited animals to develop their own environments. They have used them not only as physical/edible commodities but also in spiritual, symbolic and other cultural practices (Benton 1993; Ritvo 2004). During the growth of urban environments, for example, animals have been used as food and clothing, as vehicles for transport and construction and policing, and as objects of entertainment. Animals' presence or absence has been used to demarcate a variety of constructed sites and spaces: frontier, city, suburb, park and wilderness. Animals' 'waste products' have played a prominent role in the history and geographical siting of abattoirs and in the development of hygiene practices (e.g. Vialles 1994; Laporte 2000). Occasionally, too, animals have been identified as causal agents in natural, pestilential and other environmental disasters, and even formally prosecuted and executed for them (Beirne 1994).

Environmentalism, animal rights and enviro-politics often merge in an animal dimension or focus. Examples of this coincidence include struggles over conservation and sustainability; loss of biological diversity and the preservation of threatened or fragile ecosystems; deforestation; soil erosion caused by effluent from large-scale pig production; genetic engineering; cruelty to animals in public or outdoor sites (e.g. the poisoning of pigeons in New York City, of dogs in Hong Kong, and of the maiming of horses and cows in Wales and England); and certain contagious diseases (see also Ritvo 2004). To instantiate the last of these, animals occur prominently in the transmission of rabies, AIDS, variant Creutzfeldt-Jakob disease, West Nile virus, bovine spongiform encephalopathy (BSE), SARS, Lyme disease and avian flu. A variety of other social processes and harms are sometimes associated with outbreaks of these diseases, such as ill and deceased humans, slaughtered animals, moral panics, unemployed farmers and labourers, piqued national pride and cross-border commercial smuggling of viruses and vaccines.

Human–animal interaction and 'animals as an issue' are also involved in several relatively unexplored questions about the histories of state formation. Of likely interest to green criminologists are those attempts in the first two decades of the nineteenth century in Britain, for example, to criminalise not only individual acts of cruelty to cattle, horses, dogs and birds but also certain working-class blood sports – in particular, bear-baiting, badger-baiting, and dog and cock fighting. How should we understand the emergence of animal welfare laws like 'Humanity Dick' Martin's Act to Prevent the Cruel and Improper Treatment of Cattle (1822)? And, likewise, the emergence of various policing institutions, such as the Society (later, 'Royal Society') for the Prevention of Cruelty to Animals in 1824, and restrictions on hygienic practices, such as quarantine laws? Are these 'humane' interventions simply crude sites of class struggles or, rather, do they reflect the state's need to monopolise violence and thereby to seize and govern and civilise the terrain of the 'public' (and see Thomas 1983; Elias 1986; Franklin 1999; Radford 2001: 16–93)?

Moreover, how far did these new laws and policing institutions mirror changing social attitudes towards animals? In this regard I recommend that two recent essays on Herman Melville's great novel *Moby Dick* can very usefully be read together. Quite different in their respective emphases, and each in its own way wonderfully informative, one essay (Ruggiero 2002) addresses crimes of the economy, masculinity and the conquest of nature by the whaling industry; the other (Armstrong 2004) shows how changing material conditions influenced the development of human attitudes towards cetaceans, including anthropomorphism and compassion and, in Melville's own case, an ironic sensibility.

Global warming and intensive rearing regimes The long-term existence of *all* life on tiny planet Earth is seriously threatened by global warming. Currently, 20 billion tons of carbon dioxide are released annually into the atmosphere (Royal Society 2005: 1–21). Among the short-term results of this pollution are ocean acidification, deteriorated coral reefs, calcified plankton, and declining and threatened populations of larger animals. Among the biggest producers of environmental harms, including global warming, are intensive rearing regimes for the mass production, slaughter and consumption of cattle and poultry by humans. To suggest why green criminologists might find common cause in opposing these regimes, I can do no better than quote from Dale Jamieson's (2002: 197–212) *Morality's Progress*.

[T]he addiction to beef that is characteristic of people in the industrialized countries is not only a moral atrocity for animals but also causes health problems for consumers, reduces grain supplies for the poor, precipitates social divisions in developing countries, contributes to climate change, leads to the conversion of forests to pasture lands, is a causal factor in overgrazing, and is implicated in the destruction of native plants and animals. (p. 203)

Clearly, the respective concerns of animal rights and green environmentalism broadly coincide on major aspects of global warming, as does their opposition to its perceived perpetrators. Among these latter are those agribusinesses, transnational corporations, profit-seeking and ignorant states and ineffective international legal/enforcement machinery that variously pollute human and animal bodies and which cause them suffering and shorten their lives.

Animal rights and environmental rights/justice Consider, for a moment, the plight of 155,000 Arctic Inuit, whose six indigenous groups inhabit the northernmost parts of Canada, Denmark, Finland, Iceland, Norway, Russia, Sweden and the United States.

In late 2005 the Inuit were seeking a ruling against the United States from the Inter-American Commission on Human Rights. In their suit the Inuit claimed that, because it tolerated heat-trapping smokestacks and automobile exhaust emissions, which directly cause global warming, the melting of the Arctic ice-cap and environmental degradation, the United States has been contributing both to the deaths of individual Inuit and also to the possible extinction of their culture (Revkin 2004: A4; 2005: A3). With a considerable body of scientific evidence to support them, the Inuit further complain that rising temperatures, disappearing glaciers and ice-caps, and wind-borne toxic pollution have adversely affected the health of Arctic seals and of the Inuit who regularly eat them. Seal hunting, it should be added, the Inuit see as an essential part of their culture and traditions and, indeed, of their physical survival.

There is no space here to discuss how animal rights and environmentalism might differ in their respective approaches to Arctic seal hunting (by whom and why? for survival? for sport? for *haute cuisine* or *haute couture*?) or to the survival of other species, like polar bears and arctic foxes. The Inuit's case is perversely instructive here precisely because they are pursuing their case against the United States not in a court of US jurisdiction but at the Organisation of American States' Inter-American Commission on Human Rights – because US Supreme Court decisions imply that no individuals have sufficient legal standing to sue the US Environmental Protection Agency or other federal agencies if environmental damage (e.g. global warming) is sustained by everyone (Mank 2005)! As such, the Inuit have been forced to pursue their case not simply because they allege an environmental crime has been committed against them; rather, they also believe that this crime violates their basic human rights.

Unlike members of the animal protection community, who champion animal rights to condemn animal abuse, environmentalists rarely use rights talk to condemn environmental harms (see Benton 1993, 1998). Perhaps this is because no positive or acceptable solution has yet been found to questions like Christopher Stone's (1972) 'should trees have [legal] standing?' Perhaps, too, the Inuit's complaint about global warming will mark a turning point in this crucial respect. If so, then green environmentalism and animal rights will be harnessed ever more firmly together.

However, if there is one thing known definitively about rights – whether for humans or other animals – it is that 'law on the books' often has little bearing on 'law in action'. Perhaps environmentalists will revisit this issue soon. There has already been some soul-searching within the animal rights movement about whether animal rights can be secured through incremental legal reform, or whether more revolutionary or drastic or dramatic action is needed (e.g. Francione 1996; Wise 2000; Nibert 2002).

But one continues to wonder whether, for example, in Tom Regan's assignation of rights to animals lie some of the same problems as those entailed in human rights. Among these problems, in particular, are that their claims to universality embody an imperialist essentialism that is vulnerable to the objections of cultural relativism and post-modernism; that, once acquired both in principle and in law, they are in practice individualist notions that do little to aid the plight of all their bearers; that they are abstract and formal rights with no necessary substantive content; and that, if enacted, as in the case of civil liberties and rights for minorities, for example, they might not be enforced or recognised. Moreover, especially in self-avowed property-owning democracies and in societies where individualism is energetically encouraged, the right of animals to be free from cruelty and abuse will ultimately be thwarted, if not altogether undermined, by human rights to privacy and to the enjoyment of private property.

How, then, should animal abuse be defined and confronted? If violations of animals' rights are to be central concepts in green criminology, then we could profitably begin by examining why, just like some harms to the environment, some harms to animals are defined as criminal, others as abusive but not criminal and still others as neither criminal nor abusive. In exploring these questions a narrow concept of crimes against animals would necessarily have to be rejected in favour of a more inclusive concept of harm. Tom Regan's notion of harms to animals as either 'inflictions' or 'deprivations' springs readily to mind here (above, p. 70; and Regan, this volume, chapter 5). Without it, the meaning of animal abuse will be overwhelmingly confined to those harms that are regarded as socially unacceptable, one-on-one cases of animal cruelty. Certainly, those cases demand our attention. But so too do those other and far more numerous institutionalised harms to animals, where abuse is routine, invisible, ubiquitous and often defined as socially acceptable.

Notes

1 I am especially grateful to Ray Michalowski and Geertrui Cazaux for their helpful comments on a draft of this chapter.
2 Adams (1999) argues that in a society where meat consumption is predominantly a masculine activity, government rationing policies reserved a consistent supply of meat for US soldiers, who were the epitome of masculine men during the 1939–45 war.
3 The progression thesis depends on the successful combination of two quite separate causal propositions: (1) those who abuse animals are more likely subsequently to act violently towards humans, and (2) those who act violently towards humans are more likely previously to have abused animals. How robust and persistent is the association in these propositions? If there is a strong association, then how is it to be explained?
4 Differing accounts of criminology's several environmentalisms are given by Halsey (2004: 833–845) and White (2003, 2005).
5 Halsey also refers to 'non-human environments' (*ibid.*: 841) but only as a tactical ploy against what he sees as Benton's (1998) erroneous 'ecocentrism'.
6 In reciting this definition I follow the general, though not altogether unproblematic, direction of its populariser Peter Singer (1990a: 6; and see Ryder 1989; Dunayer 2004), who has written elsewhere that the term refers to the view that 'species membership is, *in itself*, a reason for giving more weight to the interests of one being than to those of another' (1990b:10).
7 From roughly 1990 to 1995 there was a noisy, well-publicised moral panic in rural Hampshire about gentry- and middle-class-owned horses hideously mutilated by unknown assailants. Consider, too, the public and media indifference towards the numerous horses used in racing who have their tendons 'fired', the 200 horses who are quietly and without protest annually 'put down' after having 'fallen' on racetracks, often

breaking their legs, and then shipped to abattoirs (Yates, Powell and Beirne 2001).

8 A recent survey has identified more than 110 university and college courses in the US – representing over 20 academic disciplines – with 'Animals and Society' as one of their themes (Alagappan 2003). Presently, these courses are concentrated in just a few disciplines, especially philosophy, animal sciences and law. In this regard the social sciences are notoriously underrepresented, with only a smattering of such courses in each of anthropology, criminology, psychology and sociology (Alagappan 2003: 8–9).

9 Especially given several ambiguous references in *Animal Liberation* to 'animal *rights*', Singer later carefully stressed that the notion of rights plays no significant role in his utilitarianism and that it operates merely 'as a concession to popular rhetoric' (1978: 122).

10 However, these rights are not absolute and Regan specifies three principles that might justify overriding them: (1) we should choose to harm the innocent few to save the rights of the innocent many (the 'miniride principle'); (2) we should choose to harm the many if not doing so entails that another course of action would leave some of the few worse off than any of the many (the 'worse-off principle'); and (3) the innocent have the right to self-defence even if so doing overrides the rights of others (the 'liberty principle') (pp. 286–312).

11 Singer (1975: i–ii) once related how in England he and his wife were invited to tea by a woman who had heard he was writing a book on animals. Upon their arrival, their hostess proudly informed them that she had a dog and two cats and that she loved animals. She was therefore surprised to learn from the Singers that they themselves owned no pets. Though they were interested in the prevention of suffering and misery, they informed her that

> we were not especially 'interested in' animals … We didn't love animals. We simply wanted them treated as the independent sentient beings that they are, and not as a means to human ends – as the pig whose flesh was now in our hostess's sandwiches had been treated. (p. ii)

12 Likewise, Regan enjoins his readers to make a sustained commitment to non-sentimental rational enquiry:

> Since all who work on behalf of the interests of animals are more than a little familiar with the tired charges of being 'irrational,' 'sentimental,' 'emotional' or worse, we can give the lie to these accusations only by making a concerted effort not to indulge our emotions or parade our sentiments. (1983: xii)

References

Adams, C. (1994) *Neither Man Nor Beast: Feminism and the Defense of Animals*. New York: Continuum.
Adams, C. (1999) *The Sexual Politics of Meat*. New York: Continuum.
Adams, C. and Donovan, J. eds (1995a) *Animals and Women: Feminist Theoretical Explorations*. Durham, NC: Duke University Press.
Adams, C. and Donovan, J. (1995b) 'Introduction', in Adams and Donovan 1995a, pp. 1–8.
Agnew, R. (1997) 'The Causes of Animal Abuse: a Social-Psychological Analysis', *Theoretical Criminology*, 2 (2): 177–210.
Alagappan, M. (2003) 'Expanding Humane Education: the Development of "Animals and Society" Courses in Liberal Arts Colleges', unpublished MS thesis, Center for Animals and Public Policy, Tufts University School of Veterinary Medicine.
Anderson, N. (1923) *The Hobo: The Sociology of the Homeless Man*. Chicago: University of Chicago Press.
Arluke, A., Levin, J., Luke, C. and Ascione, F. (1999) 'The Relationship of Animal Abuse to Violence and Other Forms of Antisocial Behavior', *Journal of Interpersonal Violence*, 14 (9): 963–975.
Armstrong, P. (2004) 'Moby-Dick and Compassion', *Society & Animals*, 12: (1): 19–37.
Ascione, F. (2001) 'Animal Abuse and Youth Violence'. Washington, DC: US Department of Justice, Office of Juvenile Justice and Delinquency Prevention.
Baldry, A. (2003) 'Animal Abuse and Exposure to Interparental Violence in Italian Youth', *Journal of Interpersonal Violence*, 18 (3): 258–281.
Beirne, P. (1995) 'The Law is an Ass: Reading E. P. Evans' *The Medieval Prosecution and Capital Punishment of Animals*', *Society & Animals*, (1): 27–46.
Beirne, P. (2000) 'Rethinking Bestiality: Towards a Concept of Interspecies Sexual Assault', in A. Podberscek, E. Paul and J. Serpell (eds) *Companion Animals and Us*: pp. 313–331. Cambridge: Cambridge University Press.
Beirne, P. (2004) 'From Animal Abuse to Interhuman Violence? A Critical Review of the Progression Thesis', *Society & Animals*, 12 (1): 39–65.
Bentham, J. (1789) (1970) *Introduction to the Principles of Morals and Legislation*. Edited by J. H. Burns and H. L. A. Hart. University of London: Athlone Press.
Benton, T. (1993) *Natural Relations: Ecology, Animal Rights and Social Justice*. London: Verso.
Benton, T. (1998) 'Rights and Justice on a Shared Planet', *Theoretical Criminology*, 2 (2): 149–175.
Callicott, J. (1980) (1989) *In Defense of the Land Ethic: Essays in Environmental Philosophy*. Albany, NY: SUNY Press.
Carrabine, E., Iganski, P., Lee, M., Plummer, K. and South, N. (2004) *Criminology: A Sociological Introduction*. London: Routledge.

Cazaux, G. (1998) 'Legitimating the Entry of the "Animals Issue" into (Critical) Criminology', *Humanity and Society*, 22 (4): 365–385.

Cazaux, G. (2002) 'Anthropocentrism and Speciesism Regarding Animals Other than Human Animals in Contemporary Criminology'. Belgium: Faculty of Law, Ghent University. *Unpublished Ph.D. Dissertation*.

Cazuax, G. and P. Beirne (2001) 'Animal Abuse', in E. McLaughlin and J. Muncie (eds) *Sage Dictionary of Criminology*. London: Sage.

Clark, S. (1977) *The Moral Status of Animals*. Oxford: Clarendon.

Clinard, M. (1952) *The Black Market: A Study of White-Collar Crime*. New York: Rinehart.

Cohen, S. (2001) *States of Denial: Knowing About Atrocities and Suffering*. Cambridge: Polity Press.

Collard, A. (1989) *Rape of the Wild*. Bloomington: Indiana University Press.

Donovan, J. (1990) 'Animal Rights and Feminist Theory', *Signs*, 15 (2): 350–375.

Dunayer, J. (2004) *Speciesism*. Derwood, MD.: Ryce Publishing.

Elias, N. (1986) 'An Essay on Sport and Violence', in N. Elias and E. Dunning (eds), *Quest for Entertainment*: 150–174. Oxford: Basil Blackwell.

Flynn, C. (2000) 'Woman's Best Friend', *Violence Against Women*, 6 (2): 162–177.

Francione, G. (1995) *Animals, Property, and the Law*. Philadelphia, PA.: Temple University Press.

Francione, G. (1996) *Rain without Thunder: The Ideology of the Animal Rights Movement*. Philadelphia, PA.: Temple University Press.

Franklin, A. (1999) *Animals and Modern Cultures: A Sociology of Human–Animal Relations in Modernity*. London: Sage.

Gilligan, C. (1993) *In a Different Voice: Psychological Theory and Women's Development*. Cambridge, MA.: Harvard University Press.

Godlovich, S., Godlovitch R. and J. Harris (eds) (1974) *Animals, Men and Morals*. New York: Grove Press.

Halsey, M. (2004) 'Against "Green" Criminology', *British Journal of Criminology*, 44 (6): 833–853.

Jamieson, D. (2002) *Morality's Progress: Essays on Humans, Other Animals, and the Rest of Nature*. Clarendon Press: Oxford.

Jasper, J. and Nelkin, D. (1992) *The Animal Rights Crusade: the Growth of a Moral Protest*. New York, Free Press.

Laporte, D. (2000) *History of Shit*. Translated by N. Benabid and R. el-Khoury. Cambridge, MA.: MIT Press.

Leopold, A. (1949) *A Sand County Almanac*. New York: Oxford University Press.

Lombroso, C. (1876) (2006) *Criminal Man*. Translated by M. Gibson and N. Rafter. Durham, NC: Duke University Press.

Mank, B. (2005) 'Standing and Global Warming', *Environmental Law*, 35 (1): 1–84.

Mason, J. (1993) *An Unnatural Order: Uncovering the Roots of Our Domination of Nature and Each Other*. New York: Simon and Schuster.

Nagel, T. (1974) 'What is it Like To Be a Bat?', *The Philosophical Review*, October: 435–450.

Nibert, D. (2002) *Animal Rights/Human Rights; Entanglements of Oppression and Liberation*. Lanham, MD.: Rowman and Littlefield.

Noske, B. (1997) *Beyond Boundaries: Humans and Other Animals*. Montreal: Black Rose Books.

Park, R. and Burgess, E. (1921) *Introduction to the Science of Sociology*. Chicago: University of Chicago Press.

Radford, M. (2005) *Animal Welfare Law in Britain: Regulation and Responsibility*. Oxford: Oxford University Press.

Regan, T. (1983) *The Case for Animal Rights*. Berkeley, CA.: University of California Press.

Regan, T. (2001a) *Defending Animal Rights*. Urbana, Ill.: University of Illinois Press.

Regan, T. (2001b) 'The Case for Animal Rights', in C. Cohen and T. Regan, *The Animal Rights Debate*: 127–221. Lanham, MD.: Rowman and Littlefield.

Revkin, A. (2005) 'US Resists New Targets For Curbing Emissions', *New York Times*, December 8: A3.

Ritvo, H. (2004) 'Animal Planet', *Environmental History*, 9 (2): 204–220.

Rowe, D. (2002) *Biology and Crime*. Los Angeles, CA.: Roxbury.

Royal Society (UK) (2005) 'Ocean Acidification Due to Increasing Atmospheric Carbon Dioxide', *Policy Document* 12/05. Clyvedon Press: Cardiff. Available at www.royalsoc.ac.uk

Ruggiero, V. (2002) 'Moby Dick and the Crimes of the Economy', *British Journal of Criminology*, 42 (1): 96–108.

Ryder, R. (1989) *Animal Revolution: Changing Attitudes Towards Speciesism*. Oxford: Basil Blackwell.

Shapiro, K. (2002) 'Editor's Introduction: The State of Human–Animal Studies', *Society & Animals*, 10 (4): 331–337.

Shepard, P. (1996) *The Others: How Animals Made Us Human*. Washington, DC: Island Press.

Silverstein, H. (1996) *Unleashing Rights: Law, Meaning and the Animal Rights Movement*. Ann Arbor: University of Michigan Press.

Simon, D. (2006) *Elite Deviance*. Boston: Pearson.

Singer, P. (1975) (1990a) *Animal Liberation*. New York: Avon.

Singer, P. (1990b) 'The Significance of Animal Suffering,' *Behavioral and Brain Sciences*, 13: (1) 9–12.

South, N. and Beirne, P. (2006) 'Editors' Introduction', in South and Beirne (eds), *Green Criminology*, International Library of Criminology and Criminal Justice: xiii–xvii. Aldershot, Hants.: Dartmouth.

Stone, C. (1972) 'Should Trees Have Standing?: Toward Legal Rights for Natural Objects', *Southern California Law Review*, 45 (Spring): 450–501.

Tester, K. (1991) *Animals and Society: The Humanity of Animal Rights*. London: Routledge.

Thomas, K. (1983) *Man and the Natural World: Changing Attitudes in England 1500–1800*. Oxford: Oxford University Press.

Thrasher, F. (1927) *The Gang: A Study of 1,313 Gangs in Chicago*. Chicago: University of Chicago Press.

Vialles, N. (1994) *Animal to Edible*. Translated by J.A. Underwood. Cambridge: Cambridge University Press.

White, R. (2003) 'Environmental Issues and the Criminological Imagination', *Theoretical Criminology*, 7 (4): 483–506.

White, R. (2005) 'Environmental Crime in Global Context: Exploring the Theoretical and Empirical Complexities', *Current Issues in Criminal Justice*, 16 (3): 271–285.

Wilson, J. and Herrnstein, R. (1985) *Crime and Human Nature*. New York: Simon and Schuster.

Wise, S. (2000) *Rattling the Cage: Toward Legal Rights for Animals*. Cambridge, MA.: Perseus Books.

Yates, R. (2004) 'The Social Construction of Human Beings and Other Animals in Human–Nonhuman Relations', Unpublished Ph.D. thesis, Department of Sociology, University of Wales at Bangor.

Yates, R., Powell, C. and Beirne, P. (2001) 'Horse Maiming in the English Countryside: Moral Panic, Human Deviance and the Social Construction of Victimhood', *Society & Animals*, 9 (1): 1–23.

Part II

Animal rights and animal abuse

Chapter 4

Labelling animals: non-speciesist criminology and techniques to identify other animals

Geertrui Cazaux

Being humans, we do not live in a vacuum of the social realm or the cultural world, as if this territory is separated or neatly distinguishable from the biological terrain or the natural world. Humans' lives are inextricably bound with those of other animals. Through a multitude of relationships with humans, other animals are interwoven in society, be it on occasions when their bodies are eaten by humans or, vice versa, when they are lovingly caressed as companions and taken in as part of the family; when they are hunted for trophies or exterminated as 'pests'; when they are used as models in laboratory experimentations or even when humans stand in sheer awe and marvel at the splendour which the 'animal kingdom' offers us. However, social scientific inquiries – and in extension criminological investigations – have manifested a nearly total blind spot where these issues are concerned.

The project of a non-speciesist criminology attempts to transcend the mere incorporation of human–animal relationships. On occasion these topics have indeed been the subject of criminological investigations, although it would seem that the impact of these relations on the animals' lives was nearly totally overlooked or viewed as vehicles or indicators of human–human interactions (see Beirne 1995). The status of the animals concerned does not exceed that of commodity, object, thing or product, ignoring the fact that they partake in the equation as sentient conscious beings. Informed by the growing body of 'animal philosophy' and 'animal ethics', a non-speciesist criminology exactly seeks to scrutinise those instances in which animals have to endure pain or suffering, or in which their welfare is otherwise impaired through human acts; instances which are brought together under the multifaceted dome of 'animal abuse' (Cazaux and Beirne 2001).

Constructing topics from a non-speciesist angle is allied with the project of a green criminology, although animal ethics and environmental ethics certainly do not always share similar premises (see Beirne in this volume, pp. 72–3). In addition, it is imperative to see the body of green criminology as more than just a topic-widening to include 'greenish' issues. Direct or indirect human victimisation through pollution, fragmentation or other infringements of the environment should not be the assembling smithery of a green criminology. If green criminology fails to integrate the impacts of such processes beyond the human-centred criterion of victimisation, it will be no more than just another horizontal broadening. Although we humans cannot escape epistemological anthropocentrism in the way we look at the world and describe others and our surroundings, the growing body of both animal ethics and environmental ethics has given us ample incentives to break through and transcend a normative anthropocentrism. In this way, green criminology can truly turn out to be a vertical breakthrough in criminological research.

The focus of my chapter is not on a particular domain of interactions between humans and other animals. In this regard, we think of the more commonly used demarcations such as animals in husbandry or fisheries, animals used in laboratory experiments, animals as companions for humans, animals in zoos, etc. Rather, I focus on a technique that is employed throughout many encounters of humans with other animals: the identification or labelling of animals.

Identifying animals

The individual labelling of animals to tangibly differentiate them is no hallmark of the modern era. Items in Hammurabi's Code suggest that individual identification by means of marking the bodies of animals has been practised for over 3,800 years (Blancou 2001). The motivations to tangibly label animals – as a means of telling them apart – are versatile. It can serve as an easily discernible method of claiming ownership, helping to prevent theft (animals being often viewed as property) or reuniting the human and animal whenever the latter has gone lost. In pastoral societies, the marking of animals may go beyond the significance of claiming ownership, and incorporate the marked animals in the clan. The effort to control and even prevent epizootics has served as a significant impetus to mark and register animals and remains so today. The first compulsory requirements in some European countries to present written documents to certify the origin of certain animals in husbandry can be traced back to the eighteenth century (*ibid.*: 421-422). The traceability of 'cattle' in husbandry became a legal requirement in all countries of the European Union in late 1999, in Canada in 2001, and was followed by a nationwide proposal in the United States in 2004. From the stable to the table, from pig to pork, the state-imposed identification schemes of these animals seems informed by the rationale of food security and prevention and control of epizootics with an economic momentum. Beyond disease control, retailers and consumers demand guarantees on health and welfare status and the feed supplied to the animals (Madec *et al.* 2001). Next to husbandry, from the eighteenth century onwards, many European countries made the identification of dogs obligatory in an effort to control rabies (Blancou 2001: 423). In this respect, Ritvo points to some 'political considerations' regarding dog licensing in nineteenth-century England, denying paupers the ability to keep dogs or to prevent the rural working class from keeping poaching dogs (Ritvo 1987: 167–202). Identification of individual animals may also be required by the methodological scheme of scientific research, or employed as a pivotal instrument in the monitoring of endangered species.

Although the identification of animals can nowadays be achieved with the help of sophisticated technological appliances such as microchips, methods dating back thousands of years such as branding or ear cutting are still practised. Identification can be obtained by the attachment or insertion of a body-foreign device or can be acquired through mutilation of the animal's body. However, not all devices fitted on to animals serve the purpose of identifying them. In this respect, we think of shock collars fitted to dogs, which can be used to train the dog behaviourally (the trainer shocks through a remote control unit, whenever the dog steps out of line). Shock collars can also be used as part of a containment system, when a buried boundary wire creates an invisible fence. When the dog moves near this area, he will hear a warning tone and, if not leaving the area, will receive a shock. Such systems have a negative impact on dogs' welfare (Schilder and van der Borg 2004),[1] making them interesting research topics for a non-speciesist perspective. Although not directly aimed at individually identifying the dog, the invisible fence system could be seen as a means of claiming ownership of the animal (forcing the animal to stay on the premises), and as such an indirect identification labelling. Similarly, systems have been developed to contain cattle and other grazers through GPS (Global Positioning System) – delineated grazing patches that use analogous noise warning and shocking collars or tags (Butler *et al.* 2004).

In what follows, I discuss some techniques that are used to identify animals, such as branding and tattooing, radio collaring, ear tagging, toe amputation and the insertion of microchips or transponders into animals' bodies, and their possible impact on the welfare of the animals concerned.

Branding

Animals are labelled with permanent identification marks by means of hot-iron branding, freeze branding or chemical branding. With hot-iron branding, a mark is burnt on the animal's skin with a hot iron, in freeze branding (cryobranding) a super-cooled iron (in liquid nitrogen or a mixture of dry ice and alcohol) is applied to an area of the body; the hair and skin growing back after this procedure are permanently coloured differently from the rest of the area, because the pigment-producing melanocytes of the skin are destroyed (Powell and Proulx 2003: 272). Chemical branding employs caustic material to destroy the hair in the area of application. Identification of individuals in a group of millions cannot be attained through branding because of the lack of variation in branding marks, making branding an often-used method for group identification.

For animals incorporated in husbandry systems, branding is one of the earliest known forms of identification and can be traced back to the Neolithic period (Landais 2001: 465). Blancou (2001) presents data on the branding of the horses of Alexander the Great, the horses used in Roman chariot races, the postal horses in seventh-century China, to the horses of the royal stables in seventeenth-century Persia. The branding of cows and bulls is still widely used in the United States and Western Canada, often more than once as a result of changing ownership (Schwartzkopf-Genswein *et al.* 1997: 361). While the practice of branding 'the living stock' of farmers still seems common practice, the meagreness of research into possible welfare effects of this custom is surprising. Lay *et al.* (1992) compared freeze branding to hot-iron branding with respect to distress and pain in cows. While both methods produced pain sensations, there was a greater escape avoidance reaction and heart rate in hot-iron branding. Consequently they proposed freeze branding as preferable to hot-iron branding when feasible. Similar results were found in the 1990s by Schwartzkopf-Genswein *et al.* (1997) although they also assert that branding may not be a severe enough stressor to negatively affect long-term indicators of welfare such as average daily gain or health.[2]

Branding of animals as an identification technique is employed not only in husbandry but also in the methodology of field research. An Australian government report refers to the thousands of seals labelled through hot-iron branding in past decades. Since 2000, however, this practice has been stopped 'because of serious concerns over animal welfare', and research is now moving to less invasive marking techniques (Commonwealth of Australia 2004: 43–44). Sherwin et al. developed a technique to freeze brand bats and found no adverse effects during or after branding, although acknowledged that 'this technique should not be used on bats that are federally (USA) threatened or endangered until long-term effects of branding are known' (2002: 99). The research of Saura (1996) and Winder (2004) on juvenile pikeperch and carabid beetles, respectively, illustrate that branding is not confined to mammals.

The American Veterinary Medical Association remains careful in its position on branding of animals, neither endorsing nor rejecting it. It states that 'high priority be given to the development of alternatives to hot-iron branding' (AVMA-online). A New Zealand report on methods of marking animals adds that hot branding of animals is also aesthetically unpleasant. Notwithstanding initial sterilisation of the wound due to the heat, there is, given the severity of the tissue damage and the time required for wound healing, an increased risk of later infection in comparison to less invasive methods (Beasoleil et al. 2004: 29).

Tattooing

Similarly to branding, tattooing is an identification technique through which a permanent mark is put on the body. In a review essay on methods to trap and mark terrestrial animals, tattooing is described as follows:

> A tattoo, applied with special pliers or an electric tattooing pencil, is a series of tiny perforations in the skin into which a dark dye is rubbed or injected to produce a visible pattern. Any body part that is visibly free of hair and remains fairly clean can be tattooed. Animals of all sizes can be tattooed, from small mammals to deer and bears. (Powell and Prouxl 2003: 272)

Tattooing is used in different domains in which humans come into contact with other animals, from animals in the laboratory, farmed animals, to animals appointed as companions for humans, or animals described as 'living freely in the wild'. For example, Animal Identification and Marking Systems, Inc. portray tail tattooing of neonate mice as 'a practical and non-invasive alternative to toe clipping' (AIMS-online). Identification of horses is sometimes achieved by a tattoo on the inside surface of their lips (Neary and Yager 2004: 8). In husbandry, cows, goats and sheep can be identified through tattoos in their ears. Pigs can have tattoos imprinted with a hammer in their rear or shoulder. However, tattooing is not so commonly used in husbandry as it is not considered economically profitable. Stanford *et al.* denote the practice as 'time consuming and laborious', and thus limited to small herds and flocks. The tattoo can also be difficult to read, especially in dark-pigmented ears (2001: 515–516). The practice is not so commonly used for amphibians, because the marks often last only a few weeks or months (Denardo 1995). Although not directly an identification system, tattooing of pigs has also found a niche in the art scene, with Belgian artist Wim Delvoye tattooing pigs on his art farms in China. The tattooed pigs live their natural life span, with their multicoloured and patterned skins being sold as exclusive art objects after death.

There is little scientific research on the welfare impacts of tattooing animals. Sometimes, tattooing is seen as a more animal-friendly alternative to other identification methods, for example for the identification of mice in laboratory research where it is weighed against ear tagging as being 'more humane' (Guilloud and Johnson 1990) or presented as being 'more humane and less invasive' than toe amputation (Yacowitz *et al.* 1997). Especially important in field research is the potential negative impact of the capture and handling in itself: less permanent marks necessitate repeated capture to refresh the marks. Although acknowledging that 'more permanent marks such as brands and tattoos tend to cause pain and stress at the time of application', some researchers believe this momentary, once-in-a-lifetime pain to be more humane than repeated capture and marking (Beausoleil *et al.* 2004: 7). However, tattoos are not readily discernible from a distance, often compelling capture and handling for identification. If the tattoo site is not properly disinfected beforehand, tattoos on dirty skin can result in infection or warts (*ibid.*: 32). Consider the following description in a review paper on 'Methods of Livestock Identification': 'For carcass tattoos in swine, a tattoo hammer is used, and is swung toward the tattoo site with enough force, so that the needles will penetrate the skin. The animal can be released after the number has been recorded. Tattoo equipment should be disinfected between each use.' (Neary and Yager 2004: 8). Although reference to the 'carcass' might suggest that this practice is performed on the body of a dead animal, tattooing living pigs with a tattoo hammer is a commonly used identification technique. The same authors state: 'Tattooing is the best permanent method of identification for registered animals because it does not harm the animal's appearance or reduce its [sic] value in any way' (*ibid.*).

Ear tagging

Attaching an identification tag to an animal's body is a widely used method. Tags can be made from a variety of materials, most commonly metal or plastic. Tags can be applied to ears, webs, flippers, fins, jaws and toes, depending on the anatomy of the animal (Beausoleil *et al.* 2004: 23; Stanford *et al.* 2001). The tags can be inscribed with an alphanumerical code or bar-code, or with the development of recent technology they can be the carriers of transponders with electronic identification devices. In the European Union, it is mandated that pigs, sheep and goats be identified with an ear tag or a tattoo; bovine animals have to carry a tag in each ear (Ammendrup and Füssel 2001).

From a layman's perspective, the attachment of ear marks (or tags on other body parts) seems to be a harmful procedure. An investigation into the use of ear marks on mice in field research concludes that it led to higher infestations by larval ticks, most likely because the tags reduced grooming efficiency (Ostfeld *et al.* 1993). Alternatively, in a research on prairie voles comparing ear tagging to toe amputation as identification methods, ear tagging is considered 'relatively harmless' (Wood and Slade 1990: 252). Powell and Prouxl mention that the tags must be loose enough so they do not interfere with blood circulation and that puncture marks should be appropriately treated not to cause infection (2003: 271). Tags can be pulled out by grooming animals, ripped from the ear, or get snagged in vegetation or enclosures. Because of the conspicuousness of coloured tags and disrupting camouflage, the extra visibility can influence prey ratio for certain animals (Beausoleil *et al.* 2004: 23–24). Regarding efficiency, recurring factors are they are relatively inexpensive in comparison to the more recently developed electronic identification methods, that they are easy to use, flexible in all weather conditions, usually easy to read, but they can also often get lost (Morley 2002; Stärk *et al*. 1998). Objection to compulsory ear tagging of pigs and other animals recently led to several lawsuits in the Netherlands with diverging rulings. The defendants argued that ear tagging animals negatively influences their welfare and, as such, they positioned themselves as conscientious objectors to the practice. The tags often get hooked on protrusions, tearing the animals' ears. In one case, the judge ruled the stipulations of the animal welfare legislation of greater significance than the subsidiary implementing order in which ear tagging is made obligatory (Evertsen 2005).

Radio collaring

Different animal species have been fitted with collars, although not all collars serve the purpose of identification. Sometimes the collars are fitted with devices to direct the animals' behaviour in the preferred way, as with shock collars (cf. above). Small capsules, tags or medallions attached to collars – which contain the written contact data of their caretakers – have been traditionally used to indirectly identify dogs or sometimes even cats.

The collaring of animals to identify them is a widely used technique in field studies. Sometimes, collars are simply fitted to differentiate between marked and unmarked animals, but they are often coupled with additional devices to allow individual identification of animals or have telemetric or other equipment attached. The type of collars I consider here are radio collars: the device carried by the animal transmits radio signals through which information about the animal can be determined. From crayfish to dolphins, elephants to tigers, water voles to foxes, goats to bears, radio tracking has been used to study a variety of animal species and, as such, it is a commonly used technique in field research (Beausoleil *et al*. 2004: 23; Mech and Barber 2002: 6 and 11). There seems to be no outlined instruction on the kind of material used for collars: 'Plastic, leather, vinyl, nylon, metal, metal beaded chain, rubberised machine belting and other materials can be used to fashion collars, harnesses and bands' (Beausoleil *et al*. 2004: 24). Some collars are meant to last a lifetime, others are intended to fall off after a certain amount of time to be collected by the researchers. A prerequisite for fitting radio collars is that animals must have prominent necks. Some species, such as hedgehogs, are thus installed with other radio devices, for example backpack harnesses or tail collars (see also Gregory *et al*. 2003;

Kenward *et al.* 2001). When the collar is fitted on to youngsters, expandable collars can be administered to allow for growth of the animal (Mech and Barber 2002: 14).

A number of investigations have explicitly looked into the possible effects on animals of wearing radio collars. Cypher (1997) studied the effects on San Joaquin foxes and recommended that the ratio between collar and body mass should be less than 6 per cent to have no effect on survival. Research into the effects of radio collars on European badgers suggests that at least a post-collaring acclimation period should be taken into consideration, because of lower body condition (Tuyttens *et al.* 2002). Berteaux *et al.* (1994; 1996) demonstrated social costs associated with the use of heavier transmitters on meadow voles, although they found no effect of carrying a radio collar on expenditure of energy by the same species. A recent study showed a dramatic decline of 48 per cent in the number of female water voles born at one site. The researchers suggest that the most likely cause for the female decline is a shift in the sex ratio of young raised by radio-collared females (Moorhouse and Macdonald 2005). In another study, some radio-collared mongoose showed abrasions on the neck (Palomares and Delibes 1992).

Sometimes, collaring can have an indirect effect on animal survival. For example, one study suggests that collared bears have a higher survival rate than non-collared bears because of hunter bias. This is believed to be due to the fact that hunters successfully avoid killing female bears (who were collared in this study) (Klenzendorf 2002). Similar (although opposite) effects were suggested in a study on white-tailed deer fitted with bright yellow collars: because of the bright collars, hunters could more easily spot the deer and mortality rates were therefore biased with respect to hunter pressure (Mech and Barber 2002: 31).

Other studies have found no impact of wearing these devices. Gursky (1998) states his radio collars had no appreciable effects on the behavioural patterns of the spectral tarsier (a small nocturnal primate). Côté *et al.* (1998) conclude with no significant life history effects of wearing radio collars on mountain goats. However, in their critique of 'wildlife radio tracking', Mech and Barber (2002: 29–32) enumerate many other documented effects of radio collars: animals can get snagged in vegetation and entangled or strangulated in collars that are too loose; there can be feather loss in birds; the collar can be a drag when lifting, swimming, flying or digging; and animals can have their behavioural patterns affected when spending more time in preening or less time in motion.

The American Society of Mammalogists offers some guidelines for the use of radio collars in field research. For terrestrial mammals, the radio transmitter should not exceed 5 per cent of body mass. It adds: 'Investigators are further obliged to monitor the condition of marked mammals and, if practical, remove transmitters at the completion of a study' (ASM-online 1998: 30).

Amputating toes

In laboratory research, it is not always necessary to mark an animal individually: identification is sometimes also acquired through room, rack, pen, stall or cage cards with written or bar-coded information. Besides collars, bands, plates, tabs, collared stains, ear notches, tags, tattoos, subcutaneous transponders and freeze brands, toe amputation is another means of identifying animals in the laboratory.

Toe amputation – usually a method for marking rodents – is the removal of the first bone of certain toes, corresponding to a predetermined numbering code (Lawson 2001: 45). The Association of Veterinarians for Animal Rights describes it as the following: 'Scissors or clippers are used to sever part of one or more of the digits of the feet' (AVAR-online 1988). The US Guide for the Care and Use of Laboratory Animals (National Research Council 1996) states that 'as a method of identification of small rodents, [it] should be used only when no other individual identification method is feasible and should be performed only on altricial neonates'. Although it is admitted that toe amputation may still be deemed necessary in some circumstances, the US Interagency Research Animal Committee considers it a potentially painful procedure which should be discouraged and only done with the approval of the Institutional Animal Care and Use Committee. It may only be used as a last resort, and the investigator must justify that no other marking method is possible. Furthermore, the procedure must be performed in 'the most painless and humane way' and take into consideration all accepted veterinary procedures 'including anaesthesia and antisepsis'.

In the Netherlands, toe amputation of rodents for individual identification in laboratory research received national media coverage at the end of 2005. At goudenkalf.com (Golden Calf), the director of a research centre was nominated 'animal tyrant' of the year, 'for cutting off toes of living animals and torturing animals in his job'. The pilloried director filed a complaint, resulting in the removal of the website and compensation of 1,000 Euros.[3] It was stated that at the research unit, 'toe clipping' is used as a permitted means of identifying neonate mice for cancer research in mammals. Moreover, the removed toe tissue is used for genotypic research, turning otherwise-performed tail amputations redundant. The judge reasoned that, in accordance with animal welfare legislation, this was not a matter of 'unnecessary suffering' – let alone 'torture' – and the performed procedures were in accordance with the legislation on animal experimentation. This position was later followed by the authorised Minister clarifying that 'toe clipping' is allowed when no alternative marking methods are available. Exemplifying, the Minister stated that neonate mice cannot be chipped, they have no fur to be dyed or shaved off or it is impossible to remove a part of their auricle (Ministerie van Volksgezondheid, Welzijn en Sport 2005).

Toe amputation is however not without welfare consequences. Next to the pain and suffering caused by the cutting of skin, bones and joints, the Association of Veterinarians for Animal Rights state that when the anaesthetic has worn off, there would be pain until the lesions heal, intensified because the animals must stand on their feet. Other possible consequences are haemorrhage leading to debilitation or death and osteomyelitis and cellulitis from open wounds in contact with contaminated bedding. 'There is no scientific justification or need for toe clipping, with or without anaesthesia. The suffering associated with it is completely gratuitous and inhumane.' (AVAR-online 1988). In similar vein, researchers presenting an alternative identification system for neonate and pre-weanling rodents consisting of tail tattooing, state that 'toe clipping of animals is invasive and inhumane' (Yacowitz et al. 1997: 1865).

The issue has received some more attention in field experimentation research,[4] where the technique of amputating digits or toes is a long-used identification method of some species of rodents, amphibians and reptiles. The International Society for Applied Ethology states: 'Mutilatory forms of identification (e.g. toe amputation), or those which injure substantial amounts of tissue should be assumed to cause substantial acute and perhaps chronic pain, and would therefore generally be considered unacceptable.' (ISAE-online, 2003). In similar vein, the Association for the Study of Animal Behaviour – although not unambiguously excluding the practice – suggests this is an ethically questionable method of identification (ASAB-online 2005: 6). In guidelines for research of other national or international field study societies specific guidelines for the (exceptional) use of toe amputation are often provided. The American Society of Mammalogists, for example, states:

> When no other marking methods are feasible, ear punching and
> toe-clipping are quick, long term marking methods that cause
> only brief and minor discomfort to small mammals (shrew to
> rat-sized). [...] All clipping methods should be performed with
> sharp instruments. No more than one toe per foot should be
> clipped. (ASM-online 1998: 29)

Nevertheless, toe amputation is still the most common marking
method for amphibians and reptiles (Beausoleil *et al*. 2004: 12 and 37).
One of the earliest studies of the impact of toe amputation suggests
adverse effects on survival of Woodhouse's Toad (Clark 1972).
More recent research shows that toe amputation of natterjack toads
potentially leads to infection and necrosis (Golay and Durrer 1994). A
specific factor among amphibians is that some species have the ability
to regenerate their toes, making toe amputation an impermanent
marking technique and necessitating repetition in long-term studies
(Denardo 1995). Furthermore, to read the identification codes, marked
animals must almost always be recaptured (Beausoleil *et al*. 2004: 37)
possibly inducing additional impact from handling. In another study,
it was suggested that toe amputation may reduce the life span of
male meadow voles (Pavone and Boonstra 1985). However, Dodd
(1993) concludes that amputation of a few toes has no immediate or
long-term effects on the sprint performance of the studied lizard, and
should not affect the lizard's survival, and Wood and Slade (1990)
found no detrimental effects of toe amputation that in their opinion
would preclude its use in field studies of prairie voles.

Identifying animals with transponders

In recent years, electronic identification of animals has evolved from
conspicuous devices attached to collars to tiny microchips inserted
into an animal's body. The implants, measuring one or two millimetres
in diameter and just over a centimetre long, are typically implanted
into the body with the help of a special syringe. The implant consists
of an electromagnetic coil and microchip sealed in a biologically-inert
glass capsule. When an external PIT-reader is passed over the animal
to activate the otherwise passive transponder (hence its name: Passive
Integrated Transponder, or 'PIT'), it reveals a unique identification
number on the reading device.[5] Next to being inserted in the body,
transponders can also be imbedded in tags attached to an animal's ear
(Gibbons and Andrews 2005; Low, Eason and McInnes 2005; Stanford
et al. 2001: 516–518). Although originally applied in studies in which

fish were electronically identified, the application of PIT tags for individual identification has found its way into many other domains, being applied worldwide in husbandry identification schemes, in laboratory experiments and field studies, on animal companions and on captive animals in zoos or rehabilitation centres (Elbin and Burger 1994). PIT tags can also be a fruitful supporting technique in wildlife law enforcement and in detecting illegal trafficking of endangered species (Buhlmann and Tuberville 1998: 102). From fish to crustaceans, amphibians, reptiles, birds and many mammals, millions of animals have already been injected with these identifying transponders (Eradus 2001: 16).

Several studies have specifically examined the impact of this identification technique on the animal's life and many report no effect on body functioning, behaviour or well-being. Becker and Wendeln report that the implementation of the transponder on common terns takes little time and they found no influence on the tern's behaviour (1997: 537). Another study explicitly suggests PIT tagging as an alternative to ear tagging and toe amputation for marking small mammals, having found no mortalities and little incidence of infection at the implant site (Schooley et al. 1993). Similar data result from studies of sea horses (Woods 2005), kakapo (Low et al. 2005), turtles (Buhlmann and Tuberville 1998: 103), so-called 'poultry chicks' (Jamison et al. 2000), rabbits, guinea pigs, woodchucks and some species of amphibians for laboratory experimentation (Mrozek 1995) and even tarantulas (Reichling and Tabaka 2001). 'Tags are internal, permanent, and have virtually no negative impact on animals, provided the organism has sufficient body size and its ecological activities are not prohibited by tagging and monitoring' (Gibbons and Andrews 2004: 451). However, Gibbons and Andrews do warn not to use the technique on diseased animals, 'because of the invasive nature of the procedure' (2004: 451–452). When used on amphibians, it must also be taken into consideration that these creatures have the ability to extrude foreign material from their body, especially if the material is placed subcutaneously (Denardo 1995). Although the insertion of the tag still necessitates capture and handling, the need for recapture can be reduced if the chipped animal can be voluntarily made to enter the field of a scanner (e.g. feeding or nesting site). It can also be a helpful and interesting tool in predation studies, as the tags of eaten prey animals can still be read inside predators (Petersen and Barfoot 2003).

In husbandry, microchip identification is often considered an improvement with respect to visual identification. Generally, this refers not to the welfare aspects of the identification system, but to the elimination of labour costs and the decrease of incorrect readings. This technology is said to combine 'the advantages of the conventional loose housing systems (relative freedom for the animals) with the advantages of the stanchion barns (control of single animals)' (Eradus and Jansen 1999: 92). However, the possible migration of the implant in the animal's body and the trouble of locating the implant for removal after slaughter remain inhibiting factors (Frost *et al*. 1997: 144). As an alternative, rumenal boluses have been applied. The capsule containing a transponder is swallowed and remains in the pit of the stomach, making it more easily traceable after death (Eradus 2001: 16; McAllister 2000: 384). Following electronic devices attached to collars and injected electronic transponders, a third generation of identification devices includes read-and-write possibilities for storage of life history indicators of the animal and also sensor technologies for automatic monitoring of animal health and performance (Eradus and Jansen 1999: 91–92; McAllister 2000: 384). The migration of PIT tags could also pose a risk to internal organs (Beausoleil *et al*. 2004: 34). Other mentioned disadvantages of PIT tags are that they cannot be read from a large distance, are expensive, require special equipment and that the transponder can be ejected through the insertion hole soon after implantation (*ibid*.: 33–35). Applying a biologically safe adhesive to close the puncture wound can solve this (Low *et al*. 2005: 33; Morley 2002: 147). Furthermore, the integration of different systems is needed to ensure compatibility and international standardisation (Buhlmann and Tuberville 1998: 104; Eradus 2001: 15).

Identification marks, animal welfare and unnecessary suffering

This overview of some marking methods to identify animals demonstrates that this practice, whether obtained through bodily mutilations or insertion or attachment of body-foreign devices, is not restricted to a delineated set of animal species. Spiders, polar bears, lizards, penguins, cows, cats, horses, falcons, goats, sea horses, or even beetles and many other animal species have been subjected to one or another form of tangible identification. Due to the versatility of the species labelled by humans, an overview of the outcome of marking techniques on animal welfare is no unambiguous effort and will evidently vary across species boundaries and techniques used. The use of radioactive markers, fur clipping and dyeing, retinal scanning and DNA fingerprinting, nasal discs or even the use of nose prints of cows and sheep are some other employed identification techniques (see Calvo and Furness 1992; Neary and Yager 2004; Powell and Prouxl 2003: 270–272).

Although identification techniques are ubiquitously applied in humans' dealings with other animals, the impact of these procedures on the animals' welfare seems to occupy a scantly developed area in scientific research or in the literature on animal ethics. The bulk of publications on welfare issues associated with marking techniques can be situated in field research, pertaining to studies into the so-called 'instrument effect' on the lives of the research 'objects'. As the mere presence of humans – however low profile this might be – potentially influences the animals' lives in a harmful way, handling and marking them can derivatively be presumed to have a negative impact on their lives (Goodall 1986; Bekoff 2000). Besides the actual marking and marks in themselves, the capturing, handling, recapturing or the mere presence of humans to read the data can be influencing factors. For example, in the case of radio tracking, this technique not only requires the capturing of live animals and fitting them with a collar or other device, but the emitted signals must also be monitored, usually necessitating people in the field in vehicles, aircraft or on foot (Mech and Barber 2002: 6). An issue rarely considered is the influence of handling and marking on the social relationships of the handled and marked individuals (Putman 1995: 911). Some marking techniques are indeed permanent, possibly leading to a lifetime of suspicion from conspecifics or notability for predators. Research into the welfare aspects of marking animals can be impeded by the absence of any reference point since unmarked animals often simply cannot be monitored.

Attention to the instrument effect – with concern for correct research data most closely reflecting the animals' natural behaviour as the core impetus (Mech and Barber 2002: 29) – seems to be slowly percolating into the scientific community. In a practical guide of methods for marking amphibians, reptiles and marine mammals from the New Zealand Department of Conservation, we are warned:

> Although it is encouraging to see studies systematically evaluating the effects of marking, their paltry number in relation to the thousands of investigations that use artificial marks to identify wild animals suggests that insufficient attention has been given to this area. In addition, many of the studies intended to evaluate mark-related effects have been plagued by flaws in experimental design. (Beausoleil *et al.* 2004: 12)

The scantiness of these investigations may have less to do with the actual absence of any welfare effects than with the predisposition of the researchers themselves. As Reaser (1995) notes, the small number of examinations 'may stem from biologists' reluctance to report results that indicate that their work impinges on the life of their subjects and, as a result, potentially bias their data'. Notwithstanding the importance of the instrument effect on the output of research data, the fact that these practices (might) have detrimental welfare effects (even when they would not influence data output) could in itself be the core of the matter, surpassing even an anthropocentric-informed motive. As Farnsworth and Rosovsky say: 'It would be interesting to know how many experiments have been constrained or modified out of concern for the organism itself' (1993: 467).

Increased attention to this matter in field research is contrasted with the nearly complete disregard in other domains. Investigations into the impact of marking techniques on animal welfare in laboratory research, husbandry, or even its use on animal companions resemble the impression of a pristine desert with some sparsely dotted oases of research. There are more references to the positive or negative technical or economic traits of marking techniques, e.g. whether they are easy to read, simple to apply, raise problems at slaughter or are financially lucrative (see e.g. Stärk *et al.* 1998; Ammendrup and Füssel 2001). Maybe this blind spot can be attributed to the fact that animals incorporated in husbandry, laboratory experiments or even animals referred to as companions have to deal with a whole series of invasive human-imposed techniques, of which the procedures used to mark them may in comparison turn out to be one of the lesser welfare threatening – but nonetheless welfare threatening – practices. These practices include force feeding geese or ducks for the production of fatted liver (foie gras); the dire transport conditions – sometimes even across continents – of sheep and cows, the living conditions of hens in battery cages; the life-shortening and body-mutilating practices on animals in the laboratory; the unanaesthetised tail amputation, castration or teeth clipping of pigs in husbandry; and the training methods used to straitjacket the behaviour of working dogs, guard animals or animals imprisoned to perform for human pleasure in circuses (see further Singer 2006). These are just a few of the examples which, when weighed against tagging, collaring or chipping, may show the latter to have a relative marginal influence on the animal's welfare. With a seeming abundance of acute issues, it is no surprise that pressure groups', legislative and animal welfare science's attention has focused on techniques that seem to have a more profound impact on the animals' lives. From the animals' point of view, however, the trade-off to a lesser evil still leaves them with exactly this violation to cope with.

Similarly, making decisions informed by either environmental ethics or animal rights frameworks represents analogous balancing operations. With greater value appointed to the survival of species – and certainly endangered species – in environmental ethics, would it not be an acceptable method to remove (parts of) the tusks of elephants or rhinos' horns in an effort to make them unattractive to poachers? As such, can causing harm to some individuals be justified if the extinction of an entire species is prevented? Likewise, the amputation of toes of rare lizards, toads and frogs to prevent them from being sold illegally for extortionate prices, could be proposed as a justifiable means to protect them. So, could the elimination of some fingers or toes of gorillas be condoned to prevent their hands being chopped off and sold as ashtrays? How should we weigh the welfare violations inflicted on the individual animals against the overall benefits to the survival of the species?

Many animal welfare regulations worldwide lay down strict stipulations on authorised and prohibited dealings with animals, for example in laboratory settings, in husbandry, in circuses, or in zoos. However, with no option to encompass all probable dealings with other animals in statutory provisos, general stipulations are also provided, not uncommonly outlawing the 'unnecessary suffering' or the 'socially unacceptable abuse' of animals. As such, an anthropocentric-imposed distinction is made between animal abuse and animal use, given the acceptability or necessity of the animal suffering to be overridden with economic or scientific imperatives. Most often, what is considered as necessary suffering is deemed necessary with the yardstick of anthropocentric value systems, muting the voices of the suffering animals and ignoring their proverbial view of necessity. Also, taking into respect environmental ethics, the consideration is no straightforward cost-benefit analysis:

> No simple guidelines exist regarding how to weigh the effects of research (positive and negative) on individuals versus groups versus populations versus communities. Likewise, no guidelines exist about how to weigh research funding versus effects on animals (injury) versus importance of results (e.g. for individual animals, animal populations, and humans). (Powell and Proulx 2003: 260)

Different studies have shown there to be serious welfare threats from labelling mechanisms. As Putman says: 'all available methods are associated with at least some level of risk greater than zero. Therefore there remains always the subsidiary question of what is an "acceptable" level of "suffering", of mortality or fitness loss beyond which one should abandon the research' (Putman 1995: 912). In setting out the normative boundaries of our treatment of animals, this issue is not to be relegated to an ancillary point, but stands at the heart of the matter. The precautionary principle could serve as a restraining flag with respect to species or situations which are yet uncultivated, given the available research results (Bekoff 2000). If no overruling trump is used in protecting the animal's welfare, there can always be an overriding necessity to claim superiority over the animal's interest, whether informed by a full-blown anthropocentric rationale or by an ecological-inspired ethics focused on the environment.

Dominance and colonisation

Beyond the welfare impact on the individual animals concerned, the marking of animals prompts other queries of a non-speciesist or green criminology. Driven by an abstract urge to order the natural chaos of animals and plants, theoretical classifications, taxonomies and evolution patterns still in use today find their roots in categorising efforts as far back as the seventeenth century. These categorisations can be seen as more than a mere academic effort in classifying nature; they embody 'a sweeping human claim to intellectual mastery of the natural world' (Ritvo 1987: 12). Similarly, the neatly delineated exhibits with animals in zoos in nineteenth-century England could be seen to stand for the 'imposition of human structure on the threatening chaos of nature' (Ritvo 1987: 218).

Though this chapter has not concentrated on the abstract categorisation of the natural world, the individual identification of animals can be approached on similar grounds. Through these labelling techniques, animals are assigned an identity, a human-allotted uniqueness that distinguishes them from their congeners. However, incorporated into mass production systems or scientific inquiries, the identification of animals does not pertain to the assignment of a life history or the embodiment of the personality of the animal, as can be the case when animals are embraced in the family as companions. In the former case, the identification is not really a positive identification, the allocation of an identity, but a mere differentiation among the masses incorporated in the system. As such, it is not the purpose in itself, but a means of facilitating the objectifying system in which the animals are included. Through these identification techniques, the animals can be monitored and controlled every step along the way, from birth (or even before), to their death. As a production unit in husbandry, the cow's 'yield' can be carefully supervised and if necessary adjusted.[6] When an outbreak of an epizootic threatens the economic viability of the sector, decisions can be enforced to kill all cognisable animals in a state-enforced geographical or network radius, irrespective of whether the animals are contaminated or not, sick or not, or incorporated in the husbandry scheme or living as companions of rural hobbyists.[7] Deemed as a dangerous creature wandering beyond the imposed boundaries of the nature reserve, the roaming and GPS-monitored bear can be forced to revert to his human-delineated living space. In similar vein, the monitoring of so-called wildlife with the assistance of labelling techniques fits neatly into the same scheme of human control or even – to revert to a terminology in the editor's contribution (South, this volume, p. 237) – 'the colonisation' of the natural realm. In tagging, branding, collaring or otherwise labelling animals, humans impose their dominance on the order of 'things' and display their mastership on the identification or differentiation of animals (see also Tuan 1984).

And yet, the representation of humans colonising the natural world is not such a straightforward analysis. An article in the *Los Angeles Times* mentions that in Yellowstone Park the number of reintroduced wolves who are collared has been decreased due to visitors' objections to seeing animals wearing plastic collars. It is poignantly – although relegating the animal to an asexual object status – remarked 'Is an animal still wild if it's wearing a glorified dog collar?' (Japenga 2005). Conversely, an overview and critique on the use of radio-tracking in national parks states there is no scientific research into the public's perceptions of tagged or collared animals (Mech and Barber 2002: 36). Then again, the query goes beyond the spectators' disapproval or authorisation of animals having their bodily appearance altered, associating them with either 'wild' or 'tame' creatures. Does the category of the 'wild animal' living in the 'wilderness' still – if it ever has – relate to any ontological reality? If the boundaries between pristine nature and human-made culture are blurred or shown from an outright constructionist approach never to have existed at all, what are the consequences for the interpretation and application of a non-speciesist or green criminology?

Labelling humans and other animals

Pointing to the welfare effects of tangibly labelling animals – although a scarcely documented area – is just one side of the picture. Indeed, not being labelled and incorporated into human devised identification systems can also hold dire consequences for animals. Having no certifying papers or identifying marks implies having no identity, which can denote an illegal alien, which in the case of animals commonly incorporated into husbandry schemes possibly leads to the death penalty. In Belgium in 2005, a man was given a suspended prison sentence and a 1,000 Euro fine, for having a cow under his care who was not properly ear tagged. In his defence, he argued that he had a list of all cows on his premises and that the identity of that particular animal could thus be traced and that his son had grown fond of the animal. But the Food Agency stated that the sound health status of the cow could not be proved and the court ordered immediate slaughter of the cow because her origin could not be traced (Belga 2005). Unmonitored animals cannot enter the food chain, being categorised as suspect animals and possible spreaders of disease. Moreover, the strict identification schemes in the European Union (and many other countries) for what are categorised as husbandry animals (bovines, pigs, goats, sheep) rule out many veterinary procedures or examinations on these animals (for example sending a blood sample for analysis to the lab) since these require an authorised identified animal. But when keeping sheep, pigs or cows – even with no breeding, farming or selling intentions but as companions of their human caretakers – with all the registrations and identifications required, the animals run the risk of being collected and deported to the slaughterhouse if there is an outbreak of an epizootic deemed dangerous. Outbreaks of foot and mouth disease, bird flu, swine fever, and mad cow disease have thus resulted in the killing of billions of animals in recent years.

Labelling and marking methods as a *modus operandi* to control, monitor and exercise authority over others is no technique that is reserved for other animals. In similar vein, marking techniques have been compellingly administered to humans. Although tattooing, collaring, piercing and even branding the human body can be a self-chosen adornment, these practices have also been forcefully applied to humans in order to readily differentiate between the pure and the vile, the master and the slave, the owner and the property. In *The Dreaded Comparison* Spiegel (1996) points to the many similarities in the treatment of oppressed groups, such as the treatment of slaves in eighteenth- and nineteenth-century America and the treatment of other animals continuing to this day. Burning ownership marks on their bodies is just one analogous method in their treatment, next to resemblances in muzzling, immobilising, trading and transporting methods. The marking of slaves and captives was still a common practice in Sudan and Central Africa in 1900 (Landais 2001: 473). Closer in the collective memory are the distinguishing tattoos of serial numbers inscribed on prisoners in the concentration camps in the Second World War.[8] Although such practices illustrate the similar objectifying practices of the oppressors – regardless of whether the victimised groups are humans or other animals – the fierce societal reaction when such comparisons are made emphasises the fact that pointing to such analogies is indeed a 'dreaded' comparison.[9]

Nonetheless, revealing the practices that objectify and oppress humans and other animals, and pointing to possible parallels between the two, can further the analysis and help undermine both the discriminatory operations between humans (racism, sexism, ageism and other -isms) and a prejudiced attitude against other animals, i.e. speciesism. Cultivating what has been raised in this chapter, it would be an interesting experiment to ponder the issues surrounding the legal, economic and societal status of human illegal aliens, political refugees or other 'sans papiers' who have no state-authorised or sanctioned identity. Does having no authorised identity categorise them as less than human? Can they obtain the benefits of the social security system, health care provisions and judicial assistance as can legally identified humans? Similarly, can – as an alternative to the traditional prison sentence – the development of electronic monitoring of offenders with wrist or ankle collars be analysed in similar vein as the shift away from eighteenth-century-originating zoo incarcerations to the electronic monitoring and demarcation of the movements of animals in natural parks? Another example takes us to electronically identified humans, which a couple of years ago would have been classified as science fiction. A popular beach club with branches in Spain and the Netherlands has introduced a subcutaneous 'VIP Chip', offering privileges to chip carriers and equally functioning as a credit card.[10] The development of electronic identification techniques has already raised many ethical issues (see EGE 2004) although it seems that the debate is mainly confined to human-centred concerns. It is now time to take up this issue from a non-speciesist perspective as well, since Big Brother's all-seeing eye is surely not restricted to the monitoring and control of the lives of humans.

Notes

1 A suggested negative impact of the invisible fence system is that the dog may still be lured past the fence if the reward to the dog is great enough. Once outside, the dog will have great difficulty coming 'home', precisely because of the fence barrier. Also, when shocked, the dog may associate this negative stimulus with anything or anyone visible to him at that time. In 2004, the Austrian government outlawed the invisible fence mechanism (Kole 2004).

2 They published several papers in the *Journal of Animal Science* and the *Canadian Journal of Animal Science*. References upon request.

3 LJN: AU5318, Rechtbank's-Gravenhage, KG 05/1317, Civiel Recht, Kort geding, Vonnis 1 November 2005 (http://zoeken.rechtspraak.nl).

4 Toe amputation is also performed on turkeys in husbandry, although in this case not for identification purposes, but to reduce injuries due to fighting (see Moran 1985).

5 The PIT tags thus differ from telemetric devices commonly used in field studies in that they must be scanned nearby to reveal the identification number. Telemetric devices can be used to position the location of animals from afar.

6 Many examples of monitoring animals in husbandry are supplied by Frost *et al.* (1997).

7 Previously, we labelled these emergency mass killings of other animals due to an epizootic a genocide of animals. These mass killings were aimed at destroying the polluted, the contaminated or otherwise deemed suspicious and impure animals. Framing the concept genocide beyond the human-centred realm from a non-speciesist perspective, it can legitimately be applied here because it is aimed at eliminating and exterminating all unwanted elements out of the group to retain a category of desirable and pure 'husbandry animals' (Cazaux 2001 and 2002).

8 On the similarities in the treatment of victims of the Nazis and the way animals are treated see Patterson (2002).

9 PETA's (People for the Ethical Treatment of Animals) 2003 'Holocaust on Your Plate' and 2005 'Slavery' campaigns encountered fierce opposition and outcry from civil rights groups. The 2003 exhibit graphically compared the treatment of farm animals to the victims of the Nazi concentration camps in an effort to show that the logic and methods employed in factory farms and slaughterhouses are analogous to those used in concentration camps. The 2005 campaign 'We are All Animals' juxtaposes images from human slavery and oppression to practices in modern-day husbandry. See the websites of PETA and Tolerance.org, an internet project to fight hate and promote tolerance (www.peta.org and www.tolerance.org).

10 See the website of the Verichip corporation (www.verichip.org) and the Baja beach club (www.baja.nl).

References

Ammendrup, S. and Füssel, A. E. (2001) 'Legislative Requirements for the Identification and Traceability of Farm Animals within the European Union', *Revue Scientifique et Technique de L'Office International des Epizooties*, 20 (2): 437–442.

Beausoleil, N. J., Mellor, D. J. and Stafford K. J. (2004) *Methods for Marking New Zealand Wildlife Amphibians, Reptiles and Marine Mammals.* Wellington: Department of Conservation.

Becker, P. H. and Wendeln, H. (1997) 'A New Application for Transponders in Population Ecology of the Common Tern', *The Condor*, 99: 538–543.

Beirne, P. (1995) 'The Use and Abuse of Animals in Criminology: A Brief History and Current Review', *Social Justice*, 22 (1): 5–31.

Bekoff, M. (2000) 'Field Studies and Animal Models: The Possibility of Misleading Inferences', in M. Balls, A. M. van Zeller and M. E. Halder (eds), *Progress in the Reduction, Refinement and Replacement of Animal Experimentation*: 1553–1560. Amsterdam: Elsevier Science.

Belga (2005) 'Rechtbank Laat Koe Zonder Oormerk Slachten', *News Archive of VILT – Vlaams Informatiecentrum over Land- en Tuinbouw*, 21 February 2005 (www.vilt.be).

Berteaux, D. *et al.* (1994) 'Can Radio Collars Affect Dominance Relationships in *Microtus*?', *Canadian Journal of Zoology*, 72: 785–789.

Berteaux, D. *et al.* (1996) 'Effect of Carrying a Radio Collar on Expenditure of Energy by Meadow Voles', *Journal of Mammalogy*, 77 (2): 359–363.

Blancou, J. (2001) 'A History of the Traceability of Animals and Animal Products', *Revue Scientifique et Technique de L'Office International des Epizooties*, 20 (2): 420–425.

Buhlmann, K. A. and Tuberville, T. D. (1998) 'Use of Passive Integrated Transponder (PIT) Tags for Marking Small Freshwater Turtles', *Chelonian Conservation and Biology*, 3 (1): 102–104.

Butler, Z. *et al.* (2004) *From Robots to Animals: Virtual Fences for Controlling Cattle*, submitted to the *International Journal of Robotics Research* and also in Proceedings of the 2004 International Symposium on Experimental Robotics.

Calvo, B. and Furness, R. W. (1992) 'A Review of the Use and the Effects of Marks and Devices on Birds', *Ringing and Migration*, 13: 129–151.

Cazaux, G. (2001) 'Massaslachting in de Veeteelt is Genocide', *Tijdschrift voor Criminologie*, 43 (3): 287–295.

Cazaux, G. (2002) 'Anthropocentrism and Speciesism Regarding Animals Other than Human Animals in Contemporary Criminology' (unpublished Ph.D. dissertation), Faculty of Law, Ghent University.

Cazaux, G. and Beirne, P. (2001) 'Animal Abuse', in E. McLaughlin and J. Muncie (eds), *The Sage Dictionary of Criminology*: 8–10. London: Sage Publications.

Clark, R. D. (1972) 'The Effect of Toe-Clipping on Survival in Fowler's Toad (Bufo woodhousei fowleri)', *Copeia*, 1: 182–185.

Commonwealth of Australia (2004) *Biology, Threats and Conservation Status of the Sub-Antarctic Fur Seal and Southern Elephant Seal in Australian Waters.* Canberra: Department of the Environment and Heritage.

Coté, S. D., Festa-Bianchet, M. and Fournier, F. (1998) 'Life-History Effects of Chemical Immobilization and Radiocollars on Mountain Goats', *Journal of Wildlife Management*, 62 (2): 745–752.

Cypher, B. L. (1997) 'Effects of Radiocollars on San Joaquin Kit Foxes', *Journal of Wildlife Management*, 61 (4): 1412–1423.

DeNardo, D. (1995) 'Amphibians as Laboratory Animals', *ILAR Journal*, 37 (4): 173–181.

Dodd, K. C. (1993) 'The Effects of Toeclipping on Sprint Performance of the Lizard Cnemidophorus Sexlineatus', *Journal of Herpetology*, 27 (2): 209–213.

EGE (2004) *The Ethical Aspects of ICT Implants in the Human Body. Proceedings of the Roundtable Debate.* Amsterdam: European Group on Ethics in Science and New Technologies to the European Commission, 21 December 2004.

Elbin, S. B. and Burger, J. (1994) 'Implantable Microchips for Individual Identification in Wild and Captive Populations', *Wildlife Society Bulletin*, 22: 677–683.

Eradus, W. (2001) 'Keeping a Tab on Livestock. Standardization of Electronic Animal Identification', *ISO Bulletin*, January 2001: 15–18.

Eradus, W. J. and Jansen, M. B. (1999) 'Animal Identification and Monitoring', *Computers and Electronics in Agriculture*, 24: 91–98.

Evertsen, N. (2005) 'Oormerken Varkens als Overtreding van Artikel 36 Gwwd', *Review of Animal Rights: Case Law and Literature*, Digitale Nieuwsbrief Stichting Dierenrecht Nederland, 1(0): 20 October 2005 (www.lawandroar.nl).

Farnsworth, E. J. and Rosovsky, J. (1993) 'The Ethics of Ecological Field Experimentation', *Conservation Biology*, 7 (3): 463–472.

Frost, A. R. *et al.* (1997) 'A Review of Livestock Monitoring and the Need for Integrated Systems', *Computers and Electronics in Agriculture*, 17 (2): 139–159.

Gibbons, W. J. and Andrews, K. M. (2004) 'PIT Tagging: Simple Technology at its Best', *BioScience*, 54 (5): 447–454.

Golay, N. and Durrer, H. (1994) 'Inflammation Due to Toe-Clipping in Natterjack Toads (Bufo Calamita)', *Amphibia-Reptilia*, 15 (1): 81–83.

Goodall, J. (1986) *The Chimpanzees of Gombe: Patterns of Behavior.* Cambridge MA: Harvard University Press.

Gregory, M. J. P., Gordon, A. G. and Moss, R. (2003) 'Impact of Nest-Trapping and Radio-Tagging on Breeding Golden Eagles Aquila Chrysaetos in Argyll, Scotland', *Ibis*, 145 (1): 113–119.

Guilloud, N. B. and Johnson, A. N. (1990) 'Albino Rodent Tail Tattooing: Two Years of Experimental Data and Observations', *Lab Animal Science*, 19 (3): 36–37.

Gursky, S. (1998) 'Effects of Radio Transmitter Weight on a Small Nocturnal Primate', *American Journal of Primatology*, 46: 145–155.

Jamison, B. E. *et al.* (2000) 'Passive Integrated Transponder Tags as Markers for Chicks', *Poultry Science*, 79: 946–948.

Japenga, A. (2005) 'Wildlife distress signals. Radio collars help scientists gather data, but some say they harm animals', *LA Times*, 5 July (www.latimes.com).

Kenward, R. E. *et al.* (2001) 'Setting Harness Sizes and Other Marking Techniques for a Falcon with Strong Sexual Dimorphism, *Journal of Field Ornithology*, 72: 244–257.

Klenzendorf, S. A. (2002) 'Population Dynamics of Virginia's Hunted Black Bear Population' (unpublished Ph.D. dissertation), Virginia Polytechnic Institute and State University.

Kole, W. J. (2004) 'Austria Enacts Strict Animal Rights Laws', *Associated Press*, 27 May 2004.

Landais, E. (2001) 'The Marking of Livestock in Traditional Pastoral Societies', *Revue Scientifique et Technique de L'Office International des Epizooties*, 20 (2): 463–479.

Lay, D. C. *et al.* (1992) 'A Comparative Physiological and Behavioral Study of Freeze and Hot-Iron Branding Using Dairy Cows', *Journal of Animal Science*, 70: 1121–1125.

Lawson, P. T. (2001) *Assistant Laboratory Animal Technician Manual*. Memphis TN: American Association for Laboratory Animal Science.

Low, M., Eason, D. and McInnes, K. (2005) 'Evaluation of Passive Integrated Transponders for Identification of Kakapo, Strigops Habroptilus', *Emu*, 105: 33–38.

Madec, F. *et al.* (2001) 'Traceability in the Pig Production Chain', *Revue Scientifique et Technique de L'Office International des Epizooties*, 20 (2): 523–537.

McAllister, T.A. *et al.* (2000) 'Electronic Identification: Applications in Beef Production and Research', *Canadian Journal of Animal Science*, 80: 381–392.

Mech, L. D. and Barber, S. M. (2002) *A Critique of Wildlife Radio-Tracking and its Use in National Parks. A Report to the US National Park Service*. Jamestown, ND: US Geological Survey, Northern Prairie Wildlife Research Center.

Ministerie van Volksgezondheid, Welzijn en Sport (2005) *Antwoorden op kamervragen van het kamerlid Van Velzen (SP) aan de ministers van Volksgezondheid, Welzijn en Sport en van Landbouw, Natuur en Voedselkwaliteit over het afknippen van tenen van proefdieren*, Kamerstuk, 24-11-2005, De Voorzitter van de Tweede Kamer der Staten-Generaal, Den Haag, DBO-K-U-2630404.

Moran, E. T. (1985) 'Effect of Toeclipping and Pen Population Density on Performance and Carcass Quality of Large Turkeys Reared Sexes Separately', *Poultry Science*, 64: 226–231.

Moorhouse, T. P. and MacDonald, D. W. (2005) 'Indirect Negative Impacts of Radio-Collaring: Sex Ratio Variation in Water Voles', *Journal of Applied Ecology*, 42 (1): 91–98.

Morley, C. G. (2002) 'Evaluating the Performance of PIT Tags and Ear Tags in a Capture-Recapture Experiment', *New Zealand Journal of Zoology*, 29: 143–148.

Mrozek, M. *et al.* (1995) 'Microchip Implant System Used for Animal Identification in Laboratory Rabbits, Guineapigs, Woodchucks and in Amphibians', *Laboratory Animals*, 29: 339–344.

National Research Council (1996) *Guide for the Care and Use of Laboratory Animals*. Washington DC: National Academy Press.

Neary, M. and Yager, A. (2004) 'Methods of Livestock Identification', *Farm Animal Management @ Purdue*, Purdue University, Educational Materials Online (www.ces.purdue.edu/extmedia/AS/AS-556-W.pdf).

Ostfeld, R. S., Miller, M. C. and Schnurr, J. (1993) 'Ear Tagging Increases Tick (Ixodes Dammini) Infestation Rates of White-Footed Mice (Peromyscus Leucopus)', *Journal of Mammalogy*, 74 (3): 651–655.

Palomares, F. and Delibes, M. (1992) 'An Evaluation of Techniques for Capturing and Radio-Collaring Large Grey Mongooses', *South African Journal of Wildlife Research*, 22 (3): 76–79.

Patterson, C. (2002) *Eternal Treblinka. Our Treatment of Animals and the Holocaust*. New York: Lantern Books.

Pavone, L. and Boonstra, R. (1985) 'The Effects of Toe Clipping on the Survival of the Meadow Vole (Microtus Pennsylvanicus)', *Canadian Journal of Zoology*, 63: 499–501.

Petersen, J. H. and Barfoot, C. A. (2003) 'Evacuation of Passive Integrated Transponder (PIT) Tags from Northern Pikeminnow Consuming Tagged Juvenile Chinook Salmon', *North American Journal of Fisheries Management*, 23 (4): 1265–1270.

Powell, R. and Prouxl, G. (2003) 'Trapping and Marking Terrestrial Mammals for Research: Integrating Ethics Performance Criteria, Techniques, and Common Sense', *ILAR Journal*, 44 (4): 259–276.

Putman, R. J. (1995) 'Ethical Considerations and Animal Welfare in Ecological Field Studies', *Biodiversity and Conservation*, 4: 903–915.

Reaser, J. (1995) 'Marking Amphibians by Toe-Clipping: A Response to Halliday', *Newsletter Froglog*, (12: March), IUNC/SSC/Declining Amphibian Population Task Force (www.open.ac.uk/daptf/froglog).

Reichling, S. B. and Tabaka, C. (2001) 'A Technique for Individually Identifying Tarantulas Using Passive Integrated Transponders', *The Journal of Arachnology*, 29: 117–118.

Ritvo, H. (1987) *The Animal Estate. The English and Other Creatures in the Victorian Age*. Cambridge, MA: Harvard University Press.

Schilder, M. B. H. and van der Borg, J. A. M. (2003) 'Training Dogs with Help of the Shock Collar: Short and Long Term Behavioural Effects', *Applied Animal Behaviour Science*, 85 (3–4): 319–334.

Schooley, R. L., Van Horne, B. and Burnham, K. P. (1993) 'Passive Integrated Transponders for Marking Free-Ranging Townsend's Ground Squirrels', *Journal of Mammalogy*, 74 (2): 480–484.

Schwartzkopf-Genswein, K. S. *et al.* (1997) 'Effects of Branding on Weight Gain, Antibiotic Treatment Rates and Subsequent Handling Ease in Feedlot Cattle', *Canadian Journal of Animal Science*, 77: 361–367.

Sherwin, R. E. *et al.* (2002) 'Freeze-Branding to Permanently Mark Bats', *Wildlife Society Bulletin*, 30 (1): 97–100.

Singer, P. (ed.) (2006) *In Defense of Animals. The Second Wave.* Oxford: Blackwell.

Spiegel, M. (1996) *The Dreaded Comparison. Human and Animal Slavery.* New York: Mirror Books/IDEA.

Stanford, K. *et al.* (2001) 'Traceability in Cattle and Small Ruminants in Canada', *Revue Scientifique et Technique de L'Office International des Epizooties*, 20 (2): 510–522.

Stärk, K. D. C., Morris, R. S. and Pfeiffer, D. U. (1998) 'Comparison of Electronic and Visual Identification Systems in Pigs', *Livestock Production Science*, 53: 143–152.

Swain, D. L., Wilson, L. A. and Dickinson, J. (2003) 'Evaluation of an Active Transponder System to Monitor Spatial and Temporal Location of Cattle within Patches of a Grazed Sward', *Applied Animal Behaviour Science*, 84: 185–195.

Tuan, Y.-F. (1984) *Dominance and Affection. The Making of Pets.* New Haven: Yale University Press.

Tuyttens, F. A. M., Macdonald, D. W. and Roddam, A. W. (2002) 'Effects of Radio-Collars on European Badgers', *Journal of Zoology*, 257: 37–42.

Winder, L. (2004) 'Marking by Abrasion or Branding and Recapturing Carabid Beetles in Studies of Their Movement', *International Journal of Pest Management*, 50 (3): 161–164.

Wood, M. D. and Slade, N. A. (1990) 'Comparison of Ear-Tagging and Toe-Clipping in Prairie Voles, Microtus Ochrogaster', *Journal of Mammalogy*, 71 (2): 252–255.

Woods, C. M. C. (2005) 'Evaluation of VI-alpha and PIT-Tagging of the Seahorse Hippocampus Abdominalis', *Aquaculture International*, 13: 175–186.

Yacowitz, H. *et al.* (1997) 'Tail Tattoo Identification System for Neonate and Pre-Weanling Rodents', *Fundamental and Applied Toxicology*, 36 (1): 1865.

Chapter 5

Vivisection: the case for abolition

Tom Regan

Animals[1] are used in laboratories for three main purposes: education, product safety testing, and experimentation, including medical research. Unless otherwise indicated, my discussion is limited to their use in harmful, non-therapeutic experimentation or research (which, for simplicity, I sometimes refer to as 'vivisection'). Experimentation of this kind differs from therapeutic experimentation, where the intention is to benefit the subjects on whom the experiments are conducted. In harmful, non-therapeutic experimentation, by contrast, subjects are harmed, often seriously, or put at risk of serious harm, in the absence of any intended benefit for them; instead, the intention is to obtain information that might ultimately lead to benefits for others.

Human beings, not only non-human animals, have been used in harmful, non-therapeutic experimentation. In fact, history is replete with examples of human vivisection, and it is doubtful whether the ethics of animal vivisection can be fully appreciated apart from the ethics of human vivisection, a topic to which I return below. Unless otherwise indicated, however, the current discussion of vivisection, and my use of the term, are limited to harmful, non-therapeutic experimentation using non-human animals. Moreover, unless otherwise indicated, my remarks apply to vivisection as it is conducted in the United States (adding parenthetically that there is little reason to believe that the culture of vivisection differs dramatically in other nations).

If asked what we think of using animals in research, most of us probably will answer in terms of their use in medical research, the sort of research that promises to yield important advances in combating diseases like cancer and diabetes, research frequently featured on the evening news or in the morning newspaper. However, research of this type is only part of a larger reality. Not to go unnoticed is research that is hardly ever covered by the media. Here are some examples.[2]

Eye research: monkeys, rabbits, dogs, cats and other animals are used. The animals' eyes are burned, or injured in other ways; sometimes lids are sutured shut or eyes removed.

Burn research: animals (guinea pigs, rats, mice, dogs, for example) are burned using chemicals or radiation, or they may experience 'thermal burns', ranging in severity from mild to third degree. Thermal burns are caused by immersing all or part of the animals' bodies in boiling water, or pressing a hot plate against their skin, or by using steam.

Radiation research: all or part of an animal's body is subjected to radiation or, in some cases, the test animals are forced to inhale radioactive gases. Dogs, monkeys, rats, mice, and hamsters are among the animals used.

Brain research: brain activity and behaviour are studied in cats, dogs, monkeys, rabbits and rats, for example. The animals suffer experimental trauma (usually produced by direct physical injury to the head), undergo surgical manipulation, or are stimulated electrically (for example, after undergoing surgical implantation).

Electric shock research: the physiological and psychological responses to electric shock are studied in various animals, principally rats. Electric shock of varying degrees, and at various intervals, is administered primarily through the feet or tail.

Aggression research: the effects of such factors as social isolation, induced brain dysfunction, and sleep deprivation on aggressive behaviour are investigated.

Stress research: test animals are exposed to extremes of cold or heat, deprived of REM sleep, immobilised, or malnourished, for example, to investigate physiology and behaviour.

Military research: funded by the US Department of Defense, various animals, including non-human primates, are subjected to conventional, biological and chemical weapons, nuclear radiation, lasers, and high-power microwaves.

That animals are harmed by such research, no reasonable person will deny. When (to cite other outcomes) animals are drowned, suffocated, and starved to death; when they have their limbs severed and their organs crushed; when they are the recipients of induced heart attacks, ulcers, paralysis, and seizures; when they are forced to inhale tobacco smoke, drink alcohol, and ingest various drugs, such as heroin and cocaine – when animals are on the receiving end of treatment of this kind, no reasonable person will say, 'Yes, but are they ever harmed?'

It is important to realise that what I have just described is routine. From eye removal to thermal burns, suffocation to crushed organs, nothing I have described is the least bit unordinary. No law is broken, no codes are breached. Every experimental procedure listed is perfectly consistent with 'the humane care and treatment' of animals used in research. Those are the words of the Animal Welfare Act, the only applicable United States federal legislation. When drowning, suffocating, starving, blinding, paralysing, and the other outcomes sketched above count as 'humane care and treatment', the suspicion will arise in some people that things are not as they should be. Again, I return to this matter below.

The vivisection industry's professional and lobbying organisations defend the practice with great earnestness and dismiss those who protest against it in the name of animal rights in less than commendatory terms. The same is true of vivisection's principal philosophical ally, Carl Cohen. People who believe in animal rights are 'out of their mind', he writes, and what they believe is 'silly', 'absurd', 'preposterous', and 'a fanatical conviction'. (Cohen 2001: 24, 39, 35, 65, 25).

I make no charges of the same kind, either against Cohen or any other spokesperson for the vivisection industry. My charge is that the defence of vivisection they offer is rationally deficient, not in one or a few respects, but in every respect. After explaining why this is true, I sketch my argument for human rights, do the same for my argument for my 'fanatical conviction' that animals have rights, and conclude by explaining why vivisection should be against the law – why it should be recognised for the grievous crime it is.

The benefits argument

There is only one serious moral defence of vivisection.[3] That defence proceeds as follows.[4] Human beings are better off because of vivisection. Indeed, we are *much* better off because of it. If not all, at least most of the most important improvements in human health and longevity are indebted to vivisection. Included among the advances often cited are open heart surgery, vaccines (for polio and smallpox, for example), cataract and hip replacement surgery, and advances in rehabilitation techniques for victims of spinal cord injuries and strokes. Without these and the many other advances attributable to vivisection, proponents of the Benefits Argument maintain, the incidence of human disease, permanent disability, and premature death would be far, far greater than it is today.

Yes, vivisection's apologists concede, humans sometimes are harmed as a result of medicine's reliance on vivisection. For example, drugs that were shown to be safe when administered to animals sometimes turn out to be harmful when used by humans. However, this happens very rarely, and the harms humans suffer are negligible, all things considered.

Defenders of the Benefits Argument are not indifferent (at least they say they are not indifferent) to how animals are treated. They agree that animals used in vivisection sometimes are harmed, both during the research itself and because of the restrictive conditions of their life in the laboratory. These harms are regrettable, vivisection's defenders acknowledge, and everything that can be done should be done to minimise them. For example, to prevent overcrowding, animals should be housed in larger cages.

Moreover, proponents insist that every reasonable precaution should be taken to ensure that animals are treated humanely and responsibly. This includes having adequate laws to regulate the practice as well as an adequate inspection system to ensure that these laws are observed. And, too, review procedures should be in place that permit harming animals only when the promise of benefits for humans is proportionately much greater.

But (so the argument goes) because there is no other way to secure the important human health benefits that vivisection yields so abundantly, benefits that greatly exceed any harms that animals endure, vivisection should be permitted to continue and, indeed, to flourish. As I hope to show, this defence of vivisection fails on every count.

The inadequacy of federal law

Advocates of the Benefits Argument insist that the laws regulating vivisection are adequate. This is very far from the truth. In the United States, various federal or state laws apply to the animals used in research, but none offers serious protection. At the federal level, the Animal Welfare Act (AWA)[5] addresses only the care and treatment of animals outside research itself; it explicitly removes the federal government from playing any role in the 'design, outlines, guidelines, or performance of actual research or experimentation by a research facility as determined by such a research facility'. Moreover, the AWA defines 'animal' to mean 'any live or dead dog, cat, monkey, [non-human] primate, guinea pig, hamster, rabbit, or other such warm-blooded animal as the Secretary [of the Department of Agriculture] may determine is being used, or is intended for use, for research, testing, experimentation or exhibition purposes'. Conspicuously absent from the list are rats and mice, as well as all birds, farmed animals, and fish which together account for approximately 95 per cent of the animals used in a research context.

No one really knows how many animals are used for scientific purposes in the United States. Still, everyone agrees the number runs in the millions. So the dispute is over how many million. Fifteen? Fifty? Somewhere in between? Somewhere in between, somewhere between 25 and 50 million, may not be an unreasonable estimate. Worldwide, the figure must run into the hundreds of millions.

In 2000, federal legislation was introduced in the US Congress that would have included rodents and birds within the meaning of 'animal'. The amendment was defeated, to the great relief and delight of the animal research community. Never mind that the insincerity of the United States Government's commitment to 'humane care and treatment' was never more evident. When more than 95 per cent of animals used in research *don't even count as animals,* any serious claim to adequacy on behalf of the AWA lacks credibility.

The inadequacy of federal enforcement

The Animal and Plant Health Inspection Service (APHIS) is responsible for enforcing the AWA in America's laboratories.[6] Facilities that do not use any of the regulated species are exempt from the Act, as are those facilities that do not receive federal funds and utilise animals they raise themselves. Despite these limitations, roughly 9,000 research facilities, animal dealers, animal shippers, and others are legally subject to inspection for compliance. It has been estimated that APHIS inspectors, whose primary responsibility is to prevent interstate shipments of diseased plants and livestock, devote a maximum of 6 per cent of their time to enforcing the AWA.

As a result of steadily increasing budget cuts, the first half of the 1990s witnessed more than a 20 per cent decline in the number of APHIS inspections performed. By 2001, only 100 APHIS inspectors remained on the job; as of June 2005 their number had declined to 70.

Internal audits of APHIS, conducted in 1992 and 1995 by the Office of the Inspector General, found that 'APHIS was still not able to make all the required inspection visits' to facilities *already* reported in violation of AWA. In response, APHIS officials noted that 'some of the follow-up visits were not made due to staffing limitations and budgetary cutbacks ... ' Past violators were thus able to continue to treat animals in ways that [in APHIS's own words] could 'jeopardise the health and safety of their animals without APHIS intervention'. No reasonable person would believe that things are better today, given the decline in the number of inspectors since these internal audits were performed.

All considered, then, the legally mandated and enforced protection afforded animals in labs is anything but adequate. Certainly it would be naive in the extreme to assume that 'all is well' behind the locked doors blocking the day-to-day activities in America's laboratories from public view. We have no better authority for this than the words of APHIS's own auditors.

The inadequacy of selection procedures

Most research institutions are required by law to have Animal Care and Use Committees. IACUCs are charged with the task of reviewing research protocols before they can go forward. Depending on the committee's assessment, the research may proceed as proposed, or it may have to be modified, or (theoretically) it can be disallowed. Among the criteria IACUCs use, some concern the invasiveness of the proposed research and the amount and intensity of the pain it will cause. The underlying principle is of the cost–benefit variety. Animals should not suffer 'unnecessarily'. Roughly speaking, invasive research that causes serious pain (or death) should only be permitted if the research promises important results.

The illusion of IACUC protection of animals was pierced by a study published in the prestigious journal *Science* (Plous and Herzog 2001).The study showed that, in the majority of cases, proposals that were approved by one IACUC were rejected by another. This does nothing to inspire confidence in 'humane use' and 'responsible care'. As the study shows, IACUC reviews are no more reliable, judged on their merits, than a coin toss. The claim to adequacy made on behalf of the selection process is nothing short of preposterous.

Benefits and harms

The Benefits Argument conveniently overlooks much and includes little. Any argument that rests on comparing benefits and harms must not only state the benefits accurately; it must also do the same for the relevant harms. Advocates of the Benefits Argument fail on both counts. Independent of their lamentable tendency to minimise the harms done to animals and their fixed resolve to marginalise non-animal alternatives, advocates overestimate the human benefits attributable to vivisection and all but ignore the massive human harms that are an essential part of vivisection's legacy. Even more fundamentally, they uniformly fail to provide an intelligible methodology for comparing benefits and harms across species. Let me address each of these three failures in turn.

Overestimation of benefits

Proponents of the Benefits Argument would have us believe that most of the truly important improvements in human health could not have been achieved without vivisection. The facts tell a different story. Public health scholars have shown that animal experimentation has made at best only a modest contribution to public health. By contrast, the vast majority of the most important health advances have resulted from improvements in living conditions (in sanitation, for example) and changes in personal hygiene and lifestyle, none of which has anything to do with animal experimentation.[7]

These matters aside, supporters of the Benefits Argument apparently have not been listening to what experts within the pharmaceutical industry are telling us. Allen Roses is international vice-president of genetics at GlaxoSmithKline, among the largest pharmaceutical companies in the world. Addressing a scientific meeting in December 2003, Dr Roses dared to say out loud what many in the drug industry wished he had kept to himself. When it comes to benefits derived from prescription drugs, the overall record is modest at best. 'The vast majority of drugs,' Dr Roses declared,' – more than 90 per cent [of them] – only work in 30 or 50 per cent of the people' (Connor 2003). Specific examples given by Dr Roses are drugs for cancer (helpful to only one in four patients) and for Alzheimer's (helpful to only one in three).

Writing in Britain's *The Independent*, Science Editor Steve Connor observes that '[s]ome industry analysts said Dr Roses' comments were reminiscent of the 1991 gaffe by Gerald Ratner, ... who famously said that his High Street [jewellery] shops are successful because they sold "total crap". But [Connor continues] others believe Dr Roses deserves credit for being honest about a little-publicised fact known to the drug industry for many years'(*ibid.*): most drugs don't help most patients most of the time. In fact, the odds of being helped in most cases are worse than a coin toss.

People would think otherwise if proponents of the Benefits Argument were correct. After all, all prescription drugs must first be shown to be effective when administered to animals. If the 'animal model' truly was a reliable gauge of the effectiveness of drugs for humans, it would be reasonable to believe that what is effective in their case will be effective in ours, if not all of the time then at least most of the time. However, if Dr Roses and other pharmaceutical experts are correct, this is very far from the truth. Overall, only in a comparatively small percentage of cases do prescription drugs actually benefit the humans who use them. When it comes to human benefits, therefore, proponents of the Benefits Argument greatly overstate their case.

Underestimation of harms

Advocates of the Benefits Argument conveniently ignore the hundreds of millions of deaths and the uncounted illnesses and disabilities that are attributable to reliance on the 'animal model' in research. Sometimes the harms result from what reliance on vivisection makes available; sometimes they result from what reliance on vivisection prevents. The deleterious effects of prescription medicines are an example of the former.

The Food and Drug Administration is charged with ensuring the safety and effectiveness of medical procedures and products, including prescription drugs. A staff of 100 is responsible for monitoring the 3,200 drugs currently available; another 700 oversee drug approval. Total costs for monitoring and evaluation represent only 4 per cent of the FDA's annual budget (Frontline 2001). Even if the methods the agency used to ensure safety and effectiveness were adequate, critics of American drug policy note that too few people are given too little money to do far too much.

As it happens, the FDA's methods are anything but adequate. The FDA defines an 'adverse event' as 'any undesirable experience associated with the use of [a] drug that is both serious and unexpected' (FDA 2005). Specific examples of 'undesirable experience' are 'death, a life-threatening adverse drug experience, inpatient hospitalisation or prolongation of existing hospitalisation, a persistent or significant disability/incapacity, or a congenital anomaly/birth defect'. In other words, 'adverse events' can involve much more than a runny nose or itchy feet. By definition, then, adverse events precipitated by prescription drugs (adverse drug reactions or ADRs) can be quite serious.

Among the adverse reactions patients have to prescription drugs, some are fatal. The drugs people take sometimes kill them, and do so more often than the public might suspect. A study published in 1998 found that approximately 100,000 hospitalised patients die annually because of ADRs, making prescription drugs the fourth leading cause of death in America, ranking behind only cancer, heart attack, and stroke (Lazarou, J. *et al.* 1998). And this figure does not include the number of *non*-hospitalised patients who have fatal reactions to the drugs they are taking.

According to FDA guidelines, adverse events, including all ADRs, 'should be reported'. The problem is, what 'should' be done often is not. The FDA's voluntary system of reporting (Medwatch) receives upwards of a thousand reports each working day, approximately 260,000 a year. Yet David Kessler, former director of the FDA, estimates that only 1 per cent of ADRs are reported (Kessler 1993). In other words, for every adverse drug response reported, 99 are not. If true, that figure of 260,000 (and the same is true of FDA's estimate of 2 million hospitalisations due to ADRs) does not reflect anything like the true dimensions of the problem.

Can the incidence of ADRs really be worse than the FDA says it is? Before answering, consider the following. In his book, *Prescription for Disaster: The Hidden Dangers in Your Medicine Cabinet*, Thomas J. Moore reports on a study done using the files of medical doctors in Rhode Island. The study revealed that patients had experienced 26,000 ADRs; of that number, 11 were reported (Moore 1998). When Dr Kessler says that perhaps only 1 per cent of ADRs are reported he may be giving an excessively inflated estimate. Clearly, before vivisection's defenders can reasonably claim that human benefits greatly exceed human harms, they must first acknowledge how often and how much reliance on the 'animal model' leads to prescribed therapies that cause massive human harm.

Massive harm to humans also is attributable to what reliance on vivisection prevents. The role of cigarette smoking in the incidence of cancer is a case in point. As early as the 1950s, human epidemiological studies revealed a causal link between cigarette smoking and lung cancer. Nevertheless, repeated efforts, made over more than 50 years, rarely succeeded in inducing tobacco-related cancers in animals. Despite the alarm sounded by public health advocates, governments around the world for decades relied on the findings of researchers using the 'animal model'. As a result, educational campaigns geared to informing smokers about the grave risks they were running were delayed. And what have we reaped? Today, one in every five deaths in the United States is attributable to the effects of smoking, and fully 60 per cent of direct health care costs in the United States go to treating tobacco-related illnesses.

How much of this massive human harm could have been prevented if the results of vivisection had not (mis)directed government health care policy? It is not clear that anyone knows the answer beyond saying, 'A great deal. More than we will ever know.' One thing we do know, however: advocates of the Benefits Argument contravene the logic of their argument when they conveniently omit these harms in their defence of vivisection.

Research ideology

Not to go unmentioned, finally, is the universal failure of vivisection's defenders to explain how we are to weigh benefits and harms across species. Before we can judge that vivisection's benefits for humans greatly exceed vivisection's harms to other animals, someone needs to explain how the relevant comparisons should be made. How much animal pain equals how much human relief from a drug that was tested on animals, for example? It does not suffice to say, as Cohen does, that 'the suffering of our species does seem somehow to be more important than the suffering of other species' (Cohen 2001: 60–61). Not only does this fail to explain how much more important our suffering is supposed to be, it offers no reason why anyone should think that it is. (Cohen's views are discussed at greater length in the discussion of speciesism, below.)

Plainly, unless or until those who support the Benefits Argument offer an intelligible methodology for comparing benefits and harms across species, the claim that human benefits derived from vivisection greatly exceed the harms done to animals is more in the nature of unsupported ideology than demonstrated fact.

Summary

All things considered, then, vivisection's defenders fail to justify the practice, not because they fail in one respect, but because they fail in all respects:

- They *say* the laws regulating the practice are adequate; in fact they are not.
- They *say* the laws are adequately enforced; in fact they are not.

123

- They *say* the procedures used to evaluate what research should be done are adequate; in fact they are not.
- They *say* vivisection is a reliable methodology; in fact it is not.
- They *say* humans benefit greatly from vivisection; in fact we do not.
- They *say* humans are rarely harmed because of vivisection; in fact we are harmed often.
- They *say* human benefits greatly outweigh the harms done to animals; in fact no basis for making the comparison is offered.

The very best that can be said for vivisection (and this is being generous) is that some people sometimes benefit from using some medicines or procedures that were first either given to or used on animals. And for this hundreds of billions of dollars are spent; hundreds of millions of animals are denied their freedom, are subjected to debilitating physical injury, are made to suffer, only to be killed in the end; and uncounted millions of human beings are harmed, in ways both minor and major, even to the point of death. Vivisection as it is practised today is not the panacea for the world's ills its champions would have us believe; instead, it poses a very serious threat, not only to animals, but to humans as well.

'But' (it may be said) 'the problems you have described are surmountable. Laws can be changed. Inspections can be increased. Better selection procedures can be put in place. In all, vivisection can be reformed and improved. When this happens, *then* what will be the objections to having the practice continue?' My short answer is, 'Because it is wrong.' My longer answer follows.

Human vivisection and human rights

The Benefits Argument suffers from an even more fundamental defect than those enumerated in the above. Despite appearances to the contrary, the argument begs all the most important moral questions; in particular, it assumes that animals lack rights without providing any reason for why we should agree. In so doing the argument obscures the role rights play in assessing vivisection. One way to understand its failure in this regard is to situate the argument against the backdrop of human vivisection and human rights.

Human beings have been used in harmful, non-therapeutic experiments for thousands of years.[8] Not surprisingly, most human 'guinea pigs' have not come from the wealthy and educated, not from the dominant race, not from those with the power to assert and enforce their rights. No, most of human vivisection's victims have been coercively conscripted from the ranks of young children (especially orphans), the elderly, the severely developmentally disabled, the insane, the poor, the illiterate, members of 'inferior' races, homosexuals, military personnel, prisoners of war, and convicted criminals, for example. One such case will be considered below.

The scientific rationale behind vivisecting human beings needs little explanation. Using human subjects in research overcomes the difficulty of extrapolating results from another species to our species. If 'benefits for humans' establishes the morality of animal vivisection, should we favour human vivisection instead? After all, vivisection that uses members of our own species promises even greater benefits.

No serious advocate of human rights (and I count myself among this number) can support such research. This judgement is not capricious or arbitrary; it is a necessary consequence of the logic of basic moral rights, including our rights to bodily integrity and to life. This logic has two key components.[9]

First, possession of these rights confers a unique moral status. Those who possess these rights have a kind of protective moral shield, an invisible 'No Trespassing' sign, so to speak, that prohibits others from injuring their bodies, taking their life, or putting them at risk of serious harm, including death.[10] When people violate our rights, when they 'trespass on our moral property', they do something wrong to us directly.

This does not mean that it must be wrong to hurt someone or even to take their life. When terrorists exceed their rights by violating ours, we act within our rights if we respond in ways that can cause serious harm to the violators. Still, what we are free to do when someone violates our rights does not translate into the freedom to override their rights without justifiable cause.

Second, the obligation to respect others' rights to bodily integrity and to life trumps any obligation we have to benefit others.[11] Even if society in general would benefit if the rights of a few people were violated, that would not make violating their rights morally acceptable to any serious defender of human rights. The rights of the individual are not to be sacrificed in the name of promoting the general welfare. This is what it means to affirm our rights. It is also why the basic moral rights we possess, as the individuals we are, have the great moral importance they do.

Why the benefits argument begs the question

Once we understand why, given the logic of moral rights, respect for the rights of individuals takes priority over any obligation we might have to benefit others, we can understand why the Benefits Argument fails to justify vivisection on non-human animals. Clearly, all that the Benefits Argument *can* show is that vivisection on non-human animals benefits human beings. What this argument *cannot* show is that vivisecting animals for this purpose is morally justified. And it cannot show this because no amount of human benefits settles the question, 'Do animals have rights?' If they do not, then there is no reason in principle to object to the Benefits Argument. But if they do, then there is a principled reason for objecting, an objection explained more fully below. So, which is it: Do animals have rights, or do they not? On this question, the Benefits Argument must remain absolutely moot. The benefits humans do or do not derive from vivisection are logically irrelevant to the question of animal rights.

It will not suffice (and this for three reasons) for advocates of the Benefits Argument to insist that 'there are no alternatives' to vivisection that will yield as many human benefits. First, this reply is more than a little disingenuous. The greatest impediment to developing new scientifically valid non-animal alternatives, and to using those that already exist, is the hold that the ideology of vivisection currently has on medical researchers and those who fund them. Second, to reiterate the main point of the previous paragraph: whether animals have rights is not a question that can be answered by insisting that vivisection benefits human beings. No matter how great the human benefits might be, the practice is morally wrong if animals have rights that vivisection violates. Lastly, there is an alternative to animal vivisection that others have sometimes preferred: human vivisection. I turn to one example, examine its rationale, and explore why, despite the benefits others have derived, human rights were violated. Then I address the question of animal rights.

The children of Willowbrook

Now closed, Willowbrook State Hospital was a mental hospital located in Staten Island, one of New York City's five boroughs. For 15 years, from 1956 to 1971, under the leadership of New York University Professor Saul Krugman, hospital staff conducted a series of viral hepatitis experiments[12] on thousands of the hospital's severely retarded children, some as young as three years old. Among the research questions asked: Could injections of gamma globulin (a complex protein extracted from blood serum) produce long-term immunity to the hepatitis virus?

What better way to find the answer, Dr Krugman decided, than to separate the children in one of his experiments into two groups. In the one, children were fed the live hepatitis virus and given an injection of gamma globulin, which Dr Krugman believed would produce immunity; in the other, children were fed the virus but received no injection. In both cases, the virus was obtained from the faeces of other Willowbrook children who suffered from the disease. Parents or guardians were asked to sign a release form that would permit their children to be 'given the benefit of this new preventive'.

The results of the experiment were instrumental in leading Dr Krugman to conclude that hepatitis is not a single disease transmitted by a single virus; there are, he confirmed, at least two distinct viruses that transmit the disease, that today we know as hepatitis A and hepatitis B, the latter of which is the more severe. Early symptoms include fatigue, loss of appetite, malaise, abdominal pain, vomiting, headache, and intermittent fever; then the patient becomes jaundiced, the urine darkens, the liver swells, and enzymes normally stored in the liver enter the blood. Death results in 1 to 10 per cent of cases.

Everyone agrees that many people have benefited from this knowledge and the therapies Dr Krugman's research made possible. Some question the necessity of his research, citing the comparable findings that Baruch Blumberg made by analysing blood antigens in his laboratory, where no children were harmed or put at risk of grievous harm. But even if we assume that Dr Krugman's results could not have been achieved without experimenting on his uncomprehending subjects, what he did was wrong.

The purpose of his research, after all, was not to benefit each of the children. If that was his objective, he would not have withheld injections of gamma globulin from half of them. *Those* children certainly could not be counted among the intended beneficiaries. (Thus the misleading nature of the release form: not *all* the children were 'given the benefit of this new preventive'.)

Moreover, it is a perverse moral logic that says, 'The children who received the injections of gamma globulin but who did not contract hepatitus – *they* were the real beneficiaries.' Granted, if these children already had the hepatitis virus and failed to develop the disease because of the injections, it would make sense to say that they benefited from Dr Krugman's experiment. But these children did not already have the virus; they were given the virus by Dr Krugman and his associates. How can they be described as 'beneficiaries'? If I hide a time bomb under your bed, armed with an experimental device that I think will defuse the bomb before it is set to go off, and if the device works, I do not think you would shake my hand and thank me because you 'benefited' from my experiment. I think you would (if you could) wring my neck for placing you in grave danger. Would that the children of Willowbrook could have done the same to Dr Krugman and his associates.

No serious advocate of human rights can accept the moral propriety of Dr Krugman's actions. By intentionally infecting all the children in his experiment, he put each of them at risk of serious harm. And by withholding the suspected means of preventing the disease from half the children, he violated their rights twice over: first, by wilfully placing them at risk of serious physical illness; second, by risking their very life. This grievous breach of ethics finds no justification in the benefits others derived. To violate the moral rights of the few is never justified by adding the benefits for the many.

The basis of human rights

Those who deny that animals have rights frequently emphasise the uniqueness of human beings. We not only write poetry and compose symphonies, read history and solve maths problems; we also understand our own mortality and make moral choices. Other animals do none of these things. That is why we have rights and they do not.

This way of thinking overlooks the fact that many human beings do not read history or solve maths problems, do not understand their own mortality or make moral choices. The profoundly retarded children Dr Krugman used in his research are a case in point. If possession of the moral rights to bodily integrity and life depended on understanding one's mortality or making moral choices, for example, then those children lacked these rights. In their case, therefore, there would be no protective moral shield, no invisible 'No Trespassing' sign that limited what others were free to do to them. Lacking the protection that rights afford, *the moral status of the children themselves* would not have prohibited Dr Krugman from injuring their bodies, taking their life, or putting them at risk of serious harm. Since they lacked the protection that rights afford, Dr Krugman did not – indeed, he could not – have done anything wrong *to the children* (though his work might have outraged *others*, for example). Again, this is not a position any serious advocate of human rights can accept.

But what is there about those of us reading these words, on the one hand, and the children of Willowbrook, on the other, that can help us understand how they can have the same basic rights we claim for ourselves? Where will we find the basis of our moral equality? Not in the ability to write poetry, make moral choices, and the like. Not in human biology, including facts about the genetic make-up humans share. All humans are (in some sense) biologically the same. However, biological facts are indifferent to moral truths. Who has what genes has no moral relevance to who has what rights. Whatever else is in doubt, this we know.

But if not in some advanced cognitive capacity or genetic similarity, then where might we find the basis of our equality? Any plausible answer must begin with the obvious: the differences between the children of Willowbrook and those who read these words are many and varied. We do not denigrate these children when we say that our life has a richness that theirs lacked. Few among us would trade our life for theirs, even if we could.

Still, as important as these differences are, they should not obscure the similarities. For, like us, these children were the *subjects-of-a-life, their* life, a life that was experientially better or worse for the child whose life it was. Like us, each child was a unique somebody, not a replaceable something. True, they lacked the ability to read and to make moral choices, for example. Nevertheless, what was done to these children, both what they experienced and what they were deprived of, mattered to them, as the individuals they were, just as surely as what is done to us, when we are harmed, matters to us.

In this respect, as the subjects-of-a-life, we and the children of Willowbrook are the same, are equal. Only in this case, our sameness, our equality is important morally. Logically, we cannot claim that harms done to us violate our rights, but that harms done to these children do not. Logically, we cannot claim our rights to bodily integrity and to life, then deny these same rights in the case of the children. Relevantly similar cases must be judged similarly. This is among the first principles of rational thought, a principle that has immediate application here. Without a doubt, the children of Willowbrook had rights, if we do.

Why animals have rights

We routinely divide the world into animals, vegetables and minerals. Amoebae and paramecia are not vegetables or minerals; they are animals. No one engaged in the vivisection debate thinks that the use of such simple animals poses a vexing moral question. By contrast, everyone engaged in the debate recognises that using non-human primates must be assessed morally. All parties to the debate, therefore, must 'draw a line' somewhere between the simplest forms of animate life and the most complex, a line that marks the boundary between those animals that do, and those that do not, clearly matter morally. Understandably, because so much of importance hinges on 'where we draw the line', it is unlikely that everyone will draw it in the same place. For this reason, I will adopt a conservative strategy. The animals for whose rights I will argue are mammals, not because I believe there are no other animals further down the phylogenic scale who have the psychological complexity necessary for possessing rights, but because *wherever* any line is reasonably drawn, these animals – mammals – will be on or above it. By restricting my remarks to mammals, therefore, I hope to forestall the many controversies engendered by questions about line drawing.

Charles Darwin is helpful in this context. When he compares (these are his words) 'the Mental Powers of Man and the Lower Animals',[13] he restricts his explicit comparisons to humans and other mammals. His reasons for doing so depend in part on structural considerations. In all essential respects, these animals are physiologically like us, and we, like them. Now, in our case, an intact, functioning central nervous system is associated with our capacity for subjective experience. For example, injuries to our brain or spinal cord can diminish our sense of sight or touch, or impair our ability to feel pain or remember. By analogy, Darwin thinks it is reasonable to infer that the same is true of animals who are most physiologically similar to us. Because our central nervous system provides the physical basis for our subjective awareness of the world, and because the central nervous system of other mammals resembles ours in all the relevant respects, it is reasonable to believe that their central nervous system provides the physical basis for their subjective awareness.

Of course, if attributing subjective awareness to non-human mammals (henceforth 'animals', for reasons of linguistic economy) clashed with common sense, made their behaviour inexplicable, or was at odds with our best science, Darwin's position would need to be abandoned. But just the opposite is true. Every person of common sense agrees with Darwin. All of us understand that dogs and pigs, cats and chimps enjoy some things and find others painful. Not surprisingly, they act accordingly, seeking to find the former and avoid the latter. In addition, both humans and other mammals share a family of cognitive abilities (we both are able to learn from experience, remember the past, anticipate the future) as well as a variety of emotions (Darwin lists fear, jealousy, and sadness). Not surprisingly, again, these mental capacities play a role in how they behave. For example, other animals behave one way rather than another because they remember which ways of acting had pleasant outcomes in the past, or because they are afraid or sad.

Moreover, that these animals are subjectively present in the world, Darwin understands, is required by evolutionary theory.[14] The mental complexity we find in humans did not arise from nothing. It is the culmination of a long evolutionary process. We should not be surprised, therefore, when Darwin summarises his general outlook in these terms: 'The differences between the mental faculties of humans and the higher animals, great as it is, is one of degree and not of kind.'[15]

The psychological complexity of animals plays an important role in arguing for their rights. As in our case, so in theirs: they are the subjects-of-a-life, *their* life, a life that is experientially better or worse for the one whose life it is. Each is a unique somebody, not a replaceable something. True (like the children of Willowbrook), they lack the ability to read, write, or make moral choices. Nevertheless, what is done to animals, both what they experience and what they are deprived of, matters to them, as the individuals they are, just as what was done to the children of Willowbrook, when they were harmed, mattered to them.

In this respect, as the subjects-of-a-life, other mammals and the children of Willowbrook are the same, are equal. And in this case, this sameness, this equality, is important morally. Logically, we cannot claim that harms done to the children violate their rights, but that harms done to these animals do not. Logically, we cannot claim rights to bodily integrity and to life, on behalf of the children, then deny these same rights in the case of animals. Relevantly similar cases must be judged similarly. This is among the first principles of rational thought, a principle that has immediate application here. Without a doubt, animals have rights, if the children of Willowbrook do.

Challenging human and animal equality: speciesism

The argument for animal rights sketched in the preceding implies that humans and other animals are equal in morally relevant respects. Some philosophers (Carl Cohen principal among them) repudiate any form of species egalitarianism. According to Cohen, whereas humans are equal in morally relevant respects, regardless of our race, gender or ethnicity, humans and other animals are not morally equal in any respect, not even when it comes to suffering. Here are a few examples that will clarify his position.

First, imagine a boy and girl suffer equally. If someone assigns greater moral weight to the boy's suffering because he is a white male from Ireland, and less moral weight to the girl's suffering because she is a black female from Kenya, Cohen would protest – and rightly so. Human racial, gender and ethnic differences are not morally relevant differences. The situation differs, Cohen insists, when it comes to differences in species. Imagine that a cat and dog both suffer as much as the boy and girl. For Cohen, there is nothing morally prejudicial, nothing morally arbitrary in assigning greater importance to the suffering of the children, because they are human, than to the equal suffering of the animals, because they are not.

Proponents of animal rights deny this. We believe that views like Cohen's reflect a moral prejudice against animals that is fully analogous to moral prejudices, like sexism and racism, that humans often have against one another. We call this prejudice speciesism.[16]

For his part, Cohen affirms speciesism (human suffering does 'somehow' count for more than the equal suffering of animal suffering) but denies its prejudicial status. Why? Because (he thinks) while there are no morally relevant differences between human men and women, or between whites and blacks, 'the morally relevant differences [between humans and other animals] are enormous'(Cohen 2001: 62). In particular, human beings are, but other animals are not 'morally autonomous'; that is, we can, but they cannot, make moral choices for which we are morally responsible.

This defence of speciesism is no defence at all. Not only does it conveniently overlook the fact that a very large percentage of the human population (children up through many years of their life, for example) are not morally autonomous; moral autonomy is not relevant to the issues at hand. An example will help explain why.

Imagine someone says that Jack is smarter than Jill because Jack lives in Syracuse, Jill in San Francisco. Where the two live is different, certainly; and where different people live sometimes is a relevant consideration (for example, when a census is being taken or taxes are levied). But everyone will recognise that where Jack and Jill live has no logical bearing on whether Jack is smarter. To think otherwise is to commit a fallacy of irrelevance familiar to anyone who has taken a course in elementary logic.

The same is no less true when a speciesist says that Toto's suffering counts for less than the equal suffering of Dorothy because Dorothy, but not Toto, is morally autonomous. If the question we are being asked is whether Jack is smarter than Jill, we are given no relevant reason for thinking one way or the other if we are told that Jack and Jill live in different cities. Similarly, if the question we are being asked is, 'Does Toto's pain count as much as Dorothy's?', we are given no relevant reason for thinking one way or the other if we are told that Dorothy is morally autonomous, Toto not.

This is not because the capacity for moral autonomy is never relevant to our moral thinking about humans and other animals. Sometimes it is. If Jack and Jill have this capacity, then they (but not Toto) will have an interest in being free to act as their conscience dictates. In this sense, the difference between Jack and Jill, on the one hand, and Toto, on the other, *is* morally relevant. But just because moral autonomy is morally relevant to the moral assessment of *some* cases, it does not follow that it is relevant in *all* cases. And one case in which it is not relevant is the moral assessment of pain. Logically, to discount Toto's pain because Toto is not morally autonomous is fully analogous to discounting Jill's intelligence because she does not live in Syracuse.

The question, then, is whether any defensible, relevant reason can be offered in support of the speciesist judgement that the moral importance of human and animal pain, equal in other respects, always should be weighted in favour of the human being over the animal being? To this question, neither Cohen nor any other philosopher, to my knowledge, offers a logically relevant answer. To persist in judging human pains (I note that the same applies to equal pleasures, benefits, harms, and so on, throughout all similar cases) as being more important than the like pains of other animals, because they are human pains, is not rationally defensible. Speciesism is a moral prejudice, and judgements of inequality based upon it are wrong, not right.

Criminalising vivisection

As was noted at the outset, animals are used in laboratories for three main purposes: education, product safety testing, and experimentation, harmful non-therapeutic experimentation in particular. Of the three, the latter has been the object of special consideration. However, the implications for the remaining purposes should be obvious.[17] Any time any animal's rights are violated in pursuit of benefits for others, what is done is wrong. Perhaps some uses of animals for educational purposes (for example, having students observe the behaviour of rehabilitated animals when they are released back into their natural habitat) might be justified. By contrast, using animals in product testing is not. Harming animals to establish what brands of cosmetics or combinations of chemicals are safe for humans is an exercise in power, not morality. In the moral universe, animals are not our tasters, we are not their kings.

The implications of animal rights for vivisection are both clear and uncompromising. Vivisection is morally wrong. It should never have begun and, like all great speciesist evils, it ought to end, the sooner, the better. To reply (again) that 'there are no alternatives' not only misses the point, it is false. It misses the point because it assumes that the benefits humans derive from vivisection are derived morally when they are not. And it is false because, apart from using already existing and developing new non-animal research techniques, there is another, more fundamental alternative to vivisection. This is to stop doing it. When all is said and done, the only adequate moral response to vivisection is empty cages, not larger cages.

The Preamble of the Universal Declaration of Human Rights declares that 'human rights should be protected by the rule of law', a precept honoured, in aspiration if not in fact, by representative democracies throughout the world. Our moral rights to bodily integrity, to liberty, to life are mere words if they lack the protection provided by the force of law. Those who would, without provocation, injure our body, deny us the exercise of our freedom, or take our life must be subject to criminal prosecution, the harshness of the punishment to fit the severity of the crime.

In the particular case of non-therapeutic human experimentation, the law is called upon to protect all who are subject to abuse. The more vulnerable the potential subjects, including orphaned children and the mentally disadvantaged, the weightier are the obligations to endeavour to prevent their abuse and to punish those who cause it. The 'benefits for others' claimed by those who would harm humans in non-therapeutic experimentation does not right the wrong done to the victims. Human vivisection should be, and throughout the world human vivisection is, recognised as the grave moral and legal crime that it is.

The same is not true of vivisection on non-human animals. Nowhere in the many documents issued by the United Nations do we find anything remotely like the Universal Declaration of Rights that includes the rights of animals. Vivisection using non-human animals not only is widespread; it is supported by most people – three out of four of those recently polled (Coalition for Medical Progress 2005; Foundation for Biomedical Research 2005). Moreover, those who engage in it often are bathed in the glow of public admiration and professional esteem, every bit of it painfully undeserved, when viewed through the prism of animal rights. Vivisection violates the rights of animals. As such, the animal victims, as is true of their human counterparts who are subjected to non-therapeutic vivisection, ought to be protected by the rule of law. Vivisection *should* be recognised for the crime it is, and those who engage in it *should* be recognised as the criminals they are.

In saying this I add my voice to those who have expressed the same findings before me, most famously the nineteenth-century English philosopher Jeremy Bentham. Recall his stirring words (emphasis added): that '[t]he day *may come*, when the rest of animal creation may acquire those rights which never could have been withholden from them but by the hand of human tyranny' (Bentham 1892). The day *'may come'*, he writes, not the day *'will come'*. Whether *may* becomes *will* obviously depends on many factors, a change in public perception of animals perhaps chief among them.

Is public perception changing? If it is, is this change having any influence when it comes to criminalising vivisection? The answers to both questions would seem to be the same: yes. By way of example: in December 2005, the Austrian parliament agreed to ban all vivisection conducted on great apes: chimps, bonobos, gorillas, orang-utans, and all eight gibbon species. Since 1 January 2006, it has been illegal, a crime, to conduct any experiment on any of these animals except when the experiment is undertaken in the hope of benefiting the animals themselves. Austria thereby joins New Zealand, the Netherlands, and Sweden in criminalising vivisection using these animals.

It is, of course, a long march from making some forms of vivisection illegal to criminalising all forms. Still, anti-vivisectionists like myself will not be satisfied until this destination is reached. We concur with Gandhi when he observes that 'vivisection is the blackest of all the black crimes' (Gandhi 1959). A crime so black that the evil it represents is beyond regulation. A crime so black that it is beyond reform. A crime so black that only its total abolition, through the state power of the criminal law if necessary, bespeaks an adequate moral response.

Notes

1 I follow the common usage that distinguishes between humans and animals, noting that humans *are* animals.

2 The summary of procedures and outcomes is based on Jeff Diner, *Behind the Laboratory Door* (Washington, DC: Animal Welfare Institute, 1985).

3 One could attempt to justify animal vivisection by arguing that it is interesting, challenging, and yields knowledge, which is intrinsically good even when it is not useful. However, a defender of human vivisection could make the same claims, and no one (one hopes) would think that this settles any moral question in that case. Logically, there is no reason to judge animal vivisection any differently. Even if it is interesting and challenging, and even if it yields knowledge (which is intrinsically good), that would not make it right.

4 For representative statements of the Benefits Argument, consult the websites of Americans for Medical Progress (www.ampef.org/) and the National Association for Biomedical Research (www.nabr.org/). See also Cohen 2001.

5 The Animal Welfare Act and Regulations will be found at http://www. nal.usda.gov/awic/legislat/usdaleg1.htm For information about the number of reportable animals used in research, see http//:www.aphis. usda.gov

6 Data about the number of facilities subject to APHIS inspection, and the shortcomings of these inspections, as described in this and the following paragraph, are quoted from Office of the Inspector General's *Animal and Plant Inspection Service Enforcement of the Animal Welfare Act*, Audit Report No. 33600-1-Ch. (Washington, DC: US Government Printing Office, January 1995). An informed overview of APHIS practices will be found in Michael Budke, 'Are Laboratory Animals Protected in the US?', *The Animals' Voice Magazine* (Spring 1996): 6–9. Gary Francione offers a sustained critique of the Animal Welfare Act and APHIS's enforcement of its provisions in *Animals, Property, and the Law*. (Philadelphia: Temple University Press, 1995). See also http://www.aphis.usda.gov/lpa/pubs/ fsheet_faq_notice/fs_awinspect.html

7 For an overview of how much the benefits of animal research are exaggerated, see Hugh LaFollette and Niall Shanks, *Brute Science: Dilemmas of Animal Experimentation* (New York: Rowman and Littlefield, 1996). In addition, see C. Ray Greek, MD and Jean Swingle Greek, DVM,

Sacred Cows and Golden Geese: The Human Costs of Experiments on Animals (New York: Continuum, 2000) and *Specious Science: How Genetics and Evolution Reveal Why Medical Research on Animals Harms Humans* (New York: Continuum, 2002).

8 Representative studies of human vivisection include George J. Annas and Michael A. Grodin (eds), *The Nazi Doctors and the Nuremberg Code: Human Rights in Human Experimentation* (New York: Oxford University Press, 1992), Chapters. 1–7, 11; Allen M. Homblum, *Acres of Skin* (London: Routledge, 1999); James Jones, *Bad Blood: The Tuskegee Syphilis Experiment* (New York: Free Press, 1993); Coral Lansbury, *The Old Brown Dog: Women, Workers, and Vivisection in Edwardian England* (Madison, Wisconsin, 1985), Chapters 1–4; Susan E. Lederer, *Subjected to Science: Human Experimentation in America before the Second World War* (Baltimore, 1995), Chapters 2, 4–5.

9 More complete explanations of my analysis of rights will be found in Regan 1983 and Regan 2004.

10 The analogy of rights with 'No Trespassing' signs I owe to Robert Nozick, *Anarchy, State and Utopia* (New York: Basic Books, 1974).

11 The analogy of rights with 'trump' I owe to Ronald Dworkin, *Taking Rights Seriously* (Cambridge, MA: Harvard University Press, 1977).

12 The best general account of the research conducted on the children of Willowbrook is David and Sheila Rothman, *The Willowbrook Wars* (New York: Harper & Row, 1984).

13 For Darwin's views, see his 'Comparison of the Mental Powers of Man and the Lower Animals', in Tom Regan and Peter Singer (eds), *Animal Rights and Human Obligations* (Englewood-Cliffs, NJ: Prentice Hall, 1976), pp. 72–81.

14 Many people of good will do not believe in evolution. They believe that human existence is the result of a special creation by God, something that took place approximately 10,000 years ago. For these people, the evidence for animal minds provided by evolutionary theory is no evidence at all. Despite first impressions, the rejection of evolution need not undermine the main conclusions summarised in the previous paragraph. All of the world's religions speak with one voice when it comes to the question before us. Read the Bible, the Torah, the Koran. Study Confucianism, Buddhism, Hinduism, or Native American spiritual writings. The message is everywhere the same. Mammals *most certainly* are psychologically present in the world. These animals *most certainly* have both preference and welfare interests. In these respects, all the world's religions teach the same thing. Thus, while the argument I have given appeals to the implications of evolutionary theory, the conclusions I reach are entirely consistent with the religiously based convictions of people who do not believe in evolution. And for those who believe both in God and in evolution? Well, these people have reasons of both kinds for recognising the minds of the other animals with whom we share a common habitat: the Earth.

15 Darwin, *op. cit.*, p. 80. Elsewhere I argue that this same argument can be extended to birds. In addition, I argue that fish and other vertebrates should be given the benefit of the doubt. (See Regan 2004: Chapter 4.) Because of space constraints, I limit my argument here to mammals only.
16 The term *speciesism* was coined by Richard Ryder. See his *Victims of Science: The Use of Animals in Science* (London: David-Poynter, 1975).
17 I explore the use of animals in education and product testing in Regan 220: Chapter 10.
18 The present essay adapts material from my 'Empty Cages: Animal Rights and Vivisection', in Tony Gilland (ed.), *Animal Experimentation: Good or Bad?* (London: Hodder & Stoughton, 2002) and from my contribution to *The Animal Rights Debate, op. cit.*

References

Bentham, J. (1892) *An Introduction to the Principles of Morals and Legislation*, Chapter XVII, Section 1. Cambridge: Clarendon Press.
Coalition for Medical Progress (2005) 'Reference: Facts and Figures CMP/MORI Research 2005'. http://www.meicalprogress.org/reference/mori.cfm
Cohen, C. (2001) 'In Defense of the Use of Animals', in C. Cohen and T. Regan, *The Animal Rights Debate*. Lanham, Maryland: Rowman and Littlefield.
Connor, S. (2003) 'Glaxo chief: Our drugs do not work on most patients'. *The Independent*, 8 December. http://www.drugintel.com/pharma/many_ar_treated.htm
FDA (2005) Code of Federal Regulations. Title 21, Volume 5; revised as of 1 April. CITE: 21CFR312.32. 'Drugs for Human Use'. http://www.accessdata.fda.gov/scripts/cdrh/cfdocs/cfcfr/CFRSearch.cfm?fr=312.32
Foundation for Biomedical Research (2005) 'Poll Shows Majority of Americans Support Animal Research'. http://www.fbresearch.or/journalist/press-release/Polls/HartPoll 4 15 05.htm
Frontline (2001) 'Dangerous Prescription'. http://www.pbs.org/wgbh/pages/frontline/shows/prescription/etc/limks.html
Gandhi, Mohandes K. (1959) *The Moral Basis of Vegetarianism*, compiled by R. K. Prabhu. Ahmedabad: Navajivan Publishing.
Kessler, D. (1993) 'Introducing Medwatch: A New Approach to Reporting Medication and Device Adverse Effects and Product Problems', *Journal of the American Medical Association*, 269: 2765–68.
Lazarou, J., Pomeranz, B. H., and Corey, P. N. (1998) 'Incidence of Adverse Drug Reactions in Hospitalized Patients: A Meta-analysis of Prospective Studies', *Journal of the American Medical Association*, 279: 1200–04.

Moore, T. J. (1998) *Prescription for Disaster: The Hidden Dangers in Your Medicine Cabinet.* New York: Simon and Schuster.

Plous, S. and Herzog, H. (2001) 'Reliability of Protocol Reviews for Animal Research', *Science* 27 (July 2001): 608–9.

Regan, T. (1983) *The Case for Animal Rights.* Berkeley: University of California Press.

Regan, T. (2004a) *Animal Rights, Human Wrongs: An Introduction to Moral Philosophy.* Lanham, Boulder, New York, Oxford: Rowman and Littlefield.

Regan, T. (2004b) *Empty Cages: Facing the Challenge of Animal Rights.* Lanham, Boulder. New York, Oxford: Rowman and Littlefield.

Chapter 6

Debating 'animal rights' online: the movement–countermovement dialectic revisited

Roger Yates

Whereas recent social movement theorists speak of activist 'networks' and 'communities', others have defined a social movement as, 'a collectivity acting with some continuity to promote a change or resist a change in the society or group of which it is a part' (Turner and Killian 1957: 308). This notion of a struggle to effect and resist change is captured in relation to animal protectionism by Guither's concept of the success of the 'animal rights crusade' being firmly met by 'the emerging counterforce' of animal interest groups and scientists (Guither 1998: 132).

While some have suggested that sociologists neglect the study of the interplay between social movements (Meyer and Staggenborg 1996), the issue has not been entirely ignored. For example, Mottl (1980) has described the connection between social movement and countermovement as 'a continuous dialect of social change', Lilliston and Cummings (1997) further explore the 'movement–countermovement dialectic' and Munro (1999) examines the contest over 'moral capital' in the relationships between social movements and their opponents. Goode (1992) also concentrates on how competing social movements strive to accumulate 'moral capital' or 'moral resources', noting how the former involves the building of a 'reservoir of goodwill'. One way groups can build moral capital is by trying to establish a 'respectable' public image, a factor that tends to push social movement organisations towards aspiration moderation. A commitment to 'respectability' also goes some way to explain their constant interest in the way they are portrayed in the media

(Gamson 1995), and the current penchant for labelling all opponents 'terrorists'.

In relation to the sociology of crime, the social construction of deviance provides a productive framework for exploring the movement–countermovement dialectic. The social construction of deviance approach is premised on the notion that much of reality is a construction emerging from and sustained by social interaction and language use. In such a view, society may be regarded as an arena of conflict and change as opposed to – or as well as – one of consensus and stability. Miller and Holstein's (1993) 'contextual constructionism' provides a further refinement for researching the issue at hand. According to Miller and Holstein (ibid.: 11), such a perspective does not refuse 'to evaluate the accuracy of claims-makers' claims', something the 'strict-strong' social constructionist formulation is disinclined to do. They note that contextual constructionists attempt to 'contribute to public and academic debates about social problems', something that Mills (1967), Christie (1997), Seidman (1998) and others, who argue that sociologists should actively engage in the social, political and moral issues of the day, would enthusiastically applaud.

As implied in Miller and Holstein (1993), a constructionism modelled on Berger and Luckmann's 'classical' version (1966) is useful. Validity is amplified via Rik Scarce's (1998) development of Berger and Luckmann's original 1960s approach, whereby he seeks to 'bridge the literatures on environmental sociology and the sociology of human–animal relationships' (ibid.: 121). Scarce's project involves theoretically understanding the social construction of both a single animal species and 'nature' as a general category. Further study in this area of interest is noteworthy. For example, Munro (1998) notes that a social constructionist stance and orientation have been employed in the study of both 'animal rights' and environmentalist claims about 'defending the natural world' (see Yearly 1992; Hannigan 1995; Henkle 1995; Munro 1998).

New approaches to the study of harm, be it in zemiology or green criminology, will be greatly interested in the claims-making of such groups as Corporate Watch[1] and Multinational Monitor.[2] In a paper entitled 'Corporate Crimes Against Animals', animal activist pattrice jones (2004) uses data from Multinational Monitor, on the 'Top 100 Corporate Criminals of the 1990s', to highlight the number of 'animal abuse' industries in the list. In other words, she notes the frequency in the list of oil, pharmaceutical and agribusiness corporations who cause harm and destruction to both human and nonhuman animals.

The oil industry alone, jones argues, harms nonhumans as it pollutes ecosystems, contributes to climate change and fosters 'the cultural attitudes that underlie their oppression' (*ibid.*). Jones's perspective interfaces with green criminology by defining harms caused by corporations as crimes committed against all animals. Claiming animal produce-free diets require considerably fewer petroleum resources than meat-based ones, she urges environmentalists 'to extend their environmentalism by going vegan' . Similarly she states that ethical vegans 'must extend [their] veganism by being more careful to reduce, reuse, and recycle in relation to petroleum products (which include plastics as well as gasoline)' (*ibid.*).

As indicated above, the 'contextual' form of constructionism is somewhat distinct from the so-called 'strict' (Spector and Kitsuse 1987; Kitsuse and Schneider 1989) or 'strong program' constructivism frequently employed in studies of the social construction of science and technology. Exploring the various strands of constructionism is complex and involved (see Best 1995; and Scarce 1998). However, a degree of general agreement exists, following Berger and Luckmann, that research should focus on social *processes* that give *meaning(s)* to what is seen as material reality. In addition, as noted above, 'contextual constructionist analyses turn on distinguishing between "warranted" and "unwarranted" social problem claims, a distinction that implicitly involves treating some putative conditions as "real" social problems' (Miller and Holstein 1993: 12).

The focus on process and meaning is largely what makes Berger and Luckmann's approach a sociology of knowledge. They encourage researchers to consider the historical context of their subject as well as appreciating 'both interactional and macrolevel forces as they examine the emergence and maintenance of meaning' (Scarce 1998: 120). However, it is also important to avoid what Scarce characterises as a 'serious shortcoming' in both 'classical' and 'strong program' constructivism by engaging a necessary 'critical' element to the analysis. Essentially, this involves examination of the role played by powerful social institutions in shaping, and often systematically reinforcing, dominant ideological constructions of the social world. This seems to be a potentially fruitful avenue for the green criminologist. It is precisely what Scarce did in his investigation of the social construction of salmon; what jones touched on in her recent investigation of crimes against animals; and what is proposed here in relation to the mass media, social movement mobilisation, and countermovement activity.

Activists for nonhuman animals and their countermovements

Not surprisingly, those involved in social movement activity take a great deal of notice of what countermovements are saying, just as they diligently monitor how the 'battle of ideas' they are involved in is playing out in the mass media (see Gamson (1995) on social movement activists as 'media junkies'). This chapter revisits the movement–countermovement dialectic and, in particular, it investigates how countermovement messages about 'animal rights' are reflected in a public online forum called 'Animal_Rights_ Debate' located on the internet server Yahoo (http://groups.yahoo.com/group/ Animal_ Rights_Debate/post). A number of key issues emerge from the discourse on the list, such as the meaning of terms such as 'animal rights', 'animal welfare', the status of utilitarian philosopher Peter Singer, and the idea that 'animal rights' is an extremist philosophy that promotes violence and terrorism.

Animal rights theorist Tom Regan (2004) is one of the latest to suggest that the countermovements to animal protectionism are enjoying some success in a campaign to characterise 'animal rights' as an extremist mobilisation and terroristic idea. At the same time, countermovement interests constantly reassert the centrality of orthodox or traditional animal welfarism in assessments of human–nonhuman relations. Regan claims that the general public have a negative image of animal rights advocates ('ARAs'), one that has been created and sustained by the public relations efforts of 'major animal user industries' (*ibid*: 11).

Essentially, Regan is echoing the findings of others who have taken an interest in social movements and their countermovements. For example, Guither (1998: 132) suggests that a 'counterforce' has 'awakened' to the threat posed by the animal protection community. Guither, like Regan, notes that the counterforce concentrates on discrediting 'animal rights' while supporting the notions of 'humane treatment' and conventional animal welfarism. For his part, Munro (1999) uses the umbrella terms 'animal liberation movement' and 'animal protectionism' to mean moderate welfarists,[3] pragmatic animal liberationists (citing Singer's book *Animal Liberation* here), and radical abolitionists who advocate animal rights. This movement attacks the rightness of experimentation on nonhuman animals, intensive farming, 'recreational hunting' and other forms of nonhuman 'use' – practices which the countermovements are set up to defend in a 'values war' about the human treatment of other animals. The overall battle over ideas about human–nonhuman relations serves to create and maintain a radical differentiation between 'sensible animal welfarism' and 'militant', 'violent' and 'terroristic animal rights'.

Regan (2004: 11–14) suggests that the meat, fur, animal entertainment and biomedical research industries speak with one voice in their construction of the 'animal rights extremists'. He dates the origins of the pro-use counteroffensive in the USA to the publication of a white paper by the American Medical Association (AMA) in 1989, subtitled 'The Challenge of Animal Rights'. This document suggests that people who believe in nonhuman rights 'must be shown to be not only anti-science but also (a) responsible for violent and illegal acts that endanger life and property, and (b) a threat to the public's freedom of choice' (*ibid*: 12).

The AMA strategy was both simple and inspired, Regan suggests, adding that '[i]f the public's perception of using animals in research could be structured as a contest between know-nothing animal rights extremists who hate humans and have an insatiable appetite for violence, on the one hand, and wise scientific animal welfare moderates, true friends of humanity, on the other, ARAs would be repudiated and the ideology of humane, responsible use would prevail' (*ibid*.) Regan claims that, since 1989:

> a steady stream of press releases, memos, e-mail messages, press conferences, and website miscellany, denouncing ARA extremists and lauding reasonable animal welfarists, has flowed from the AMA's and other biomedical research industry's public relations offices straight into the hands of reporters, news directors, and editors. (*ibid*.)

Regan cites information from the Foundation for Biomedical Research (FBR) internet pages that reveal the provision of 'journalist resources' and an aspiration that scientists and journalists can be brought together to inspire 'exceptional, outstanding and ongoing' media coverage. Essentially, this means media texts aimed at convincing the general public of both the morality and utility of using nonhuman animals in research. The message claims such use is 'humane', 'responsible' and 'essential'. When it comes to identifying those who could possibly oppose that, Regan says that the FBR itself provides the answer: fanatical animal rights activists who are engaged in illegal and violent acts. This, he argues, is the construction of welfare moderates versus 'know-nothing ARAs'; wise and humane scientists versus extremists.

Not surprisingly, Regan suggests that it did not take long before other nonhuman animal user groups followed the biomedical industry's apparently-successful lead:

> The meat industry. The animal entertainment industry. Sport hunters and rodeo enthusiasts. The story is everywhere the same. Animal welfare moderates versus animal rights extremists. Law-abiding citizens versus law-breaking terrorists. (*ibid.*: 14)

The fur industry is also 'on-message', as this contribution to the Fur Information Council of America's website attests:

> The majority of Americans support animal welfare groups, but do NOT support [any] out-of-touch-with-reality, publicity-hungry animal rights groups ... Animal welfare groups support humane treatment and responsible care of animals while the animal rights philosophy not only condemns the use of all animals for any purpose but also is known for its increasingly terroristic tactics. The current mind-set of the animal rights movement is, 'Believe what I believe ... or else.' (cited in *ibid.*: 15)

The utility and frequency of countermovement strategies may possibly be judged by recent developments in Britain. Following the so-called hunting 'ban' in England, Wales and Scotland in 2004 and 2005, which supposedly prohibits the hunting of foxes, minks, deer and hares with packs of hounds, the shooting and fishing lobbies have expressed worries that anti-hunting mobilisations, having seen off 'hunting with dogs', will turn their fire on them. There is some suggestion that organisations such as the League Against Cruel Sports (LACS) are proposing alterations to their constitutions in order to mount such a campaign. In July 2005, *The Scotsman*[4] ran an article entitled '"Animal terrorists" in bid to ban shooting' which claimed that 'Campaigners lobbying for a ban on the use of guns in rural sports were labelled "animal terrorists" by a former Labour agriculture minister yesterday'. Apart from utilising the 'terrorist' construction, Lord Donoughue appears to appreciate fully the importance of countermovements. He warned landowners that they had 'a window of ten years or less' to 'mount a counter campaign to ensure that shooting did not follow hunting into the list of banned activities' . Oddly, while acts of terrorism are normally regarded as the most extreme extra-parliamentary activities imaginable, Donoughue, a former lecturer at the London School of Economics before he joined the Wilson Labour government, suggests such acts may be of use to gain the support of individual members of the House of Commons:

> This is just half to two thirds of the way through the next Parliament and it is by then that the animal terrorists will have mounted a major campaign to get back-bench support and will have someone to bring a Private Member's Bill into the House. (*ibid.*)

Lord Donoughue claimed he calls lobbyists 'animal terrorists' because their aim is 'to destroy the countryside as we know it'.

Welfare and rights on ARD

Discourse on animal welfare and animal rights, as described by Regan above, is alive and well on Yahoo's Animal_Rights_Debate forum and can be traced back at least three years in the message archive. To some extent this is not surprising given the long-term presence on the ARD site of Norma Bennett Woolf, who works for the National Animal Interest Alliance (NAIA). The NAIA's mission statement reads, 'Our mission is to promote a more abundant life for all the people of this planet through a wise and compassionate human relationship with animals and the environment' (http://www.naiaonline.org/body/about_naia.htm).

The NAIA claim that they:

> Recognize that human–animal interactions take many forms; Recognize that man is an integral part of any solution to an animal or environmental issue; Serve as a resource for groups and individuals dedicated to responsible animal care; Provide information to reporters and writers for articles, news broadcasts and books; Host conferences to highlight topical issues, expose animal rights and environmental extremism and share animal welfare efforts and successes; Support the victims of animal and environmental extremism; Have a speakers' bureau and provide experts to media, classrooms and public policy makers; Counter the rhetoric of the animal rights movement; Support the wise and thoughtful use of natural resources. (*ibid.*)

Moreover, they state that they:

Provide this website to alert animal owners and others about the differences between animal rights and animal welfare and the battle for reasonable laws, regulations, and guidelines affecting animal treatment, use and ownership. (*ibid.*)

What Bennett Woolf says in ARD contributions differs little from the above:

ARD message 30336, 'Norma Bennett Woolf' to 'Jim' : AW and AR are not on the same scale. AW is an animal use philosophy; AR is a no-use philosophy. The twain doesn't meet no matter how deep your belief that it does. NAIA falls into the same category of AW support as AVMA, various specialty veterinary groups, AKC, groups specializing in research animal care, many humane societies, etc., etc., i.e., we support animal use; believe that those who own and interact with animals tend to be experts in their care and training; and work hard to make and support improvements where improvements are necessary ... The goal of AR is to end animal use (no instrumental control, remember?) and the goal of AW is to give animals a decent life and a quick death while we benefit from their presence in our lives. These are two completely incompatible sets of goals. (*ibid.*)

While the NAIA notes that 'meeting the animal rights challenge' amounts to educating the public about the 'critical difference' between animal welfare and animal rights, an organisation known as 'Putting People First' (PPF) defines its objectives as enlightening 'middle America about the work of animal rights groups, to provide balanced education about animals and their use with school-age children, and to protect human health through disease control and support for biomedical research' (PPF, cited in Guither 1998: 140–41). According to Guither, the founder of PPF, Kathleen Marquardt, characterises her materials produced for school use as 'balanced', while she dismisses what the People for the Ethical Treatment of Animals (PeTA)[5] has to say about human–nonhuman relations as a form of 'brainwashing' (*ibid.*: 141).

Although the NAIA and other organisations have acknowledged that they provide classroom speakers for educational purposes, ARD contributors have used animal welfare and animal rights distinctions to suggest that a *rights* advocate's presence in an educational setting is illegitimate. For some, it is akin to 'terrorism' in and of itself:

ARD message 16978, 'Kathy': Well, if hanging a dead animal should be a crime, why shouldn't distributing literature (known to be filled with inflammatory statements) to children be considered a terrorist crime? It's meant to be used to terrorize children into changing their lifestyles. You can hand out anything you want to adults, but NOT children and certainly not MY children.

ARD message 19715, 'Norma Bennett Woolf': I don't care if you or anyone else believes that animals have rights, I care only if those who believe try to push their opinion on the rest of us via laws, regulations, indoctrination of kids, or terrorist tactics.

'Terrorism' discourse on Animal-Rights-Debate

Guither (1998) describes how the North American Farm Animal Welfare Coalition (FAWC) was formed in 1981 to 'promote education against animal rights activism'. This organisation is made up of 45 'major farm animal associations' whose mission is to:

- unite all farm organisations into a coalition committed to continued well-being and safe treatment of farm animals;
- study public opinion, attitudes, and knowledge about farm practices and modern farm technology; and
- educate the consumer, public officials, media, and other audiences about the farmers' essential concern for the well-being of their animals and the production of safe, low-cost food. (quoted in *ibid.*: 133)

This umbrella organisation appears to be agitated and apparently gravely concerned by the effects, potential or real, of present-day 'animal rights' campaigning. It identifies 'six basic issues' within 'animal rights' advocacy, including the promotion of vegetarianism, arguments about food shortages in 'developing' nations and the 'humane treatment' of animals. The FAWC responds to such issues with a campaigning programme that includes commitments to:

- continuing to monitor the direction of the animal rights movement, its attempts at coalition building, and themes used to alter public perceptions;
- establishing an effective system of monitoring state legislative and legal action;

- monitoring all studies on animal stress and advising members on implications for farming practices related to animal rights issues;
- developing positive themes to neutralise what coalition members see as irresponsible attacks on animal farming practices by animal rights groups;
- maintaining communications with other animal-rearing or user groups, particularly those concerned with laboratory animals;
- preparing their organisations to deal effectively with the challenge of the animal rights movement and implementing an ongoing communications programme, and
- researching the attitudes and knowledge level about animal rights issues prevailing in the wider circle of agribusiness. (*ibid.*: 133–34)

Guither (*ibid.*: 136) goes on to detail other pro-animal farming organisations set up to counter dangerous and unwarranted 'animal rights' views, with descriptions of some of their campaigns. For example, there is the 'I care' programme run under the auspices of the 'American Farm Bureau Federation' designed to 'foster humane treatment of animals' and to 'demonstrate that young people do believe in good animal welfare'. This particular federation publishes handbooks such as *Meeting the Animal Rights Challenge* and *Handling the 20 Toughest Animal Rights Assertions*.

Another pro-use organisation, the 'Pork Producers' Council', advises members to respond to 'animal rights' claims in measured tones, suggesting lines such as: 'We share with them their concern about the welfare of farm animals. We wish they were better informed about the way pork producers take care of their livestock' (*NPPC Handbook*, quoted in Guither 1998: 136). The handbook concludes with good advice for all those fashionably waging 'war against terrorism': 'The animal rights movement is acquiring the earmarks [!] of international terrorism ... animal rights activists want the entire farm industry to live in a state of anxiety. Don't give them the satisfaction. On the other hand, don't be careless' (*ibid.*: 137).

Not surprisingly, there has been much talk on ARD about 'animal rights terrorism'. This discourse is often prompted either by individual contributors' personal concerns or by what activities are heavily featured in media reports about animal advocates:

ARD message 39724, 'bint': We do spend a great deal of time talking about AR terrorism but that's just the way the world works. No one needs to be worried about the ARAs who just go about their life being vegans and trying to convince their friends to do the same.

ARD message 34660, 'Lisa': PS – The reason I post articles that refer to violent ARAs is due to them being in the news.

The discourse about animal advocacy and terrorism is seen by some to prevent real debate on ARD:

ARD message 36475, 'Norma Bennett Woolf' to 'Jim': 'It is 'reactionary' to speak out against violence? To consider that ELF, ALF, etc. are domestic terrorists?'
'Jim' in reply: Norma – WHAT a hugely stupid question! *I* (as well as Rags and Pro B) have spoken REPEATEDLY against such violence! ... However what YOU do – Ms. Propagandist – isn't to simply 'speak out' against the violence. What YOU do – is to repeatedly refer to the violence for the purposes of casting prejudice against the whole of the rights movement. THAT is quite dishonest – Norma!

ARD message 28273, 'Jim' to 'Lisa': Can't you just disagree (about rights) without saying something so off the edge as implying I'm supporting TERRORISM? Surely YOU know better by now.

ARD message 15868, 'Peachybean' to 'Norma': I have never bombed, threatened, committed arson, etc. I work at a public aquarium, I eat meat, I don't want to end pet breeding, etc. Just want to see the animals and consumers protected. And I am considered an AR by you and I am grouped in the same 'terrorist' category you give.

ARD message 8800, 'Aimee' to 'Lisa': You've said this once before, in your fight to make AR look like a bunch of terrorists, so I will explain again ...

ARD message 15817, 'Jim': Norma – are we going to talk about ideas OR are you just going to keep ranting about how bad and terroristic some ARs are?

The dominant discourse about terrorism appears to have led some to conclude that individuals are or are not terrorists depending on whether or not they adhere to welfare or rights principles:

ARD message 8919, 'Balddog': Animal welfarists are not what we are calling terrorists. Animal rights activists, animal liberators, and their supporters ... THOSE I call terrorists.

ARD message 16165, 'Randolph Critzer': Same folks defending ar terrorism and chicken rights!

ARD message 17207, 'Kathy': the AR movement SUPPORTS VIOLENCE in seeking its goals. Oh, not every individual does. But PeTA is the largest AR organization and they PAY MONEY to CONVICTED CRIMINALS. They support VLASAK who calls for assassination. They pay a SALARY to men who advocate TERRORISM.

ARD message 26701, 'Kim': We, whom don't believe animals have rights, don't have anything to worry about as we are not classified as terrorists by the USA government. Think about it.

ARD message 13206, 'Steve': *IF* animals do have any rights, it would not benefit those on our side to concede even in the smallest degree. Given the current societal confusion, and the obvious insanity of many within the ar movement (re: the recent write up on peta and the holocaust – and the large percentage of ar's that support terrorist organizations, for example), it seems that the smallest concession would only inspire ar's to steamroll any opposition.

Can't seem to do without Peter Singer

Australian philosopher Peter Singer is not an advocate of rights and, despite finding some political utility in its use, does not particularly regard 'animal rights' talk as a good way of advocating for change in human–nonhuman relations. It would not take too long on the internet to find Singer himself saying just that.[6] Although he is not a rights advocate, the publication of Singer's *Animal Liberation* in 1975 is often credited with stimulating the modern movement that calls itself 'animal rights'. There is an irony to register here. For, while many advocates for nonhuman interests seem to care little about the philosophical consistency of their own movement, pro-use countermovements appear incredibly anxious to ensure that Singer is irrevocably regarded as an out-and-out animal rights advocate. While academic commentators (e.g. Garner 1993; Benton and Redfearn 1996) may identify Peter Singer as a non-rights utilitarian animal welfarist, this description will definitely *not* do for pro-use advocates in nonhuman user industries. The latter are happiest when there is no question that Singer is characterised as the 'father of AR' and, likewise, when *Animal Liberation* is uncritically labelled as the 'bible of the animal rights movement'.[7]

Singer is a controversial figure in applied ethics. If *Animal Liberation* was to mark him out as a radical thinker, his views on biomedical ethics and recently on 'bestiality' (interspecies sexual assault (Beirne 1997)) have prompted opponents to call him a 'Nazi' and 'maybe the most dangerous man in the world today'.[8]

How does the Peter Singer construction play out on the Animal_Rights_Debate (ARD) forum? There appears to be a general attempt by ARD contributors to discredit non-orthodox nonhuman advocacy, especially the 'animal rights movement', by associating Singer as a controversial character with the philosophical theory of animal rights. For example, in ARD message 37880, 'KC' writes:

> It [interspecies sexual assault] does sicken me – almost as much as child molestation or pedophilia … But of course with someone of Peter Singer's stature recommending it, who knows anymore.

> *ARD message 36245, 'Lisa':* Singer's view of bestiality disgusts me I will say.

In another contribution (ARD message 36354) 'Lisa' writes of Singer's *Animal Liberation*: 'A book that initiated others to seek 'animal liberation' while at the same time excuses bestiality?', despite the fact that other contributions of hers had established that she was aware that *Animal Liberation* was published in 1975 while Singer's views on interspecies sexual assault came to light much later in 2001.[9]

In a discussion on Singer, the ARD moderator re-posted a typical pro-use take on his philosophy and position in the animal protection movement:

> *ARD message 18431, 'Kim' cites an article by Daniel J Flynn in which the author writes:* Is the self-righteousness of animal rights activists, or their tactics, at all surprising given the popularity of Singer's writings? Singer has even coined a term – speciesists – to place the fight for animal rights on the same plane as the fight against racism and sexism.[10]

In other exchanges about what Singer stands for as a philosopher, such as this one contained in ARD message 28653, there is a marked reluctance to forego the perceived advantage of having Singer characterised as a rights advocate:

'Pro.B': Singer believes, for example, that one animal might be replaced with another animal. If the replacement has an equally pleasant or more pleasant life than the original had, then the death of the first does not necessitate ethical concern.

'KC': I thought Singer wasn't an AR advocate? You guys want it both ways, eh?

'Pro.B': No, I don't want it both ways. NB: 1. I do not agree with Singer. 2. Singer is not a rights advocate, but a utilitarian philosopher.

Even when it is pointed out that Singer himself acknowledges that he is not an animal rightist, there is a reluctance to accept it:

ARD message 28678, 'KC': Okay, let me see if I have this right. Peter Singer says he is NOT an ARA so that means he's not.

Similarly, the opinion of academic commentators counts for little:

ARD message 19049, 'bint': Just because Garner[11] believes that Singer is not an advocate of rights doesn't mean that this belief should be 'clear' to anyone else.

In ARD message 19045, 'Rags' wrote: In second edition of Animal Liberation, Singer writes 'the language of rights is a convenient political shorthand'. When she appeared on Philosophy Talk (radio show), Singer's co-author Lori Gruen [Gruen and Singer 1987] said exactly the same thing in her rejection of rights. The same ARD contributor resorted to the minutiae of semantics:

ARD message 19049, 'bint': The quote from Singer also doesn't prove that he doesn't believe in rights. To say that something is political shorthand doesn't mean you don't believe in this particular political shorthand. Even if he says that claims of rights are irrelevant, it doesn't mean that he doesn't believe in them.

In ARD 27802, 'bint' makes this point: 'It isn't the AW [animal welfare] advocates that call Singer the Father of the AR movement. It is those who are within the AR movement who are responsible for that.' However, while this statement is correct, it is only partly correct.[12] Any short internet search will reveal that pro-use countermovements persist in labelling Singer as an animal rights advocate. Again, it is difficult to interpret this consistent fundamental error in any other way than to suggest that such organisations appear to believe that the controversies surrounding Singer can be used against the movement for nonhuman rights.

Conclusion

Of the counterforce to 'animal rights', Guither (1998: 132) writes: 'Through educational efforts with their members and to the general public through the media, they are challenging and attempting to discredit the animal rights doctrines and beliefs'. Regan (2004: 10) says that opponents have been 'untruthful in labelling' in the construction of the violent 'animal rights extremist'.

It seems fair to acknowledge that the anti-'animal rights' countermovement(s) have met with a certain degree of success in their aim to assert a radical divide between sensible, i.e. orthodox, animal welfarists and extremist and violent animal rightists. They have apparently profitably tuned into the current 'war on terrorism' and seem to have been fairly successful in framing any concern for nonhuman animals beyond the confines of conventional animal welfarism as illegitimate, beyond the pale, unnecessary, and terroristic in nature. With some irony, they even seem to have co-opted the confusion and controversy surrounding a radical animal welfarist, Singer, in order to further attack and undermine what 'animal rights' is taken to mean. Apart from being successful in getting their messages out to the general public via the mass media, through their own specialised media, such as websites, they appear to have successfully armed traditional animal welfarists with all the arguments they require to make deviant and discredit the philosophy and followers of animal rights.

Notes

1 http://www.corporatewatch.org
2 http://www.corporatepredators.org/top100.html.
3 Very different organisations claim to be animal welfarists, ranging from groups such as the National Animal Interest Alliance (NAIA) in the

USA – which defends virtually any form of nonhuman 'use' – to organisations such as the British-based Compassion In World Farming (CIWF), set up by a dairy farmer, which has an abolitionist attitude towards the most intensive forms of farming, or 'factory farming' as it is known.

4 http://business.scotsman.com/agriculture.cfm?id=1670572005

5 The acronym 'PETA' is sometimes written 'PeTA' in various internet forums by both friends and enemies of People for the Ethical Treatment of Animals (this quite apart from the existence of the anti-animal rights site deliberately named People Eating Tasty Animals to produce the acronym PETA). The 'e' is often presented in lower case because PeTA's 'e' in its title is italicised. Alternatively, countermovemnt supporters may use the lower case 'e' to suggest that PeTA are not an ethical organisation.

6 For example, this from http://www.citypaper.net/articles/100799/feat.20q.shtml: Q: Could there be a basic problem in referring to animals' 'rights'? PS: You know, Americans tend to look at almost every issue as if it's a question of rights; I don't. People describe me as an 'animal rights advocate' and that's not strictly correct … While the language of rights has a use, particularly in political contexts, I don't really like it as the foundation of moral argument, because it's too intuitive, and people's intuitions are different … I'd rather look at the interests of animals and the wrongness of ignoring those interests by inflicting suffering or death unnecessarily.

7 In a Thorsons Publishers' undated edition of *Animal Liberation* (includes a copyright notice to Peter Singer, 1975, and references to a Jonathan Cape edition in 1976 and a First Trade paperback in 1983), Jean Pink, the founder in 1977 of the British national organisation Animal Aid, is quoted describing the book as 'the Bible of the new animal rights movement'.

8 http://www.mofed.org/Who%20is%20Peter%20Singer.htm

9 See Singer, 'Heavy Petting' at http://www.nerve.com/Opinions/Singer/heavyPetting and Beirne (2001).

10 In fact it was Richard Ryder who coined this term and first explored its connection to racism.

11 This is a response to the following point revealing that Garner was stating what Singer had said about his utilitarian philosophical position: 'In 1993, political scientist Robert Garner published a book called *Animals Politics and Morality*. On page 27, Garner writes, "Singer is clear … that he is not an advocate of rights."'

12 This contribution from 'bint' is only partly correct for a second, more complex, reason. ARD list members, including 'bint', have frequently discussed the perspective of rights theorist Gary Francione (1995; 1996; 2000). In his controversial thesis on the animal protection movement, *Rain Without Thunder* (1996), Francione describes advocates who label themselves animal rightists as 'new welfarists'. There is great resistance

in the 'animal rights movement' to this term (as there is hurt dismissal of Dunayer's (2004) name for the same people: 'new speciesists'). This despite the fact that most 'ARAs' do not take a consistent rights line on human–nonhuman relations and do indeed often frame their major claims about the human treatment of other animals within the precepts of animal welfarism. Such factors tend to support Francione's assertion that the 'animal rights movement' does not really exist. Thus, when talking of 'those who are within the AR movement', 'bint' is most likely speaking about non-traditional or radical animal welfarists, or at least some type of non-rightist campaigners.

References

Beirne, P. (1997) 'Rethinking Bestiality: Towards a Concept of Interspecies Sexual Assault', *Theoretical Criminology*, 1 (3): 317–340.

Beirne, P. (2001) 'Peter Singer's "Heavy Petting" and the Politics of Animal Sexual Assault', *Journal of Critical Criminology*, 10 (1): 43–55.

Benton, T. and Redfearn, S. (1996) 'The Politics of Animal Rights – Where is the Left?', *New Left Review*, Jan/Feb: 43–58.

Berger, P. L. and Luckmann, T. (1966) *The Social Construction of Reality*. New York: Anchor.

Best, J. (1995) 'Debates about Constructionism' in E. Rubington and M. S. Weinberg (eds), *The Study of Social Problems*, 5th edn. Oxford: Oxford University Press.

Christie, N. (1997) 'Four Blocks Against Insight: Notes on the Oversocialisation of Criminologists', *Theoretical Criminology*, 1 (1): 13–23.

Dunayer, J. (2004) *Speciesism*. Derwood, MD.: Ryce Publishing.

Francione, G. (1995) *Animals, Property, and the Law*. Philadelphia, PA.: Temple University Press.

Francione, G. (1996) *Rain without Thunder: The Ideology of the Animal Rights Movement*. Philadelphia, PA.: Temple University Press.

Francione, G. (2000) *Introduction to Animal Rights: Your child or the Dog?* Philadelphia, PA: Temple University Press.

Gamson, W. A. (1995) 'Constructing Social Protest' in H. Johnson and B. Klandermans (eds), *Social Movements and Culture*. London: University College of London Press.

Garner, R. (1993) *Animals, Politics and Morality*. Manchester: Manchester University Press.

Goode, E. (1992) *Collective Behaviour*. Florida, FA.: Harcourt Brace Jovanovich.

Gruen, L. and Singer, P. (1987) *Animal Liberation – A Graphic Guide*. London: Camden Press.

Guither, H. D. (1998) *Animal Rights: History and Scope of a Radical Social Movement*. Carbondale, IL. : Southern Illinois University Press.

Hannigan, J. (1995) *Environmental Sociology: A Social Constructionist Perspective*. London: Routledge.

Henkle, K. (1995) 'Down on the Farm: Rationale Expansion in the Construction of Factory Farming as a Social Problem', in J. Best (ed.) *Images of Issues: Typifying Contemporary Social Problems*. New York: Aldine de Gruyter.

Kitsuse, J. I. and Schneider, J. W. (1989) Preface, in J. Best (ed.) *Images of Issues: Typifying Contemporary Social Problems*. New York: Aldine de Gruyter.

Lilliston, B. and Cummins, R. (1997) 'The Food Slander Laws in the US: The Criminalization of Dissent', *The Ecologist*, vol. 27 (6): 216–220.

Marshall, G. (ed.) (1994) *Oxford Concise Dictionary of Sociology*. Oxford: Oxford University Press.

Meyer, D. S. and Staggenborg, S. (1996) 'Movements, Countermovements, and the Structure of Political Opportunity', *American Journal of Sociology*, 101 (May) (6): 1628–1660.

Miller, G. and Holstein, J. A. (1993) 'Reconsidering Social Constructionism', in J. A. Holstein and G. Miller (eds), *Reconsidering Social Constructionism: Debates in Social Problems Theory*. New York: Aldine De Gruyter.

Mills, C. W. (1967) *The Sociological Imagination*. New York: Oxford University Press.

Mottl, T. L. (1980) 'The Analysis of Countermovements', *Social Problems*, 27 (5): 620–634.

Munro, L. (1999) 'Contesting Moral Capital in Campaigns Against Animal Liberation', *Society and Animals*, 7 (1): 35–53.

Regan, T. (2004) *Empty Cages: Facing the Challenge of Animal Rights*. Oxford: Rowman and Littleflield.

Scarce, R. (1998) 'Socially Constructing Pacific Salmon', *Society and Animals*, 5 (2): 117–135.

Seidman, S. (1998) *Contested Knowledge: Social Theory in the Postmodern Era* (2nd edn). Oxford: Blackwell.

Spector, M. and Kitsuse, J. I. (1987) *Constructing Social Problems*. Menlo Park, CA: Cummings.

Turner, R. H. and Killian, L. M. (1957) *Collective Behaviour*. Englewood Cliffs, NJ: Prentice-Hall.

Yearly, S. (1992) *The Green Case: A Sociology of Environmental Issues, Arguments and Politics*. London: Routledge.

Part III

Ecological systems and environmental harms

Chapter 7

'At risk': climate change and its bearing on women's vulnerability to male violence

Sandra Wachholz

Over the last two decades a vast body of literature has emerged that sheds light on how human activity since the Industrial Revolution has significantly altered global climate systems (Dore 2005; Hulme *et al.* 2002; Knutson and Tuleya 2004; Lempinen and Pinholster 2004; Wilson 2002).[1] Although there are regional variations in the degree and extent of climate disruption, we now have a collective picture of a world that is experiencing rising ocean and surface temperatures, increasing variability in precipitation, and more intense tropical cyclones (Salinger 2005; United Nation's Intergovernmental Panel on Climate Change (IPCC) 2001).

Vulnerabilities to the adverse impacts of climate change, however, are not evenly distributed around the world. The asymmetries in social, political and economic power that exist both between and within countries are influencing how individuals experience, respond to, and recover from the environmental hazards and the natural disasters that climate change brings in tow (Dankelman 2002; Enarson and Morrow 1998a; Blaikie *et al.* 1994). Drawing attention to this point, the IPCC (2001) has warned that the harmful effects of climate change will fall disproportionately on developing nations and the poverty-stricken within all countries – thereby exacerbating existing inequalities in material resources and socio-economic power.[2] In this sense, then, climate change must also be understood as a social process that is situated within the context of unequal distributions of power and privilege.

The bearing of gender inequality on women's vulnerabilities to the adversities associated with climate change, however, has been largely ignored (Denton 2002a; Masika 2002; Skutsch 2002). Although climate change is unfolding within the context of unequal gender relations, discussions of how women experience the risks and hazards associated with this phenomenon are rarely the focus of concern. A growing body of research signals, nonetheless, that one of the risks that women face within the context of climate change is increased levels of violence by men. Indications of this gender-based vulnerability are emerging in the work of feminists writing in the area of disaster science who have documented rises in reported levels of violence against women after natural disasters such as hurricanes, floods, and droughts (Clemens *et al.* 1999; Enarson 1999; Frasier *et al.* 2004; Wilson *et al.* 1998). Drawing on this research, I examine the prevalence and incidence of violence against women after slow and sudden-onset climate-related natural disasters and argue that since these forms of extreme weather events are increasing, climate change is likely to be correlated with rises in violence against women. In doing so, I highlight how climate change, like other forms of disaster, 'affirms, reflects, disrupts and otherwise engages gendered social relationships' (Enarson and Morrow 1998b: 4).

To lay the foundation for a conceptual understanding of the issues at hand, the chapter begins with an overview of climate change and its bearing on natural disasters. This is followed by a discussion of some of the various gender-based vulnerabilities that climate change poses for women, both in developing and developed nations. Emphasised throughout this section is the view that these vulnerabilities are not shared uniformly by women but rather are shaped by inequalities between nations and the complex interplay of class, caste, race, ethnicity, sexuality and age. The chapter then turns to a review of various studies and agency reports that examine levels of violence against women during and after weather-related disasters. This section takes as its starting point the position that while such factors as heightened levels of stress and anxiety among men during and after disaster are thought to facilitate violence against women, they are not a sufficient condition to initiate this violence. Its underpinning is masculine entitlement to violence: the idea that it is legitimate for men to solve 'problems' though violence (Connell and Messerschmidt 2005; Wilson *et al.* 1998; Messerschmidt 1997). The chapter concludes with a discussion of the remarkable agency and resiliency that women have demonstrated in the wake of natural disasters and provides an overview of some of the initiatives they have taken to address climate change. Although discussions about disasters are often framed within gender stereotypes, it is not the case that during and after disasters 'men must work and women must weep' (Fordam and Ketteridge 1998: 81).

Global climate change and its bearing on extreme weather events

Simply put, the world is warming. The average global surface temperature has increased over the past one hundred years by approximately 0.8 degrees C. Three quarters of this warming has occurred since the 1970s, and at a rate in many parts of the world that is greater than at any other time during the last 1,000 years (Henson 2005; IPCC 2001). As a consequence, most of the world's glaciers are in rapid retreat, freeze-free periods in most mid- and high–latitude regions are lengthening, Arctic ice is thinning, deserts are advancing, and sea levels are rising (Arctic Council 2005; IPCC 2001). There is no getting around it – the Earth is getting hotter (Geographical 2005).

Although some of the trend towards warmer conditions can be attributed to natural warming processes, the overwhelming scientific consensus is that the increase in surface temperatures is largely due to anthropogenic influences on the atmosphere (Henson 2005; IPCC 2001; Spray and McGlothlin 2002). Concentrations of carbon dioxide, methane, tropospheric ozone and nitrous oxide have reached their highest levels in recorded history, primarily due to the combustion of fossil fuels, agriculture, and deforestation. Atmospheric concentrations of carbon dioxide, in particular, have risen quite sharply over the last two centuries. Pre-industrial rates of carbon dioxide were 280 parts per million (ppm) compared to the current concentration of 368 ppm. This rate of increase is unprecedented in at least the last 20,000 years (IPCC 2001).

Data from ice cores drawn from the deep underbelly of the Arctic regions also provide evidence of our dangerous interference with the atmosphere. In 2005, the European Project for Ice Coring in Antarctica (EPICA) drilled two miles below the surface of east Antarctica and recovered the oldest frozen core samples to date. Analyses of the air extracted from the cores revealed that carbon dioxide levels are 27 per cent higher than they have been in 650,000 years and methane levels are 130 per cent higher (Brook 2005; McFarling 2005; Siegenthaler 2005). The significant rise in levels of carbon dioxide and other greenhouse gases has meant that the atmosphere is absorbing more of the outgoing terrestrial radiation from the Earth's surface – thereby increasing global surface and ocean temperatures (IPCC 2001; Salinger 2005).

There are significant regional variations, however, in the rate at which the world is warming. Increases in the average temperatures in the Arctic regions have been more rapid due to a complex global warming feedback process that is triggered by melting ice, snow and permafrost.[3] While a few areas of the Arctic have cooled slightly, the average annual temperature in this region has risen by approximately 2–3 degrees C since the 1950s. Essentially, the Arctic is warming at least twice as fast as the rest of the world (Arctic Council 2005). Reflecting this trend, ice thickness over the entire Arctic Ocean has declined by 40 percent since the 1950s (McCarthy and McKenna 2000).

As research indicates, global warming is already thought to be fostering increases in the frequency and intensity of certain types of natural disasters (Parks and Roberts 2006). Since greenhouse gases in the atmosphere are predicted to double or quadruple by 2100, our planet is likely to undergo an unparalleled period of global climatic change during the twenty-first century (Aalst 2006; Dore 2005; Epstein 2005; Knutson and Tuleya 2004; ICPP 2001; Union of Concerned Scientists 2005).

In the sections that follow I discuss some of the observed and predicted changes in the global climate system and address their relationship to four types of climate-related natural disasters: heat waves, hurricanes, droughts, and floods. It is important to stress that these disasters may occur in tandem (e.g. heat waves and drought), and are often exaggerated by other forms of environmental degradation, such as deforestation, soil erosion, and desertification.

Heat waves

With the projected rises in greenhouse gases this century, surface temperatures around the world are likely to increase quite significantly. The IPCC (2001) estimates that the average surface temperature will rise within the range 1.4 to 5.8 degrees C over the next 100 years, which is an increase that is unprecedented during at least the last 10,000 years.

Heat waves are one of the extreme weather events accompanying rising surface temperatures. Researchers have documented increases in the intensity, frequency, and duration of heat waves in many regions of the world during the latter half of the twentieth century, and have attributed this trend to the rise in heat-trapping greenhouse gases in the atmosphere (IPCC 2001; Meehl and Tebaldi 2004; Schar *et al.* 2004; Wagner 2004). Stott *et al.* (2004) estimate that the increase in greenhouse gases over the last 200 years has at least doubled the risk of heat waves like the one in Europe during the summer of 2003, which research suggests was intensified by the impact of greenhouse gases on an unusual atmospheric circulation pattern that was observed in Europe during that time period (Meehl and Tebaldi 2004; Wagner 2004).

Robust climate-model simulation studies predict that advances in global warming will produce hotter, longer and more frequent heat waves in the twenty-first century (IPCC 2001). According to a recent study by Meehl and Tebaldi (2004) – who work at the US National Center for Atmospheric Research (NCAR) – cities such as Paris and Chicago could experience at least 25 per cent more heat waves by 2090. Unlike floods and hurricanes, heat waves do not create dramatic physical destruction, but they are one of the deadliest natural disasters. Heat waves accounted for more deaths in the US between 1960 and 1995 than all other climate events combined (Klinenberg 2002). Reflecting the capacity of heat waves to kill large numbers of people over a short period of time, the extreme heat in Europe during the summer of 2003 is blamed for between 22,000 and 35,000 deaths (IFRC 2004). This level of mortality, however, reflects two kinds of policy failure – one tied to climate control and the other to social equity initiatives. Heat waves primarily kill the dispossessed – those who are poor, isolated, alone, or forgotten.

Hurricanes

Over the last 40 years, global ocean surface temperatures have risen on average 0.5 degrees C. There is now considerable evidence that this warming trend is a product of human influences on the atmosphere (Sci-Tech Today 2005). For example, scientists at Scripps Institution of Oceanography at the University of California recently compared the observed rise in ocean temperatures over the last 40 years with predictions from two well-known computer climate models and found that greenhouse gases were the best predictors of this warming trend in virtually every ocean of the world (Barnett *et al.* 2005).

Numerous studies also provide rather strong indications that the warming oceans are generating more powerful and destructive hurricanes (Emanuel 2005a; Emanuel 2005b, Knutson and Tuleya 1999; Knutson and Tuleya 2004; Union of Concerned Scientists 2005; Webster *et al.* 2005).[4] In the simplest of terms, heat fuels hurricanes. A warming of the ocean's surface leads to more evaporation and hence increases in water vapour (McCarthy and McKenna 2000). In regions susceptible to hurricanes, water vapor and heat serve as octane for this type of extreme weather event. The change in intensity of Hurricane Katrina in 2005 perfectly illustrates this scientific principle. It made landfall in Florida as a Category 1 storm; however, as it passed over the exceedingly warm waters of the Gulf Coast it spun into a super storm, reaching the level of Category 5 (Union of Concerned Scientists 2005).

Hurricanes have been intensifying in every ocean basin since the 1970s, which is a pattern that corresponds to the increase in ocean surface temperatures (Webster *et al.* 2005). Emanuel (2005a: 686) has attributed most of this warming to human-induced climate change and warned that there may be 'a substantial increase in hurricane-related losses in the twenty-first century [with rising temperatures]'. Similarly, Webster *et al.* (2005) found that the number of Category 4 and 5 hurricanes in all ocean basins has nearly doubled over the last 35 years, and noted that this is not inconsistent with climate model simulations that show a substantial intensification of hurricanes with increases in global warming gases.

Drought

The observed change in precipitation patterns around the world is thought to be another 'signature' of global warming (Breshears *et al.* 2005; Dai *et al.* 2004; Dore 2005; Trenberth *et al.* 2003). Although the rates and types of change differ across regions and continents, analyses of observational data from the twentieth century show an increase in precipitation variance across the planet, with greater extremes of drying and heavy precipitation. Research also suggests that this trend is producing an upward swing in extreme weather events like droughts (Aalst 2006; IPCC 2001).

According to Dai *et al.* (2004) at the US National Center for Atmospheric Research, the amount of land categorised as experiencing drought has more than doubled since the 1970s. These researchers examined global climate records from 1870–2002 using the Palmer Drought Severity Index – which measures the cumulative departure in atmospheric moisture supply and demand – and found that the proportion of land experiencing very dry conditions rose from 15 per cent in the early 1970s to approximately 30 per cent by 2002. Their data also provide evidence of widespread drying over Europe, Asia, Canada, and parts of Africa and Australia.

Although Dai *et al.* (2004:129) note that some of the tendency towards drier conditions can be attributed to El Niño-induced precipitation-decline in the 1980s, they identify global warming as the primary factor driving the rise in droughts. Consistent with this position, IPCC (2001) climate models predict an increase in drought conditions over most mid-latitude continental interiors as climate change progresses in the twenty-first century. Dore (2005) believes that this projection deserves the most systematic and urgent attention as the current drying trends in various regions of the world are already placing significant constraints on food production, water resources, and hydroelectricity. As a case in point, the food scarcity produced by the drought conditions in Africa's Sahel desert during the later half of the twentieth century is blamed for at least 150,000 deaths (Collier and Webb 2002).

Floods

As Collier and Webb (2002: 17) emphasise, 'Floods don't just happen because it rains'. A broad of array of hydrological, meteorological, and geophysical conditions produces flood events, and research indicates that global warming is already having a significant impact on many of these triggers (Milly *et al.* 2002; UNEP 2002). This section explores the relationship between global warming and two types of flood events: glacial lake outburst flooding and coastal sea flooding.[5]

Glacial lake outburst floods

During the last three decades there has been an increase in the frequency of glacial lake outburst floods (GLOF) in several regions of the world, which reports suggest is attributable to climate change (UNEP 2002; Cyranoski 2005). According to the United Nations Environmental Program (2002) (UNEP), over the next decade there could be a dramatic rise in the number of GLOFs, particularly in the Himalayas. Using ground surveys and satellite images, UNEP researchers have identified 44 lakes in Nepal and Bhutan that are in danger of bursting their natural dams within the next 5–10 years. If this happens, catastrophic flooding will occur as glacial lake floods can release several million to a billion cubic meters of water in a few hours (McDowell 2002; Cyranoski 2005). Beyond the threat of floods, the current level of alpine glacial retreat is a grim threat to water supplies – 50 per cent of the freshwater humans consume comes from mountains (Hall and Fagre 2003; Liniger *et al.* 1998).

Coastal sea flooding

Sea-level rise from melting polar ice sheets is believed to be one of the gravest threats of climate change as millions of people live near coastlines and are thus conceivably vulnerable to flooding over the next century (Overpeck *et al.* 2006). In the past 30 years, Arctic surface temperatures have increased by 0.5 degrees C each decade and this has rapidly accelerated the melting of Arctic ice.

The predicted level of sea rise over the next one hundred years is the source of great debate. The IPCC (2001) has suggested a rise of 0.09 to 0.88 m by 2100, while more recent studies point to an increase of 0.30 to 0.91 m (Otto-Bliesner *et al.* 2006). Overpeck *et al.* (2006) warn, however, that future melting and related sea-level rises could be much faster than previously anticipated. At the current rate of warming, their climate models predict the oceans will rise between 3.9–6.09 meters by the end of this century. Rising sea levels are already threatening countries like Tuvalu, the Maldives, and the Marshall Islands; salt water has begun to contaminate freshwater supplies making parts of these islands uninhabitable (Parks and Roberts 2006; Spear 2003).

Uncharted waters

As this discussion of slow and sudden-onset natural disasters suggests, we appear to be sailing the planet into uncharted waters, most likely in the direction of more extreme weather events. We are in the middle of a large, uncontrolled experiment that poses many risks to humans, and is also likely to foster the extinction of an enormous number of plant and animal species (Jensen 2004; Woodruff and McMichael 2004).

In the sections that follow I begin with a discussion of some of the gender-differentiated impacts of climate change, and then I examine its bearing on women's vulnerability to violence.

In the eye of the storm: exploring the gender-differentiated impacts of climate change

Although climate change is not a gender-neutral problem, gender issues have largely been ignored in the wider climate change discourses and policy initiatives (Masika 2002; Skutsch 2002). Women have a key stake in the effective management of our environment and yet, as Denton (2002b: 17) laments, 'Mainstreaming gender issues into debates on climate change and sustainable development is happening piecemeal, extremely slowly, and with varying degrees of success, and often as an afterthought.'

As a small but growing body of literature suggests, there are a number of gender-differentiated impacts of climate change, and many are embedded in the deep roots of gender inequality (Cannon 2002; Denton 2002b; Masika 2002; Nelson *et al.* 2002). Women's vulnerability to these impacts, however, is not shared uniformly, but rather is influenced by the powerful way in which other attributes, such as class, race, ethnicity, sexuality, and age, intersect with gender. Unsustainable global development and inequalities between nations also create conditions where certain groups of women carry different and disproportionate 'vulnerability bundles' (Cannon 1994). As the proceeding discussion underscores, many of the current and potential gender-differentiated impacts of climate change are intrinsically tied to women's material conditions and socially constructed gender practices and responsibilities.

Gender division of labour

As climate change unfolds, there is accumulating evidence that it is having an adverse impact on women's experiences within various forms of paid and unpaid labour. The added strain that climate change is imposing on women's work in agriculture illustrates this point. In most developing nations, women perform the majority of the labour related to subsistence farming. It has been estimated that in many countries women spend up to 16 hours a day in agricultural work and that approximately 60 per cent of the world's food production rests squarely on women's shoulders (Denton 2000; Morrow and Phillips 1999). In various parts of the world women are increasingly faced with the arduous challenge of cultivating arid land that has been damaged by rising temperatures and other forms of environmental degradation. This is a particularly salient problem for women in the Sahel region of Africa (Denton 2000; Masika 2002).

Women who have traditionally gathered and managed household biomass fuels and water are also vulnerable to the negative impacts of climate change. Due to land clearing, over-harvesting, and a host of other forms of environmental degradation, many women are forced to travel long distances in search of these resources. This task can harm women's bodies – given the weight of their loads and the distances they must now travel. It also reduces their opportunities for personal and social development as long hours are devoted to the collection process. Climate change is likely to enhance existing shortages of biomass fuels and water, thereby fostering conditions where women spend even more time in search of diminishing natural resources (Denton 2000; Easterling and Apps 2005; Masika 2002; IPCC 2001; United Nations Development Programme 2001).

Many believe that climate change will have a significant effect on women's care-giving activities. Around the world, women bear disproportionate responsibility for raising children and caring for the ill, disabled, and elderly (Enarson and Morrow 1998b). Climate change is predicted to generate a rise in various types of illnesses, which would intensify women's care-giving forms of labour. For example, researchers estimate that rising temperatures will facilitate an increase in certain types of infectious diseases – water-, food- and vector-borne – and this will magnify the amount of time and energy women devote to caring for the ill.

The extreme weather events tied to climate change are also likely to increase women's domestic and care-giving responsibilities. Around the world women are the primary care-givers within disaster-impacted families. In the wake of natural disasters women generally spend more time caring for family members and securing food, fuel and water (Enarson and Morrow 1998b; Nelson *et al.* 2002; United Nations Development Programme 2001). However, in these situations demands on some women expand much more dramatically than for others. As Enarson and Morrow (1998b: 2) remind us, 'When the dust clears or the water recedes, poor [women and families] around the world suffer the greatest losses and have access to the least public, as well as private, recovery assets.' Underscoring this point, when the water began to recede in New Orleans after Hurricane Katrina, it was largely poor, African-American women who were left to care for their families in the Superdome and plead for food and water (Enarson 2005).

Women and poverty

Throughout the world, women are disproportionately living in poverty. According to the United Nations (2000), women account for the majority of the 1.5 billion people who currently live on one dollar or less a day. The poverty that women endure, which arises from the complex interplay of gender inequality with other forms of oppression, is considered to have a profound impact on their capacity to cope with and recover from the impacts of climate change. Many women face the vagaries of climate change from the starting point of acute need and limited resources; this makes them more dependent on disaster relief and compromises their access to medical care, food, and physical protection. As Fothergill (1998: 23) emphasises, '[Women's] lack of economic power in so called "normal" times has serious ramifications in a disaster situation.'

Since women are in general poorer than men and many engage in livelihoods that are most threatened by climate change (e.g. agriculture, catching fish), it is likely that women's poverty will be compounded by rising surface and ocean temperatures (Easterling and Apps 2005; Francisco 2003). The IPCC (2001) has warned that climate change is likely to accentuate gaps between the world's rich and poor, and women are already among the poorest (Denton 2000).

As this brief review has shown, gender is not incidental to climate change. The symbiosis of climate change and gender inequality places women literally 'in the eye of the storm', and exposes them to an array of risks and hazards – which includes increased levels of vulnerability to violence, as the following section demonstrates.

Violence against women after climate-related natural disasters

It is increasingly clear that much can be gleaned from studies of gender issues within disaster science and environmental management (Masika 2002). Feminists writing in these areas have documented increases in reported levels of violence against women in post-disaster communities (Enarson 2006). As their research suggests, the predicted rise in natural disasters tied to climate change is likely to be correlated with increases in violence against women within the regions that experience extreme weather events (Enarson 2006; Fordam 2003; Marshall 2005; Wilson *et al.* 1998).

However, like so many issues tied to gender inequality, the research addressing violence against women after natural disasters is far from complete. Many important questions remain largely unanswered. For example, most studies have relied on data from police departments, court records, evacuation centres and battered women's shelters – only a small number have entailed direct surveys of men and women after natural disasters. In turn, much more needs to be known about how factors such as socio-economic status and access to resources affect women's vulnerability to violence after disaster events – particularly those who may be more isolated such as women in poverty, refugees, single mothers, widows, and disabled women (Enarson 1999; Fothergill 1999). Finally, many studies may significantly underestimate levels of violence against women. It is very hard to measure this violence due to the extent of population dislocation and changes in law enforcement resources and priorities after disasters (Morrow and Enarson 1996). However incomplete, though, the existing research sheds light on a gender-differentiated vulnerability that women face in the wake of natural disasters. It serves as fair warning to the discipline of criminology that climate change, and its gender-differentiated impacts, will be an increasingly important area for research.

In this section I summarise various studies and agency reports that examine violence against women during and after three types of natural disasters: hurricanes, floods, and drought. Although this violence may be heightened by such factors as increased levels of stress, depression and anxiety among men and shortages of housing, they are not a sufficient condition to initiate it. At the core of this behaviour is masculine entitlement to violence – the idea that it is legitimate for men to solve 'problems' though violence (Connell and Messerschmidt 2005; Messerschmidt 1997).

Hurricanes

As noted, over the last three decades there has been a significant increase in the strength and duration of hurricanes (Webster *et al.* 2005). In the wake of two very powerful hurricanes in this time period, Hurricane Andrew in 1992 and Hurricane Mitch in 1998, various researchers collected data on women's experiences with violence.[6] Their studies suggest that in the year following both hurricanes it is very probable that violence against women increased in the regions they damaged.

Hurricane Andrew
In August 1992, Hurricane Andrew spun through Louisiana and the southern part of Dade County, Florida, killing 15 people. It caused $30 billion in damages, destroyed over 49,000 homes, and displaced 250,000 people. The flora and fauna in southern Dade County were also ravaged. For example, approximately one-third of the coral reefs of Biscayne Bay National Park were severely denigrated. At the time, Andrew was only the third Category 5 hurricane to hit the United States, and up until Hurricane Katrina, was the costliest (*St Petersburg Times* 2002). Low-income, single mothers were among those most severely impacted by Andrew as the majority of public housing in Dade County was destroyed and the government was slow to repair

and rebuild these units. Fully two years after the storm only 20 per cent had been rebuilt – leaving many poor women in crowded apartments and small FEMA trailers for years (Enarson and Morrow 1997).

By most accounts, levels of violence against women rose in Dade County after Hurricane Andrew (Wilson *et al.* 1998). Six months after the disaster, Miami's Helpline experienced a 50 per cent increase in spousal abuse calls.[7] This support service had been providing counselling and referral information to woman abuse victims for over 20 years, but the number of calls from battered women after Hurricane Andrew was unrivalled in the agency's history. Dade County's domestic violence programmes reacted by providing free support groups for women and holding public forums about domestic violence (Laudisio 1993).

Various reports generated by the Dade County criminal justice system also provide evidence that violence against women probably increased after Hurricane Andrew. Court records reveal that in 1992 spousal abuse cases in the Dade Circuit Court were 98 per cent higher than the previous year (*Miami Herald* 1993). In turn, the battered women's shelter in South Dade was forced to add extra staff to address the increased demand (Enarson and Morrow 1997; Wilson *et al.* 1998).

Hurricane Mitch
Hurricane Mitch, the fifth most powerful Atlantic hurricane of the twentieth century, swept through Nicaragua and Honduras in October 1998. The disaster affected 3.5 million people and left 18,000 dead or, by official count, 'disappeared'. It was one of the worst disasters to hit Central America in over 200 years (Bradshaw 2001). In Nicaragua, the hurricane directly impacted approximately 22 per cent of the population; many farmers that subsist from one growing season to the next lost everything (Metoyer 2001). In response to the crisis, the Civil Coordinator for Emergency Reconstruction (CCER) was established as a coalition of 350 national NGOs and various social justice organisations (Bradshaw 2001).

Among its many tasks, CCER began to study the needs of Nicaraguans through large-scale studies. The first piece of research, conducted in February 1999, surveyed 10,500 households in 16 of the most heavily damaged municipalities. The findings demonstrated that women were affected by the hurricane in very gender specific ways, and highlighted the fact that many believed violence against women had escalated. One in four women (N=27 per cent) told the surveyors that woman battering had increased in families within their community after the hurricane; 21 per cent of the men also expressed this belief. Almost a third of the community leaders (68 per cent of whom were men) felt that woman battering had increased, as did 42 per cent of the mayors (46 men and two women) (CCER 1999; Enarson 2006).

Writing on behalf of the Word Bank, Delaney and Shrader (2000: 39) provide additional information about violence against women after Hurricane Mitch. They argue that it increased, but do not include any statistical information in their report to support this claim. They note, however, that some temporary shelters 'reported an increase in sexual violence as well as coerced prostitution among adolescent girls'.

Floods

In floods, as Dobson (1994) has stated, human relationships are laid bare – their strengths and weaknesses come into sharp focus. Violence against women is one of the weaknesses floods expose, as research from the 1993 Missouri Flood and the 1997 Grand Forks Flood indicates. After the water receded, data emerged suggesting that violence against women had probably risen in the communities that had endured flooding.

1993 Missouri Flood

Huge, costly, and devastating flooding across Missouri occurred during the summer of 1993. This disaster was part of the largest and most significant flood event ever to occur in the United States. Between April and October of that year over 600 rivers in the Midwest passed their flood stage – producing 50 flood deaths and creating damages in excess of $15 billion. Extreme weather and hydrological conditions led to the flooding. The Midwest had experienced a very wet autumn in 1992 that created above normal levels of soil moisture, and in many parts of the region this was followed by several feet of rain during the spring and summer of 1993. In St Louis, Missouri, where the Mississippi, Missouri, and Illinois Rivers meet, rivers were 20 feet above flood stage for over one hundred days (National Weather Service 2006).

Data from battered women's shelters across Missouri indicate that women may have experienced greater levels of violence following the flooding. The average state turn-away rate at the battered women's shelters in the aftermath of the flooding was 111 per cent higher than during the corresponding months in 1992.[8] In an effort to address the increased demand for services, the Missouri Coalition Against Domestic Violence modified an existing federal grant so that it could provide extra funding to 35 flood-affected domestic violence programmes. These programmes expected to shelter an estimated 660 victims of domestic violence (220 women and 440 children) in the twelve months after the flood but ended up housing approximately 3,400 victims, which was 400 per cent higher than anticipated (Constance and Coble 1995; Enarson 1999).

1997 Grand Forks Flood

In April 1997, after a winter of extreme blizzards, the Red River crested at 54 feet and flooded the city of Grand Forks, North Dakota. The city was particularly vulnerable to flooding as it sits on an ancient lakebed that now serves as a flood plain. Approximately 60,000 residents were evacuated and 90 per cent of the city was severely damaged. This flood event ranks as one of the worst natural disasters in US history (Fothergill 1999).

Approximately six months after the flooding, researchers at the University of North Dakota conducted a cross-sectional, random survey of 140 adults to assess whether domestic violence had increased in Grand Forks. It had. They found a statistically significant increase in violence against women after the flood event. Not surprisingly, their findings indicate that the perpetrators were most likely to be men who felt they had limited emotional support from friends and family, had values more approving of violence and domination over women, and had previously abused a woman. Income did not explain any of the variance in post-flood violence (Clemens et al. 1999).

Agency reports also signal that there may have been heightened levels of violence against women after the flooding. For example, an additional 18 per cent more protection orders were filed in August 1997 than in August 1996. Concomitantly, the Grand Forks Community Violence Intervention Center received more crisis calls after the flooding. Their year-end report indicates they experienced a 21 per cent increase in crisis calls and a 59 per cent increase in counselling of on-going clients over the previous year (Enarson 1999).

Droughts

Droughts can pose significant threats to food security, water resources and hydroelectricity production (Dore 2005). In some regions of the world, droughts are also an engendering condition for wars and violent conflicts (Homer-Dixon 1994; Johnson 2003). Although the factors driving the current civil war in Sudan are complex and multifaceted, droughts have played a role in this conflict. They have fostered large-scale migration that has evolved into violent conflicts between groups over agricultural land and water. As such, the droughts that have plagued Sudan over the last three decades have an intrinsic link to the increased levels of violence women have experienced during the civil war, which erupted in 1983 (Johnson 2003; Lacey 2004; Amnesty International 2004).

Drought conditions, Sudan, and the civil war
Since the mid-1970s, Sudan has endured a series of life threatening, crippling droughts. The devastating drought in 1984/85, which was one of the most severe in Sudan's history, killed thousands and fostered malnutrition among 1.3 million people. This crisis was followed by droughts in 1989, 1990, 1997, 2000, and 2004. The territory of Darfur has been particularly hard hit. Over the last two decades the mean annual average rainfall has dropped by 64 per cent. In northern Darfur, which is situated at the edge of the Sahara desert, rain has been exceptionally erratic since the 1980s and this has led to significant reductions in agricultural productivity. Well over 90 per cent of the population in this area experience food insecurity (Intermediate Technology Development Group 2006).

As a result of extended drought in Sudan over the last three decades, tens of thousands of semi-nomadic pastoralists from northern Darfur and Chad have moved south into the central farming belt of Darfur in search of land and water. The migration started in the mid-1970s, but conflict soon followed. Battles over land developed between the migrant pastoralists, who are largely Arab, and sedentary agriculturalist groups, who are largely African. By 1989 over 5,000 agriculturalists had been killed and 40,000 had lost their homes during conflicts with pastoralists who were trying to secure orchards, farms, and fields (Johnson 2003).

The conflict over land in Darfur remains unresolved, and is now interwoven with what many identify as government-sponsored genocide. Arab militia called the Janjawid, who are thought to be supported by the government, are killing African farmers and seizing their land. What is happening in Darfur, however, is only one part of an exceptionally complex crisis. It is not simply a war between north and south, Muslim and Christian, Arab against African (Nasong'o and Murunga 2005). Nonetheless, it is clear that the large, drought-induced migrations that have occurred in Sudan over the last several decades have significantly configured this war and that violence against women is being used as a weapon during the conflict (Johnson 2003; Lacey 2004).

Violence against Sudanese women: a weapon of war

The decades-old civil war in Sudan has led to the deaths of millions of people. Since the outbreak of intense fighting in Darfur in 2003, well over 180,000 have been killed in that region alone. Violence against women is part of the suffering and horror of war-torn Sudan. Reports from humanitarian organisations and UN agencies indicate that Sudanese women are being beaten and raped during armed conflict, while fleeing from conflict, and in refugee camps (*The Lancet* 2004).

In 2004, Amnesty International delegates travelled to Chad and interviewed Sudanese men and women in three UN refugee camps about violence against women in Darfur. Although many women were reluctant to talk about their experiences, the delegates were able to obtain over 100 personal testimonies about rapes that had occurred within the context of conflict in Darfur. These accounts came from rape victims as well as from those who had witnessed rapes. The delegates were also able to collect the names of over 250 women who had been raped during fighting. Based on this study and other pieces of evidence, both Amnesty International and the UN High Commissioner for Refugees assert that rape and other forms of gender-based war crimes are widespread in Sudan, and may possibly be systematic (Amnesty International 2004).

Many Sudanese women who have fled armed conflict also run directly into a new peril: rape and other forms of violence within refugee camps. Studies indicate that refugee camps can be very dangerous places for women (Olsen and Scharffscher 2004). A United Nations study of rape in refugee camps in Kenya reported that these crimes were occurring 75 times more often than would be expected in a community of 100,000 (Off Our Backs 1999). A recent report by Médecins Sans Frontières indicates that refugee camps in Sudan are also settings where women are at increased vulnerability to rape. In this report they document 500 rapes over a four-month period in the Kalma refugee camp, and also note that women who venture beyond this camp in search of firewood also run the risk of being raped (Dealey and Abeche 2005).

Conclusion

The research on violence against women after slow and sudden-onset natural disasters serves as a poignant reminder of the fact that while the environment, infrastructures and buildings are damaged during such events, women are also subjected to a great deal of harm

(Morrow and Enarson 1996). Life for many women after natural disasters is punctuated by violence, and this fact needs to be more deeply integrated into discussions about climate change as well as criminological perspectives on violence against women.

Although women face an array of gender-differentiated vulnerabilities during and after natural disasters, they also play an important role in rescue and relief initiatives in disaster-impacted communities. All too often though, the media portrays women simply as tearful and exhausted mothers during such events. They fail to highlight the proactive and instrumental work that women perform as 'mitigators, preparers, rescuers, care-givers, sustainers, and rebuilders' (Enarson and Morrow 1998b: 6). After Hurricane Andrew, for example, women in Florida formed a coalition to redirect recovery funds away from business interests and were able to successfully funnel more money into the immediate health and social needs of women and children (Enarson and Morrow 1998b).

Women have also shown remarkable levels of resilience and resourcefulness in their responses to climate change. The work of Wangari Maathai is a poignant example of these efforts. In 2004 she won the Nobel Peace Prize for her work on the reforestation of Kenya, which serves as an important carbon dioxide offset initiative. She was also instrumental in forming the Green Belt Movement that has now been launched in many countries in Africa; it is dedicated to revitalising flora and fauna (Frangsmyr 2005). Women have also established an array of programmes that promote sustainable energy development. To that end, the Global Network on Gender and Sustainable Energy (ENERGIA) was formed in 1995 after the Fourth United Nations Conference on Women. This organisation is involved in capacity-building activities such as training, site visits, and energy needs assessments (Makhabane 2002).

As we spiral forward into climate change, however, more research needs to be done to develop a better understanding of its bearing on women, particularly on their vulnerability to violence. Climate change has typically been seen as a technical problem that will be solved through technical solutions. It must also be understood as a social process that is situated within the context of unequal distributions of power and privilege. My hope is that this chapter will stimulate others to explore the bearing of climate change on violence against women.[9]

Notes

1   Following the United Nations Framework Convention on Climate Change (UNFCC), I define climate change in this chapter as 'a change of climate which is attributable directly or indirectly to human activity that alters the composition of the global atmosphere and which is in addition to natural climate variability observed over comparable time periods' (FCCC/CP/1997/7 at www.unfcc.de).

2   The Intergovernmental Panel on Climate Change report (2001) is an assessment of the science of climate change. It was prepared by 122 scientists and includes documents written by an additional 515 scientists; 420 scientists reviewed the draft report. Many consider it to be the most thorough and credible summary of climate change; it is the largest and most rigorously peer-reviewed scientific collaboration in history. It is relied on rather extensively throughout this chapter.

3   This process releases several different types of global warming gases, including water vapour.

4   The common name for tropical cyclones is hurricanes (van Aalst 2006). There is significant debate in the literature about the bearing of climate change on hurricane intensity and duration. For example, Piekle et al. (2005) argue that the observed changes in hurricane intensity over the last 30 years are within the range of observed variability over the last one hundred years.

5   I selected to write about glacial flooding as glaciers are thought to be excellent barometers of climate change given that they do not respond to year-to-year climate variability. They are thought to be the 'canary in the mine' for climate change (Hall and Fagre 2003).

6   Research on violence against women after Hurricane Katrina was not available at the time of this publication. Enarson (2006: 4) notes, 'in the first four months after the US Gulf Coast hurricanes, 38 rape cases were reported to women's shelters' services that initiated documentation projects to capture sexual assaults of disaster-displaced women.'

7   These studies use the term 'spouse abuse', but appear to be addressing women abused by a husband or male cohabiter.

8   It may be that larger numbers of women used the shelters as their friends and family members who traditionally had provided shelter may have lost their housing in the flood. However, it could also be the case that some women were forced to return to unsafe living conditions with violent partners (Enarson 1999).

9   For their thoughtful review of this chapter I would like to thank Dr Marcia Cohen, Dr Jim Messerschmidt, Dr Fred Padula, Dr Deb van den Hoondaard, and Dr Travis Wagner.

References

Aalst, M. (2006) 'The Impacts of Climate Change on the Risk of Natural Disasters', *Disasters*, 30 (1): 5–18.

Amnesty International (2004) 'Rape as a Weapon of War: Sexual Violence and its Consequences' (online). Available from: www.amnestyusa/refugee (cited 4 April 2006).

Arctic Council (2005) *Arctic Climate Impact Assessment*. Cambridge: Cambridge University Press.

Barnett, T., Pierce, D., AchutaRao, K., Gleckler, P., Santer, B., Gregory, J. and Washington, W. (2005) 'Penetration of Human-Induced Warming into the World's Oceans' (online). Available from: www.sciencemag.org/cgi/content/full/1112418/DC1 (cited 2 March 2006).

Bradshaw, S. (2001) 'Reconstructing Roles and Relations: Women's Participation in Reconstruction in Post-Mitch Nicaragua', *Gender and Development*, 9 (3): 79–87.

Breshears, D., Cobb, N., Rich, P., Price, K., Allen, C., Balice, R., Romme, W., Kastens, J., Floyd, M., Belnap, J., Anderson, J., Meyers, O., and Meyer, C. (2005), 'Regional Vegetation Die-Off in Response to Global-Change-Type Drought', *PNAS*, 102 (42): 15144–15148.

Brook, E. (2005) 'Tiny Bubbles Tell All', *Science*, 310: 1285–1286.

Blaikie, P., Cannon, T., Davis, I. and Wisner, B. (1994) *At Risk: Natural Hazards, People's Vulnerability, and Disaster*. London: Routledge.

Cannon, T. (1994) 'Vulnerabilities Analysis and the Explanation of Natural Disasters', in A. Varely (ed.) *Disasters, Development, and Environment*, pp. 13–30. London: Belhaven Press.

Cannon, T. (2002) 'Gender and Climate Hazards in Bangladesh', in R. Masika (ed) *Gender, Development, and Climate Change*, pp. 45–50. Oxford: Oxfam.

CCER (1999) 'Social Audit for Emergency and Reconstruction, Phase 1 – April', Coordinadora Civil para la Emergencia y la Reconstruccion (CCER). Managua, Nicaragua.

Clemens, P., Hietala, J., Rytter, M., Schmidt, R. and Reese, J. (1999) 'Risk of Domestic Violence after Flood Impact: Effects of Social Support, Age, and History on Domestic Violence', *Applied Behavioral Science Review*, 7 (2): 199–206.

Collier, M and Webb, R. (2002) *Floods, Droughts, and Climate Change*. Tucson: The University of Arizona Press.

Connell, R. and Messerschmidt, J. (2005) 'Hegemonic Masculinity: Rethinking the Concept', *Gender and Society*, 19 (6): 829–859.

Constance, V. and Coble, C. (1995) *The Missouri Model: The Efficacy of Funding Domestic Violence Programs as Long-Term Disaster Recovery*. Jefferson City, MO: Missouri Coalition Against Domestic Violence.

Cyranoski, D. (2005) 'The Long-Range Forecast', *Nature*, 438 (17): 275–276.

Dai, A., Trenberth, K. and Quan, T. (2004) 'A Global Dataset of Palmer Drought Severity Index for 1870–2002: Relationship with Soil Moisture and Effects of Surface Warming', 5, *Journal of Hydrometeorology*: 1117–1130.

Dankelman, I. (2002) 'Climate Change: Learning from Gender Analysis and Women's Experiences of Organizing for Sustainable Development', in R. Masika (ed.), *Gender, Development, and Climate Change*, pp. 21–29. Basingstoke, England: Oxfam.

Dealey, S. and Abeche, K. (2005) 'Who Speaks for Her? Rape is the Weapon of Choice in Darfur, but Sudan's Government Doesn't Want to Help'. *The UN Refugee Agency* (online). Available from: http://www.unrefugees. org/archives.sfm?ID=3279&catID=2 (April 1 cited 2006).

Delaney, P. and Shrader, E. (2000) 'Gender and Post-Hurricane Reconstruction: The Case of Hurricane Mitch in Honduras and Nicaragua' (online). Available from: http://gdnonline.org/wot_papers.htm (cited 8 April 2006).

Denton, R. (2000) 'Gendered Impacts of Climate Change – A Human Security Dimension', *Energia*, 3 (3): 13–14.

Denton, R. (2002a) 'Climate Change Vulnerability: Impacts, and Adaptation: Why Does Gender Matter?', *Gender and Development*, 10 (2): 10–20.

Denton, R. (2002b) 'Climate Change Vulnerability, Impacts, and Adaptation: Why Does Gender Matter?', in R. Masika (ed.), *Gender, Development, and Climate Change*, pp. 10–20. Oxford: Oxfam.

Dobson, N. (1994) 'From Under the Mud-Pack: Women and the Charleville Floods', *The Australian Journal of Disaster Management*, 9 (2): 11–13.

Dore, M. (2005) 'Climate Change and Changes in Global Precipitation Patterns: What Do We Know?', *Environment International*, 31 (8): 1167–1181.

Easterling, W. and Apps, M. (2005) 'Assessing the Consequences of Climate Change for Food and Forest Resources: A View from the ICCP', *Climate Change*, 70, pp. 165–189.

Emanuel, K. (2005a) 'Increasing Destructiveness of Tropical Cyclones Over the Past 30 Years', *Nature*, 436(4): 686–688.

Emanuel, K. (2005b) *Divine Wind: The History of Hurricanes*. Oxford: Oxford University Press.

Enarson, E. and Morrow, B. (1997) 'A Gendered Perspective: The Voices of Women', in W. Peacock, B. Morrow and H. Gladwin (eds), *Hurricane Andrew: Ethnicity, Gender, and the Sociology of Disasters* pp. 116–140. London: Routledge.

Enarson, E. and Morrow, B. (eds) (1998a) *The Gendered Terrain of Disaster*. Westport, Connecticut: Praeger.

Enarson, E. and Morrow, B. (1998b) 'Why Gender? Why Women? An Introduction to Women and Disaster', in E. Enarson and B. Morrow (eds), *The Gendered Terrain of Disaster*. Westport, Connecticut: Praeger.

Enarson, E. (1999) 'Violence Against Women in Disasters', *Violence Against Women*, 5 (7): pp. 742–768.

Enarson, E. (2005) 'Women and Girls Last: Averting the Second Post-Katrina Disaster' (online). Available from: http://understandingkatrina.ssrc.org/Enarson/pf/ (5 December cited 2005).

Enarson, E. (2006) 'Violence Against Women in Disasters' (online). Available from: http://gdnonline.org/wot_papers.htm (cited 4 August 2006).

Epstein, P. (2005) 'Climate Change and Human Health', *The New England Journal of Medicine*, 353(14): 1433–1436.

Fordam, M. (2003) 'Gender, Disaster and Development', in M. Pelling (ed.) *Natural Disasters and Development in a Globalizing World* pp. 57–74. London: Routledge.

Fordam, M. and Ketteridge, A. (1998) 'Men Must Work and Women Must Weep', in E. Enarson and B. Morrow (eds), *The Gendered Terrain of Disaster*, pp. 81–94. Westport, Connecticut: Praeger.

Fothergill, A. (1998) 'The Neglect of Gender in Disaster Work: An Overview of the Literature', in E. Enarson and B. Morrow (eds), *The Gendered Terrain of Disaster*, pp. 11–25. Westport, Connecticut: Praeger.

Fothergill, A. (1999) 'An Exploratory Study of Women Battering in the Grand Forks Flood Disaster: Implications for Community Responses and Policies', *International Journal of Mass Emergencies and Disasters*, 17 (1): 79–98.

Frasier, P., Belton, L., Hooten, E., Campbell, M., DeVellis, B., Benedict, S., Carrillo, C., Gonzalez, P., Kelsey, K. and Meier, A. (2004) 'Disaster Down East: Using Participatory Action Research to Explore Intimate Partner Violence in Northern Carolina', *Health Education and Behavior*, 31 (4): 69–84.

Frangsmyr, T. (2005) *The Nobel Prizes in 2004.* Stockholm: Nobel Foundation.

Francisco, E. (2003) 'Warming Takes Toll on Tanganyika', *Science Now*, 8 (15): 1–2.

Geographical (2005) 'Life in a Warmer World', *Geographical Dossier*, 12 (77): 36–37.

Hall, M. and Fagre, D. (2003) 'Model Climate-Induced Glacier Change in Glacier National Park, 1850–2100', *Bioscience*, 53 (2): 131–141.

Henson, R. (2005) 'The Heat Was On in 2005', *Nature*, 438 (7071): 1062.

Homer-Dixon, T. (1994) 'Environmental Scarcities and Violent Conflict', *International Security*, 19 (1): 5–40.

Hulme, M. (2002) 'Climate Change: A Sober Assessment', in T. Gillard, M. Hulme, P. Sammonds, C. Secrett, and J. Morris (eds), *Nature's Revenge? Hurricanes, Floods and Climate Change* pp. 1–17. Abingdon, England: Hodder & Stoughton.

IFRC (International Federation of Red Cross and Red Crescent Societies) (2004) 'Heat Waves, the Developed World's Hidden Disaster', *World Disasters Report 2004*. Geneva: IFRC.

Intermediate Technology Development Group (ITDG) (2006) 'Challenging Climate Change: Terracing Technology in Darfur' (online). Available from: http://itdg.org/id=s6_cresent (cited 4 April 2006).

Jensen, M. (2004) 'Climate Warming Shakes up Species', *Bioscience*, 54 (8): 722–729.

Johnson, D. (2003) *The Root Causes of Sudan's Civil Wars*. Oxford: James Currey.

Klinenberg, E. (2002) *Heat Wave: A Social Autopsy of Disaster in Chicago*. Chicago: University of Chicago Press.

Knutson, T. and Tuleya, R. (1999) 'Increased Hurricane Intensities with CO_2-induced Warming as Simulated using the GFDL Hurricane Prediction System', *Climate Dynamics*, 15: 503–519.

Knutson, T. and Tuleya, R. (2004) 'Impact of CO_2 Induced Warming on Simulated Hurricane Intensity and Precipitation: Sensitivity to the Choice of Climate Model and Convective Paramerization', *Journal of Climate*, 17: 3477–3495.

Lacey. M. (2004) 'In Sudan, Militiamen on Horses Uproot Millions', *The New York Times*, Tuesday 4 May, A1–A10.

Laudisio, G. (1993) 'Disaster Aftermath: Redefining Response – Hurricane Andrew's Impact on I & R', *Alliance of Information and Referral Systems*, 15: 13–32.

Lempinen, E. and Pinholster, G. (2004) 'Facing Global Warming', *Science*, 304 (5679): 1921–1922.

Liniger, H., Weingartner, R. and Grosjean, M. (1998) *Mountains of the World: Water Towers for the 21st Century*. Switzerland: Paul Haupt.

Makhabane, T. (2002) 'Promoting the Role of Women in Sustainable Energy Development in Africa: Networking and Capacity-Building', in R. Masika (ed.), *Gender, Development, and Climate Change* pp. 84–91 Oxford: Oxfam.

Marshall, L. (2005) 'Were Women Raped in New Orleans? Addressing the Human Rights of Women in Times of Crisis', *Off Our Backs*, 35 (9/10): 14–15.

Morrow, B. and Phillips, B. (1999) 'What's Gender "Got to Do With It"?', *International Journal of Mass Emergencies and Disasters*, 17 (1): 5–11.

Masika, R. (ed.) (2002) *Gender, Development, and Climate Change*. Oxford: Oxfam.

McCarthy, J. and McKenna, M. (2000) 'How the Earth's Ice is Changing', *Environment*, 42 (10): 8–19.

McDowell, N. (2002) 'Melting Ice Triggers Himalayan Flood Warning', *Nature*, 416 (25): 776.

McFarling, U. (2005) 'Core evidence that humans affect climate change', *Los Angeles Times*, 25 November: A24.

Meehl, G. and Tebaldi, C. (2004) 'More Intense, More Frequent, and Longer Lasting Heat Waves in the 21st Century', *Science*, 305 (5686): 994–997.

Messerschmidt, J. (1997) *Crime as Structured Action: Gender, Race, Class and Crime in the Making*. Thousand Oaks, California: Sage.

Miami Herald (1993) 'Andrew by the numbers', 22 August: 10D.

Milly, P., Wetherald, R., Dunne, O. and Delworth, T. (2002) 'Increasing Risk of Flood in a Changing World', *Nature*, 415 (6871): 514–517.

Metoyer, C. (2001) 'Hurricane Mitch, Aleman, and Other Disasters for Women in Nicaragua', *International Studies Perspectives*, 2: 401–415.

Morrow, B. and Enarson, E. (1996) 'Hurricane Andrew Through Women's Eyes: Issues and Recommendations', *International Journal of Mass Emergencies and Disasters*, 14 (1): 5–22.

Nasong'o, S. and Murunga, G. (2005) 'Lack of Consensus on Constitutive Fundamentals: Roots of the Sudanese Civil War and Prospect for Settlement', *African and Asian Studies*, 4 (1–2): 51–82.

National Weather Service (2006) 'The Great USA Flood of 1993' (online). Available from: www.nwrfc.noaa.gov/floods/papers/oh_2/great.htm (cited: 6 April 2006).

Nelson, V., Meadows, K., Cannon, T., Morton, J. and Martin, A. (2002) 'Uncertain Predictions, Invisible Impacts, and the Need to Mainstream Gender in Climate Change Adaptations', in R. Masika (ed.) *Gender, Development, and Climate Change*, pp. 51–59 Oxford: Oxfam.

Off Our Backs (1999) 'Somali Refugees: Rape in the Camps', *Off Our Backs*, 29 (7): 3.

Olsen, O. and Scharffscher, K. (2004) 'Rape in Refugee Camps as Organizational Failures', *International Journal of Human Rights*, 8 (4): 377–397.

Otto-Bliesner, B., Marshall, S., Overpeck, J., Miller, G., Hu, A. and CAPE Interglacial Project Members (2006) 'Simulating Arctic Climate Warmth and Icefield Retreat in the Last Interglaciation', *Nature*, 311 (5768) 1751–1753.

Overpeck, J., Otto-Bliesner, B., Gifford, M., Miller, G., Muhs, D., Alley, R. and Kiehl, J. (2006) 'Paleoclimatic Evidence for Future Ice-Sheet Instability and Rapid Sea-Level Rise', *Science*, 311 (5768): 1747–1750.

Parks, B. and Roberts, J. (2006) 'Globalization, Vulnerability to Climate Change, and Perceived Injustice', *Society and Natural Resources*, 19: 337–355.

Pielke, R., Landsea, C., Mayfield, M., Laver, J. and Pash, R. (2005) 'Hurricanes and Global Warming', *Bulletin of American Meteorological Society*, 86 (11): 1571–1575.

Salinger, M. (2005) 'Climate Variability and Change: Past, Present, and Future – An Overview', *Climate Change*, 70 (1/2): 9–29.

Schar, C., Vidale, P., Luthi, D., Frei, C., Haberli, C., Linger, M. and Appenzeller, C. (2004) 'The Role of Increasing Temperature Variability in European Summer Waves', *Nature*, 427 (22): 332–336.

Sci-Tech Today (2005) 'Ocean Warming Supports Model' (online). Available from: www.scie-tech-today.com/story (cited 6 March 2006).

Siegenthaler, U., Stocker, T., Monnin, E., Luthi, D., Schwander, J., Stauffer, B., Raynaud, D., Barnola, J., Fischer, H., Masson-Delmotte, V. and Jouzel, J. (2005) 'Stable Carbon Cycle–Climate Relationship During the Late Pleistocene', *Science*, 310: 1313–1317.

Skutsch, M. (2002) 'Protocols, Treaties, and Action: The "Climate Change Process" Viewed through Gender Spectacles', in R. Masika (ed.) *Gender, Development, and Climate Change*, pp. 30–39 Oxford: Oxfam.

Spear, S. (2003) 'Refugees Escape Ravages of Climate Change', *Journal of Environmental Health*, 66 (1): 38–39.

Spray, S. and McGlothlin, K. (2002) *Global Climate Change.* Lanham: Rowman and Littlefield Publishers, Inc.

St. Petersburg Times (2002) 'Hurricane Andrew after the storm: Ten years later' (online). Available from: http://www.sptimes.com/2002/webspecials02/andrew (cited 4 April 2006).

Stott, P., Stone, D. and Allen, M. (2004) 'Human Contribution to the European Heat Wave of 2003', *Nature,* 432 (2): 610–613.

Trenberth, K., Aiguo, D., Rasmussen, R. and Parsons, D. (2003) 'The Changing Character of Precipitation', *Bulletin of the American Meteorological Society,* 84 (9): 1205–1217.

The Lancet (2004) 'Sudan and its New Weapon of War', *The Lancet,* 364: 390.

Union of Concerned Scientists (2005) 'Global Warming Lending Strength to Hurricanes: Warmer Waters Fueling More Powerful Storms' (online). Available from: http://www.ucsusa.org/news/press_release/Global-Warming-Lending-Strength.html?print=t (cited 2 February 2006).

United Nations Framework Convention on Climate Change (1997) (online). Available from: www.unfcc.de. (cited 3 March 2006).

United Nations (2000) 'Feminization of Poverty' (online). Available from: http://www.un.org/womenwatch/daw/followup/session/pressit/fs1.htm (cited 22 April 2006).

United Nations Intergovernmental Panel on Climate Change (IPCC) (2001) *Climate Change 2001: The Scientific Basis.* Cambridge: Cambridge University Press.

United Nations Development Programme (2001) *Generating Opportunities: Case Studies on Energy and Women.* New York: United Nations.

United Nations Environmental Programme (UNEP) (2002) *Inventory of Glacial Lakes and Lake Outburst Floods, Monitoring and Early Warning System in the Hindu Kush–Himalayan Region* (online). Available from: http://www.rrcap.unep.org/issue/glof/

Wagner, C. (2004) 'Hotter Heat Waves Foreseen', *The Futurist,* November–December: 7–8.

Webster, P., Holland, G., Curry, J. and Chang, H. (2005) 'Changes in Tropical Cyclone Number, Duration, and Intensity in a Warming Environment', *Science,* 309: 184–186.

Wilson, E. (2002) *The Future of Life.* New York: Alfred Knopf.

Wilson, J., Phillips, B. and Neal, D. (1998) 'Domestic Violence After Disaster', in E. Enarson and B. Morrow (eds) *The Gendered Terrain of Disaster: Through Women's Eyes,* pp. 115–122 Westport, Connectituct: Praeger.

Woodruff, R. and McMichael, T. (2004) 'Climate Change and Human Health: All Affected, But Some More Than Others', *Social Alternatives,* 23: (4) 17–22.

Chapter 8

Crime, regulation and radioactive waste in the United Kingdom

Reece Walters

Introduction

Britain's programmes for the development of nuclear weaponry and energy emerged in the 1940s and 1950s. The race for international nuclear superiority dominated political debates with little regard for issues of pollution, contamination or waste removal. As Griffiths (1997: xi) argues, 'whilst the need for appropriate radioactive waste management and disposal arrangements was recognised, the topic lacked the glamorous appeal of the prestigious projects and took on something of the character of the Cinderella of the industry'.

Prime Minister Tony Blair has recently reignited the nuclear debate by stating that nuclear power was 'back on the agenda with a vengeance', suggesting that if his government was to shirk the long-term energy issue it would be 'a dereliction of duty' (BBC News 2006). Such comments have provoked widespread criticism during a time when the world remembers the tragedy at Chernobyl and near-disaster of Three Mile Island. These events serve to remind the energy-consuming world of the risks and costs associated with nuclear power and its toxic residue. With an estimated 80,000 cubic metres of solid radioactive waste currently in storage across the UK, the issue of waste disposal has become an ongoing political, environmental and economical concern (CoRWM 2005). Radical responses have been proposed, including the recently rejected options of radioactive waste disposal in space or at the bottom of the sea (BBC News 2005). The siting of radioactive waste disposal areas has been an issue of contestation and conflict across several nuclear active countries for some time (Solomon *et al.* 1987) and the safety of long-term disposal of radioactive waste both in the UK and abroad remains fraught with risks and uncertainties. While some risk management strategies may be politically palatable and based on persuasive scientific evidence, there are no guarantees against long-term environmental degradation (Uggla 2004).

In this chapter the regulation and administration of radioactive waste in Britain is examined and it is then argued that green criminology internationalises the domain of criminological discourse by focusing on actions that threaten the ongoing development and sustainability of the planet.

Eco-crime and radioactive waste

Eco-crime involves acts of 'environmental harm and ecological degradation. It is a term often used synonymously with "green crime" or "environmental crime"' (Walters 2005: 146). Situ and Emmons, (2000: 3) situate eco-crime within domestic and international legal frameworks, arguing that it is 'an unauthorised act or omission that violates the law and is therefore subject to criminal prosecution and criminal sanction'. Other definitions locate eco-crime within acts of environmental harm not necessarily covered in legal statute. For Westra (2004: 309) eco-crime is unprovoked aggression, 'committed in the pursuit of other goals and "necessities" such as economic advantage'. Westra's work extends the definition of eco-crime beyond ecological degradation to human health, global security and justice. She suggests that eco-crimes committed by governments and corporations in pursuit of free trade or progress are 'attacks on the human person' that deprive civilians (notably the poor) of the social, cultural and economic benefits of their environment. As a result, eco-crime is an act of violence and should be viewed as a human rights violation as citizens are deprived of freedoms and liberties. The diversity of subject matter covered under both international and national environmental law, and within notions of environmental harm, has necessitated the integration of diverse expertise and knowledges including criminology. Within criminological studies, debates about eco-crime have emerged within discourses on state and corporate crime or 'crimes of the powerful' and within developing debates of 'green and environmental criminology' (Lynch and Stretesky 2003). Moreover when eco-crime is contextualised within notions of harm or what Hillyard *et al.* (2004) refer to as 'zemiology', we observe the broadening of the criminological gaze beyond legal terrain to include discourses on risk, rights and regulation (South 1998).

Given the above, the links between eco-crime and radioactive waste are apparent. The range of risks associated with commercial enterprises in research, power production, telecommunications, medicine and pharmaceuticals as well as state activities in military defence and war, all utilise varying degrees of radioactive substances that produce waste. As a result, there is an ongoing emergence of illicit and harmful actions linked to such activities and the production of radioactive waste. The United Nations Interregional Crime Research Institute lists four international environmental crimes – one of which is 'dumping and illegal transport of various kinds of hazardous waste' (RIIA 2002: 5). Within international legal frameworks, the London Convention on the Prevention of Marine Pollution by Dumping of Wastes and Other Matter 1972 was the first significant international step in regulating and prohibiting the illegal disposal of waste. The London Convention is an international treaty with 81 nation signatories that aims to regulate the depositing of industrial waste, sewerage sludge, incinerated and dredged materials into marine environments. The disposal of radioactive waste in all its forms at sea is completely prohibited. Subsequent international laws such as the Basel Convention have imposed strict requirements on the transportation of hazardous substances and outlawed the trade and discharge of radioactive substances at sea or on land (Birnie and Boyle 2002). As a result, there is a growing body of international and environmental law identifying breaches, regulations and remedies dealing with radioactive waste.

Illegal actions involving radioactive waste – including the dumping of toxic waste at sea resulting from the above activities – have been widely documented (Ringius 2001). Parmentier (1999) identifies how nuclear and chemical industries in the US and Europe routinely burned or illegally dumped radioactive and toxic waste at sea as an alternative to the corporate-perceived view of 'impossible environmental regulations'. Moreover, the transportation and illegal trafficking of toxic waste in Italy is so widely acknowledged that an Italian dictionary has an entry for 'ecomafia' to describe organised criminal networks that profit from dumping or illegally disposing of commercial, industrial and radioactive waste (Legambiente 2003). In Russia, the dumping of radioactive waste at sea has been widely recognised and proven as common practice. Cochran *et al.* (1995) document that dozens of damaged submarine nuclear reactors and thousands of radioactive waste containers have been dumped by Russian authorities in the Barents and Kara Seas. Commercial Russian sailing vessels have also recently been reported to the International Atomic Energy Agency for transporting radioactive waste in substandard containers – which is both illegal and highly dangerous (Greenpeace 2005). The problems Russian authorities face are substantial as it has long been recognised that 50 years of nuclear technologies have produced an irreversible and unsolvable radioactive waste problem (Bridges and Bridges 1995). That said, the dumping of radioactive waste at sea is not the sole domain of Russian officials. In 2001, the Russian parliament amended domestic law permitting the importation of nuclear waste. As a result, the British nuclear industries were reported to be disposing of radioactive waste in Russia to avoid costly UK regulations (Environment News Service 2002). However, the UK is also responsible for radioactive dumping closer to home. In 2000, Greenpeace conducted independent research, involving remotely operated underwater cameras that identified 28,500 corroded barrels of radioactive waste rusting on the seabed of the Channel Islands. The waste was reportedly dumped by UK authorities and corporations between 1950–1963 in the Hurd Deep, a stretch of water 15 kilometres north-west of Cap de la Hage in France (Greenpeace 2000). Further evidence of the illegal dumping of radioactive pollution emerged in November 2005 when the Scotland Environment Protection Agency reported that Dalgety Bay contained more than 100 radioactive contaminated sites where the Ministry of Defence had dumped dismantled technology, mostly containing radium (Edwards 2005; Harvie 2005). This incident of UK marine pollution follows earlier allegations in 2005 that Dounreay, Britain's biggest nuclear research station, operated by the UK Atomic Energy Agency, had 'recklessly' released hundreds of thousands of radioactive particles into the environment and attempted to cover up the unlawful actions (Farquharson and Macaskill 2005). In addition, the UK Government's unsatisfactory record with radioactive waste regulation and management is highlighted by its pending prosecution by the European Commission in the European Court of Justice – the first-ever prosecution of a member state – for alleged failure to adhere to nuclear safety standards at Sellafield where 30 kilograms of deadly plutonium has been 'lost' and remains unaccounted for (Brown 2004; Jameson 2005).

The ocean floor has been a radioactive rubbish dump for decades. The International Atomic Energy Agency maintains a Global Inventory of Radioactive Wastes in the Marine Environment. In its report of 2001, the IAEA identified more that 4,500 GigaBequerels of corroding radioactive solids in oceans around the world that had either been 'lost or potentially released' (IAEA 2001). The widespread nature of radioactive dumping at sea and its devastating effects were made apparent after the tragic tsunami of early 2005. The United Nations Environment Programme identified that hundreds of illegally dumped barrels containing radioactive waste had washed up on the shores of Somalia causing infections, skin diseases and untold long-term cancers following the tsunami (UNEP 2005). Finally, in what could be termed 'radioactive environmental racism', the US-led invasion of Iraq has resulted in several Iraqi cities being exposed to radiation from depleted uranium weaponry at up to 2,000 times the normal level and US authorities have refused to clean up their 'waste of war', arguing that such toxic residue is not dangerous (Kirby 2003; Flounders 2003).

The above examples of eco-crime provide a brief overview of some of the illegal and harmful acts involving radioactive waste that have caused substantial environmental and human injury. Such acts require a criminological engagement that must transcend traditional disciplinary boundaries to include discourses on risk, rights and regulation. The following sections examine these three areas in relation to radioactive waste in the UK.

The UK and radioactive waste

Natural habitats and all living things are exposed to 'natural background radiation' through cosmic rays and gamma radiation. These naturally produced chemical processes contribute to the evolving dynamics of ecosystems that change over time (Arms 1994). However, radio toxicity produced through the energy release of radioactive decay raises serious problems for living matter. Radionuclides emit nuclear particles during atom transformation. This process of atom breakdown will eventually decay into stable and non-radioactive elements. However, the stabilisation of radionuclide atoms produces energy discharges and dangerous ionising substances that destroy surrounding organisms (House of Lords 1999).

Radioactive waste in Britain is classified into four categories including:

i) high level or heat-generating waste consisting of liquid nitric products from spent nuclear fuel;

ii) intermediate level waste, mainly metals but also organic compounds, generated during dismantling or reprocessing nuclear power plants;

iii) low level waste such as redundant metals and laboratory equipment – much of this waste accumulates from hospitals and research facilities;

iv) very low level waste which includes substances with very low levels of radioactivity (DEFRA 2005).

The 1981 Royal Commission on Environmental Pollution emphasised the importance of radioactive waste management through its 1976 sixth report (Flowers Report). Among other things it recommended that 'there should be no commitment to nuclear fission power until it has been demonstrated beyond reasonable doubt that a method exists to ensure the safe containment of long-lived, highly radioactive waste for the indefinite future'.

Emerging from the Flowers Report was a recommendation that the Department of the Environment should be responsible for radioactive waste management. As a result, the Radioactive Waste Advisory Committee was set up in 1978 as an independent group consisting of scientists and experienced professionals to advise government on issues of radioactive management. An important function of this multidisciplinary committee was to consider scientific evidence and social consensus for the development of radioactive waste management strategies.

In his history of radioactive regulation in the UK, Chandler (1997) points out that the regulatory and disposal systems for radioactive waste have 'struggled to keep pace with developments, and a major legacy of waste from the early years of the nuclear programme now awaits a final disposal route'. Radioactive wastes that have been produced in the UK since the 1940s are currently held in 30 different sites from Devonport in the south-west of England to Dounreay in the far north of Scotland. The waste is held in short-term storage and it is estimated that existing facilities may continue to operate for up to 50 years (CoRWM 2005: 5). However, decisions regarding long-term disposal must be made in order to safely discard radioactive wastes that remain active for thousands of years. Scientific knowledge has become a key ingredient in corporate and government practices representing, as Abell and Oxbrow (2001: 267) argue, 'the combination of explicit data and information to which is added tacit expert opinion, skills and experience to result in a valuable asset which can be used to make key decisions'. As a result, there is little democratisation in a process of risk assessment that favours political and economic interests. Within debates about radioactive waste disposal scientific views are often polarised by the competing interests of the energy industry and environmental groups and frequently blurred within politics (Papy 2003). Even so, as David Suzuki argues, the production of knowledge and scientific enquiry are becoming regulated by the vested interests of corporate entities; 'when once scientists sought answers to fundamental questions, they now seek venture-capital investors for biotech companies' (2001: 5). Indeed the Radioactive Waste Management Advisory Committee (RWMAC1989) questioned the objectivity within scientific studies, stating that 'scientists can and do feed in other more subjective interests into their own particular issues' (pp. 7–8).

The ecological risks and dangers associated with radioactive substances have been debated at length in scientific studies. Some recent studies have warned of the increasing and apparent dangers of soil migration and plant contamination in radioactive polluted water tables (Ashworth and Shaw 2005). Others have identified the potentially deleterious effects of future glaciation and deglaciation on the deep geological disposal repositories of nuclear waste (Chan et al. 2005), as well as the importance of controlling underground temperatures (see Kamei 2005). Tests are constantly being conducted to analyse neutron absorption on boron-alloyed stainless sheets used as shielding for radioactive waste disposal and to find ways to strengthen and secure waste shielding (Zawsky et al. 2004). Finally, emerging scientific work identifies deep geological disposal as the preferred disposal option, although it remains both dangerous and short term (Papay 2003).

While recognising the difficulties of scientific certainty, the RWMAC asserted the importance of obtaining scientific consensus for decision-making regarding waste disposal. Consensus was defined as 'the achievement of sufficient concurrence of view at various stages to legitimise a decision to proceed with a particular course of action' (RWMAC 1999: 5). Indeed, RWMAC stated that scientific consensus was a desirable but not essential criterion for successful waste management strategies (p. 17). That said, Warren (1998) argues that ambiguous and uncertain science is increasingly playing an important role in the development of environmental law and advocates closer links between producers of scientific knowledge and government policy makers. Moreover, while Warren argues that there is an over-reliance on scientific voices in the creation of environmental policy she endorses the need for policy to be 'translated into law by people who understand the limitations of science' (p. 186). The House of

Lords Science and Technology Committee supports this view and has recently expressed 'astonishment' at the lack of technical expertise available to CoRWM (House of Lords 2005; cf. Thorne 1993).

Earll (1992) presents an environmentalist perspective on policy and law-making regarding conservation and the precautionary principle. He suggests that an approach that 'puts the environment first' is less about precaution and more about common sense. While recognising that science and reliable programmes of research are useful tools to formulate sound policy, he argues that 'absence of evidence' is often used by commercial enterprises and developers to pursue initiatives that result in environmental damage. He asserts that the precautionary principle must direct all future environmental initiatives as well as policies and laws of regulation and control. In this sense preventing environmental harm is seen as *a priori* knowledge rather than a scientific and technical specialism.

Existing notions of precaution require both scientific and common sense analyses. For example, European Union member states are obliged under Directive 35 on environmental liability to develop legal frameworks and policies that provide commitment to preventing and remedying environmental damage (see European Union 2004). Each state is currently determining its environmental policies and law based on a combination of international experiences, emerging scientific evidence, public good and 'environmental common sense'. In his summing-up remarks to a recent workshop on Directive 35 involving senior judicial members from 29 European countries, Honourable Justice Drupsteen from the Council of State in The Hague stated that 'issues of liability, jurisdiction, competence, and enforcement remain challenges for European judicial systems when implementing Directive 35. Whatever type of pollution and contamination we are talking about we must deploy a multifaceted approach to legal reasoning that incorporates a range of expertise.' (Drupsteen 2005). Therefore, explicit in the development of policy and law related to environmental damage is a tacit understanding of openness, information sharing and multidisciplinary approaches to prevention.

UK Regulations and management of radioactive waste

Legal requirements

The European Court of Human Rights has identified the 'right to a safe environment' (Mularoni 2003), and risks posed by radioactive waste threaten this right. The Radioactive Substances Act 1993 imposes controls and regulations on radioactive materials. It is enforced by three separate agencies across the UK (Environment Agency in England and Wales, Scottish Environment Protection Authority and Environmental Heritage Service [Industrial Pollution and Radiochemical Inspectorate] in Northern Ireland) (see Health and Safety Executive 2001). Sections 13–18 of the Act address the disposal of radioactive waste. The Act details the process of authorisation and accumulation of radioactive waste but does not provide guidance on methods of storage or disposal; such matters are delegated. The Radioactive Substances Act 1993 requires certificates of registration for any persons who keep or use radioactive material on their premises, unless they are granted exemption orders.

Complementing the Radioactive Substances Act are several other sources of law providing the regulatory framework for policies and practices related to radioactive waste in Britain. These include, The Health and Safety at Work Act 1974, Nuclear Installations Act 1965, The Environment Act 1995 and the Ionising Radiations Regulations 2000. The Health and Safety Executive regulates the safe management and storage of radioactive waste on licensed disposal premises, while environmental agencies across devolved jurisdictions in the UK (mentioned above), enforce regulations on discharges to the environment and the disposal of radioactive waste (Williams 2002).

The legal requirements for radioactive waste management were articulated in judicial review in the Queen's Bench Division case of *R* v. *Secretary of State for the Environment and others*, ex parte *Greenpeace Ltd and another* [1994] 4 All ER 352. In his judgement, Justice Potts stated that the fundamental objectives of radioactive waste management in the UK were:

(a) that all practices giving rise to radioactive waste must be justified, i.e. the need for the practice must be established in terms of its overall benefit;
(b) radiation exposure of individuals and the collective dose to the population arising from radioactive waste shall be reduced to levels which are as low as reasonably achievable, economic and social factors being taken into account;
(c) the average effective dose equivalent from all sources including natural background radiation and medical procedures to representative members of a critical group of the general public shall not exceed 5 mSv (075 rem) in any one year. (Paragraph 46)

This ruling of Justice Potts, including guidelines for radiological dose assessments expressed in units of nucleus decay, has incorporated into UK law the necessity to justify the practices of creating radioactive waste before granting disposal authorisations (Chandler 1997).

Offences and Enforcement of Radioactive Substances Act 1993

In an attempt to identify the regulatory and enforcement procedures of the Radioactive Substances Act 1993, Official Information Requests were lodged with the three regulatory bodies in the UK listed above for the period 2000–2005. This official request both revealed the inadequate nature of existing databases and raised serious concerns for the regulation of radioactivity in Britain.

First, it was identified that not all establishments in Britain are required to be registered and authorised holders of radioactive substances. Exemption orders are statutory instruments that grant exemption from certain practices involving radioactivity and 'provide a degree of control, without excessive bureaucracy, over minor uses of radioactive substances where there is a clear benefit from its use'. At present there are more than 30 installations across the UK that are not required to be registered users of radioactive material. These facilities include nuclear power plants such as Chapelcross, Huntererston, Torness, and gas facilities in Scotland and Northern Ireland. Moreover, Faslane nuclear submarine base and the SUERC nuclear research institute, both in Scotland, are exempt from registration. Clearly such exemptions are a cause of serious concern as exempt facilities pose greater risks and create greater waste than those facilities requiring certificates (for example, hospitals and universities). As a result, there are currently no statutory arrangements to prosecute, fine or impose enforcement orders in respect of those radioactive substance stored at facilities that are granted exemption orders.

Second, during the period 2000–2005 a total of 3,437 certificates of registration were cancelled by the regulatory authorities. The authorities report that most of the cancellations resulted from operators ceasing to use radioactive materials and requesting a licence closure; however, this cannot be determined. As one official from the Environment Agency stated, 'we do not keep a central record of why a certificate has been cancelled, and we estimate that, to provide a definitive answer from the information on each individual file would cost in the order of £6,000' (Williams 2005). Moreover, a similar response was obtained for breaches of certificates. There is no central record that identifies violations of certificates. It is striking that operators who breach regulations while using the most dangerous substances known to humanity and the environment are not routinely recorded on a central database. That said, the Environment Agency in England and Wales has recently implemented a Compliance Classification Scheme for recording breaches of all environmental permits. During the period April 2004–June 2005 this register identified a staggering 223 offences for breaching the regulation of a registration under the Radioactive Substances Act 1993. The majority of offences (151) were classified as 'Category 4 – no actual or potential impact' – and involved records and management failure; a further 65 offences were deemed Category 3 or minor; and 8 were Category 1 or 2, namely, major or significant. Category 1 and 2 offences involve maintenance, equipment, storage and security failure. Of the 223 breaches only four resulted in prosecution. While the total number of breaches during the period 2000–2005 is not known, the authorities were able to supply the number of enforcement orders. In sum, only 37 enforcement notices and 25 prosecutions were issued by the three regulatory authorities across the UK during the five-year period under review (Frew 2005; Larmour 2005; Williams 2005). Given the small sample above from England and Wales that involved 223 breaches during a 14-month period, it is conceivable that total breaches across the UK during 2000–2005 exceeded 1,000, yet only 25 prosecutions were instigated. Naturally, this result does not include the 30 installations exempt from registrations, and highlights the ways in which the use of radioactive substances in the UK relies upon self-regulatory negotiation and partnership between private industry and the Government's environmental watchdogs.

Public opinion and waste disposal options

The Radioactive Substances Act 1993 permits UK residents to make formal complaints about the keepers and users of radioactive substances as a means of providing citizen input and oversight of these facilities. Again, the regulatory authorities were unable to provide any details about complaints, citing lack of readily available information and resources. The issue of public involvement and consultation has been frequently raised as important for the management and future handling of radioactive waste. If the general public are to understand government strategies for dealing with long-term radioactive waste management, then it is imperative that access to information be made readily available. The government has emphasised the importance of winning public confidence and operating 'in an open, transparent and inclusive manner' (House of Lords 2005: 10). Clearly public opinion has in the past influenced the disposal policies of the nuclear industry (Chandler 1997) and has proven influential in regulating global ocean dumping (Ringius 2001). To date, public opinion in the UK remains negative about the management and disposal of radioactive waste (Hunt and Simmons 2001).

The CoRWM's second consultation (4 April to 27 June 2005) sought to embrace public opinion while systematically assessing various disposal options against scientific, legal, economic and social imperatives. The consultation document provided a list of options for radioactive waste disposal from 'long-term interim storage; disposal at deep-sea, in ice sheets or in space and incineration (CoRWM 2005: 9). The selection or 'screening out' of options is based on 10 shortlisting criteria including possible harm to the environment and human health, cost, burden for future generations and possible breaches of international treaties. Importantly there is 'no proof of concept'. Namely, the chosen option need not have been implemented in the UK or elsewhere and there is no requirement that the 'international scientific community demonstrate confidence that the option can be implemented' (CoRWM 2005: 10). This is a substantial shift in the position previously held by CoRWM that all options be scientifically proven. The basis for this shift is premised on notions of 'flexibility' – to enable future technological and scientific developments to sustain viability of a given disposal strategy. In this sense there is a reduced onus on existing scientific evidence. Decision-making for radioactive waste disposal may proceed on the basis of economic imperatives, social consensus and available science. The science need not be definitive or conclusive but indicative and hence 'flexible'. The CoRWM has screened some options for various reasons relating to law, science and public opinion. Disposal in subduction zones and dilution and dispersal constituted breaches of a duty of care to the environment, while disposal in space was viewed as too costly and high risk to human health. Disposal by direct injection was seen as scientifically unknown while incineration and melting of metals were already part of a processing and not a disposal option (CoRWM 2005: 16–20). The 'land use planning process' for disposing of radioactive waste in the UK has been deemed inappropriate for some time (Kemp and O'Riordan 1988). However, it continues to remain a viable alternative. It should be noted that the decision to screen out options was more heavily reliant on international regulations and law than scientific certainty. As a result the currently preferred options include:

i)   deep geological disposal;
ii) phased deep geological disposal;
iii) near surface disposal or shallow burial of short-lived waste; and
iv) long-term interim storage.

A 'consensus conference' was convened in 1999 to allow members of the public to direct questions on radioactive waste management to scientific experts. This process aimed to enhance the democratisation of decision-making and encourage citizen participation in debates concerning human health and environmental security. The initial four-day event that reconvened for a second time in 2002 interviewed a range of senior personnel including scientists, lawyers, politicians, business proprietors and community representatives to consider consultation documents produced by DEFRA. The panel of the consensus conference concluded that 'evidence' should not be restricted to scientific inquiry only and should incorporate the experiences and views of government, commercial and community personnel. Moreover, it concluded that public consultation can only be effective if the information disseminated is 'accurate, objective and complete by all interested parties' and that the most important comment is 'the need for openness, honesty and transparency – and the need for policy-makers to be seen to be listening' (DEFRA 2002: 4–5). This view is consistent with the conclusions of RWMAC (1999) stating that the public were more likely to accept scientific analyses of radioactive waste disposal if the science was not too technical and there was 'trust in both the message and the messenger' (p. 14).

Green criminology and radioactive waste

Issues pertaining to the protection of the planet continue to capture media headlines and continually focus public and political debate. As a result, environmental law is currently the fastest growing area of international law (Galizzi and Sands 2004). The diversity of subject matter covered under international environmental law has necessitated the integration of diverse expertise and knowledges that must include criminology. With new laws, emerge new regulations and new offences. Eco-crime is, therefore, poised to be a developing area within a global criminology. As an evolving discipline criminologists must constantly be asking what criminology has to offer issues, debates and actions that threaten the preservation of the planet? Within criminological studies, debates about eco-crime have emerged within discourses on state and corporate crime or 'crimes of the powerful' (Pearce and

Tombs 1993; Tombs and Whyte 2003) and within developing debates of 'green and environmental criminology' (South and Beirne 1998; Lynch and Stretesky 2003). Green criminology provides an umbrella under which to theorise and critique the emerging terminology related to environmental and species harm.

The ongoing greening of criminology intersects with diverse narratives and disciplines and provides an interface with social movements to examine issues of environmental harm, risks and rights. A criminological scholarship committed totally to environment issues is essential and achievable by utilising a range of analytical tools in the production of a knowledge that is theoretical, empirically grounded and politically active. The emergence of a green criminology that includes diverse analyses of eco-crime provides a mandate for broadening the critical gaze and opening up the debate to alternative avenues of analysis that examine the issues within social, cultural and political frameworks (Walters 2006).

That said, it is important that green criminology must not be reduced to green party politics. It must be a position premised on the principles of environmentalism and broader issues of environmental justice. Such an approach recognises that environmental victimology is as much about issues of race, class, poverty, trade and economics as it is about the environment. Moreover, a green criminology must harness discourses in both risk and rights. It must be a 'global criminology', one that examines notions of transnational justice within expanding global economies. This is a high-wire act omitted from the criminological repertoire but essential within changing international economic and political landscapes where crime respects no sovereign domains and where crime control must be dynamic.

Conclusion

Issues of radioactive waste have global implications and require legal and policy frameworks capable of minimising risk to the environment and human health. Such risk management strategies must straddle political, economic, social, scientific and environmental concerns. This chapter concludes that proposed nuclear developments in the UK recently supported by Prime Minister Tony Blair fail to address the concerns raised by the 1981 Royal Commission on Environmental Pollution regarding radioactive waste. Nor do they conform with the landmark ruling of Justice Potts that requires 'justification' for those practices that produce radioactive waste in terms of 'overall benefit'.

It is of further concern that existing regulatory arrangements in the UK for managing and administering radioactive waste are clearly inadequate. Radioactive waste is the most dangerous set of substances known to humanity with an active life spanning thousands of years. There are currently no solutions for long-term safe storage and the ongoing and ever-present risks of human and environmental disaster. That said, the UK government does not have a central database on fundamental information about cancellations and breaches of certificates of registration nor community complaints. If community consultation is seen to be essential to policies relating to radioactive waste management, then considerable change must occur that provides efficient access to detailed information.

The current regulatory regime in the UK relies too heavily on operator self-regulation and the small number of prosecutions and fines during the past five years for installations that breach the Radioactive Substances Act demonstrates the Blair government's inability to grapple with the importance and seriousness of issues pertaining to the use and abuse of radioactive substances. This point is further compounded by the exemption of nuclear military establishments and nuclear power plants from environmental agency regulation. The fact that the most potentially damaging and risky radioactive substance using industries in the UK are devoid of close government scrutiny is an act of government negligence.

Finally, it is clear that the formulation of the long-term management of radioactive waste in the UK remains uncertain and contested. The relationships between science, policy and law within debates about radioactive waste disposal must continually emphasise environmental protection and human health. Improper or dangerous solutions may produce irretrievable consequences. The race for nuclear superiority and the quest for solutions to proposed energy shortages have resulted in a 50-year history of industries and governments contaminating the environment. The prohibitive costs associated with decommissioning radioactive facilities have created a worldwide legacy and ongoing practice of waste dumping – the effects of which are yet to be fully realised.

Criminologists must continue to engage in issues of global significance while being attentive to local and national interests. The various environmental issues broadly defined with green criminology demonstrate that criminology is capable of moving beyond domestic borders and contributing to debates of international significance.

References

Abell, A. and Oxbrow, N. (2001) *Competing with Knowledge: The Information Professional in the Knowledge Management Age.* London: TFPL.

Arms, K. (1994) 'Ecosystems and how They Change', in K. Arms (ed.) *Environmental Science.* Saunders College Publishing.

Ashworth, D. and Shaw, G. (2005) 'Soil Migration and Plant Uptake of Techetium from Fluctuating Water Table', *Journal of Environmental Radioactivity*, 81 (2): 155–171.

BBC News (2005) 'Warning on nuclear waste disposal', *BBC News World Edition*, 4 April 2005. http://news.bbc.co.uk/2/hi/science/nature/4407421.stm

BBC News (2006) 'Blair backs nuclear power plans', 16 May 2006, news.bbc.co.uk/1/hi/uk_politics/4987196.stm

Birnie, P. and Boyle, A. (2002) *International Law and the Environment.* 2nd edn. Oxford: Oxford University Press.

Bridges, O. and Bridges, J. (1995) 'Radioactive Waste Problems in Russia', *Journal of Radiological Protection*, 15: 223–234.

Brown, P. (2004) 'UK faces court action for nuclear safety failings', *The Guardian*, 4 September 2004: 9.

Chan, T., Christiansson, R., Boulton, G., Ericsson, L., Hartikainen, J., Jensen, M., Mas Ivars, D., Stanchell, F., Vistrand, P. and Wallroth, T. (2005) 'Decovalex 111 BMT3/BENCHPAR WP4: The thermo-hydro-mechanical responses to a glacial cycle and their potential implications for deep geological disposal of nuclear fuel waste in a fractured crystalline rock mass', *International Journal of Rock Mechanics and Mining Sciences*, 43 (1): advanced online publication.

Chambers, W. and Green, J. (eds) (2005) *Reforming International Environmental Governance. From Institutional Limits to Innovative Reforms.* Washington DC: United Nations University Press.

Chandler, S. (1997) *Radioactive Waste Control and Controversy. The History of Radioactive Waste Regulation in the UK.* London: Gordon and Breach Science Publishers.

Cochrane, T., Norris, R. and Bukharin, O. (1995) *Making the Russian Bomb: From Stalin to Yeltsin.* Boulder: Westview Press.

Committee on Radioactive Waste Management (2005) 'Learning from the Past – Listening for the Future. How should the UK manage radioactive waste?' Second Consultation Document, 4 April to 27 June 2005. London: CoRWM.

Connor, S. (2004) 'US Climate Policy Bigger Threat to World than Terrorism', *The Independent*, 9 January 2004.

Department for Environment, Food and Rural Affairs (2002) *Managing Radioactive Waste Safely. Summary of Responses to the Consultation September 2001 – March 2002.* London: HMSO.

Department for Environment, Food and Rural Affairs (2005) *Radioactive Waste Management*, www.defra.gov.uk/environment/radioactivity/waste/index.htm

Dripsteen, T. (2005) Summary remarks. International Court of the Environmental Foundation (2005) *Workshop on Environmental Law. Prevention and Remedying of Environmental Damage.* 27 May 2005, Ostia Antica, Rome.

Earll, R. (1992) 'Commonsense and the Precautionary Principle – An Environmentalist's Perspective', *Marine Pollution Bulletin*, 24(4): 182–186.

Edwards, R. (2005) 'Dalgety Bay awash with radioactive military waste – but the MoD refuses to clean it up', *Sunday Herald*, 6 November 2005: 3.

Environment News Service (2002) 'Russia May Import British Nuclear Waste', *Environment News Service. International Daily Newswire*, 10 April 2002, www.ens-newswire.com/ens/apr2002/2002-04-10-01.asp

European Union (2004) *Directive 2004/35/CE of the European Parliament and of the Council of 21 April 2004.* Official Journal of the European Union.

Farquharson, K. and Macaskill, M. (2005) 'Reckless nuclear waste on beaches', *The Times*, 6 March 2005.

Flounders, S. (2003) 'Another U.S. War Crime? Iraqi City "Hot" with Depleted Uranium', *Workers World*. www.workers.org/ww/2003/iraqdu0821.php

Frew, J. (2005) 'Request For Information', Official Information Request to the Scottish Environment Protection Agency, Reference number F0090478.

Galizzi, P. and Sands, P. (2004) *Documents in International Environmental Law.* 2nd edn. Cambridge: Cambridge University Press.

Greenpeace (2000) 'Thousands of Radioactive Waste Barrels Rusting Away on the Seabed: Greenpeace Research Unveils Nuclear Energy'. www.archive. greenpeace.org/pressreleases/nucreprocess/2000jun19.html

Greenpeace (2005) 'Illegal Nuclear Waste Shipment Blocked', 1 December 2005. www.greenpeace.org/international/news/illegal-nuclear-waste-shipment.

Griffiths, R. (1997) Foreword, in Chandler, S. (1997) *Radioactive Waste Control and Controversy. The History of Radioactive Waste Regulation in the UK.* London: Gordon and Breach Science Publishers.

Harding, R. (1983) 'Nuclear Energy and the Destiny of Mankind – Some Criminological Perspectives', *The Australian and New Zealand Journal of Criminology*, (16): 81–92.

Harvie, D. (2005) *Deadly Sunshine: The History and Fatal Legacy of Radium.* London: Tempus.

Health and Safety Executive (2001) *Guidance for Inspectors on the Management of Radioactive Waste Materials and Radioactive Waste on Nuclear Licensed Sites.* Nuclear Safety Directorate.

Hillyard, P., Pantazis, C., Tombs, S. and Gordon, D. (2004) (eds) *Beyond Criminology. Taking Harm Seriously.* London: Pluto.

Houghton, J. (2003) 'Global warming is now a weapon of mass destruction. It kills more people than terrorism, yet Blair and Bush do nothing', *The Guardian*, 28 July 2003.

House of Lords (1999) *Science and Technology – Third Report*, 10 March 1999. London: The Stationery Office.

House of Lords (2005) *Radioactive Waste Management: Government Response*, 5 April 2005. Science and Technology Committee. Second Report of Session 2004–05. London: The Stationery Office.

Hunt, J. and Simmons, P. (2001) *The Front of the Front End: Mapping Public Concerns about Radioactive Waste Management Issues*. Lancaster: Centre for the Study of Environmental Change.

Jameson, A. (2005) 'Nuclear Audit Says Sellafield has "Lost" 30kgs of plutonium', Timeonline, 17 February 2005, www.timesonline.co.uk/article/0,,2-1487789,00.html

Kamei, G., Mitsui, M., Futakuchi, K., Hashimoto, S. and Sakuramoto, Y. (2005) 'Kinetics of Long-term Illitization of Montmorillonite – a Natural Analogue of Thermal Alteration of Benonite in the Radioactive Waste Disposal System', *Journal of Physics and Chemistry of Solids*, 66(1): 612–614.

Kemp, R. and O'Riordan, T. (1988) 'Planning for Radioactive Waste Disposal – Some Central Considerations', *Land Use Policy*, 5(1): 37–44.

Kirby, A. (2003) 'US Rejects Iraq DU Clean-up', BBC Online, 14 March 2003. http://news.bbc.co.uk/2/hi/science/nature/2946715.stm

Larmour, R. (2005) 'Environmental Information Regulations', Official Information Request to the Northern Ireland Environment and Heritage Services. Reference Number EIR/90IE145/EHS/2005

Legambiente, G. (2003) *The Illegal Trafficking in Hazardous Waste in Italy and Spain*. Rome: European Commission.

McLaughlin, A. (1998) 'Radioactive Waste ', *Interdisciplinary Science Reviews*. Special Edition. 23 (3).

Mularoni, A. (2003) 'The Right to a Safe Environment in the Case-law of the European Court of Human Rights', in A. Postiglione (ed.) *The Role of the Judiciary in the Implementation and Enforcement of Environmental Law*. Rome: International Court of the Environmental Foundation.

Parmentier, R. (1999) 'Greenpeace and the Dumping of Waste at Sea: A Case of Non-State Actors' Intervention in International Affairs', *International Negotiation. A Journal of Theory and Practice*, 4(3): 435–457.

Papay, L. (2003) 'The Science and Politics of Radioactive Waste Disposal', *The Bridge*, 33(3).

Pirro, D. (2002) Project for an International Court of the Environment – Origins and Development. www.biopolitics.gr/HTML/PUBS/VOL8/html/Pirro.htm

Radioactive Waste Management Advisory Committee (1999) *Advice to Ministers on the Establishment of Scientific Consensus on the Interpretation and Significance of the Results of Science Programmes into Radioactive Waste Disposal*. London: HMSO.

Ringius, L. (2001) *Radioactive Waste Disposal at Sea*. Cambridge: MIT Press.

Royal Institute of International Affairs (2002) *International Environmental Crime. The Nature and Control of Environmental Black Markets, Workshop Report*. Sustainable Development Programme: RIIA.

Solomon, B., Shelley, F., Pasoualetti, M. and Murauskas, G. (1987) 'Radioactive Waste Management Policies in Seven Industrialized Democracies', *Geoforum*, 18 (4): 415–431.

South, N. (1998) 'A Green Field for Criminology?', *Theoretical Criminology*, 2 (2): 211–233.

South, N. and Beirne, P. (eds) (1998) *For a Green Criminology*. Special Edition of *Theoretical Criminology*, 2 (2).

Suzuki, D. (2001) 'A Geneticist's Reflections on the New Genetics', in R. Hindmarsh and G. Lawrence (eds), *Altered Genes 11*. Melbourne: Scrine Publications.

Thorne, M. (1993) 'The Use of Expert Opinion in Formulating Conceptual Models of Underground Disposal Systems and the Treatment of Associated Bias', *Reliability Engineering and System Safety*, 42 (2–3), 161–180.

Uggla, Y. (2004) 'Risk and Safety Analysis in Long-term Perspective', *Futures*, 36 (5): 549–564.

Ulfstein, G. and Werksman, J. (2004) (eds) *Yearbook of International Environmental Law*. Oxford: Oxford University Press.

United Nations Environment Programme (2005) 'Somalia', www.enep.org/tsunami/reports/tsunami_SOMALIA_LAYOUT.pdf

Walters, R. (2005) 'Eco-Crime', in E. McLaughlin and J. Muncie (2005) *The Sage Dictionary of Criminology*. 2nd edn. pp. 146–148 London: Sage.

Walters, R. (2006) 'Crime, Bio-Agriculture and the Exploitation of Hunger', *The British Journal of Criminology*, 46 (1): 26–45.

Warren, L. (1998) 'Using Law to Define Uncertain Science in Environmental Policy', in M. Freeman and H. Reece (eds), *Science in Court*. London: Ashgate.

Williams, C. (2005) 'Request For Information on Premises Permitted Under The Radioactive Substances Act 1993', Official Information Request to the England and Wales Environment Agency. Reference number FOI 131.

Williams, L. (2002) 'The Regulation of Radioactive Waste in Great Britain', *European Parliament Committee on Petitions Safety and Impact of Processing Plants*. www.hse.gov.uk/nsd.europarl.htm

Zawisky, M., Basturk, M., Derntl, R., Dubus, F., Lehmann, E. and Vontobel, P. (2004) 'Non-destructive 10B Analysis in Neutron Transmission Experiments', *Applied Radiation and Isotopes*, 61 (4): 517–523.

Cases

R v. *Secretary of State for the Environment and others*, ex parte *Greenpeace and another*. Queen's Bench Division [1994] 4 All ER 352

Statutes

Nuclear Installations Act 1965
Radioactive Substances Act 1993
The Environment Act 1995

Chapter 9

Food crime

Hazel Croall

The phrase 'food crime' may not resonate with criminologists as well as other often-used phrases to describe categories of crime such as car crime or sex crime. Yet the many crimes which are involved in the production, distribution and selling of basic foodstuffs touch everyone as food is an essential commodity and a major part of personal expenditure. While often not associated with crime, food has been the subject of a variety of 'scandals' or 'scares' concerning the quality and contents of meat, basic ingredients and mass-produced food. It involves major health issues and manufacturers' descriptions and labelling of food has become subject to calls for greater regulation in the wake of concerns about obesity. Consumers express concerns about the risks of food poisoning (*Which?* 2004a), wish to avoid food containing Genetically Modified (GM) ingredients (*Which?* 2004b), and are often confused about the information provided by labels. The globalisation of food production and manufacture and the use of new technologies and chemicals in farming and food processing have created a variety of risks to humans, non-human animals, the environment and health, many of which, like the long-term effects of GM foods are ill understood (Walters 2004). This paper will explore the different forms of crime which are related to the food chain by providing illustrative and selective examples from farming and manufacturing through to sales and marketing. It will then raise a number of issues about how food crime can best be analysed within criminology, and briefly outline the socio-economic context within which food crime occurs.

A wide range of offences is involved in the food chain, involving economic and physical harms, issues of personal safety and health and many different kinds of frauds, from the evasion of subsidies and quotas and the avoidance of revenue, to food adulteration and misrepresenting through written and pictorial indications, the quality and contents of food. Consumers have been poisoned by food unfit for human consumption or adulterated food. This can lead to death and serious illness. Two hundred and fifty-nine Spanish consumers were killed and many more made seriously ill after consuming cooking oil mixed with industrial oil (Croall 1992) and 21 old-age pensioners in Wishaw in Scotland died after consuming meat contaminated by E.coli, supplied by a local butcher who was found to have neglected food hygiene regulations (Croall 2001). Some food additives have been associated with cancer risks, as was the case with the recent food 'scare' about Sudan 1 which was found in a wide variety of food products.

Many of these practices are also fraudulent as they involve adulterating food with cheaper ingredients – adulterating food with water is one of the oldest forms of fraud which persists today with many forms of 'legalised adulteration' by a range of additives (Lawrence 2004a). Many other frauds have been associated with food – current concerns include 'meat laundering', the passing of adulterated, unfit or 'illegal meat' into a variety of meat products. Agricultural subsidies, the imposition of fishing quotas, export and import controls and taxes on different kinds of food also give rise to a host of frauds. Food laws also cover food labelling and food packaging and the many ways in which the quality or contents of food can be misrepresented. As will be seen below, a variety of practices have been identified which systematically deceive consumers. Many of these practices lie on the fringes of legality and illegality raising issues about the definition of fraud and deception and the use of expert scientific knowledge in relation to food safety.

A wide range in the UK of enforcement agencies and government departments are involved in the regulation of food. While the police and customs and excise may be involved in what are defined as 'serious' frauds, which may involve what they define as organised crime, most food regulation is the responsibility of inspectorates such as Environmental Health Services, Trading Standards officers (who operate locally) and the Meat Hygiene Service (which operates nationally). Food is covered by a variety of government departments such as:

Food Standards Agency (FSA);
The Office of Fair Trading (OFT);
Department for Environment, Food and Rural Affairs (DEFRA),
Trade and Industry and Health.

Following devolution, elements of food policy are also the responsibility of the Scottish Executive and the National Assembly for Wales.

Some agencies seek to work across this rather disparate regime. In February 2005, for example, the Welsh Food Fraud Co-ordinating Unit, described as a 'food crime task force', was set up and is related to a number of Departments. It is supported by Welsh Local Authorities and the Welsh Assembly, organised by the Welsh Food Standards Agency and funded by the Agriculture and Health Department. It will share information across enforcement agencies in Wales and also across the UK (*Western Mail* 6th January 2005; Doig 2006).

This gives some indication of the wide variety of offenders involved, ranging from some of the largest 'corporate giants' involved in food manufacture, distribution and retailing to small individual businesses selling out-of-date food or failing to comply with hygiene regulations. Farmers, fishing businesses, abattoirs and meat packers are all involved along with gang masters, organised criminals and opportunistic entrepreneurs. In this way, the study of crime involving food crosses several areas of white-collar, corporate and organised crime.

While no definition of food crime has been attempted at this stage, it is clear that the amount and variety of crimes involved in food are considerable. Some of the major forms will be outlined below. As is the case with many forms of white-collar, corporate or environmental crime, the borderlines between the legal, the illegal and the criminal can be very narrow ones, and a major issue is what practices should be included or excluded (Croall 2001; Nelken 2002; Lynch and Stretesky 2003). On the grounds that exploring how particular forms of crime are constructed and whose interests are involved in analysing, for example, the required content of food labels and the descriptions of foods, this paper will include examples of 'misleading' and 'unsafe' practices which are not at present covered by criminal law but which have been the subject of calls for legislation and which lie at the fringes of the law.

This paper represents both a development of the author's previous research in this area (Croall 1987; 1989), and a preliminary, more focused investigation of the range and context of food crime. Researching and gaining information about this form of crime involves using a wide variety of sources, many lying well beyond traditional criminological methods such as criminal statistics or victim surveys. This paper, and subsequent research, have identified a wide variety of sources including:

- the media: searches using different key words were undertaken. Investigative journalism is a particularly useful source of information, particularly the detailed investigation of the food industry carried out by writers such as Felicity Lawrence of *The Guardian* (Lawrence 2004a), and the critique of supermarket concentration and power carried out by food writer Joanna Blythman (Blythman 2005);

- the websites of the government agencies and enforcement agents referred to above which contain much useful information along with summaries of research;

- research and investigations carried out by a range of interest groups such as the Consumers' Association and the Food Commission;

- a range of relevant academic literature which of necessity moves outside criminological literature.

Following the food chain – crimes involving food

To illustrate the variety and extent of food crime, the following examples trace crime from production (involving farming, fishing and food manufacture) through distribution and food preparation to the selling and marketing of food. The examples are selective and by no means exhaustive and many more examples, statistics and reports could well be included. This paper has focused primarily (for reasons of space) on what might be described as 'solid' food – water, wine and other drinks are also the subject of many forms of fraud and adulteration which have not been included here and there are many more misleading practices in the production and selling of food.

Food production

Farming

At the start of the food chain lie the many forms of crime associated with agriculture and the planting and growing of crops. Safety issues involve the planting of genetically modified (GM) crops, the use of pesticides and other chemicals, the overuse of crops such as soya or rapeseed oil which are heavily subsidised and which become part of processed food not recognised on the label (Lawrence 2004). The use of subsidies and the Common Agricultural Policy (CAP) have for long been associated with a variety of frauds (Passas and Nelken 1993; Doig 1995; 2005), and other frauds have been perpetrated in the wake of BSE and the foot-and-mouth outbreak (Croall 2001). Cruel and inhumane practices used by farmers, particularly those associated with the factory farming of chickens, have raised considerable concern as have illegal and inhumane practices in slaughterhouses (Lawrence 2004a). The concentration of buying power in the hands of a small number of supermarket chains and the pressures this places on suppliers, farmers and packers, has been blamed, as will be seen below, for the use of gang masters and illegal immigrant labour, and the drive for cheaper production and the growth of sales of 'out of season' crops has been associated with not only the exploitation of labour in developing countries but damage to the environment in countries growing such crops (Lawrence 2004a; Blythman 2005). Some examples include:

Subsidies frauds

While assumed to be widespread, the extent of subsidies fraud in the European Union (EU), once estimated to amount to around 10 per cent of its budget (Clarke 1994) is difficult to estimate. Indeed in 2002, the European Court of Auditors acknowledged that Brussels cannot keep track of the vast subsidies paid to farmers under CAP. A few reported spot checks in EU states found disturbing levels of error and outright fraud including the following examples (Evans-Pritchard 2002):

- Aerial photography exposed a scam in which alpine pastures eligible for subsidies in Austria had been inflated by 60 per cent.

- Spain and Greece, the chief recipients of £1.5 billion subsidy for olive groves, were failing to keep tabs on their olive mills, making it impossible to know how much production was fictitious.

- British farmers were drawing inflated subsidies under the £4.2 billion livestock programme, lodging premium claims that did not tally with farm records.

- A cross-check in Northern Ireland during the foot-and-mouth epidemic found that 103 farmers had claimed payments for more sheep than were actually culled and 17 had no sheep at all on their property.

One case attracting considerable publicity was that of Joseph Bowden, a Devon farmer who was given £130,000 in subsidies for non-existent land. The fictitious map references he provided would have placed his fields in Greenland, Iceland and the North Sea and he also claimed subsidies for different crops on different land. He was eventually convicted in 2000 and sent to prison for two and a half years. The MAFF regulators who failed to spot this fraud were severely criticised by the House of Commons Public Accounts Committee (Watt 2002).

A further example is provided in the fraud surrounding Spanish olives, where around £1.4 billion EU subsidies have been associated with £10 million worth of subsidy frauds, with subsidies being claimed for olives which were never produced, and for inculcating a culture of 'rural greed' (Wilkinson 2002). This has also led to an increase in planting olives, and to misrepresenting the date of planting as the EU will give no subsidies for trees planted after 1998. This has further had an adverse effect on the environment due to the high levels of water consumption (*The Economist* 2001).

Other frauds were involved in the wake of the foot-and-mouth epidemic, with farmers being accused of claiming for animals which did not exist and even for deliberately spreading the disease to gain compensation (Elliot 2001).

Gang masters and illegal immigrants

The use of gang masters to provide agricultural labour is a long-established practice and not in itself illegal. Contemporary practices, however, have been associated with 'mafia style' operations, a range of frauds and the exploitation of immigrant labour, by working labourers beyond maximum hours and below the minimum wage (Lawrence 2004a). Other forms of crime may be involved – some are involved in illegal 'trafficking', the provision of false documents, charging packhouses, factories and farmers the 'going rate' for labour plus VAT and extracting tax and insurance from workers' pay even when it has nowhere legitimate to go. Some gang masters then declare themselves bankrupt before paying any taxes and move their money offshore – only to reappear again.

Fishing

A variety of frauds and safety issues is involved in fishing, ranging from the use of chemicals in fish farming and the effects of this on the environment to the 'fish wars' which have been associated with fishing quotas, most recently by EU quotas introduced to preserve fishing stocks. This has been held responsible for the widespread practice of black market fishing. Some examples of investigations and prosecutions for these practices are outlined below.

- In 2003, two Spanish fishing firms, registered in the UK to take advantage of quotas, were fined over £1 million for illegally catching over £1 million worth of hake and declaring only 4 per cent of the catch (Smith 2003).

- 'Black fishing', the practice of catching fish which are not officially declared is said to be endemic in Scotland and other parts of Europe. It has been estimated by fish merchants to cost about £80 million in Scotland alone (Urquhart 2005). The quota system for fish such as cod has led to a situation in which any fish caught over quota must be thrown back into the sea, even if dead. 'Black fishing', involves not only fishermen but also requires the collusion of fish processors and hauliers and the extent of the practice is so great that some have estimated that catches of black fish equal those of legal fish (Mackay 2003).

- In a recent case in Scotland, the master and mate of the trawler *Altaire* were convicted after being caught landing more than 7,600 tonnes of illegal herring and mackerel into Norway over two years. They had unloaded 17,085 tonnes of mackerel over 20 landings in Norway, declaring to the Scottish Fisheries Protection Agency that they had landed just 10,031 tonnes. They also unloaded over 1,012 tonnes of herring but declared just 469 tonnes in landings. Their assets have been frozen under the Proceeds of Crime Act (Urquhart 2005).

Black fishing has attracted mixed responses, with journalistic investigations being largely sympathetic to fishermen, featuring their arguments that they need to engage in black fishing in order to survive, and describing the virtual destruction of fishing communities, particularly in northern Scotland (e.g. Mackay 2003). Others, notably enforcers, dispute this although a distinction is made between white fishing, subject to tight quotas, and pelagic fishing (mackerel and herring), the subject of the *Altaire* case above. Following this, the chief executive of the Scottish Fisheries Protection Agency commented that this sector is highly profitable and that 'greed' leads to fishing over quota (Smith 2005).

Food manufacture

Many frauds (both legal and illegal) are associated with food manufacturing. The popularity of pre-prepared meals and the practice of food manufacturers of 'value adding' – charging more for basic ingredients by preparing food (the pre-packaged salad) and adding cheap ingredients and additives (processed food) – has been associated with a variety of forms of 'legalised adulteration' and, some would argue, the 'debasement' of food by water and a whole host of additives. The borderlines between illegal and legal practices – between 'fraud', deception and 'misleading' indications – are very fine, as is the borderline between safety issues and what is counted as deception. The addition, for example, of water to specific foods in specific quantities is legal, and water in itself raises few safety implications. It should however be stated on the label. This is the case with many other additives although the long-term health implications of some additives are uncertain and some, like the notorious Sudan 1, have been associated with the risk of cancer. Modern food processing also relies on the use of Mechanically Recovered Meat (MRM) in which parts of the animal not normally associated with consumption are used and, of course, considerable concern accompanies the use of GM ingredients. Other processes and ingredients include, for example, the use of starch, hard fats and hydrogenated oils to 'bind' processed foods – all linked with health risks (Lawrence 2004a).

Food additives are used for a variety of reasons and many are the products of what Lawrence describes as the 'carbohydrate chemist'. Some, such as preservatives, are used to extend shelf life, others are used to 'mask off' unpleasant agents, some are used as bulking agents and others are used to replace expensive 'natural' ingredients. Yet more are used purely for cosmetic reasons (see, for example, Lawrence 2004a). Salt is added for flavour, other additives replace the natural flavours and colours lost in processing and to help ingredients survive. Many are not adequately tested (Lawrence 2004a) – flavourings for example are not tested for safety and currently do not have to be declared individually on the label (Millstone and Lang 2003).

Some examples of how food can be adulterated follow:

- Lawrence (2004a) cites the example of chicken nuggets, where one pack was found to contain only 16 per cent meat, 30 per cent less than indicated on the label.

- Water is often added to meat, and not only to processed meat. For example, pork chops sold in major chains such as Tesco, ASDA, Sainsbury's and the Co-op, are known to have been injected with water and additives to retain moisture. Tesco chops, for example, were found to contain only 80 per cent pork, and the supermarket chain was prosecuted in January 2002 and fined £2,800 for selling 'Tesco tender select pork leg' without declaring added water, glucose, syrup and salt on the outer label (Lawrence 2004b). The FSA, while agreeing that it is 'completely unacceptable for the consumer to be paying for water', does not see banning these practices as appropriate since the meat is not unsafe. According to Tesco the water is added to improve eating quality while ASDA blamed customers' 'poor cooking skills' – without water they argued, the meat would dry up.

- The use of sell-by dates: a different kind of issue is revealed in a *Which?* (2004c) report into the abuse of sell-by dates by manufacturers. It was informed by a source in the Meat Hygiene Service (MHS) of a chicken processing plant in which raw chicken which had not been packed and sent to retailers one day was repackaged and redated and passed on to shops as 'fresh'. This is perfectly legal as it is the responsibility of manufacturers to indicate sell-by dates. It is, they argue, nonetheless deceptive, as both consumers and supermarkets are deceived. Once food has arrived at supermarkets it is an offence, for which some have been prosecuted, to sell food past its sell-by date. The MHS however is concerned as this practice also carries safety risks.

These are only a very few, selected examples of how modern food manufacturing can threaten safety and health and also be deceptive – many more could be added including the use of non-organic ingredients in organic foods, cases in which horse meat has been found in foods imported into Britain which, while not having any safety implications, would be repugnant to many consumers, and may also involve the maltreatment of horses, and how in Japan, rice can be adulterated by the use of cheap foreign imports (Croall 2005). Many of these involve a complex chain of production and distribution, evading taxes, and cross-border frauds – some indeed involving transnational organised crime (Croall 2005).

Food distribution

A transnational and more 'local' example of frauds involving the 'food chain' of production and distribution is outlined below – sometimes described as *'food laundering'*.

- An example reported by Lawrence (2004a) involves the food processing technique known as 'tumbling' in which meat (and all parts of the animal) is tumbled and reconstituted for passing further down the chain. This can involve several kinds of fraud. In one case, Dutch food processors (the Netherlands is reported to be the centre of the tumbling industry) imported cheap frozen chicken from Thailand and Brazil. Some of this is salted in order to avoid EU tariffs on fresh meat. The meat is then defrosted, injected with water and additives and tumbled into giant machines, in the process of which the water is absorbed and the salt diluted, to make the chicken palatable. It is then refrozen and shipped on for further processing by manufacturers or caterers. Much of it is reported to end up in take-away food.

- This kind of laundering has also been associated with findings of proteins from pork in chicken and there have been some reports of cow waste also being involved, raising issues about the spread of BSE. These examples are not technically illegal. According to the FSA, adding water to chickens is legal provided it is accurately labelled and adding proteins from other animals is also legal – although they should be declared on the label. It has now accepted, however, that these practices can amount to a major 'scandal' following the discovery by Irish enforcers of pork in chicken labelled 'halal' and has pressed the EC to ban the use of proteins from other species in chicken and to limit the amount of water which can legally be added to 15 per cent.

- Other meat frauds involve more locally based criminal 'gangs'. In a widely reported case, a defendant known as 'Maggot Pete' and members of his 'gang' from the Denby Poultry Products Firm in Derbyshire were convicted following a 'meat laundering' case as a result of which meat destined for pet food, and unfit for human consumption, was sold to hospitals, schools and local supermarkets (Stringer 2003). Around 450 tons of chicken and turkey, declared as unfit even for pets, were doctored to appear healthy. The firm had been registered to receive low-risk waste for use in pet foods but it also sold laundered high-risk waste carrying hepatitis,

Staphylococci and E.coli septicaemia into the human food chain. The cleaned-up waste was sold to another company which applied illegitimate health marks to it. (Lawrence 2004a)

Food preparation

Food preparation mainly involves considerations of food hygiene in restaurants, premises selling take-away food and anywhere preparing food including the chicken packing referred to above. Hygiene regulations are directed at food poisoning – a major concern of the FSA and as seen above, also of concern to the public (*Which?* 2004a). In the FSA survey, 13 per cent reported having experienced food poisoning in the last year, mainly, they believed from food bought and consumed outside the home. The extent of food poisoning is difficult to estimate as many do not report it but it is generally assumed to be rising and associated with convenience and take-away foods. Food poisoning can of course kill, as seen most dramatically in the deaths of 21 old age pensioners in Wishaw, Lanarkshire, after they had consumed meat supplied by one butcher (Croall 2001). It is difficult, however, to trace the chain of evidence to sustain a criminal prosecution for food poisoning – therefore prosecutions, often of individual restaurants or take-away food establishments, represent only the tip of a large iceberg. E. coli has also been traced to salad crops and to lettuce.

While many breaches of hygiene regulations take place, prosecutions are relatively rare. Nonetheless, there have been recurrent calls to make these more public and to publicise the results of food hygiene inspection more widely. This could be done either by restaurants being required to place these on the doors of the restaurant, as is done in Denmark and parts of the United States ('scores on doors'), or by placing them, along with details of prosecutions, on Local Authority websites. A number of Local Authorities, such as Glasgow and Birmingham, now do this, although the practice is opposed by the restaurateurs' association (Muir 2004; Wilson 2005). This practice has revealed, for example, that Gordon Ramsay, a famous television chef, was reported for breaches of hygiene regulations. *Which?* has also carried out repeated investigations into the take-away sector, with one report (*Which?* 2004a) following visits with Environmental Health Officers (EHOs) to 12 take-aways in three areas, finding that in a small number (four) no staff had been trained, and in several only some staff were trained. This investigation revealed a variety of 'dirty deeds' including the use of dirty cloths and the presence of pests – one take-away was described as 'crawling'. This investigation also found that 42 per cent of UK food businesses visited by EHOs in 2001 failed to comply fully with food law, though fewer than 0.5 per cent were prosecuted.

Selling and marketing

As pointed out above, the contents of food raise several safety and health issues, although safety issues are often perceived to be related to labelling rather than safety, thus making them appear less serious. This raises the question of what *is* on the label, an issue which has been taken up by media and consumer groups who have highlighted many ways in which consumers are 'conned', deceived or misled – although this is not generally described as 'fraud'. Labels themselves are often seen as difficult to find, written in 'small print', difficult for older consumers to understand, and containing descriptions, figures and percentages which may also be confusing (*Which?* 2002). The borderline between 'misleading' and deceptive, between what Sutherland (1949) described as 'puff', which everyone would see through, and that which is regulated is a very fine one. The FSA for example, point out that 'everyone knows' that a 'swiss' roll is not made in Switzerland, thus this description is not held to be misleading (www.eatwell.gov.uk). Changes to labelling laws which move towards greater regulation are normally strenuously opposed by food manufacturers.

Behind the seeming triviality of many of the issues surrounding food labelling lie the attempts of manufacturers and retailers, in a highly competitive market, to encourage consumers to buy particular brands of food by using a variety of 'claims' about, for example, health, the contents of food and what they contain. Many practices lie on the fringes of the law, some exploit loopholes (as for example the repeated addition of water to meat outlined above or the use of 'meaningless' descriptions such as 'traditional-style'); new practices emerge which necessitate new regulations, and prosecutions – even where breaches are found – are costly and difficult. Descriptions are not only written but can be photographic, as manufacturers routinely use photographic techniques to portray, for example, larger portions or larger amounts of ingredients on packets and in advertisements. A practice long recognised as a means of deceiving consumers is to sell items in larger packages – which Clinard and Yeager (1980) once described as selling fresh air. Packaging not only deceives consumers but can have a serious environmental impact.

Particularly in the wake of campaigns about obesity and the consumption of 'junk food', there have been recurrent concerns with manufacturers' claims about the presence of nutrients, the percentage of different ingredients, the fat content or the origins of food. Labelling laws are enormously complicated. 'Low fat' food, for example, must contain no more than 3g fat per 100g, 'reduced' at least less than 25 per cent less, but terms such as 'light' or 'extra light' have little meaning. FSA guidelines indicate that 'a little' fat amounts to 3g per 100g whereas 'a lot' would be the equivalent of 20g per 100g (*Which?* 2005b). A notorious example was the claim used by major manufacturers that food was '90 per cent fat free' which means that it could contain 10 per cent fat which would be high fat. Such claims have been subject to a range of investigations – academic, journalistic, by enforcement agencies and government departments and in particular by the Consumers' Association. Some examples of these include:

- A *Which?* study (2005a) 'named and shamed' 'offenders' making claims such as 'low-fat', 'nutritious' or 'fortified' for foods which contained high amounts of salt, fat or sugar. For example, Nestlé claims that its Cheerios cereal 'may be an easy way to keep your heart healthy', yet it is relatively high in salt, which is linked to high blood pressure. In another example, Sainsbury's 'Be Good to Yourself' Cream Crackers are reported to have been promoted on the basis that they contained 'less than 8 per cent fat'. However, they also contained 2g of salt per 100g. (*Which?* 2005a; Poulter 2005)

- Labels can be inaccurate and guidelines may be 'loose', as seen in the example of nutrient labelling. A *Which?* (2005b) investigation found that out of 70 foods tested, only 7 per cent of 570 nutrients matched what the label said, with 17 per cent falling outside an agreed error margin. There is no specific law about how accurate information must be as there are different ways of working out contents and the 'acceptable' error margin is 20–30 per cent depending on what proportion of a product the particular ingredient amounts to. Many foods contain more calories and fat than are declared for example:

  The worst offenders – those where the discrepancy lay outside the 'acceptable error margins' – included wafers containing nearly three times more saturated fat than the label stated – two biscuits would contain 3g of saturated fat (around one sixth of women's recommended daily amount).

One beef joint contained 90 per cent more fat and 70 per cent more saturates than indicated on the label. With 4.8g fat per 100g this could not, argues the report, be described as 'less than 3 per cent fat' as claimed.

Cadbury's light trifles had 23 per cent more fat than indicated.

Even with the acceptable margin, discrepancies could be significant. An ASDA chicken korma was found to have 81 more calories than indicated – although this is considered as 'acceptable'.

Some companies admitted their 'mistakes' but others claimed they were due to inevitable variations. For example, a Bernard Matthews spokesperson, when asked about a turkey roll with 22 per cent more fat than indicated on the label, replied that 'some natural variation in fat will occur from slice to slice'.

- A widely reported *Which?* (2004d) investigation concerned 'cereal offenders'. 100 cereal products, produced by the five biggest cereal manufacturers were purchased and their claims in relation to amounts of fibre, sugar, salt and saturated fats were tested, using FSA guidelines for what's 'a little' and 'a lot'. A nutrition expert was asked to identify the worst offenders. 'On the go' cereal bars and supermarkets' own brands were also included. Some of the main findings included:

  Most products contained high fibre, as claimed.

  85 per cent contained 'a lot' of sugar, including all but one of 28 cereals marketed for children.

  A 'shocking' 40 per cent contained 'a lot' of salt, which included 18 out of 28 for children.

  Most were a good source of vitamins and minerals.

  Many were low in fat as claimed, but nine contained 'a lot' and 13 listed hydrogenated oils (associated with trans fats), 10 of which were marketed for children.

  Similar findings were reported for 'own brands', and cereal bars contained less energy and fibre than an equivalent bowl of cereal.

Many implied, through the use of symbols, specific health benefits, but were high in salt.

- GM in processed food: it has also been found that a growing number of consumers (60 per cent according to *Which?* 2004b) are worried about GM foods and that those who wish to avoid them face difficulties. This *Which?* report cites an FSA report that most processed foods contain elements of GM whether or not this is declared on the label. Again, labelling laws are complex. Food containing GM derivatives must now be labelled as GM. Foods produced using GM technology, in which bacteria and yeasts may be used as processing aids but are not present in the end product, do not however have to be labelled. Similarly, foods made using animals fed with GM feed and those containing less than 0.9 per cent GM, where efforts have been made to prevent contamination, do not have to be labelled. Almost all supermarket own brand milk and much meat comes from animals fed on GM and does not therefore have to be labelled. One study by scientists at Glamorgan University tested a variety of food products, such as vegetarian sausage mix and organic burger meat, labelled 'GM free' or 'organic' and found that around 80 per cent contained GM soya (Utton 2004).

Many food descriptions used in advertising are subject to regulation, and a number of widely used descriptions breach guidelines. An FSA study (Rowan and Kellow 2004; Uhlig 2004) carried out with Trading Standards officers, found that four out of ten samples using terms for which guidelines exist (fresh, natural, pure, traditional, original, authentic, home-made) broke these guidelines. For example:

While a 'farmhouse' product should be made in a house on a farm, or more specifically in the farmer's main dwelling, about three-quarters of products claiming to be 'farmhouse' were produced in industrial premises.

'Traditional' foods should be made from recipes, ingredients and cooking methods which have 'existed for a significant period', but Tesco was chastised for labelling its Irish Wheaten Loaf as traditional, when it was baked in store and used flour treatment agents that were 'unlikely to be part of the Irish tradition'.

Manufacturers who used 'traditional-style' as a label were castigated by the agency for using a term it said was 'meaningless'.

'Home-made' was also widely misused, in particular on The Original and Genuine Home-made Sticky Toffee Pudding made by Cartmel Village Shop, which the report said was 'believed to be produced on a large scale outside of domestic facilities'.

The head of food labelling and standards at the FSA said the report showed manufacturers targeting descriptions that shoppers particularly looked for when buying food, such as fresh, pure and natural. 'They rightly expect foods labelled with these terms to be different in some way from products that don't carry these types of descriptions,' she said. 'They don't expect items labelled fresh to have a four-week shelf life, they don't expect items labelled as pure to have added ingredients and they don't expect products with ingredients described as natural to have used artificial preservatives and additives' (cited in Rowan and Kellow 2004).

Pictorial images

Pictorial images are also 'descriptions', yet again these can be misleading and it is difficult to prosecute. For example, it is often unclear whether rules are being broken (*Which?* 2004e). Some rules are clear cut – if eight cakes are pictured when the packet contains only four, this is clearly illegal, but the use of substitute foods and other misleading images must be shown to be 'misleading' as to the 'nature, substance or quality of the food'. Thus, enhancing the look of the food may not be misleading as it represents what the food *might* be like. The *Which?* report lists a number of 'photographic tricks' such as blow torching food to give a 'grilled' or barbecued look, showing a pie full of ingredients when in reality it may not be 'full' and – the aspect complained about most – misleading indications of portions; – in some cases, small plates are used to indicate a 'full plate'. In one case, the Independent Television Commission (ITC) ruled against a McDonald's advertisement in which all the fillings of a burger were pulled to the front, making it look fuller than it really was.

Misleading packaging

Misleading packaging is also a widely recognised problem (Croall 2001). A recent *Which?* (2005c) survey reveals a range of practices which are arguably deceptive. Yet again, these breaches are difficult to prosecute as companies claim 'convincing' reasons, such as the need to prevent damage to the product, for excess packaging. The survey highlights practices such as wrapping small numbers of biscuits inside small packs, all put together in one big pack, which they liken to 'pass the parcel'. Other practices include selling food in larger packages, making it look as if more food is being bought. Suppliers are said to capitalise on consumer behaviour – according to DTI research which they cite, many consumers ignore labels indicating quantity and judge the amount of goods by look or feel. Some companies have taken action about this, and there is now more pressure as regards packaging in the face of EU rules about reducing the amount of plastic waste sent to landfill sites.

These examples are again highly selective. More could be added. They illustrate the widespread nature and some of the key features of crimes involving food, which are taken up below.

The criminological significance of food crime?

As illustrated above, food involves a vast range of crimes largely neglected by criminology, even in the areas where it might be expected to feature. Thus the major focus in the study of corporate crime has tended to be on occupational and other forms of safety and environmental crime. The literature on white-collar crime more often associates this with financial and employee frauds and tax evasion. The study of transnational crime has dealt primarily with illegal criminal industries such as drugs, organised crime, contraband goods, people trafficking, money laundering and environmental crime. It has rarely included food. Crimes involving food cross many of these categories, and many are also, as illustrated above, regarded as rather trivial, 'consumer' issues, as food 'scares' and not as crime. Possible exceptions to this are more serious frauds involving 'organised' or more conventionally 'criminal' offenders.

Is food crime of importance to criminology? Arguments in favour of including food crime in large part follow those used in relation to the criminological significance of corporate or environmental criminology (Croall 2001), green criminology (South 1998a) or specific issues such as GM foods (Walters 2004) along with those used by theorists who argue that the boundaries of criminology are 'porous' and should not be 'fixed' (Loader and Sparks 2002). In addition, as seen above, food, being a basic essential, is the subject of some very serious frauds and modern food processing raises many issues of safety – indeed, it is a key area of risk, also of concern to criminological theory (Loader and Sparks 2002). To critical criminologists, many food crimes can be seen as an example of corporate violence. The above examples also show that they raise key issues about how crimes such as 'fraud' are constructed and activities are criminalised.

A related question is where the study of 'food crime' is best situated within criminology. In some respects this may not matter (except, for example, in conferences or contributions to edited collections!) as traditional categories are often, and some would argue, increasingly, blurred, as seen in lengthy debates over definitions of organised or white-collar and corporate crime and distinctions between them (Ruggiero 1996; Croall 2001; 2005). The examples above include cases which involve transnational organised crime, white-collar crime, so called 'conventional crime', and crimes committed by small, otherwise legitimate, businesses.

Food crime, notwithstanding the presence of many small businesses, may seem closest to corporate crime and its analysis almost inevitably draws from theoretical work in that area. It involves key issues raised in the literature on corporate crime about how the definition of crime and criminalisation can be related to the interests of powerful business lobbies. One example is the widespread resistance, by large multinational food manufacturers and retailers, to forms of labelling and other regulations – also a problem noted in relation to GM food (Walters 2004). Moreover, the examples above illustrate how these groups, despite claims of corporate social responsibility (Jones *et al.* 2005), also seek to evade the 'letter of the law' by using ever complex forms of 'legalised adulteration'. In addition, as will be seen below, the analysis of food crime must incorporate the broader socio-economic context of food production and retailing, as has been done in studies of corporate crime in specific industries such as pharmaceuticals (Braithwaite 1984) or chemicals (Pearce and Tombs 1998). Food, as is the case with these industries, also raises questions about what counts as legitimate scientific knowledge, seen in the many discussions over the safety and long-term health implications of food.

There have been calls for 'greening' criminology (South 1998a; 1998b) and food crime may well belong in this area, although it is not yet fully theorised or defined (Lynch and Stretesky 2003). It also shares many elements with the study of corporate crime including questioning which activities are to be included and moving beyond the narrow confines of the criminal law by questioning the way in which some activities, particularly those of the powerful, are criminalised (Lynch and Stretesky 2003). Food production, agriculture and fishing have an enormous environmental significance and cause harm to humans and other species. The disposal of 'unfit' meat

223

and food packaging are also major environmental issues. Like both corporate crime and 'green' criminology, food crime also raises important issues of social inequality and social justice (Lynch and Stretesky 2003). The poor, for example, may have less opportunity to purchase cheap healthy food given the concentration of food retailing and the 'cheapness' and attractiveness of mass-produced, unhealthy food (Lawrence 2004).

While drawing many theoretical points from these two areas, food crime also demonstrates the limitations of fixed categories as it also involves more traditional 'organised' criminals and indeed provides an example of how both legitimate and illegitimate industries may collude or how organised crime may provide a service to legitimate industry (see, for example, Ruggiero 1996). In cases such as 'meat laundering', the use by farmers and food packaging firms of illegal immigrants, and the landing of large catches of black fish, there is collusion between legitimate and illegitimate industries. Criminal gang masters are providing a service to legitimate industry, just as illegal meat firms are taking unwanted waste out of the hands of legitimate processors and packers. And as is the case when comparing, for example, organised criminals with white-collar or corporate offenders, it is the former's activities which attract heavier forms of criminalisation while the 'legalised adulteration' of food by legitimate multinational food producers is seen as a far less serious matter.

Wherever 'food crime' fits within criminology, and whether or not it should become a 'new' criminological category, its analysis inevitably involves placing it in the context of the wider features of food production, some of which can be seen as 'criminogenic'. While time and space preclude a full analysis of these features, consider:

- Globalisation: food production is now globalised, which has given rise to many issues surrounding, for example, the use of GM crops, food miles (the miles travelled by food from crop to plate and the environmental impact of this), the widespread drive to produce and market 'out of season' food in countries in Southern Europe and Africa – which can damage the environment in these countries (Lawrence 2004a; Millstone and Lang 2003) in addition to involving the exploitation of cheap labour. And as with other areas of transnational corporate crime, those involved in the food industries may utilise the 'spaces' between laws (Croall 2005).

- Many practices are also related to issues of world trade, fair trade and subsidies. The most obvious examples of this are provided by the cases of black fishing which have emerged in response to the imposition of quotas to maintain fish stocks and the massive subsidies frauds in the EU and in other countries. The widespread use of corn, sugar, soya, palm and rapeseed in food production (much of which is widely seen as a form of adulteration) is related to their being among the most subsidised crops (Lawrence 2004a). The food industry, contests Lawrence, is provided with cheap ingredients by the 'handful of global giants' who dominate trading and processing, whose subsidies undermine farmers in developing countries. These food giants represent powerful political lobbies – the American Sugar Association, for example, lobbied the Bush administration to seek changes to advice by the World Health Organisation about the use of processed sugars.

- Food manufacturing and retailing is now heavily concentrated within large manufacturers and retailers. In the UK, for example, by 2003, the top 10 food retailers accounted for just over 82 per cent of food sales and 4 retailers (Tesco, Sainsbury's, ASDA and Morrison's) enjoyed a 65.3 per cent market share (Jones *et al.* 2005). The power that this implies has raised many issues around competition and pricing. An investigation into the activities of major supermarkets by the Competition Commission in 2000 covered the issue of the level of profits extracted by supermarkets – concluding that they were not excessively profiteering. It also considered their relationship with suppliers amidst allegations of practices such as charging suppliers for shelf space and promotions, retrospectively reducing prices, and 'bullying' suppliers. Also criticised has been the uniformity of produce which supermarkets have caused by accepting only food which fits supermarket preferences as to shape and colour (which has led in some cases to the virtual extinction of some crop varieties). Orders fluctuate and there are strong pressures for 'just in time' production. A code of practice was introduced but, while few suppliers are prepared to openly complain (fearing that their contracts will be terminated), media investigations and 'insiders' claim that abuses are widespread, and a range of groups including Friends of the Earth and FARM (a farming pressure group campaigning for independent farmers) are calling for a new Office of Fair Trading investigation (Blythman 2004; Lawrence 2004a; *Which?* 2003f; Jones *et al.* 2005).

This has also been related to the use of casual labour and low wages as the pressure on farmers and food packers is such that they need large amounts of labour to fill orders at short notice.

Their need for casual labour exceeds the supply of local labour who would in any event not be prepared to work for such low wages and long hours. According to Lawrence (2004a: 42), 'supermarkets have driven down prices and transferred the risk to suppliers; they in turn save money by not carrying the spare capacity that flexibility really demands'. She further cites an EFRA (House of Commons, Environment, Food and Rural Affairs Committee) report of 2003 which concluded that the supermarkets' dominant position was a significant contributory factor in creating an environment where illegal activity by gang masters can take root.

- Food adulteration, as seen above, is a major part of modern food processing which relies on maximising the value of basic ingredients by 'value adding' and using cheap ingredients to replace more expensive 'natural' foods – and selling them for more than the sum of their parts (Lawrence 2004a). Staggering amounts are spent by food manufacturers on additives – estimated to amount to around £20 billion. As seen above, these are often used for cosmetic reasons, but they are also used to extend the shelf life of food to enable more sales and to provide more 'convenience' food.

- Pressures on growers and suppliers to provide basic ingredients at low, sometimes less than cost price often provide the context for adulteration. Mandalia (2005) argues that the Sudan 1 scandal came as no surprise to spice traders who have long been aware of the adulteration of spices coming from India – in one case Customs officers found turmeric powder to be no more than garam flour dyed yellow. However, he argues it is not just unscrupulous suppliers who are to blame, as such practices are ultimately linked to European demand for low prices which 'more or less forces' producers – who need Western currency to survive – to cheat. Moreover, dyeing was introduced as wholesalers wanted brightly coloured spices.

These provide a few examples of how many forms of food crime are related to the structure of the food industry. It can also be argued that industrial interests have a strong effect on the law itself, regulation and, in a wider sense, on which foods, however unhealthy they may be, are more likely to be consumed.

References

Braithwaite, J. (1984) *Corporate Crime in the Pharmaceutical Industry*. London: Routledge and Kegan Paul.

Clarke, M. (1994) *EC Fraud, Issues in Sociology and Social Policy*. Occasional Paper No. 4, Department of Sociology, Social Policy and Social Work Studies, University of Liverpool.

Clinard, M. and Yeager, P. (1980) *Corporate Crime*. New York: Free Press.

Croall, H. (1987) *Crimes against the Consumer: An Analysis of the Nature, Extent, Regulation and Sanctioning of Trading Crime*. London: University of London (unpublished Ph.D. thesis).

Croall, H. (1989) 'Who is the White Collar Criminal?' *British Journal of Criminology*, 29 (2): 157–74.

Croall, H. (1992) *White Collar Crime*. Buckingham: Open University Press.

Croall, H. (2001a) *Understanding White Collar Crime*. Buckingham: Open University Press.

Croall, H. (2005) 'Transnational White Collar Crime', in J. Sheptycki and A.Wardak (eds) *Transnational and Comparative Criminology*. London: Glasshouse Press.

Doig, A. (2006) *Fraud*. Cullompton: Willan Publishing.

Elliot, V. (2001) 'Fraud spurs change in farming payouts', *The Times*, 31 July: 1.

Evans–Pritchard, A. (2002) 'Financial watchdog discloses EU fraud and error', *The Daily Telegraph*, 6 November: 19.

Jones, P., Comfort, D., Hillier, D. and Eastwood, I. (2005) 'Corporate Social Responsibility: A Case Study of the UK's Leading Food Retailers', *British Food Journal*, 107 (6): 423–425.

Lawrence, F. (2004a) *Not on the Label! What Really Goes into the Food on Your Plate*. London: Penguin Books.

Lawrence, F. (2004b) 'Supermarkets criticised over water in fresh pork', *The Guardian*, 16 July 2004. (www.guardian.co.uk/food/story/ accessed 20 December 2005).

Loader, I. and Sparks, R. (2002) 'Contemporary Landscapes of Crime, Order and Control. Governance, Risk and Globalization', in M. Maguire, R. Morgan and R. Reiner (eds), *The Oxford Handbook of Criminology*, 3rd. edn. Oxford: Oxford University Press.

Lynch, M. and Stretesky, P. (2003) 'The Meaning of Green: Contrasting Criminological Perspectives', *Theoretical Criminology*, 7 (2): 217–238.

Mackay, N. (2003) 'Fishermen have to catch black fish: Just to survive we have to break the law', *Sunday Herald*, 23 November 2003: 13.

Mandalia, S. 'The spice traders' tale', *New Statesman*, 7 March 2005: 14.

Millstone, E. and Lang, T. (2003) *The Atlas of Food*. London: Earthscan Books.

Muir, H. (2004) 'Restaurant inspectors urge "scores on doors": Councils plan public display of results of hygiene inspections to cut 1m-plus food poisoning cases a year', *The Guardian*, 14 September: 5.

Nelken, D. (2002) 'White Collar Crime' in M. Maguire, R. Morgan and R. Reiner (eds), *The Oxford Handbook of Criminology*, 3rd ed. Oxford: Oxford University Press.

Passas, N. and Nelken, D. (1993) 'The Thin Line Between Legitimate and Criminal Enterprises: Subsidy Frauds in the European Union', *Crime, Law and Social Change*, 19: 223–43.

Poulter, S. (2005) '"Healthy" foods that are high in salt and sugar', *Daily Mail*, 24 May: 27.

Rowan, D. and Kellow, J. (2004) 'Pack of porky pies', *The Times*, 20 March: 16.

Ruggiero, V. (1996) *Organised and Corporate Crime in Europe: Offers That Can't be Refused*. Aldershot: Dartmouth.

Smith, G. (2005) 'Black fishing "policeman" attacks greed of top crews. £3m discovery may only be tip of iceberg', *The Herald*, 3 May: 11.

Smith, R. (2003) '£1m fish fraud firms net fines', *The Daily Mirror*, 5 April: 20.

South, N. (1998) 'A Green Field for Criminology? A Proposal for a Perspective', *Theoretical Criminology*, 2 (2): 211–34.

Stringer, D. (2003) '"Maggot Pete" gets six years for food fraud', *The Independent*, 13 December: 13.

Sutherland, E.H. (1949) *White Collar Crime*. New York: Holt, Reinhart and Winston.

The Economist (2001) 'Europe: Glut, fraud and eco-damage', *The Economist*, 30 June, 359, (8228): 46–47.

Uhlig, R. (2004) 'Farmhouse fresh? It's more likely to have been produced on an industrial estate: Government watchdog accuses supermarkets and manufacturers of duping shoppers with misleading labels', *The Daily Telegraph*, 12 February: 4.

Urquhart, F. (2005) 'Two trawlermen may lose £3m assets from illegal fish landings', *The Scotsman*, 27 April: 23.

Utton, T. (2004) 'It may say organic, but it could be GM; Misleading labels blamed for not warning of polluted soya', *Daily Mail*, 11 March: 15.

Watt, N. (2002) 'Officials "appallingly lax" over farm subsidy checks', *The Guardian*, 22 August: 18.

Wilkinson, I. (2002) 'Olive growers ditch tradition for subsidies. EU cash has encouraged intensive farming and fraud', *The Daily Telegraph*, 10 July: 12

Wilson, I. (2005) 'Ramsay's kitchen nightmare as he falls foul of hygiene rules. Inspectors cite restaurant's poor cleanliness and food storage', *The Herald*, 16 May: 4.

Which? (2002) 'Food labelling' *Which?*, Online, Dec 2002.

Which? (2003) 'Hygiene, takeaway' *Which?*, Online, May 2003.

Which? (2004a) 'Food safety', *Which?* Online, February 2004.

Which? (2004b) 'No to GM', *Which?* Online, September 2004.

Which? (2004c) 'Food, use by dates', *Which?* Online, April 2004.

Which? (2004d) 'Cereal offenders', *Which?* Online, April 2004.

Which? (2004e) 'Trick packs?, *Which?* Online, November 2004.

Which? (2004f) 'Are we getting a raw deal?', *Which?* Online, June 2004.

Which? (2005b) 'Nutrition labelling', *Which?* Online, March 2005.

Which? (2005c) 'Food packaging', *Which?* Online, April 2005.

Chapter 10

The 'corporate colonisation of nature':[1] Bio-prospecting, bio-piracy and the development of green criminology

Nigel South

Introduction

In working towards a green criminology it is important to demonstrate that it has the characteristics that might be expected of a new direction for research. These might include differing points of origin that lead to an identifiable discourse, embracing both convergence and divergence of interests and approaches, and the related growth of citation within and external to the subject. This chapter engages with the need to review existing foundations for a green criminology but it then focuses on further prospects for study, illustrated by consideration of the particular case of corporate exploration and exploitation of biodiversity.

Global biotechnology industries have increasingly sought to identify and exploit natural products with medicinal and healing properties found in developing nations. This notion of 'finding' – locating, identifying, using – is pivotal. The biodiversity of different environments has yielded products with numerous uses for local and wider populations for centuries. The subsequent assertion by Western interests of the ownership of genetic materials and pharmacological products via Western-based intellectual property rights and patents has been criticised as a new form of piracy and colonial expropriation. Similar practices, issues and concerns are associated with the global expansion of Western bio-agricultural corporations and contestation around ownership of seeds, plants and knowledge derived from indigenous farmers. As Cleveland and Murray (1997: 477) note, 'The "globalization" of resources and the problems caused by increasing rates of resource use and degradation have increased conflict over the meaning of, and rights to, resources that have previously enjoyed somewhat separate existences in indigenous and industrial worlds.' The aim of this chapter is to take some further steps in the elaboration of a green perspective within criminology and illustrate potential contributions to the study of rights, justice, nature and globalised society. Discussion of these topics can be brought together in considering cases of activities described by supporters as bio-prospecting and by critics as bio-piracy.

Green criminology: challenges, achievements, prospects

Proposing a green perspective *for* criminology is about more than simply adding a new perspective *within* criminology, it is a call for inter-disciplinary awareness and collaboration. Characterised by Downes (1988) as a 'rendezvous subject' and remarked upon by Garland and Sparks (2000: 190) as having no monopoly on the study of crime, criminology is well positioned to expand its contribution to interdisciplinary research on local and global environmental issues.

It is not possible to review the full range of green critical inquiry here but brief examples can be provided that also serve the purpose of illustrating how the themes of justice, rights, nature and globalisation have been explored in green criminological work so far.

Environmental justice and rights versus crimes and claims of the powerful

One concept that unifies a now considerable body of work in this field is the idea of environmental justice (see also this volume, White, Lynch and Stretesky, and Benton). Many studies have drawn attention to the environmental victimisation of communities of the poor and powerless due to the frequency with which their locations are also the sites of, for example, polluting industry, waste processing plants or other environmentally hazardous facilities (Bullard 1994). Environmental injustices also include cases where local, indigenous populations have been forcibly removed from land to which they are spiritually attached or where their land has been exploited for military, agribusiness or other purposes in circumstances depriving them of any control or say (Samson 2003; Kuletz 1998). Usually the consequences are damaging, if not devastating, producing community dislocation, relationship breakdowns, mental health and substance misuse problems and so on. Hence, White (2004: 281) usefully suggests that:

> *Environmental justice* refers to the distribution of environments among peoples ... and the impacts of particular social practices on specific populations. The focus of analysis is therefore on human health and well-being and how these are affected by particular types of production and consumption. Here we can distinguish between environmental issues that affect everyone, and those that disproportionately affect specific individuals and groups (see Williams 1996).

Relevant to these observations as well as to globalisation, Simon (2000) notes the additions to the research agenda offered by Szasz and Meuser (1997) concerning topics that may have been neglected by environmental justice research to date. These include '(a) the place of the upper class in environmental research and (b) the lack of both a global and a historical perspective' (Simon 2000: 633). Major offenders against the environment such as industrial corporations and parts of government mean 'the upper class' are represented by chief executives, major shareholders and those in positions of political power, and Simon also comments that 'most large American environmental polluters are transnational in scope' (*ibid*.: 634), engaging in 'international environmental wrongdoing'. Exploring the idea of 'institutionalised insensitivity to right and wrong' (*ibid*.: 635) as an underpinning of environmental injustice, Simon lists a long record of violations of environmental and white-collar crime laws. Importantly, the scale of such insensitivity and injustice is largely unrecorded and unacknowledged in the public arena as media coverage can be 'censored' and stories massaged by the expensive public relations companies employed by corporations.[2] By such means can corporate messages manipulate opinion and employ techniques of neutralisation (Sykes and Matza 1957), the public receive reassurance, and critics be marginalised. At the global level, Simon indicts the waste industry as chronically open to corruption, all the more devastating when 'most of its victims include the least powerful people on the face of the earth, poverty-stricken people of color, most of whom are powerless to resist the environmental deviance of multinational firms' (*ibid*.: 639).

Nature: genetic modification of food and the discursive modification of 'risk'

Explicitly seeking to contribute to a green criminology, Walters (2004) seeks to integrate 'the GM debate into existing criminological discourses about chemical crimes and environmental pollution (see

Lynch *et al.* 2000) and deviant behaviour "for economic venture"'
(Ruggiero 2002). Walters synthesises the work and outcomes of
the New Zealand Royal Commission on Genetic Modification
which reported in 2001, producing four volumes and containing 49
recommendations. According to Walters (p. 153), 'the vast amount
of expert evidence ... casts doubt over GM's safety and the ability
of regulatory authorities to adequately manage potential health and
ecological risks', yet the dominant theme of the report is the need to
'keep options open'. Walters employs the work of Beck (1992) on the
global risk society and draws attention to the particular perceptions
of risk at stake here: 'In the GM debate we see that agents of power
are not identifying high risk to exert control but asserting a position
of low risk in an attempt to manipulate and monopolize world trade
in the food industry' (p. 162). In terms of future research and debate,
Walters suggests that what will be required is 'a criminological
knowledge capable of transcending disciplinary boundaries in order
to critique the multifaceted dimensions of international biotechnology'
(p. 165). Here, Walters addresses the themes of globalisation and of
risk related to corporate engineering of nature but also calls for an
interdisciplinary perspective.

Globalisation: eco-bio-genocide as transnational crime

Transnational crime is complex by its very nature (Passas 1999)
and environmental issues, in particular, demonstrate the intimate
relationship between the global and the local. One significant case-
study illustrating the intertwining of political, economic, cultural and
environmental matters has been provided by del Olmo (1987; 1998),
and she shows how 'the war on drugs' has led to 'crimes against the
environment' (1987: 30) and how very different parties engage with
different definitions and forms of criminal activity. In the 1980s, the
Reagan administration (as others before and since) maintained that
the drug problem was in large part a supply phenomenon and that
interdiction and eradication were the twin strategies to be vigorously
pursued, aimed at seizing drugs before they reached, or at, the US
border, and destroying production of e.g. marijuana and cocaine in
the fields and mountains of Latin America. The latter provides del
Olmo's focus as she investigates *'a type of crime committed on the
pretext of preventing another crime'*; this

> is a crime which has the characteristics of ecocide by virtue
> of making war with certain methods, systems, or prohibited

233

weapons. Vietnam was a good example, with napalm and Agent Orange. Today the new war is on drugs and its weapons are toxic chemicals, especially herbicides prohibited in their place of origin for causing poisoning, contamination of food, and serious environmental problems, like *paraquat, gliphosphate* and *agent orange* [all italics in original].

Crop eradication programmes have limited effectiveness as a method of curtailing drugs production but do have serious effects on the 'quality of life' and the health of local inhabitants, especially when toxic chemicals are liberally used, frequently using aerial spray methods which of course mean the chemicals can be blown across a wide area.[3] Del Olmo argues that historically such programmes fail and merely expand the drug industry into new areas 'ultimately increasing the sources of supply':

> We are thus faced with a transnational crime of broad scope which we can call *eco-bio-genocide*. [This] involves the utilization of a whole complex of toxic chemicals ... which are prohibited and/or restricted in the developed countries but have an unlimited market in Third World countries ... such chemicals are utilized widely in programs of drug eradication because the sole preoccupation is to destroy the marijuana and cocaine crops before they arrive in the United States in order to protect North American youth, regardless of the consequences for Third World youth' (p. 31) (emphasis in original).

These policies and practices continue today and not just in Latin America. The official focus is on outcomes related to the destruction or depletion of drug harvests and hence supply-reduction. What seem to be largely neglected in considerations of success or failure of such initiatives are the consequences of chemical crop eradication for those living with the residues and contamination of water, and with other affected plant-life and symptoms of ill-health. Although not explicitly proposed, del Olmo's work connects with the idea of environmental justice and we could identify here and in similar work contributions to a 'green victimology' (see Williams 1996).

The problem of protection: rights, regulation and law

The examples given so far indicate some of the diverse ways in which green criminological research can contribute to discourses around justice, nature and globalisation. However, one further set of issues is worth addressing and concerns the long-standing criminological problem of how to provide 'protection' and assurance of rights. The questions that then follow are by no means straightforward – for example, who or what is to be protected?; who or what is the protection to be afforded against?; what (if any) are the most effective ways of providing 'protection' against offending, exploitation and abuses of power and laws?

In terms of the themes of rights and justice, nature and globalisation, one obvious question is whether global and/or national laws can ever offer suitable space(s) for the protection of nature and the environment? Miller (1995) takes the case of 'environmental rights' and starting from his curiosity about a commitment from politicians and activists to promote a 'right to clean air' (at what point does such a 'right' become 'meaningful'?) he examines environmental rights in terms of relevant law in England and the European Union. Importantly, he notes difficulties in the use of existing law not least in trying to 'clarify what an anthropocentric environmental right might be' in the context of 'the several technical, political and legal obstacles to its recognition in United Kingdom law'. Nonetheless, Miller concludes that the 'benefits for public (that is, human) health which would follow from treating the atmosphere (if not, coastal waters) as a legal entity endowed with a right not to be polluted have become apparent' (p. 390).

This argument can be usefully read alongside Benton (1998 and this volume) and Beirne (1999 and this volume, on the concept of 'speciesism') for it is clear that the inter-related topics of environmental, human and animal rights present considerable further complications. To paraphrase Benton (1998), whatever the merits of rights-based arguments as applied to the environment or animals, they are unlikely to be successful unless accompanied by fundamental economic, social, political and cultural changes between humans.

One consistent theme in global political discourse about environmental rights is the need to establish a reasonable balance of interests between environmental protection and the costs of providing this. This has been seen in operation at a global level as part of the underlying opposition of the USA to the Kyoto agreement, viewed by US anti-environmental 'hawks' as a European conspiracy to damage America's competitiveness and 'reduce' its standard of living to European levels. In national and local contexts, Du Rees (2001: 115) argues that what is reflected here is:

... a question of the way environmental criminal law has been constructed as a form of legislative balancing act, which involves making compromises between different interests, i.e. economic factors and environmental considerations ... agencies whose task is to apply the law and report suspected offences have a dual role whose two sides are in competition with one another ... both helping companies to follow the environmental laws, and prosecuting their breaches of the law. This unclear role gives rise to an uneven application of the law ...

This control dilemma is well known internationally and can lead to the unsatisfactory phenomenon of 'regulatory capture' (Simon 2000: 640–642). Indeed the regulatory system can be manipulated from the outset (Szasz 1986), as the case of the relationship between the biotech company Monsanto and successive US governments has shown (Eichenwald *et al.* 2001).[4]

In this respect, White (2004: 279) argues that:

The state ... has a formal role and commitment to protect citizens from the worst excesses or worst instances of environmental victimisation. Hence the introduction of extensive legislation and regulatory procedures designed to give the appearance of active intervention, and the implication that laws exist which actually do deter such harms. The existence of such laws *may* be encouraging in that they reflect historical and ongoing struggles over certain types of activity. But how or whether they are used once again begs the questions of the relationship between the state and the corporate sector, and the capacity of business to defend its interests by legal and extra-legal means (my emphasis).

These observations offer resonance with the themes of rights, justice, nature and globalisation explored here. However, they apply particularly to advanced Western nations because they are largely concerned with the environmental problems and areas of contestation within and across such societies. The developing world, including indigenous communities with little socio-economic engagement with the West, as well as post-colonial societies still striving for stability and security, are acknowledged in such formal regulatory discourse but largely in terms of tokenism, additions to the main body of policy statements and agreements, or – significantly – admissions of difficulties posed. The exploitation of plant, animal and human genetic resources represents an arena in which different sets of economic, cultural and knowledge interests and claims can be seen to conflict. Under contemporary conditions of globalisation, the transnational mobility of corporate operations and the application of international trade and property law powerfully reshape the basis of rights and challenge indigenous concepts and cosmologies of 'nature' (whether identified with non-human living matter or natural resources or human beings themselves). In this process, knowledge becomes intellectual 'property'.

Intellectual property and 'the corporate colonisation of nature'

McCoy (2005: 48) sets out some of the context relevant to the cases and discussion that follow. In the early 1990s,

> the Agreement on Trade Related Aspects of Intellectual Property Rights (TRIPS) was established. It has since been described by some academics in the field of intellectual property as a charter for the protection of northern knowledge-based industries that want to strengthen their grip on the global control of knowledge and continue to accrue the power necessary to discipline both markets and states. The extended scope of patents, to cover, for example, discoveries made in the natural world, opens up the way for the corporate colonisation of nature.

The TRIPS agreement originates with an organisation that was perhaps little known to the wider public until the 1999 Seattle protests against the World Trade Organisation, a body that is largely invisible yet makes decisions of enormous significance for producers and consumers in both developed and developing countries.

Patenting biology

The first patent of a living organism was granted in the US on 1 June 1980 (Tsioumanis et al. 2003: 606) and, as Crespi (2000) notes, marked 'a watershed in the development of patent law, as a precedent for extension to cell lines ... and genetically modified plants and animals'. Essentially the biotechnology industry of the late twentieth and twenty-first centuries extracts value from biodiversity, natural and human resources, remaking 'the natural' into products for the commercial market (e.g. recycling skin cells into cosmetic treatments).[5] Tsioumanis *et al.* (2003: 607) observe that 'Most of the mega-biodiversity countries are developing countries, which could profit substantially in financial terms from their wealth in biodiversity.' But translating 'could' into 'will' is the problem. Furthermore, these authors note that 'in many cases, those extraordinary properties of biological resources that now get commercial interest were already known to indigenous communities and used for centuries'. Again, the problem is whether 'commercial interest' will recognise this fact and, further, whether the complex *meaning* of such properties is understood. As used by indigenous peoples these natural products have a place in cultural and cosmological systems. Their properties, of real efficacy and symbolic value, are seen as intimately woven together with tradition. How strange then that authorities that are remote and external can empower others to lay their own claims of ownership.

A few brief cases can illustrate how such 'commercial interest' in 'extraordinary properties' leads to ethical and economic dispute. Noting that 'patents are still being granted on properties which have been well known for generations', Vidal (2000: 9) provides one example in the instance of the University of Mississippi which took out 'US patent no 5,401,504 on turmeric, which Indians have long known can heal wounds faster'. Vidal also describes the case of Dr Conrad Gorinsky, ethnobotanist, prospector and environmentalist, who 'stands accused on four continents of being a "biological (or bio-)pirate" – someone who identifies and extracts material from plants for profit.' In this case Gorinsky patented a chemical protein of the greenheart tree of Guyana, submitting a description to the US patent office concerning the nut of the tree as a source of an anti-pyretic (i.e. useful for prevention or control of fever) with possible applications in treatments for malaria, cancer and possibly AIDS. Promises of cure and prevention of disease suggest that a unique and major discovery has been made. However, the Wapishana tribe with which Gorinsky spent his time in Amazonia have a well-established knowledge of and set of uses for the derivatives from the greenheart nut (e.g. grating it to stop haemorrhages, prevent infections, and use in contraception). Unsurprisingly, the Wapishana object to the patenting in an overseas country of a local resource and their traditional knowledge for the profit of a remote global enterprise. Vidal (*ibid.*) reports Gorinsky's response as 'Tough, isn't it? ... I have analysed the chemical structure but I have not patented the tree or a life process. How can I tell the Wapishana about the science? They just inherited the greenheart. They don't own it. I have invested in this with my own money.' Nonetheless, as Vidal also notes, 'Gorinsky's defence that he is realising benefits to human kind is countered by critics who argue that stealing knowledge is a question of national sovereignty.'

In another case based on exploitation of Amazonian biodiversity, in 1986 Loren Miller obtained a US patent on a purported variety of an Amazonian vine also known as Ayahuasca. In 1994 the existence of this patent was discovered with some dismay by the body representing the organisations of indigenous peoples of the Amazon Basin. Ayahuasca has been cultivated and used for medicinal and religious purposes throughout this region for centuries so the evident question was how a stranger could 'discover' its properties and claim ownership? A long dispute followed with the patent first being overturned in 1999 but then reinstated in 2001. Future continuing dispute is likely.[6]

Bio-patenting and bias

Tsioumanis *et al.* (2003: 612) argue that while the UN Convention on Biological Diversity (CBD) calls for the 'protection of indigenous knowledge', the WTO agreement on Trade Related Aspects of Intellectual Property Rights

> obligates its members to adopt patents or a *sui generis* [unique] system for plant varieties. Conservation and privatization are seen by many as contradictory goals, and the TRIPS agreement is accused for restricting the availability of genetic resources and causing risks for food security and sustainable livelihoods of local communities by jeopardizing farmers' rights. ... Furthermore, Western-style intellectual regimes do not fit the characteristics of traditional knowledge, and can therefore hardly be used for its protection.

Here lie the roots of the critique of bio-patenting and biotechnology /bio-agriculture development as forms of bio-piracy and post-colonial exploitation. The core element of injustice arises in a twofold manner:

> In the case of commercialization of products incorporating traditional knowledge, indigenous and local communities suffer a double loss. On one hand, they cannot share the benefits arising from the new product, as this right stays with the

holder of the patent. On the other hand, applications of modern biotechnology often eliminate the need for commercial growing of the original plant, depriving thus the local population from another source of income. (Tsioumanis *et al.* 2003: 608)

Among various causes for concern is that the key principle of patenting is being blatantly and repeatedly violated. Patent law is supposed to require that an invention or discovery be clearly and evidently 'novel'. Clark (2000: 9) explains that to get a patent granted:

It is not enough to identify the gene sequence there also has to be an 'inventive step'. Critics anxious about the power of a handful of Western multi-nationals who dominate ag-bio, contend that the corporations are over-zealous in their patenting and are permitted by regulators to obtain protection over crops by adding the simplest of 'inventive steps'.

The compromised and weak state of regulatory regimes has already been referred to.

Discussion: a post-colonial perspective

One of the major critics of bio-prospecting as the 'plunder of nature and knowledge' has been Vandana Shiva (1998) who has argued against the kinds of justification put forward by Gorinsky and the multinationals, citing this as the same kind of logic that has supported centuries of colonial theft and denial of rights: 'The most fundamental cause of biopiracy is the colonial syndrome of Columbus's "discovery". Just as Europeans claimed that Columbus "discovered" America and the Europeans could therefore take it away from the original inhabitants, the old colonial mentality allows the piracy of biodiversity and knowledge from non-western cultures to be claimed as "invention", needing patent protection.' (http://www. vshiva.net/archives/biopiracy/pirates.htm; 2003; Shiva 1998).

Following Shiva, parallels with the state-sponsored acts of piracy of earlier centuries can be seen. Chambliss (2005: 13) observes that:

various states permitted pirates to bring and unload pirated goods in their ports for a share of the profit. Indeed, English and European commercial enterprises in the 17th to 19th centuries were inextricably interwoven with piracy. For example, Sir

> Francis Drake and [Sir John] Hawkins were sent by an English investment company, with the blessing of the English monarchy, to get slaves from Africa and to sell them in the West Indies.

The global regimes of international law and trade have changed since the days of Drake and Hawkins but expeditions in search of materials for genetic engineering rather than gold are still about the pursuit of revenue for capital and state.

Today's pursuit of empire is of the corporate variety. In the Thatcher/Reagan years of the 1980s, market-makers and commentators talked of privateers and profiteers, risk-takers and conquerors, adapted to a winner-take-all culture (Messershmidt 1993; South 2000). The twenty-first century has seen some softening of macho corporate culture and 'greenwashing' of terminology with different metaphors performing symbolic services, as corporations herald their reports to investors and media with news of 'eco-friendly breakthroughs' ('responsible science', not testing products on animals: see Regan, this volume) and images of corporate identities as variations on 'visionaries – bringing the world closer together'. Nonetheless, both in imagery and practice, the neo-colonialist methods of expropriation and the negotiable ethics of the market, shape and drive corporate privateering and the privatisation of environmental resources and indigenous knowledge in ways that update for today the *modus operandi* of earlier centuries of empire building.

Bio-piracy represents an extension of colonial exploitation into late modernity. Where religion and pseudo-scientific notions of evolutionary hierarchies once provided the justifications for such practice, today science and law play these parts. In particular, Western science can act as an extremely effective mechanism of exclusion from discourse and hence from reasonable consultation and discussion. This can be seen above in Gorinsky's response to the Wapishana and is found in many other cases of conflict between 'expert' and 'indigenous' knowledge (Samson and Short 2006). For example, the work of Kuletz (1998: 28) strikingly reveals this process at work in a different context. In this case, radiation-related health problems face the Navajo and other peoples of desert areas of the American West where uranium has been mined and nuclear tests carried out but their 'statements are, in effect, excluded from consideration and the people who speak them are, by extension, excluded from any decision-making process bearing on their welfare' (*ibid.*). 'Anecdotal knowledge' (based on inter-generational folk wisdom as well as real contemporary experience) is de-legitimated and not weighted as strongly as 'scientific evidence' (which is privileged as inherently and evidently neutral and unbiased). This strengthens the argument made by green criminologists (Lynch and Stretesky 2001) for the development and use of science to support the case and plight of those who are victimised but frequently excluded from recourse to redress or protest. The science discourse is central to this exclusion process because the debate is so frequently dominated by the louder voice and economic power of those who can afford to mobilise expert opinion and mount a case defending their legal position and the superior scientific credibility of their claims. As Tsiounamis *et al.* (2003: 614) observe in relation to intensification of conflict regarding knowledge claims, 'As long as there is an obvious bias in favour of the Western, developed world, a – yet again – new form of colonialism cannot be considered out of the question.' Cleveland and Murray (1997: 485) broadly concur: 'International intellectual property rights law is dominated by industrial-world concepts.'

The examples and discussions above illustrate how traditional knowledge and practices handed down as an inheritance across generations increasingly become part of the modern, multi-directional 'mobilities' of ideas, knowledge, people, objects, images and so on discussed by Urry (2000), flowing across 'networked, diasporic and global economies' (p. 194). Furthermore, these are particularly interesting examples of this kind of mutation of knowledge-transfer, for the *value* of the knowledge passes beyond the control of the originating nation state and is then 'realised' in a different nation state which will guarantee the 'property rights' of its corporate bodies. This is achieved by recourse to legislation on intellectual property conceived in Western frameworks of law and science and implemented internationally by dominant Western economic interests. This process leads to the assertion of control over knowledge as property and the production of consumables for a transnational market, again flowing across borders but now as a priced commodity.

Of course, it would be naïve and foolish to deny that a great deal of global public good has followed from Western-led advances in health and agricultural sciences that owe their inspiration and origin to practices or products from developing nations. Undoubtedly, human and animal health and welfare benefit widely from the discovery and commercial investment that make modern pharmaceuticals available (Aguilar 2001; Fenwick 1998; Hamilton 2004). Notwithstanding criticisms of the behaviour of international pharmaceutical companies (Moynihan *et al.* 2002; Santoro and Gorrie 2005), such drugs can and do help fight, prevent or stabilise chronic conditions and disease in the developed and developing worlds. Many other products of value in everyday life and specialist scientific research originate in 'discoveries' made in areas of great biodiversity. In this process, Western science has revealed greater potency and possibilities than indigenous knowledge systems and resources can yield. Yet, even acknowledging all of this, the key issue is that this process usually leads to no positive benefits for the inhabitants of the areas of origin and sometimes instead produces rather dubious benefits from commercial development as well as the altogether negative outcome of the theft of traditional knowledge. The issues arising for a criminology concerned with global inequalities and injustice relate to familiar themes of property and power, ownership and control, but here identified in a new context of conflict involving a clash between differing cultural paradigms of knowledge and property.

Conclusion: towards a green criminology

In recent years criminology has been influenced by developments in law, public campaigning and social protest to embrace and take seriously 'rights' based issues , relating to human rights generally and rights of victims, women, minorities, animals more specifically. The *denial* of rights – even where not a criminal offence – has been examined in various areas of criminology (from victimology and restorative justice to crimes of war) but rights to traditional 'ways of life' and protection from exploitation of indigenous lands, culture and folklore (as foundations of traditional knowledge) have been neglected in criminology as well as ineffectively affirmed in national and international law (Orkin 2003).

With the exception of Walters (2004) who touches upon the subject of bio-prospecting versus bio-piracy, the literature *in criminology* seems to have made no contribution to discussion of the issues raised in this chapter. In contrast, the wider social and natural science literature now provides a considerable amount of relevant research and debate, often reflecting concerns and concepts quite central to criminology- matters of ownership versus theft, abuse of power and of trust, exploitation and conflict, and so forth.

In the further development of green criminology, an interdisciplinary and comparative approach (embracing, for example, understandings of context, culture, law, economics and science) will be of benefit.

243

As Hauck (this volume) observes, 'criminology is one discipline – among many – with a role to play in politicising environmental harm and mobilising action that is appropriate to sustain resources and livelihoods'. The movement toward a green criminology aims to provide a new perspective on the unjust exploitation of natural resources, ecosystems, humans and animals, and the consequences of this in terms of health, welfare and rights for all affected by such actions.

Notes

1   I take the title from a phrase in McCoy's (2005) article.
2   Sometimes referred to as 'greenwashing', as corporations likely to be criticised for activities harmful to the environment seek to promote their pro-environment credentials (Rowell 1996; Simon 2000: 642).
3   This is what happened with the use of Agent Orange in Vietnam but also occurred in New Brunswick, Canada, when the defoliant was used in the 1960s to clear brush in order to carry out military exercises and to test the chemical by agreement with the USA (Hanomansing 2000; Elliott 2005). In both cases the legacy of damage to human health remains evident.
4   On two counts, first, to pre-empt potentially hostile and restrictive regulation and, second, to have a means by which to reassure an uncertain public, in 1986 Monsanto sought rules from Washington to govern the new technology involved in genetic modification of food. Monsanto got 'the regulations it wanted ... an outcome that would be repeated ... through three administrations ... If the company's strategy demanded regulations, rules favored by the industry were adopted. And when the company abruptly decided that it needed to throw off the regulations and speed its food to market, the White House quickly ushered through an unusually generous policy of self-policing' (Eichenwald *et al.* 2001: 1).
5   Press reports have described a 'sinister trade in human tissue' (*The Week*, 1 October 2005: 19) in the Western 'beauty treatment industry': 'anti-wrinkle gels that contain an ingredient from the foreskin of a circumcised baby, lip implants made from skin tissue harvested from corpses', 'evidence that skin from executed Chinese criminals was being used as collagen for lip and wrinkle treatments' and unethical and misleading practices of private tissue banks in the USA who solicit tissue donation for medical research but hide in the small print the clause that human remains may also be used in reconstructive or cosmetic surgery.
6   For more on the cultural use of this drug see MacRae 2004.

References

Aguilar, G. (2001) 'Access to Genetic Resources and Protection of Traditional Knowledge in the Territories of Indigenous Peoples', *Environmental Science and Policy*, 4: 241–256.

Beck, U. (1992) *Risk Society: Towards a New Modernity*. London: Sage.

Beirne, P. (1999) 'For a Nonspeciesist Criminology: Animal Abuse as an Object of Study', *Criminology*, 37 (1): 117–148.

Benton, T. (1998) 'Rights and Justice on a Shared Planet', *Theoretical Criminology*, 2 (2): 149–175.

Bullard, R. (1994) *Unequal Protection: Environmental Justice and Communities of Color*. San Francisco: Sierra Club Books.

Chambliss, W. (2005) 'Piracy and Other Crimes of War', *Nathanson Centre Newsletter*, 6, Winter: 12–14.

Clark, A. (2000) 'Agribusiness sows its seeds down on the pharm', *The Guardian*, 15 November.

Cleveland, D. and Murray, S. (1997) 'The World's Crop of Genetic Resources and the Rights of Indigenous Farmers', *Current Anthropology*, 38 (4): 477–515.

Crespi, R. (2000) 'An Analysis of Moral Issues Affecting Patenting Inventions in the Life Sciences: A European perspective', *Science and Engineering Ethics*, 6 (2): 157–180.

Del Olmo, R. (1987) 'Aerobiology and the War on Drugs: a Transnational Crime', *Crime and Social Justice*, 30: 28–44.

Del Olmo, R. (1998) 'The Ecological Impact of Illicit Drug Cultivation and Crop Eradication Programs in Latin America', *Theoretical Criminology*, 2 (2): 269–278.

Downes, D. (1988) 'The Sociology of Crime and Social Control in Britain, 1960–87', in P. Rock (ed.), special issue, *British Journal of Criminology*, 28 (2): 175–87.

Du Rees, H. (2001) 'Can Criminal Law Protect the Environment?', *Journal of Scandinavian Studies*, 2: 109–126.

Eichenwald, K., Kolata, G. and Petersen, M. (2001) 'Biotechnology food: From the lab to a debacle', *The New York Times on the Web*, 25 January.

Elliott, L. (2005) 'Agent purple and agent orange', 13, 14 June *CBC News Online*: http://www.cbc.ca/news/background/agentorange/

Fenwick, S. (1998) 'Bioprospecting or Biopiracy?' *Drug Discovery Today*, 1 September, 3 (9): 399–402.

Hamilton, A. (2004) 'Medicinal Plants, Conservation and Livelihoods', *Biodiversity and Conservation*, 13: 1477–1517.

Hanomansing, I. (2000) 'Agent Orange: grim legacy', *The National*, 23 April, available on CBC News Indepth, http://www.cbc.ca/news/background/agentorange/agentorange_grimlegacy.html.

Kuletz, V. (1998) *The Tainted Desert: Environmental and Social Ruin in the American West*. Routledge: London.

Lynch, M.J. and Stretesky, P.B. (2001) 'Toxic Crimes: Examining Corporate Victimization of the General Public Employing Medical and Epidemiological Evidence', *Critical Criminology*, 10 (3): 153–172.

Lynch, M., Stretesky, P. and Hammond, P. (2000) 'Media Coverage of Chemical Crimes, Hilsborough County, Florida, 1987–97', *British Journal of Criminology*, 40: 112–26.

MacRae, D. (2004) 'The Ritual Use of Ayahuasca by Three Brazilian Religions', in R. Coomber and N. South (eds), *Drug Use and Cultural Contexts 'Beyond the West*. London: FAB.

McCoy, D. (2005) 'Strong Medicine', *RSA Journal*, June: 48–53.

Messerschmidt, J. (1993) *Masculinities and Crime: Critique and Reconceptualisation of Theory*. Lanham: Rowman and Littlefield.

Moynihan, R., Heath, I. and Henry, D. (2002) 'Selling Sickness: The Pharmaceutical Industry and Disease Mongering', *British Medical Journal*, 324: 886–891.

Orkin, A. (2003) 'When the Law Breaks Down: Aboriginal Peoples in Canada and Governmental Defiance of the Rule of Law', *Osgood Hall Law Journal*, 41 (2 and 3): 445–462

Passas, N. (ed.) (1999) *Transnational Crime*. Aldershot: Ashgate.

Rowell, A. (1996) *Green Backlash: Global Subversion of the Environment Movement*. London: Routledge.

Samson, C. (2003) *A Way of Life that Does Not Exist: Canada and the Extinguishment of the Innuit*. London: Verso.

Samson, C. and Short, D. (2006) 'The Sociology of Indigenous People's Rights', in L. Morris (ed.) *Sociological Approaches to Rights*. London: Routledge.

Santoro, M. and Gorrie, T. (2005) *Ethics and the Pharmaceutical Industry*. New York: Cambridge University Press.

Simon, D.R. (2000) 'Corporate Environmental Crimes and Social Inequality', *American Behavioural Scientist*, 43: 633–645.

South, N. (1998) 'A Green Field for Criminology: A Proposal for a Perspective', *Theoretical Criminology*, 2 (2): 211–233.

South, Nigel (2000) 'The Criminological Imagination: Late-modern Criminology from the 20th to the 21st Centuries', in M. Haralambos (ed.), *Developments in Sociology*, 6: 125–149. Ormskirk: Causeway Press.

South, N. and Beirne, P. (eds) (2006) *Green Criminology*. Aldershot: Ashgate.

Szasz, A. (1986) 'Corporations, Organised Crime and the Disposal of Hazardous Waste: An Examination of the Making of a Criminogenic Regulatory Structure', *Criminology*, 24 (1): 1–27.

Szasz, A. and Meuser, M. (1997) 'Environmental Inequalities: Literature Review and Proposals for New Direction in Research and Theory', *Current Sociology*, 45: 99–120.

Tsioumanis, A., Mattas, K. and Tsioumanis, E. (2003) 'Is Policy Towards Intellectual Property Rights Addressing the Real Problems? The Case of Unauthorized Appropriation of Genetic Resources', *Journal of Agricultural and Environmental Ethics*, 16: 605–616.

Urry, J. (2000) *Sociology Beyond Societies: Mobilities for the Twenty-First Century*, London: Routledge.

Vidal, J. (2000) 'Biopirates who seek the greatest prizes', *The Guardian*, 15 November.

Walters, R. (2004) 'Criminology and Genetically Modified Food', *British Journal of Criminology*, 44 (2): 151–167.

White, R. (2004) 'Criminology, Social Regulation and Environmental Harm', in R. White (ed.) *Controversies in Environmental Sociology*. Port Melbourne: Cambridge University Press.

Williams, C. (1996) 'An Environmental Victimology', *Social Justice*, 23 (4): 16–40

Chapter 11

Green criminology in the United States

Michael J. Lynch and Paul Stretesky

As a discipline, criminology has neglected the crimes of the powerful and the laws and regulations that define, sanction and control these offences. Despite exceptions to this observation, research on crimes of the powerful remains underdeveloped, especially in relation to the level of harm caused by, and the extensive legal and social control apparatus directed towards these offences (Friedrichs 2004). More important to the current discussion, articles examining environmental crimes are virtually non-existent (Lynch, McGurrin and Fenwick 2004). In particular, American criminologists have done a dismal job investigating environmental crimes, laws and social control mechanisms, and have paid even less attention to the sub-field of environmental crimes studies called green criminology. Indeed, at this point in time, green criminology has received greater attention from criminologists in other countries, even though the idea was first proposed by an American criminologist.

The neglect of green criminology by American criminologists poses a particular problem for us since we agreed to write a chapter on this subject. This is especially true if we limit our discussion to the definition of green criminology laid out in our earlier works. To avoid this dilemma, we organised this chapter to examine environmentally oriented research by criminologists that is compatible with our view of green criminology. Towards this end, we examine literature on eco-critical criminology, environmental justice, toxic crimes, and exposure to environmental toxins that have an impact on behaviour, and a brief examination of crimes against non-human animals.

Our examination of literature in these areas illustrates how each view is compatible with the green criminological approach we prefer.

Before embarking on this review and discussion, we summarise and extend our previous theoretical position on green criminology in order to expand that view, and to be more inclusive of the environmentally oriented research US criminologists have undertaken.

Green criminology: a developing idea

In 1990, Lynch published the first discussion of green criminology, arguing that it should be built on green political theories prevalent in Europe that viewed 'environmental destruction as an outcome of the structure of modern industrial capitalist production and consumption patterns' (Lynch 1990: 1). Taking this view, he situated green criminology within radical criminology, and mounted an effort to explore how class, race and gender structures influenced behaviours that harmed the environment, the kinds of laws and social control mechanisms that emerged to protect the environment, and whether these harms would be treated or even recognised as crimes under existing economic arrangements.

In our view, green crimes involve a wide range of actions and outcomes that harm the environment and that stem from corporate behaviours such as decisions about what is produced and how it is produced. As an example, consider paper manufacturing, which produces a widely used commodity. The process begins with harvesting and pulping trees, and bleaching the pulp. Harvesting trees harms the environment by reducing animal habitats, the ability of the ecosystem to purify air, replenish soil, or prevent erosion, and by using large volumes of water, which is polluted by the paper pulping and bleaching process (O'Brien 1997). The resulting pollutants are often emptied into large waterways without sufficient treatment. The environmental harms associated with paper milling have direct environmental costs on non-human species but also have indirect human health costs that can cause respiratory diseases and illnesses such as cancer (O'Brien 1997). From a corporate perspective, direct environmental and indirect human health costs are economically unimportant because they are externalised or socialised and become part of the costs incurred by entities and individuals outside of the corporation (Daly and Cobb 1994). For example, paper mills that cause more pollution are not penalised in ways that increase their costs of production (except in extreme cases where egregious violations of law bring substantial fines). Moreover, paper produced by heavy polluters does not cost more than paper produced by environmentally conscious corporations. In fact, the cost difference is usually reversed, since environmentally conscious companies do not externalise their production costs (for additional commentary see Hart 1997).

We must recognise, however, that paper millers are not engaged in illegal behaviours (making paper), and, moreover provide a needed product. Yet, while legitimate, paper milling produces harms that can be analysed using a green perspective. For instance, green criminology directs attention to rule-making processes that allow uncontrolled or mildly regulated tree harvesting, animal habitat destruction, water and air pollution, and exposure of human populations to toxic wastes associated with paper milling that impact on health. In the green view, these outcomes can be considered crimes because they are unnecessary consequences of paper milling. Alternative, low-pollution production techniques that cause less environmental and human harm, though widely available, are not legally required (Lynch and Stretesky 2001). Likewise, stricter regulations and more extensive recycling of paper products – a viable, though not widely used source for paper pulp – reduces the need for continued logging of old-growth forest. Finally, existing law does not require paper millers to employ sustainable tree farming techniques that produce less environmental harm. Each of these options is not only viable and environmentally friendly, but necessary to preserve the ecosystem.

In the green view, the continued existence of environmentally destructive behaviours has a great deal to do with the nature of capitalism and the influence corporations wield in political and law-making processes (O'Connor 1998). Traditional criminology fails to take the environmentally destructive behaviour of corporations seriously, and ignores the relationship between society's economic organisation, power structures and the making and enforcement of laws. In order to study environmentally destructive corporate behaviours as crimes, it is often necessary to go beyond the limits of existing laws. Green criminology also directs us to consider environmentally destructive behaviours as crime because they produce more harm than the street crimes criminologists typically study.

To be sure, some green crimes are already recognised as violations of environmental regulations. Most criminologists, however, ignore the study of these laws and the behavioural violations associated with them because the laws in question are not criminal laws (Burns and Lynch 2004; Clifford 1998). For the green criminologist, the distinction between criminal law and regulatory law can be ignored because it is a social construction; that is, the difference between a crime and a regulatory violation is definitional, resulting from a political process that reflects the application of power to constructing social definitions of harm, and as such is not a useful indicator of harm (Lynch and Stretesky 2003). In other words, the difference between a regulatory law and a crime is not found in the degree of harm but in how effectively opposing interests organise to represent an interpretation that they wish to codify. And, because law is a political process that unequally represents the interests of various groups in society, it cannot be taken as an objective measure of harm.

Having outlined some key green criminological issues, we turn our attention to specific areas of research capable of contributing to the goals of green criminology.

Eco-critical criminology

In 1999, *Criminal Justice Policy Review* published a special issue on 'eco-critical criminology' (ECC). The concerns of ECC are similar to those found in green criminology and both promote a similar analytic view. Those engaged in ECC are primarily American scholars, and it is useful to review this body of research.

According to Seis (1999a) ECC critiques environmental policies with the aim of devising meaningful policy alternatives. In the ECC view, 'environmental problems have antecedent causes embedded in a variety of political and cultural forms ranging from flawed ethical systems of human/nature interaction and punishment, to the ideological forces that drive consumer culture, to assumptions which lead to the partitioning of space into human and nature dichotomies, to the homogenizing nature of global capitalism' (Seis 1999a: 153). This view resonates well with green criminology. However, unlike the ECC approach, green criminology ties ideology, human–nature dichotomies and assumptions, and consumer cultures to economic flows of power found in structural inequalities and hierarchies (i.e. class, race and gender structures).

Wilson (1999) examined what she identifies as essential differences between ECC and green critical approaches. First, she points out that green and ECC perspectives share the view that environmental problems stem from 'human exploitation of the non-human world' (Wilson 1999: 155). The difference, Wilson argues, is found in a commitment to political analysis that is essential to the ECC perspective but not to the green approach. On this point, we disagree, and note one of the goals of advancing a green criminology was to integrate radical criminological analysis with the political action styles found in European green political movements and theoretical approaches. If there is a difference between these views, it might be in how political analysis is used, what forms are emphasised, and the goal of such analysis. These differences, however, are inconsequential and should not be held out as constituting meaningful distinctions between ECC and green theorists.

Wilson argued that a second difference between ECC and green approaches involved the discussion of the connection between politics, policy and victims. In Wilson's view, greens tend to focus on human victims, while ECC is comfortable examining the effect of policy on both human and non-human victims. Certainly greens have been criticised for 'putting humans first' while treating non-humans as secondary. However, it is important to note that green criminology has focused on the importance of examining a broad range of victims – both human and non-human. It should be acknowledged, however, that examining a broad set of issues and the relationship between human and non-human harms is not the same as focusing attention on the unique attributes of non-human species harms. This issue – how to treat human and non-human species theoretically or philosophically, and how to depict their relationship – is perhaps one of the most troubling aspects of devising any view on environmental harm and action.

In the green view, any analysis that examines the destruction or harm of natural forms or species that does not return to consider the impact both of and on humans has missed the point of the investigation altogether. In a world where species are connected, and the human species has by force come to dominate all others, it is always necessary to demonstrate how the destruction of one species encroaches on the survival and historical path of other species, and how the action of the human species may lie behind this chain of events. For example, deforestation not only harms plant life and the survival of local animal species by adversely impacting habitat, and waterway and air quality (Foley *et al.* 2005; White, this volume), but also indirectly impacts humans. Changes in water, land and air quality affect humans through increased global warming, or the loss of natural species that may hold the key to curing diseases. In the green view, the point of returning to human effects isn't to downplay or ignore non-human species harms but, rather, to illustrate that humans do not escape harm when they exploit the environment.

The environment is not an 'other', but is part and parcel of the human condition and changing the environment and affecting the sustainability of natural species has an impact that is not confined to a segment or slice of the natural world. Each time a human action harms even a small segment of the natural world, that victimisation is magnified, spreading slowly and perhaps in tiny increments, creating what is to the human eye and human perspective an imperceptible yet real and far-reaching effect; the kind of silent effects first identified by Rachel Carson (1962), or more recently, by Colborn, Dumanoski and Meyer (1997).

Barnett's (1999) contribution to ECC and green theory stems from his discussion of the philosophical basis of a 'land ethic', as well as from his earlier works on toxic waste and superfund sites. We limit our discussion to Barnett's position on the land ethic, a philosophical view defining environmental ethics, harms and rights, since he is one of the few contributors to ECC or green criminology to develop a broad philosophically grounded view. Barnett begins with a land ethic, which states that right and wrong can be distinguished by the impact of behaviour on the environment or biotic community. Behaviours that preserve the environment are right, while those that damage the environment or create environmental instability are wrongs. Barnett (1999: 162) acknowledged that this statement is overly broad, especially for criminologists interested in 'selecting the universe of acts to study in an empirical investigation'. Barnett uses the land ethics perspective to analyse (1) how statutory laws should be constructed, (2) human–nature relations, (3) technology and (4) the structure of modern markets. This discussion develops a view of the modern environmental ethic and where that ethic might take us. Barnett argues that the key to developing a sound environmental ethic involves (1) education about scientific principles and the ethics of maintaining sound natural environments; (2) altering dominant economic institutions' tendencies to treat nature as a commodity, and redesigning basic economies to promote subsistence, recycling, waste reduction, and discourage overindulgent production and consumption patterns; (3) the redesign of environmental laws to be consistent with scientific knowledge concerning harm, and (4) techniques that promote compliance with a positive land ethic that includes redesigning the use of production subsidies (e.g. eliminate subsidies to the oil industry), and curtailing punishment in favour of strategies that promote voluntary environmental compliance.

Seis's (1999b) application of ECC illustrates an important problem criminologists haven't sufficiently addressed: the ability of multinational corporations, international laws and trade agreements to weaken environmental regulations enacted within individual nations. Seis highlights how global corporations have translated their economic power into political power and influence across nations to impact environmental politics within individual nations. He argues that through global capitalism and increasingly global trade agreements and treaties, 'western nations are beginning to reduce to the lowest common denominator the regulatory structure of each others nations' (1999b: 293). Seis's observation implies that it may no longer be sufficient to analyse the impact of the immediate political and economic context within each nation in an effort to understand the array of factors impacting on environmental law, policy or polluting behaviours. Rather, it is also necessary to consider the impact of the global context, because international regulations and treaties are transforming national laws. In effect, national sovereignty over environmental law is under attack by expanding global networks of capital, resulting in weakened national environmental law (see South, this volume). Seis concludes that a system structured according to the needs of global capitalism's production, growth and consumption needs meets the inevitable limitations presented by the fixed level of natural resources found in the world's environment. Despite the extent of the predicament created by global capitalism, Seis holds out hope that renewed use of local democratic governance – a policy position consistent with green views – can provide a remedy. In particular, he suggests that bioregionalism, which could promote sustainable development practices consistent with the resources of local areas and communities, may be the best alternative.

Seis (2001: 130) has also argued that '[t]he goals of global corporations and a healthy environment are in total contradiction.' Global corporations use international laws and trade agreements to their benefit by, for example, suing nations over environmental policies that violate trade agreements. For instance, in 1996, Ethyl Corporation, a US company that produces gasoline additives, used Chapter 11 of the North American Free Trade Agreement (NAFTA) to sue the Canadian government over restrictions it places on importing gasoline containing MMT. Despite the health threats presented by MMT (Loranger, Zayed and Forget 1994), international trade agreements do not consider health claims as part of the dispute settlement mechanism. This is significant because the health issues involved appear far ranging. MMT (methylcyclopentadienyl manganese tricarbonyl) contains magnesium, a known neurotoxin that can cause irreversible diseases linked to attention deficit disorders and hyperactivity (Crinella, Cordova and Ericson 1998). Magnesium, an essential trace that is easily metabolised and excreted in its natural form, presents health concerns when inhaled, such as when it is burned in gasoline (Davis 1999). Furthermore, the magnesium found in MMT is smaller than naturally occurring magnesium, and in the process of gasoline combustion, is likely to form dangerous magnesium-based compounds. These smaller, more dangerous magnesium particles are particularly detrimental to infants and young children (Crinella, Cordova, Ericson 1998). Despite these health issues, decisions concerning MMT as a gasoline additive have been made on the basis of commerce, not public health. Likewise, in 1996, the World Trade Organisation required the US to increase permitted air pollution allowances, arguing that the air pollution standards restrained trade in commodities that violated new, more restrictive pollution levels.

As Seis (1999b) points out, it may be inadvisable to analyse environmental policy without paying attention to the impact of global contexts on domestic law. In Seis's view, globalisation benefits capital at the expense of human health and the ability of local populations to determine their own pollution emission standards. In addition, globalisation has increased the income gap between nations, making it more difficult for poorer nations to defend themselves from global corporations. For example, the income gap between the top 20 per cent of nations and the bottom 20 per cent grew from 30 to 1 in 1970 to 74 to 1 by 1997 (Seis 2001: 136). Globalisation also justifies extensive inequality across nations, illustrated by differences in levels of consumption and differential contributions to environmental destruction across nations. As an example, Seis (2001: 134) notes that the average American child causes twice the environmental damage as a child in Sweden, 13 times more damage than a Brazilian child, 35 times more damage than an Indian child, and 280 times more environmental damage than a child from Chad or Haiti.

Howard's (1999) contribution to the ECC literature examines waste management law as ideology and a symbolic exercise in a manner consistent with radical criminology. For Howard, waste laws are symbolic to the extent that while they recognise health and environmental threats posed by hazardous waste and municipal waste sites, they ignore these threats by codifying and privileging corporate interests. For example, the impact of waste laws can be minimised through enfeebled enforcement efforts or restricted punishments. In either case, the result is that the law becomes incapable of remedying the problem it was designed to address.

The works of eco-critical criminologists are to be applauded for the analytic styles they have brought to the study of environmental law, policy, crime and ethnics. The tendency of ECC research to connect environmental issues to economic and political structures and hierarchies is consistent with the premises of green criminology. Existing ECC studies serve as an excellent example of the diverse forms of environmentally related research criminologists can engage in under the rubric of green criminology. Unfortunately, criminologists have largely ignored ECC, and those who have engaged in promoting this view have not developed a consistent literature within criminology.

Environmental justice

The environmental justice (EJ) movement began in the early 1980s as an expression of grievances related to the unequal distribution of environmental hazards across diverse races and classes. Unlike the primarily white, middle-class, pro-environmental movement that raised public awareness about environmental issues during the 1960s and 1970s, the EJ movement reflects the experiences of minorities and the poor (Taylor 2000).

The American EJ movement emerged in 1978 in Warren County, North Carolina (McGurty 2000: 373), triggered by a criminal violation of the Toxic Substance Control Act, illustrating one way in which criminology and EJ can be linked (Taylor 2000). The event began when waste hauler Robert Burns conspired with Ward Transformer Company to intentionally spray 31,000 gallons of polychlorinated biphenyls (PCBs) along nearly 270 miles of state roads in North Carolina (Begley 1980). PCBs are a dangerous chemical group known to cause birth defects, liver and skin disorders and are suspected carcinogens. The state of North Carolina did not immediately clean up the contaminated soil, and waited until health issues, such as those described in a 1980 *Newsweek* article (Begley 1980: 25) emerged.

After initiating the clean up, North Carolina officials disposed of the PCB-contaminated soil in a landfill site it had purchased from a farmer in Warren County facing foreclosure and bankruptcy (*New York Times* 1982). Warren County residents discovered the plan and began to protest. As Bullard (1994: 5) noted, these 'protests marked the first time African Americans had mobilized a national broad-based group to oppose what they defined as environmental racism'.

The Warren County protests produced governmentally conducted EJ studies. The US General Accounting Office (1983) undertook the first study of the relationship between proximity to hazardous landfills and community race and socio-economic characteristics. This study, which focused on the eight southern states that comprise the Environmental Protection Agency's Region IV, found that 'blacks make up the majority of the population in three of the four communities where the landfills are located' (USGAO 1983: 1). Moreover, socio-economic effects also appeared to be associated with location of toxic landfills.

In 1987, the United Church of Christ (UCC) commissioned the first national study of the relationship between community racial and socio-economic status and proximity to commercial hazardous waste facilities (Goldman and Fitton 1994; UCC 1987). Using zip codes as the unit of analysis, the study demonstrated that race was the most significant factor associated with proximity to hazardous waste facilities.

Since the late 1980s, numerous EJ studies have been undertaken. There are two broad categories into which EJ research falls. The first focuses on the fairness of procedural rules rather than outcomes (Bullard 1990; Liu 2001; Mank 1999; Rhodes 2003) and includes studies of laws, legal procedures and policies. The question that is asked concerns whether or not the procedure being employed is fair.

The second type of study focuses on outcome evaluations or distributive justice concerns. At issue in distributive EJ studies is whether the distribution of environmental hazards (e.g. toxic waste sites; municipal land fills; treatment, storage and disposal facilities, hazardous waste production, storage and disposal sites) have a spatial pattern that causes the health risks and social consequences associated with those sites and facilities to be unequally distributed across population subgroups. Of primary concern is whether toxic hazards are more proximate to lower income and minority communities, thus causing exaggerated health and social impacts on these communities. Theoretically, low income and minority communities are hypothesised to be more proximate to hazardous waste sites because they lack the economic power that translates into the forms of political power that would protect them from adverse conditions produced by existing structures of power such as corporate capitalism (Saha and Mohai 2005).

There is extensive empirical evidence suggesting that environmental injustices exist in terms of procedures and outcomes – though evidence of injustice is stronger in the south-east and western regions of the US (Bowen 2002; Stretesky 2003). As evidence of procedural and distributive environmental injustice becomes more pervasive, researchers have begun to focus more on the mechanisms that produce environmental inequalities (Pellow 2000, 2002; Sara and Mohai 2005).

The vast majority of EJ literature has been produced by sociologists, geographers and political scientists, and few criminologists have used EJ hypotheses to examine distributive justice questions. Those that have are associated with green criminology (e.g. Lynch, Stretesky, Burns, Hogan). To be sure, criminologists have not framed EJ studies against a green criminological backdrop but have used this view in an effort to promote the study of environmental issues among radical and critical criminologists. Despite this oversight, there are a number of points of unification between the green criminological and EJ literatures. Especially relevant is the shared focus on race and class structures and inequality as influential determinants of justice procedures and outcomes. For green criminologists, EJ studies illustrate that the impacts and effects of environmental pollution are not evenly distributed across populations, and that the effects on pollution cannot be treated as universal. Indeed, the EJ literature produces fairly persistent results correlating racial and socio-economic characteristics of an area's inhabitants to proximity to hazardous waste sites in ways that might have significant life course impacts. For example, the life course of young minority children may be disrupted by proximity to environmental hazards that affect learning ability (Stretesky 2003; Stretesky and Lynch 2003) and alter behaviour (Stretesky and Lynch 2001, 2004) in ways that delay school progress and maturation, perhaps leading to poor school performance, an increased likelihood of dropping out, and a diminished ability to obtain a well-paying, satisfying job, or enter a legitimate career path. In such a case, unequal exposure to environmental pollution, hazards and toxins not only carries health risks (e.g. elevated levels of diseases such as cancer, and illnesses including asthma) for unequally exposed populations, but behavioural modification risks that could increase levels of aggression, criminal offending and victimisation in minority communities. These outcomes, which are among the central issues in green criminology, are omitted from traditional criminology.

Like EJ researchers, green criminologists have investigated both procedural and distributive justice questions. For example, are there fewer inspections of potentially dangerous manufacturing processes in poor and minority neighbourhoods? Are penalties for violating environmental regulations lower in these neighbourhoods? Such questions have implications for the victims of environmental crime. If poor and minority neighbourhoods are not equally protected by organisations responsible for policing environmental crimes then this lack of enforcement effort could send a signal to potential criminal polluters that crime in these areas is acceptable. Despite compatibility with EJ research, green criminologists have performed few empirical studies on unequal enforcement patterns as they might affect diverse races and classes.

Toxic hazards, toxic crimes

For decades, biologists, chemists, toxicologists, epidemiologists and even journalists have warned political leaders, academics and the public about the toxic dangers humans have produced, incorporated into commercial products and dumped as waste into natural and humanly constructed environments. In 1962, armed with new evidence of the harms produced by toxic chemicals, especially pesticides marketed as safe, Rachel Carson documented these concerns in her book, *Silent Spring*. Carson, a biologist, noted that 'For the first time in the history of the world, every human being is now subjected to contact with dangerous chemicals, from the moment of conception until death. In less than two decades of their use ... synthetic pesticides have been so thoroughly distributed throughout the animate and inanimate world that they occur virtually everywhere' (1962: 15). Today, evidence of Carson's claims are more widespread. Recently, Colborn, Dumanoski and Myers (1997: 15) suggested that evidence of harm was not as 'visible and straightforward' as Carson believed and is now more serious than Carson could ever imagine. Furthermore, the problem is not simply related to the harms associated with the release and dispersal of chemical toxins – it also involves the politics of regulating those chemicals. In other words, the decisions concerning which chemicals and toxins ought to be regulated, banned, or considered safe, go beyond scientific evidence to include influential political processes and forms of economic power. Credible scientific evidence (i.e. non-corporate, 'unspun' experimental and epidemiological evidence; see Fagin and Lavelle 1999; Stauber and Rampton 1995) exists in numerous studies documenting the global problem of toxic hazards, chemical and waste exposure that impacts on all living things on earth. From a criminological perspective, exposure to toxins produces a variety of victims – humans, animals, insects, plants, land masses, air and water

259

bodies – which are rarely the subject of criminological investigation. Nor does the criminological literature include many studies of the legal, regulatory and political forces involved, or discussions of the scientific evidence that details these harms. One of the goals of green criminology is to rectify this neglect.

Criminologists are rarely also qualified biologists or toxicologists or epidemiologists, so they cannot be expected to produce unique experimental results concerning the effects of toxic chemicals on living things or the environment, or to identify emerging health threats through scientific experiments. Rather, criminologists must rely on existing toxicological and biological evidence of harm by drawing, for example, on the vast literature examining populations exposed to toxic health threats undertaken by epidemiologists (who study the spread of disease within populations). As an example of this style of research, Lynch and Stretesky (2001) reviewed over 100 studies from the medical, epidemiological and toxicological literature on the health impacts of exposure to environmental toxins. They grouped these studies into three areas: pesticides, toxic waste and toxic accidents, and dioxin exposure. Their goal was to illustrate how green criminologists could employ chemical toxicity and population exposure studies to describe and discuss the scope of chemical victimisation and harm. Lynch and Stretesky point out that unlike the data criminologists typically employ (which contains aggregate estimations of criminal offences, offenders and victims), epidemiological and toxicological evidence is not aggregated into uniform reporting sources that describe the extent of toxic crimes or victimisations. As a result, it is impossible to rely on a single data source to obtain this type of information. There is, however, a wealth of information that can be used to examine the extent of chemical crime and victimisation. This literature also helps illustrate the claims made by Carson (1962), Davis (1999) and Colborn *et al.* (1997) concerning the extent of toxic victimisation.

In recent years, the study of environment law, crime and social control has expanded greatly, especially among legal scholars. As O'Hear (2004) notes, despite the increased interest in environmental law, few studies have examined the sentencing of environmental offenders. As in ordinary criminal cases, the majority of cases involving 'green' defendants are settled by plea rather than trial. In both instances, judges exercise their discretion in sentencing offenders who plead guilty. Judicial discretion, while limited by federal sentencing guidelines, may still significantly impact the sentences defendants receive. To determine if offender status influenced judicial discretion, O'Hear (2004: 205) studied sentences handed out to green collar and non-green collar defendants in federal courts between 1996 and 2001. During this period, the percentage of green collar offenders sentenced to prison declined from nearly 52 per cent in 1996, to 23 per cent by 2001. At the same time, and consistent with general observations in the criminological literature, the percentage of all other defendants sent to prison increased from 79 per cent to 84.5 per cent. When sent to prison, green collar offenders received shorter prison terms than non-green collar offenders. For instance, nearly 80 per cent of green collar offenders received prison sentences of less than two years, while only 2 per cent received sentences longer than six years. For non-green collar offenders, 42 per cent received sentences less than two years, while 23 per cent received sentences longer than six years (O'Hear 2004: 206–207). Finally, O'Hear (2004: 208) discovered that judges were more likely to abide by federal minimum sentences for green collar offenders (81.5 per cent of the time) compared to non-green collar offenders (60.7 per cent), and that judges were more likely to employ downward departures (employ sentences below guideline limits) for green collar offenders (48.2 per cent of the time) as opposed to non-green collar offenders (32.6 per cent; O'Hear 2004: 209–211).

Linking toxic exposures to criminal behaviour

Medical and epidemiological researchers have collected extensive evidence linking exposure to certain environmental toxins to behavioural changes (Pueschel, Linakis, and Anderson 1996; Colborn, Dumanoski and Meyer 1997). Several chemicals are associated with behavioural changes that generate increased levels of aggression and violence. Prominent among these are heavy metals – lead, cadmium, and mercury – which may alter behaviour by inhibiting brain development (e.g. impacts on vascular morphology, or disrupted synaptogenesis), causing a loss of brain matter, scarring of the brain (e.g. gliosis), or through a disruption of cognitive development and motor skills (Bellinger, Needleman, Bromfield and Mintz 1984; Bellinger, Stiles and Needleman 1992; Denno 1990). Other research implicates pesticide exposure as another cause of violent and aggressive behaviour. In this case, pesticides act as 'hormone mimics' which may either stimulate aggressive behaviours, or cause cognitive malfunctions that are more likely to produce aggressive behavioural outcomes (Colborn, Dumanoski and Meyer 1997). While the exact causal pathway is unknown, research establishing an association between exposure to environmental toxins and behaviour change is growing rapidly.

Examining the relationship between exposure to toxins and alterations in behaviour may seem far removed from the discussion of green crimes. In reality, this discussion is not as far removed as one might initially think. Above, we reviewed the idea of EJ, which examines how the racial and class characteristics of communities correlate with the likelihood that residents of those communities will be proximate to various environmental hazards, and thus more likely to be exposed to toxic chemicals than other groups. The idea that exposure levels influence behaviour is simply the next step in this type of analysis. Under such conditions researchers must connect factors related to exposure probabilities (such as race and class) with health and behavioural outcomes (such as aggression and crime). Thus, it is not the biological processes themselves that are important since these are rather uniform across a population (though there is still variation here as well); rather it is the probability of exposure determined by race and class indicators which becomes the focus.

Extending this idea, Stretesky and Lynch (2004) argued that the political economy of race and class affects pollution exposure probabilities (Stretesky 2003) which, in turn, can alter individual behaviour in ways that produce higher rates of crime in areas with elevated levels of toxic hazards. To test this assertion, Stretesky and Lynch (2001, 2004) examined the relationship between lead pollution measures and crime rates across all counties in the United States. Controlling for the effects of numerous other criminological explanations and general levels of pollution, they found an association between lead levels and crime rates.

Crimes against non-humans as green criminological subject matter

More so than any other criminologist, Piers Beirne's work has been instrumental in extrapolating the historical and philosophical dimensions of harms against non-human animals and situating these offences within a green criminological perspective (2002, 1999, 1995, 1994). While other criminologists have addressed crimes against animals as an offence in itself, as a pathway to human violence, or as a means for exploring the psychology of criminal offenders (Merz-Perez and Heide 2003), in contrast, Beirne has examined how crimes against non-human animals are defined in practice. Beirne's work has explored this in both contemporary and historical circumstances, employing a natural rights perspective to forward a critique of prevailing human–animal relations used to justify the mistreatment of animals on the basis of human superiority. Beirne's approach (see this volume) represents an example of one method of applying a green criminological view to crimes against animals. Below, we describe two alternatives to illustrate the variety of ways in which a green approach to non-human animals and crime could be grounded.

Frank and Lynch (1992) have argued that a green criminology that considers how human political-economic arrangements affect the kinds of harms humans commit against the environment can also be applied to studying crimes against animals: for example, human actions that produce animal victimisation both directly (hunting baby seals) and indirectly (species extinction through environmental pollution). Furthermore, in this view, solutions to the problem of crimes against animals could be located in green political activism, efforts to reform human–animal interactions and hierarchies, and efforts to reshape human political economies.

Though Frank and Lynch's primary concern was to illustrate how economic structures and interests shaped environmental crimes, they also highlight how environmental crimes and crimes against animals overlap. In particular, they noted that humans often failed to consider how environmental damage affects animal populations. Three factors influence this tendency. First, humans fail to see the environment as an interconnected whole, and fail to appreciate the feedback between environmental and human health. Second, humans view their needs as paramount and superior to all others. Third, human use of the environment as a resource for human pleasure and consumption is dictated by the nature of political-economic arrangements. For example, using nature's raw materials such as lumber to support the expanding housing market with the aim of extending profitability has short-term human benefits. Behind these short-term benefits are substantial long-term environmental costs that have negative impacts on human health and survival by damaging the natural environment. The problem is that modern societies are built on economic systems that require continued environmental destruction to satisfy the ideas of 'progress' and 'economic achievement' that they embrace, meaning that 'healthy' economic positions will be favoured over healthy environmental conditions. Green criminology takes environmental threats more seriously and recasts circumstances normally taken as indicators of a healthy economy as evidence of pathways to environmental destruction. Consider, for instance, a common indicator of US economic health: housing starts. The construction of housing causes various forms of environmental damage that include habitat destruction associated with both clearing land for housing and harvesting of timber. In addition, producing the other raw materials used to construct housing, especially cement, generates extensive environmental costs (e.g. global warming). Moreover, the environmental damage caused by home construction creates indirect forms of violence against animals. That is, humans do not harvest a forest in order to harm animals but they nevertheless harm animals when they do so. Not only does the process of home building destroy animal habitats, the entire ecosystem on which animals relied may disappear, creating the potential for species extinction.

For Frank and Lynch, the human actions that lead to environmental destruction can feed back, causing harm to both humans and animals. To address this problem, it is necessary to understand that the motives behind these harms are found in political-economic arrangements. In this view, political economy configures the ways in which harms against animals will be defined, and how relevant laws will be enforced. To develop this approach, we can say that human–animal relationships mirror the kinds of conflicts that typify class relationships. In place of class conflict, however, the emphasis is shifted to species conflict and the way this is shaped by humanly constructed economic systems. Clearly, for instance, these systems advantage human interests over animal interests, and do so by defining human forms of production and consumption as being of more value and existing at a 'higher level' than animal production and economic activity. In addition, from the viewpoint of human political economy, animals are primarily raw materials and commodities, to be used to fulfil human desires. In some instances, fulfilling human desires requires doing violence to and wasting the lives of animals.

As another example, consider an activity humans do not often regard as a harm or crime against animals: laboratory experimentation. The whole system of laboratory animal experimentation is built around economic interests. These interests include but are not limited to: those of the experimental animal research sector (supply, housing, food and service); the need for rapid intergenerational, low-cost, multi-subject experimentation desired by the pharmaceutical industry; and creating product safety marketing information. Outside of a handful of 'ethical rules' regarding 'humane' treatment of animal subjects, the pain and suffering of experimental animals is rarely considered and when it is, it is typically treated as secondary to human concerns, or defined as non-existent.

An alternative for analysing crime against non-human species can be derived from the work of economist James O'Connor. O'Connor (1998: 137) argues that discussions of ecological/environmental crises appear objective because they are typically based on empirical data that pit facts representing different views against one another. However, the facts tend to hide the subjective interests involved in crises debates. Rather than objective battles, O'Connor suggests that ecological conflicts are political turning points where the interests of competing groups are played out. The opposing positions taken in an ecological crisis define human interests and power struggles. More often than not, interests supporting economic expansion rather than environmental preservation tend to receive political support, and core economic interests rather than environmental preservation interests tend to be legitimised regardless of the quality or quantity of objective data employed. In this way, ecological conflicts support economic interests over preservation interests.

Following O'Connor's logic, ecological crises are acts of social construction involving efforts to legitimise one of the competing interests in the debate – either the side making the harm claim, or the side attempting to show that proof of the harm is insufficient. Green criminology could employ this view to examine competing economic versus ecological interests, and how economic conditions influence the outcomes of these processes. This approach could be applied to a variety of harms against animals, including animal experimentation, species extinction, or harms against farm animals. For example, with respect to animal experimentation, the 'pro' side consists of pharmaceutical firms, animal laboratory breeding and supply companies, medical equipment firms, medical experimentation groups, and united groups of medical, toxicological and biological researchers who employ animals in their daily work. Some of these interest groups control substantial monetary resources, including the pharmaceutical field, medical equipment firms and animal laboratory supply houses. Animal tests are valued for the data they produce, shorter turnaround times compared to *in vitro*, computer or epidemiological studies, even though animal tests are more harmful and not required by law.

Conclusion

Green criminology, first suggested by a US criminologist over 15 years ago, has become a more popular means for studying crime, law and forms of victimisation in other nations. There is, however, a growing body of research in environmental sciences and other disciplines that can be employed to stimulate the further development of green criminology in the USA and internationally. Within criminology, several developing areas can be joined under the rubric of green criminology including eco-critical criminology, environmental justice and the study of toxic hazards to name but a few.

As ecological crises intensify – as global warming progresses, levels of environmental toxins rise, the unequal nature of exposure to environmental harms becomes more evident – the need for incorporating an environmental science perspective within criminology expands. While the need for an environmental vision and knowledge has been recognised in other fields, criminology has been extraordinarily slow to respond to and recognise the need to reorient itself to include more extensive studies of environmental issues, becoming one of the last fields to become cognisant of the relationship between its subject matter and the environmental status of the world. It is time for criminologists to take environmental problems more seriously and engage with the various ways in which environmental and criminological issues intersect. Green criminology provides the means and method whereby this may occur.

References

Barnett, H. (1994) *Toxic Debts and the Superfund Dilemma*. Chapel Hill, NC: University of North Carolina Press.

Barnett, H. (1999) 'The Land Ethic and Environmental Criminology', *Criminal Justice Policy Review*, 10 (2): 161–192.

Begley, S. (1980) 'Toxic Waste Still Pollutes Roadways', *Newsweek*, 27 October: 5 (update).

Beirne, P. (1994) 'The Law is an Ass: Reading E.P. Evans' The Medieval Prosecution and Capital Punishment of Animals', *Society and Animals*, 2 (1): 27–46.

Beirne, P. (1995) 'The Use and Abuse of Animals in Criminology: A Brief History and Current Review', *Social Justice*, 22 (1): 5–31.

Beirne, P. (1999) 'For a Nonspeciesist Criminology: Animal Abuse as an Object of Study', *Criminology*, 37 (1): 117–147.

Beirne, P. (2002) 'Criminology and Animal Studies: A Sociological View', *Society and Animals*, 10 (4): 381–386.

Bellinger, D., Needleman, H., Bromfield, R. and Mintz, M. (1984) 'A Follow-Up Study of the Academic Attainment and Classroom Behavior of Children with Elevated Dentine Lead Levels', *Biological Trace Element Research*, 6: 207–223.

Bellinger, D., Stiles, K. and Needleman, H. (1992) 'Low-Level Lead Exposure, Intelligence and Academic Achievement: A Long-Term Follow-up Study', *Pediatrics*, 90: 855–861.

Bowen, W. (2002) 'An Analytical Review of Environmental Justice Research: What Do We Really Know?', *Environmental Management*, 29 (1): 3–15.

Bullard, R. (1990) *Dumping in Dixie: Race, Class and Environmental Quality* Boulder, CO: Westview.

Bullard, R. (1994) 'Environmental Justice for All', in R. Bullard (ed.), *Unequal Protection: Environmental Justice and Communities of Color*. San Francisco, CA: Sierra Club.

Burns, R.G. and Lynch, M.J. (2004) *Environmental Crime: A Sourcebook*. New York, NY: LFB Scholarly.

Carson, R. (1962 [1994]) *Silent Spring*. Boston, MA: Houghton Mifflin.

Clifford, M. (ed.) (1998) *Environmental Crime: Enforcement, Policy, and Social Responsibility*. Gaithersburg, MD: Aspen.

Colborn, T., Dumanoski, D. and Myers, J.P. (1997) *Our Stolen Future: Are We Threatening Our Fertility, Intelligence and Survival?* New York, NY: Plume.

Crinella, F.M., Cordova, E.J. and Ericson, J.E. (1998) 'Manganese, Aggression, and Attention-Deficit Hyperactivity Disorder', *Neurotoxicology*, 19 (3): 468–469.

Daly, H.E. and Cobb, J.B. (1994) *For the Common Good: Redirecting the Economy toward Community, the Environment, and a Sustainable Future*. Boston, MA: Beacon.

Davis, M. J. (1999) 'Inhalation Health Risks of Manganese: An EPA Perspective', *Neurotoxicology*, 20: 511–518.

Denno, D. (1990) *Biology and Crime*. Cambridge: Cambridge University Press.

Fagin, D. and Lavelle, M. (1999) *Toxic Deception: How the Chemical Industry Manipulates Science, Bends the Law and Endangers Your Health*. Monroe, ME: Common Courage Press.

Foley, J. A., DeFries, R., Asner, G. P., Barford, C., Bonan, G., Carpenter, S. R., Chapin, F.S., Coe, M.T., Daily, G.C., Gibbs, H.K., Helkowski, J. H., Holloway, T., Howard, E. A., Kucharik, C. J., Monfreda, C., Patz, J.A., Prentice, I.C., Ramankutty, N. and Snyder, P. K. (2005) 'Global Consequences of Land Use', *Science*, 309: 570–574.

Frank, N. and Lynch, M. J. (1992) *Corporate Crime, Corporate Violence*. Albany, NY: Harrow and Heston.

Friedrichs, D.O. (2004) *Trusted Criminals: White Collar Crime in Contemporary Society*. Belmont, CA: Wadsworth.

Goldman, B.A. and Fitton, L. (1994) 'Toxic Wastes and Race Revisited: An Update of the 1987 Report on the Racial and Socioeconomic Characteristics of Communities with Hazardous Waste Sites'. Washington DC, Center for Policy Alternatives National Association for the Advancement of Colored People and United Church of Christ Commission for Racial Justice.

Gottschalk, M. (1999) 'Monkeywrenching as Punishment', *Criminal Justice Policy Review*, 10 (2): 193–212.

Hart, S.L. (1997) 'Beyond Greening: Strategies for a Sustainable World', *Harvard Business Review*, 75 (1): 66–78.

Howard, G.J. (1999) 'Garbage Law and Symbolic Policy: Governmental Responses to the Problem of Waste in the United States', *Criminal Justice Policy Review*, 10 (2): 257–290.

Liu, F. (2001) *Environmental Justice Analysis: Theories, Methods, and Practice.* Boca Raton, FL: Lewis.

Loranger, S., Zayed, J. and Forget, E. (1994) 'Manganese Contamination in Montreal in Relation with Traffic Density', *Water, Air, and Soil Pollution*, 74 (3–4): 385–396.

Lynch, M.J. (1990) 'The Greening of Criminology: A Perspective on the 1990s', *The Critical Criminologist*, 2 (3): 1–4 and 11–12.

Lynch, M. J., McGurrin, D. and Fenwick, M. (2004) 'Disappearing Act: The Representation of Corporate Crime Research in Criminology Journals and Textbooks', *Journal of Criminal Justice*, 32 (5): 389–398.

Lynch, M.J. and Stretesky, P.B. (2001) 'Toxic Crimes: Examining Corporate Victimization of the General Public Employing Medical and Epidemiological Evidence', *Critical Criminology*, 10 (3): 153–172.

Lynch, M.J. and Stretesky, P.B. (2003) 'The Meaning of Green: Towards a Clarification of the Term Green and Its Meaning for the Development of a Green Criminology', *Theoretical Criminology*, 7: 217–238.

Mank, B. (1999) Title VI, in M. Gerrard (ed.) *The Law of Environmental Justice.* Chicago, IL: American Bar Association.

McGurty, E. (2000) 'Warren County, NC, and the Emergence of the Environmental Justice Movement: Unlikely Coalitions and Shared Meanings in Local Collective Action', *Society and Natural Resources*, 13: 373–387.

Merz-Perez, L. and Heide, K.M. (2003) *Animal Cruelty: Pathway to Violence against People.* Walnut Creek, CA: Altamira.

New York Times (1982) 'Carolinians angry over PCB landfill', *The New York Times*, Late city final edition, 11 August 1982: 17, Section D.

O'Brien, M.H. (1997) 'Alternatives to Risk Assessment: The Example of Dioxin', in C. Levenstein and J. Wooding (eds), *Work, Health, and Environment: Old Problems, New Solutions.* New York, NY: Guilford.

O'Connor, J. (1998) *Natural Causes: Essays in Ecological Marxism.* New York, NY: Guilford.

O'Hear, M. (2004) 'Sentencing the Green Collar Offender: Punishment, Culpability and Environmental Crime', *The Journal of Criminal Law and Criminology*, 95 (1): 133–276.

Pellow, D. (2000) 'Environmental Inequality Formation', *American Behavioral Scientist*, 43 (4): 581–601.

Pellow, D. (2002) *Garbage Wars: The Struggle for Environmental Justice in Chicago*. Cambridge, MA: MIT.

Pueschel, S.M., Linakis, J.G. and Anderson, A.C. (eds) (1996) *Lead Poisoning in Childhood*. Baltimore, MD: Paul H. Brooks.

Rhodes, E.L. (2003) *Environmental Justice in America: A New Paradigm*. Bloomington, IN: University of Indiana Press.

Saha, R. and Mohai, P. (2005) 'Historical Context and Hazardous Waste Facility Siting: Understanding Temporal Patterns in Michigan', *Social Problems*, 52 (4): 618–648.

Seis, M. (1999a) 'Guest Editor's Statement', *Criminal Justice Policy Review*, 10 (2): 153–154.

Seis, M. (1999b) 'A Community-Based Criminology of the Environment', *Criminal Justice Policy Review*, 10 (2): 291–317.

Seis, M. (2001) 'Confronting the Contradiction: Global Capitalism and Environmental Health', *International Journal of Comparative Sociology*, 42 (1–2): 123–144.

Stauber, J. and Rampton, S. (1995) *Toxic Sludge is Good for You: Lies, Damn Lies and the Public Relations Industry*. Monroe, ME: Common Courage.

Stretesky, P.B. (2003) 'Environmental Inequity and the Distribution of Air Lead Levels across U.S. Counties: Implications for the Production of Racial Inequality', *Sociological Spectrum*, 23: 91–118.

Stretesky, P.B. and Lynch, M.J. (2001) 'The Relationship between Lead and Homicide', *Archives of Pediatric and Adolescent Medicine*, 155 (5): 579–582.

Stretesky, P.B. and Lynch, M.J. (2003) 'Environmental Hazards and School Segregation in Hillsborough', 1987–1999, *Sociological Quarterly*, 43 (4): 553–573.

Stretesky, P.B. and Lynch, M.J. (2004) 'The Relationship between Lead and Crime', *Journal of Health and Social Behavior*, 45 (2): 214–229.

Taylor, D.E. (2000) 'The Rise of the Environmental Justice Paradigm', *American Behavioral Scientist*, 43 (4): 508–580.

United Church of Christ (1987) 'Toxic Wastes and Race in the United States'. *A National Report on the Racial and Socio-Economic Characteristics of Communities with Hazardous Waste Sites*. United Church of Christ.

United States General Accounting Office, USGA (1983) *Siting of Hazardous Waste Landfills and Their Correlation with Racial and Economic Status of Surrounding Communities*. Washington DC: United States General Accounting Office.

Wilson, N.K. (1999) 'Eco-Critical Criminology: An Introduction', *Criminal Justice Policy Review*, 10 (2): 155–160.

Chapter 12

Non-compliance in small-scale fisheries: a threat to security?[1]

Maria Hauck

Introduction

This chapter explores the nature and complexity of small-scale fisheries non-compliance with environmental law and regulations in South Africa. In this context, adopting a 'green criminology' perspective has meant the bridging of disciplines to understand how law is defined, and by whom, and the exploration of the intricacies between the social, political, economic and institutional dynamics of the defined environmental 'crime'. Key to this research has been the recognition of the need to move beyond a traditional understanding of what is considered 'illegal' and beyond traditional approaches to regulating the environment. Debates within the green criminology discourse have explored these positions through the eco-human rights approach (Halsey 1997) and environmental justice approach to criminology (Lynch and Stretesky 2003). Although there are debates within these perspectives (Halsey 2004), general principles relate to the strong links between human rights and environmental rights, the importance of the role of law in defining environmental 'harm' and the necessity to embed an understanding of harm, and responses to such harm, with a broader contextual frame (South, this volume, 1998). Interestingly, in the green criminology literature, there seems to be little direct reference thus far to the discourse on human security, non-traditional security, or more specifically, environmental security, which also encompass some of the tenets of these approaches. The aim of this chapter is to discuss these new concepts of security, to reflect on this discourse in relation to small-scale fisheries, with a particular emphasis on South Africa, and to examine how fisheries' conflicts and compliance can be understood in the context of green criminology.

Non-traditional security

Traditional perceptions of security, concerned mainly with a state's ability to counter external threats, have been broadened in recent years to include a wide range of threats, as well as a concern for the security of individual people and communities. This broadening of security discourse has highlighted the importance of redefining security beyond a military context, to include political, economic, social and environmental threats (Buzan *et al.* 1998). Examples of non-traditional security issues include terrorism, drugs, arms and people trafficking, AIDS, environmental degradation, ethnic violence, migration, terrorism and growing income disparities (Akaha 2002; Thakur and Newman 2004; Tan and Boutin 2001). Within this broad understanding of security is the concept of 'human security'. Human security specifically focuses on humans (whether as individuals or groups) as the referent of security concerns and policies, moving away from a state-centric focus. This concept became popularised by the United Nations Development Programme's (UNDP) Human Development Report (UNDP 1994), which emphasised the importance of livelihoods and the individual as the centre of development (Curley 2002; Thakur and Newman 2004). The Commission on Human Security (2004) emphasises that human security is about protecting people's fundamental rights, such as freedom, peace and safety, access to resources and the basic necessities of life and an environment that does not threaten health and well-being. Although both approaches attempt to redefine security, human security focuses specifically on the individual as the referent object, whereas non-traditional security can be broader (including the source of the threat and the response to the threat).

With such a diversity of issues, a key concern within the security debate is the danger of encapsulating all welfare and development issues under the conceptual umbrella of 'non-traditional security'. However, it is argued that when issues become life-threatening, or considered an 'existential threat' (Buzan *et al.* 1998), then they become a security issue. Thakur and Newman (2004) explain that non-traditional security 'does not include all health, welfare and development challenges. But these issues *become* security concerns

271

when they reach crisis point, when they undermine and diminish the survival chances of significant proportions of the citizens of society and when they threaten the stability and integrity of society' (p. 3).

Fisheries and security

Fisheries, which involves the direct utilisation of natural resources, falls within the growing discourse of 'environmental security'. The notion of environmental security became established in the mid-1980s but gathered renewed interest in the mid-1990s (Myers 2004) and is now firmly embedded within the discourse of non-traditional security. Environmental decline or degradation and resource depletion are often cited as examples of non-traditional security issues (Thakur and Newman 2004; Tan and Boutin 2001; Emmers 2004; Buzan *et al.* 1998). Thakur and Newman (2004) argue that the links between the environment and security are clear, specifically emphasising the threat of environmental deterioration on human well-being. Buzan *et al.* (1998) identify two referent objects within the environmental security paradigm: (1) the environment itself and (2) human civilisation. With examples of environmental security threats including emission of hazardous gases, pollution, resource degradation and biodiversity loss, it is clear that there are direct biophysical and socio-economic repercussions (see also Lynch and Stretesky, Wachholz, White, this volume). Further, there is a widespread recognition in the literature that environmental security encompasses many other aspects of security (including political, economic and social) and therefore is intertwined with social inequity and injustice, poverty, societal vulnerability, weak political structures, population growth, unsustainable economic growth, industrialisation and growing demands for resources (Elliott 2001; Najam 2004; Myers 2004; Haque 2004).

Proponents of environmental security recognise that the linkages are complex and there is a move towards a broader conceptual understanding of the environment through the notion of human security. Embedded within this approach is the fundamental 'right to food', which is increasingly being highlighted as justification to protect the livelihoods of small-scale fishers around the globe (Ziegler 2004). Small-scale fisheries have not been universally defined but generally encapsulate the terms 'subsistence', 'traditional' and 'artisanal'. Although each context will be different, small-scale fisheries can be broadly characterised as employing labour intensive harvesting to exploit fishery resources by operating from shore or from small fishing vessels. Furthermore, it is recognised that fishers within this sector live in fishing communities with relatively fragile livelihood conditions (Manning 2001).

It is estimated that 99 per cent of the world's fishers are small-scale fishers, and 95 per cent reside in developing countries (Food and Agriculture Organisation (FAO) 1999a). Approximately one billion people rely on fish as a major source of animal protein (Ziegler 2004). Berkes *et al.* state that it is clear that 'the importance of the world's fisheries, and especially the small-scale fisheries, in providing food, income and livelihood cannot be overemphasised, especially in developing countries' (2001: 223). The crisis within fisheries becomes real when one realises that fisheries resources, and the ecosystems on which they depend, are being degraded and over-exploited. Roughly 70 per cent of fish stocks are fully exploited or overfished (FAO 1999b).

The focus of this chapter will be on non-compliance with formal laws governing the fisheries. Non-compliant activities can include overfishing, ignoring restrictions on types of fishing gear and closed seasons, transcending zones and fishing without a licence. Within the non-traditional and human security paradigms, non-compliance in small-scale fisheries could potentially be defined as a 'security issue' based on the threat of environmental degradation, the threat of jeopardising a fundamental right to food security and, in some cases, due to violent conflict. But what does this mean?

The process of identifying how and when an issue becomes 'securitised' is an ongoing debate within security discourse. In fact, Thakur and Newman (2004: 15) argue that a key area of future research is to 'grapple with the challenging question of securitisation of issues'. Nevertheless, within existing theory, the Copenhagen School (Buzan *et al.* 1998) accepts that an act of securitisation justifies the need to implement 'extraordinary measures'. From a traditional perspective, by identifying something as a security threat, the state legitimises the use of whatever action seems necessary (e.g. military force) to block the threat. By broadening the concept of security, however, Buzan and colleagues argue that any public issue can be securitised, shifting the issue beyond its political domain due to its declared urgency. Thus, in determining the appropriateness of identifying fisheries non-compliance as a security threat, the implications of 'endorsing emergency measures beyond rules that would normally bind' (Emmers 2004: 5) need to be carefully considered.

The discussion below highlights the perceived crisis within small-scale fisheries that is emanating from the literature. However, there is a strong critique of government responses to this crisis and a realisation that new approaches need to be pursued that understand the problem in its entirety – not just as a direct response to conflict and non-compliance. As Berkes *et al.* explain, 'if we are to ensure food security and livelihoods of small-scale fishers and conserve the biodiversity of the resources on which they depend, we must consider new directions' (2001: 225). A review of small-scale fisheries below will highlight the conflicts that have emerged from illegal fishing and the responses implemented by governments.

Small-scale fisheries

A myriad of conflicts exist within small-scale fisheries, contextualised within a diverse range of political, socio-economic and institutional dynamics. Conflicts are often intertwined with non-compliant activities, relating to issues of resource access and allocation, enforcement of rules and regulations (or lack thereof), interaction (sometimes violent) between different fishery sectors (i.e. small-scale *v.* industrial fisheries) and inconsistent government policies (Ghee 1990; Hauck and Sowman 2003; Bennett *et al.* 2001; Squires *et al.* 2003; Silvestre *et al.* 2003).

These conflicts, some of which have had severe repercussions on both livelihoods and resources, have rarely led to traditional security threats. However, an exception is the case of sea border conflicts between Pakistan and India, where the respective governments identify the crossing of sea borders by the other country's fishers as a direct threat to state sovereignty (Gupta and Sharma 2004). As a result, fishers who cross borders are subject to an extreme violation of human rights (including torture, arrest, jail for several years and treatment as prisoners of war). This securitisation, which has been justified as a means to 'preserve the state's territorial integrity and ... to protect the nation' (p. 13), has not only led to human rights abuses, but has also had significant social implications (such as separation of families). The irony is that despite the security measures taken by the two states, and the risks involved, fishers from both nations continue to cross boundaries to access resources as a means of survival.

This case sets the scene for the shift in security being advocated by the non-traditional security and human security paradigms. As Gupta and Sharma argue: 'the attention of these countries has to shift from the security of the borders to the security of the people' (2004: 24). In other words, the fundamental threat to fishers in Pakistan and India (from their perspective) is not the crossing of borders but that of food security and the reliance on increasingly declining fish stocks for their survival.

Generally speaking, small-scale fisheries worldwide have been marginalised by governments (Berkes *et al.* 2001). Fisheries non-compliance in this sector seems to be elevated to a higher political level only when violence and loss of life are involved. Thus, a key trigger to identifying a 'crisis' in fisheries is related to the presence of violent conflict. In the case of some South-east Asian countries, for example, the perception of conflicts 'gained ground only when these conflicts erupted into violence' (Mathew 1990: 59). In some cases, violent conflict resulted in an immediate response by government to militarise the fishery (such as in South Africa: Hauck 2000), and in some cases it catalysed new government policies (Ghee 1990; Fisheries Action Coalition Team 2001; Mathew 1990). In Malaysia, for example, a ban on trawler fishing was imposed in response to escalating violence between trawler fishers and inshore fishers because trawlers were not complying with inshore zoning regulations. However, the ban was short-lived and the overarching modernisation policies of the government continued to trigger conflicts (Ghee 1990).

This issue of conflicting policies has emerged in many fisheries. For example, there is the problem of preferential policies that favour large-scale, industrialised fishers over small-scale, traditional fishers (Ghee 1990; Gupta and Sharma 2004; Fisheries Coalition Action Team 2001; Mathew 1990; McGoodwin 1987; Sunderlin and Gorospe 1997; Silvestre *et al.* 2003). This problem was identified as a key issue by the FAO Advisory Committee on Fisheries Research: 'One of the main policy thrusts in the past has been to promote economic growth at a national level, based on the assumption that all sectors of society (including small-scale fishers) will benefit. In fisheries, this has tended to favour the development of large-scale approaches over small-scale ones and the resources being concentrated in fewer and fewer hands' (2003: 9).

In Malaysia, Ghee (1990) clearly highlights how the rapid development of heavily capitalised, export-oriented fisheries has had severe consequences for the well-being of small-scale fishers. Although the development of new policies aimed to 'advance' small-scale fishers through social development and economic upliftment, little progress was achieved due to ineffective implementation and poor institutional structures. In essence, these policies developed and encouraged large-scale trawling operations. This led to overfishing, conflicts between trawler operators and traditional fishers (due to the encroachment of trawlers in coastal waters, which sometimes led to violence), and exclusion of small-scale fishers in this sector (non-fishing entrepreneurs were benefiting from the trawler operations with little, or no, employment to inshore fishers). This inequity, which discriminates against the small-scale fishers, was also discussed by Gupta and Sharma (2004), who argued that it was the élites that retained the power in fisheries, resulting in more and more resources being concentrated in the hands of a few. As a result, these 'commercialisation' or 'modernisation' policies were triggering non-compliance by creating greater competition for resources and leading to conflicts between large-scale and small-scale fishers. This view is supported by Elliott (2001: 450) who states that policies that have conflicting objectives can 'exacerbate rather than overcome inequities'. Essentially, governments are focusing on resolving the immediate conflict rather than addressing the principles and contradictions rooted in the policies themselves.

A South African perspective

South Africa's coastline is more than 3,000 kilometres in length, stretching from the west coast border of Namibia to the east coast border of Mozambique (see Figure 1, page 289). It is estimated that approximately 10,000 species of marine plants and animals reside in these waters, with some being commercially exploited. Although South Africa's fisheries sector only contributes 0.25 per cent of the GNP, and the first-hand sale value amounts to R3.1 billion (£298 million),[2] a significant number of coastal communities rely on marine resources for their livelihoods (Chandler 2003). Direct employment in fisheries is estimated to be about 29,000, with a further 29,000 estimated to be small-scale fishers largely located on the south and east coasts. An examination of this latter group highlights many of the same triggers to non-compliance and conflict that have been identified in the cases above.

First, determining how laws are defined and by whom, is critical in the South African context. Prior to the 1998 Marine Living Resources Act (MLRA: the first post-apartheid fisheries legislation following the democratic elections of 1994), subsistence fishers in South Africa were not legally recognised. They had no legal rights to access resources and were either regulated as recreational fishers (if they complied with the stipulated bag or size limits) or they were considered poachers and were fined or jailed. The policies and practices of apartheid effectively excluded black[3] ethnic groups from accessing marine resources and participating in the fishing industry. The distribution of marine resources was heavily skewed in favour of the white, large-scale operators over the black, small-scale fishers (Hauck and Sowman 2005). This was the case in 1994 when only 0.75 per cent of the Total Allowable Catch of all species was allocated to blacks and of the 2,700 registered fishing boats, only 7 per cent were owned by blacks (Hersoug 2002). However, from the perspective of these subsistence or 'informal' fishers (historically disadvantaged individuals (HDIs)[4] who were denied legal access to resources under apartheid), they believed they had a 'right' to access marine resources that they lived adjacent to (Hauck *et al.* 2002). Furthermore, during the fisheries policy development process (which began in 1995), informal fishers took part in 'protest fishing', which was considered illegal fishing by government authorities but was a mechanism for the informal fishers to put pressure on government to allocate legal access rights (Hauck and Kroese 2006; Tarr 2000). Although the new fisheries policy (1997) and the resulting MLRA (1998) embrace the concepts of broadening access and addressing past inequities, the process of implementation has been cumbersome and slow (van Sittert *et al.* 2006).

The greatest challenge of government was to reallocate fishing rights in a way that would reflect the national population ratio of 80 per cent black and 20 per cent white. Government embarked on this process by redistributing access rights from apartheid-era companies to HDIs, in addition to encouraging the restructuring of historically established companies to increase ownership and management by HDIs. To a large extent, post-apartheid transformation has succeeded in broadening access to marine resources and 'blackening' the fisheries (van Sittert *et al.* 2006). For example, in 1994 access rights were almost exclusively owned by 300 white-owned companies but by 2004 rights had been allocated to 5,837 individuals and fishing companies. Small-scale fishers have been accommodated through the limited commercial or subsistence sectors, in which access rights have been allocated for the first time. Ownership among HDIs has risen from 0.75 per cent in 1994 to 62 per cent in 2004 (Branch and Clark 2006).

However, despite the significant increase in the numbers of new entrants in the fishing industry, and the inclusion of HDIs as rights holders or managers, the so-called 'transformation process' has also led to considerable conflict between traditional fishers and new entrants in coastal communities (van Sittert *et al.* 2006). Key to this conflict has been the fact that many *bona fide* fishers have not secured access to resources but have been out-competed by higher skilled or well-connected peers who also happen to fit the HDI status (Isaacs 2006). Thus, lack of a policy for applying, verifying and allocating rights to small-scale fishers often led to new entrepreneurs entering the fisheries at the expense of traditional fishers. As a result, in many cases, the informal fishers continue to fish with no legal rights. From the government's perspective however, the broadening of access rights has removed the political justification for illegal fishing (Tarr 2000) and has provided greater legitimacy for strengthening law enforcement (Hauck and Kroese 2006).

A second trigger related to non-compliance is conflicting policies. Fisheries in South Africa have been significantly affected by national and sectoral policies that have as their objectives social equity, economic stability and ecological sustainability. In most cases these objectives are contradictory, and in the fisheries they have 'neither been explicitly defined nor prioritised, leading to their fragmentary and contradictory implementation' (van Sittert *et al.* 2006). For example, in some cases, the goal of social equity has been favoured (through the process of broadening access rights), at the expense of economic stability (through the allocation of non-viable quotas or catch limits). In a survey of both small-scale and large-scale fishers in South Africa, rights holders with small quotas or catch limits were considered more likely to overfish, in some cases simply to 'break even' (Hauck *et al.* 2005). Similarly, government policies to encourage investment in the fisheries have often led to over-capitalisation and excess fishing effort, which has also been identified as a trigger for increased illegal fishing (Raakjaer-Nielsen and Hara 2006).

Third, research in South Africa has indicated that conflicts, specifically between fishers and the authorities, are often fuelled by the exclusion of fishers from management decision-making. Fishers have widely advocated for greater participation in decisions ranging from the allocation of rights to the framing of rules and regulations governing those rights (Hauck and Sowman 2003). This partnership arrangement between fishers and government to manage resources is known as co-management (Pomeroy and Williams 1994). Fishers in South Africa, with a wide diversity of circumstances, have strongly indicated that the perceived legitimacy of both the rules and the management authority were key to enhancing compliance in the fisheries (Hauck and Sowman 2003; Hauck *et al.* 2005). In essence, 'legitimacy' refers to what is considered 'fair' and, in the case of fisheries, resource users are more likely to comply with regulations that are considered appropriate by them and conform to their values and expectations (Hara 2003). The pattern of fishers transgressing rules that are not accepted by them has been documented (Jentoft 2000; Kuperan *et al.* 1997), and highlighted in recent South African research (Hauck *et al.* 2005).

Government's response to non-compliance

The three triggers to non-compliance discussed above reflect the normative approach to compliance, which recognises the important role that norms, morals and legitimacy of law and governance play in fisher decision-making (Raakjaer-Nielsen 2003; Hatcher *et al.* 2000; Gezelius 2002). Although these are not the only motivators of small-scale fisheries non-compliance in South Africa (Hauck and Sowman 2003; Hauck *et al.* 2002; Hauck *et al.* 2005; Godfrey *et al.* 2005), they have been highlighted in order to emphasise a shift that is taking place in understanding fisheries compliance and conceptualising appropriate responses to non-compliant behaviour (Raakjaer-Nielsen 2003; Hatcher *et al.* 2000; Gezelius 2002; Flewwelling *et al.* 2003). Traditionally, fisheries compliance literature was built upon Becker's neoclassical model of rational criminality (Becker 1968), arguing that non-compliance was determined by the balance of expected gains and losses from illegal activities (Sutinen and Andersen 1985; Anderson and Lee 1986). This instrumental approach argues that external influences (such as rewards and punishment) prompt individual fishers to act in their own immediate self-interest. Based on this perspective, fishers will choose to comply (or not) based on economic gains, the likelihood of detection and the severity of sanctions. Fisheries management systems worldwide have embraced this approach and governments often respond to non-compliance by increasing law enforcement efforts in order to increase the probability of detection and conviction (Raakjaer-Nielsen 2003; Sutinen *et al.* 1990).

In South Africa, there has been a clear move by the fisheries authority to strengthen law enforcement capacity as the primary objective and means to achieve compliance (Hauck and Kroese 2006). From 1999 a new institutional structure prioritised fisheries Monitoring, Control and Surveillance (MCS) to the level of a Chief Directorate within the national Department of Environmental Affairs and Tourism, also leading to a 400 per cent budget increase over the past decade. This has contributed to a highly skilled investigative team, the appointment of state prosecutors to focus on marine crime, a strengthening of inter-agency law enforcement cooperation and the procurement of four new patrol vessels. The focus has been on strengthening the 'policing' function of the fisheries directorate.

From a security perspective, illegal fishing has been prioritised by the government and a security discourse has been used to wage 'war' on poachers (Cape Argus, 28 February 2002). In fact, to some extent, fisheries regulation has been militarised, with a focus on intelligence gathering, use of high-tech surveillance gear (such as CCTV cameras in harbours and night goggles for patrolling) and the increased cooperation (and sometimes secondment) of military personnel. However, as has been highlighted by debates on securitisation and militarisation (Emmers 2004; Lutterbeck forthcoming), the implications of such responses raise serious questions.

Fishing for abalone in South Africa can be used as an example that highlights important concerns regarding this approach to fisheries compliance (Hauck and Sweijd 1999). Since 1995, this fishery has been identified by the media as the 'abalone war'. Due to the eruption of violent conflict, the government responded with armoured vehicles, helicopters and the army and navy to quell violence in coastal communities and to send a tough message to poachers. However, following the democratic elections of 1994, the country was immersed in policy transformation and fisheries reform (as discussed above). This had significant implications and potential opportunities for small-scale fishers who were significantly marginalised during apartheid (Hauck and Sowman 2003). As a result, amidst the violent confrontations with the authorities, abalone poachers were lobbying government for legal access to resources. Although there have subsequently been significant changes to the industry, broadening and redistributing access to the resource, the most concentrated government effort has been on policing and law enforcement. Despite this focus, the past decade has seen international organised crime syndicates becoming firmly entrenched in the abalone trade as the demand for this lucrative product in the Far East outweighs supply. In addition, the resource has been severely degraded, the commercial industry is likely to collapse in the next five years and coastal communities have been infiltrated by gangs and affected by social upheaval. The immediate response of government to the 'abalone war' was to *respond* to conflicts, without embracing a long-term approach that would impact on the fundamental triggers to the problem. Thus, the collapse of the fishery, the impact on the marine ecosystem and the socio-economic repercussions to fishers and coastal communities, are now almost inevitable (Hauck and Kroese 2006). This example raises concerns about the efficacy of the security label in fisheries, including the danger of reacting to non-compliance without considering the diversity of issues that may be influencing non-compliant behaviour.

Conclusion

The intention of this chapter was not to provide a comprehensive analysis of the underlying factors that lead to fisheries non-compliance, nor to engage in a critical reflection on the merits of green criminology. Rather, it has been to highlight that in our attempt (criminologists or otherwise) to understand environmental harm, and to develop appropriate responses to sustain both the environment and human livelihoods, a number of key points need to be considered.

First, in order to understand environmental harm, it is necessary to explore the role of formal law in defining what is 'illegal'. The definition of an environmental crime can be contested. For example, legal activities, such as forms of production to sustain industrial society, may have a more detrimental impact on the environment than activities deemed illegal by the state (Halsey and White 1998; Halsey 1997). Inversely, environmental harm may be perpetuated by declaring certain activities to be criminal. This is the case of criminalising indigenous people's rights of access to natural resources, and has been seen in the discussion of small-scale fisheries in South Africa. Rather than limiting resource exploitation, harm was exacerbated by 'protest fishing' which not only resulted in significant damage to resources but led to violent conflict and animosity between fishers and the authorities, which still exists in many places today (Hauck and Sowman 2003; Hauck and Kroese 2006).

This relates to the second point, namely that the understanding of environmental harm requires it to be situated in its social, economic, political and institutional contexts. There is broad acknowledgement that environmental protection and/or degradation are influenced by, among others, power, poverty, political structures, governance arrangements and economic growth and industrialisation (Elliot 2001; Najam 2004; Halsey 1997; Lynch and Stretesky 2003; White 2003). Research on fisheries compliance has only recently begun to explore the variety of relevant variables in its attempt to understand fishers' behaviour (Gezelius 2002; Raakjaer-Nielsen and Mathiesen 2002; Honneland 2000; Kuperan and Sutinen 1998; Roncin et al. 2004; Herrera 2004). These investigations have not only identified the complex interactions taking place in fisheries but have begun to highlight a concern for contemporary strategies to respond to, and address, resource over-exploitation and decline.

Thus, the approaches by governments to address environmental crime need to be investigated and understood. Examples of illegal fishing in this chapter clearly highlight that governments are reacting directly to immediate conflicts. It seems evident that a contextual understanding of non-compliance, as discussed above, is not embraced when government strategies are developed. Furthermore, governments are increasingly responding to illegal fishing with military-type responses (Gupta and Sharma 1990; Hauck and Sweijd 1999; McGoodwin 1987; Phyne 1992; White 2003). This has led to the 'militarisation' of fisheries to address access to resources, conflicts between sectors and over-exploitation. Elliott (2001) explains that this approach will do little to resolve the broader security challenges. Rather, there should be an attempt to 'respond to both cause and consequence in a way that emphasises preventive, collective and common security' (Elliott 2001: 450).

This leads to the overarching question of whether a small-scale fisheries 'crisis' should be labelled a security threat. Due to the diverse circumstances related to each fishery issue, and the local context where illegal fishing and conflicts emerge, it is not possible to answer this question with much confidence. Nonetheless, through a broad overview of the literature and an analysis of illegal fishing in South Africa, many small-scale fisheries issues, particularly those in poor, developing countries, could be considered threats to security within the non-traditional and human security paradigms. According to these approaches, the degradation of resources, the reliance of developing countries on fisheries for their livelihoods, the severity and impact of conflicts within and between fisheries sectors (sometimes violent in nature) and the inequality and imbalance of power and access to resources legitimise a 'security' label.

Emmer (2004) argues that it is the *response* that is the critical component of securitisation. Thus, he proposes that a full security action 'demands both a discourse of securitisation and the implementation of extraordinary measures' (p. 15). However, the danger of relying on security measures that are 'extraordinary' is that they may result in short-term impacts that impinge on human rights. The militarisation of fisheries, for example, legitimises governments' use of power, and sometimes violence, to respond to a so-called internal 'war'. This shift from democratic governance to a military model of crime control is taking place in America and Europe with respect to the militarisation of policing and criminal justice (Lutterbeck forthcoming; Kraska 1999). Similar concerns about the implications of this response have been highlighted by these authors. As Buzan *et al.* caution, one has to 'weigh the always problematic side effects of applying a mind-set of security against the possible advantages of focus, attention and mobilization' (1998: 29).

A concern with regard to the securitisation of fisheries is the recognition that this identifies issues as urgent, requiring decisive and immediate action (Buzan *et al.* 1998). Fisheries issues are extremely complex. As a result, it is believed that fisheries policies and management strategies need to be interdisciplinary, integrated and involve the participation of resource users if they are to be effective (Hauck and Sowman 2003; Berkes *et al.* 2001; Pinkerton 1994; Jentoft 1989). It is questionable whether these approaches can be incorporated into a security response that is reactionary.

It is necessary to question whether the act of securitising small-scale fisheries conflicts will in fact lead to appropriate responses. Although an immediate or urgent response may be necessary to react to violent conflicts in order to prevent immediate loss of life or safety, the response to fisheries non-compliance should rather focus on developing long-term strategies. As Buzan *et al.* (1998) state: 'National security should not be idealized. It works to silence opposition and has given power holders many opportunities to exploit "threats" for domestic purposes, to claim a right to handle something with less democratic control and constraint ... [hence], desecuritisation is the optimal long-range option' (p. 29).

As Emmers highlights, the challenge is to 'create a sense of urgency while still avoiding the possible excesses of securitisation' (2004: 83). Therefore, effort should be placed on identifying strategies to *politicise* these issues and to secure the necessary political will to implement policies that will prevent resource degradation and secure fisher livelihoods. So, what is the role of criminology in all of this? Well, surely criminologists have a role to play in heightening an understanding of the severity of environmental harm and its implications. However, as Garland and Sparks (2000: 190) aptly state, the discipline of criminology cannot 'monopolize' research on crime. Rather, criminology is one discipline – among many – with a role to play in politicising environmental harm and mobilising action that is appropriate to sustain resources and livelihoods.

Notes

1 This chapter is a revised and adapted version of a report completed for the WorldFish Center in 2004. Financial support to conduct this research is acknowledged from the South African National Research Foundation and the NORSA-South African regional cooperation agreement. The opinions expressed are those of the author and are not necessarily to be attributed to the organisations above.

2   As of February 2006, the exchange rate is R1: £10.40.
3   'Black' is a generic term in South Africa for those ethnic groups identified by apartheid policy as 'Indian', 'African' or 'Coloured'.
4   The term 'historically disadvantaged individual (HDI)' is a post-apartheid South African term used to refer to black South Africans (see note 3), the sector of the population disenfranchised by apartheid.

References

Akaha, T. (2002) Non-traditional Security Issues in Northeast Asia and Prospects for International Cooperation. Paper presented at 'Thinking outside the security box: non-traditional security in Asia: governance, globalisation and the environment'. United Nations University Seminar, United Nations, New York, 15 March 2002.

Anderson, L.G. and Lee D.R. (1986) 'Optimal Governing Instruments, Operation Level, and Enforcement in Natural Resource Regulation: The Case of the Fishery', *American Journal of Agricultural Economics*, 68 (3): 678–690.

Bennett, E., Neiland, A., Anang, E., Bannerman, P., Rahman, A.A., Huq, S., Bhuiya, S., Day, M., Fulford-Gardiner, M. and Clerveaux, W. (2001) 'Towards a Better Understanding of Conflict Management in Tropical Fisheries: Evidence from Ghana, Bangladesh and the Caribbean', *Marine Policy* 25: (365–376).

Berkes, F., Mahon, R., McConney, P., Pollnac, R. and Pomeroy, R. (2001) *Managing Small-scale Fisheries: Alternative Directions and Methods*. Ottawa: International Development Research Centre.

Branch, G. M. and Clark, B.M. (2006) 'Fish Stocks and their Management: The Changing Face of Fisheries in South Africa', *Marine Policy*, 30: 3–17.

Buzan, B., Waever, O. and de Wilde, J. (1998) *Security: A Framework for Analysis*. Boulder: Lynne Rienner Publishers.

Cardoso, P., Fielding, P. and Sowman, M. (2005) 'Overview and Analysis of Social, Economic and Fisheries Information to Promote Artisanal Fisheries Management in the BCLME Region – South Africa. Final report and recommendations'. Environmental Evaluation Unit, University of Cape Town, South Africa.

Chandler, T. (2003) *Fishing Industry Handbook: South Africa, Namibia and Mozambique*. Cape Town: George Warman Publications.

Commission on Human Security (2004) *Human Security Now*. New York: United Nations.

Curley, Melissa (2002) 'The Role of NGOs in Non-traditional Security in Northeast Asia', Centre of Asian Studies, University of Hong Kong, Hong Kong, Japan.

Elliott, L. (2001) 'Regional Environmental Security: Pursuing a Non-traditional Approach', in T.H. Tan and J.D.K. Boutin *Non-Traditional Security Issues in Southeast Asia*: 438–467. Singapore: Select Publishing.

Emmers, R. (2004) *Non-Traditional Security in the Asia-Pacific: The Dynamics of Securitisation*. Singapore: Eastern Universities Press.

FAO (1999a) 'Guidelines for the Routine Collection of Capture Fishery Data', FAO Fisheries Technical Paper No. 382. Rome: Italy.

FAO (1999b) 'Assessment of the World Food Security Situation', Report CFS: 99/2. Prepared for the 25th Session of the Committee on World Food Security, 31 May–2 June 1999. Rome: FAO.

FAO Advisory Committee on Fisheries Research (2003) A discussion paper for the ACFR Working Party on small-scale fisheries: draft. Prepared for the ACFR working party meeting October 2003, Bangkok, Thailand.

Flewwelling, P., Cullinan, C., Balton, D., Sautter, R.P. and Reynolds, J.E. (2003) 'Recent Trends in Monitoring, Control and Surveillance Systems for Capture Fisheries'. FAO Fisheries Technical Paper 415. FAO, Rome.

Garces, P.A.A. (2000) 'The Artisanal Fishery Reserve Zone: A Right Almost Forgotten by the State and Large Industry – the Case of Chile'. Paper presented at the Constituent Assembly of the World Forum of Fish Harvesters and Fishworkers, 2-6 October 2000, Loctudy, France.

Garland, D. and Sparks, R. (2000) 'Criminology, Social Theory and the Challenge of our Times', *British Journal of Criminology* 40: 189–204.

Gezelius, S. (2002) 'Do Norms Count? State Regulation and Compliance in a Norwegian Fishing Community', *Acta Sociologica* 45: 305–314.

Ghee, L.T. (1990) 'Conflict Over Natural Resources in Malaysia: The Struggle of Small-scale Fishermen', in L.T. Ghee and M.K. Valencia (eds), *Conflict over Natural Resources in South-east Asia and the Pacific*. Singapore: United Nations University Press.

Ghee, L.T. and Valencia, M.J. (1990) *Conflict over Natural Resources in South-east Asia and the Pacific*. Singapore: United Nations University Press.

Godfrey, B., Raemaekers, S. and Britz, P. (2005) 'Eastern Cape Province Abalone Resource Survey'. Final report prepared for Marine and Coastal Management (DEAT), February 2005.

Gupta, C. and Sharma, M. (2004) 'Blurred Borders: Coastal Conflicts between India and Pakistan', *The Economic and Political Weekly*, 3 July 2004.

Halsey, M. (2004) 'Against "Green" Criminology', *British Journal of Criminology*, 44: 833–853.

Halsey, M. (1997) 'Environmental Crime: Towards an Eco-human Rights Approach', *Current Issues in Criminal Justice*, 8 (3): 217–242.

Halsey, M. and White, R. (1998) 'Crime, Ecophilosophy and Environmental Harm', *Theoretical Criminology*, 2 (3): 345–371.

Harris, J.M., Sowman, M., Branch, G.M., Clark, B.M., Cockroft, A.C., Coetzee, C., Dye, A.H., Hauck, M., Johnston, A., Kati-Kati, L., Maseko, Z., Salo, K., Sauer, W.H.H., Siqwana-Ndulu, N. and Beaumont, J. (2002) 'The Process of Developing a Management System for Subsistence Fisheries in South Africa: Recognising and Formalising a Marginalised Fishing Sector in South Africa', *South African Journal of Marine Science*, 24: 405–424.

Haque, M.S. (2004) 'How Critical is "Environmental Security" as a Non-Traditional Security Issue in Northeast Asia?', in R. Thakur and E. Newman (eds), *Broadening Asia's Security Discourse and Agenda: political, social and environmental perspectives*: 174–195. Tokyo: United Nations University Press.

Hara, M. (2003) 'Co-management of Natural Resources: Theory and Attendant Assumptions,' in M. Hauck and M. Sowman (eds), *Waves of Change: coastal and fisheries co-management in South Africa*: 13–36. Cape Town: University of Cape Town Press.

Hatcher, A., Jabbar, S., Thebaud, O. and Bennett, E. (2000) 'Normative and Social Influences Affecting Compliance with Fishery Regulations', *Land Economics*, 76 (3): 448–62.

Hauck and Kroese (2006) 'Fisheries Compliance in South Africa: A Decade of Challenges and Reform 1994–2004', *Marine Policy* 30: 74–83.

Hauck, M., Hara, M. and Mather, D. (2005) Economic Aspects of MCS South Africa: compliance/legitimacy investigation, SADC Monitoring Control and Surveillance of Fishery Activities Programme, Lux Development SA.

Hauck, M. and Sowman, M. (eds) (2003) *Waves of Change: coastal and fisheries co-management in South Africa*. Cape Town: University of Cape Town Press.

Hauck, M. and Sowman, M. (2005) 'Coastal and Fisheries Co-management in South Africa: Is there an Enabling Legal Environment?', *South African Journal of Environmental Law and Policy*, 12 (1): 1–21.

Hauck, M., Sowman, M., Clark, B., Russell, E., Harris, J.M., Venter, A., Beaumont, J. and Maseko, Z. (2002) 'Perceptions of Subsistence and Informal Fishers in South Africa Regarding the Management of Living Marine Resources', *South African Journal of Marine Science*, 24: 463–474.

Hauck, M. and Sweijd, N.A. (1999) 'A Case Study of Abalone Poaching in South Africa and its Impact on Fisheries Management', *ICES Journal of Marine Science*, 56: 1024–1032.

Hersoug, B. (2002) *Fishing In a Sea of Sharks: Reconstruction and development in the South African fishing industry*. Delft: Eburon.

Hønneland, G. (2000) 'Compliance in the Barents Sea Fisheries. How Fishermen Account for Conformity with Rules', *Marine Policy*, 24: 11–19.

Isaacs, M. (2006) 'Small-scale Fisheries Reforms: Expectations, Hopes and Dreams for "A Better Life for All"', *Marine Policy*, 30: 51–59.

Jentoft, S. (1989) 'Fisheries Co-management: Delegating Government Responsibility to Fishermen's Organisations', *Marine Policy*, 13: 137–154.

Jentoft, S. (2000) 'Legitimacy and Disappointment in Fisheries Management', *Marine Policy*, 24: 141–8.

Kraska, P.B. (1999) 'Militarising Criminal Justice: Exploring the Possibilities', *Journal of Political and Military Sociology*, 27: 205–215.

Kuperan, K. and Sutinen, J.G. (1998) 'Blue Water Crime: Deterrence, Legitimacy and Compliance in Fisheries', *Law and Society Review* 32 (2): 309–37.

Kuperan, K., Abdullah, N.M.R., Susilowati, I., Siason, I.M. and Ticao, C. (1997) 'Enforcement and Compliance with Fisheries Regulations in

Malaysia, Indonesia and the Philippines.' Research report, Department of Natural Resource Economics, University Pertanian Malaysia.

Lutterbeck, D. (forthcoming) 'Blurring the Line: The Convergence of Internal and External Security in Western Europe', *European Security*.

Lynch, M.J. and Stretesky, P.B. (2003) 'The Meaning of Green: Contrasting Criminological Perspectives', *Theoretical Criminology* 7 (2): 217–238.

Manning, P. (2001) 'Small-scale Fisheries Management in Sub-Saharan Africa'. A background document for the FAO Expert Consultation on Small-scale Fisheries Management in Sub-Saharan Africa, December 2001. Accra, Ghana.

Mathew, S. (1990) 'Fishing Legislation and Gear Conflicts in Asian Countries', SAMUDRA Monograph No. 1. International Collective in Support of Fishworkers (ICSF), Chennai, India.

McGoodwin, J.R. (1987) 'Mexico's Conflictual Inshore Pacific Fisheries: Problem Analysis and Policy Recommendations', *Human Organization*, 46 (3): 221–232.

Myers, N. (2004) 'Environmental Security: What's New and Different?' Background paper for The Hague Conference on Environment, Security and Sustainable Development, 9–12 May 2004. The Hague, The Netherlands.

Najam, A. (2004) 'Sustainable Development and Human Security: Lessons from South Asia', in R. Thakur and E. Newman (eds) *Broadening Asia's Security Discourse and Agenda: political, social and environmental perspectives*: 147–173. Tokyo: United Nations University Press.

Phyne, J. (1992) 'Changes from Compliance to Deterrence among Federal Fishery Officers: An Atypical Case of Regulatory Policing?', *The Canadian Review of Sociology and Anthropology*, 29 (4): 524–534.

Pinkerton, E. (1994) Summary and conclusion. In C.L. Dyer and J.R. McGoodwin (eds), *Folk Management in the World's Fisheries: lessons for modern fisheries management*: 317–337. Colorado: University of Colorado Press.

Pomeroy, R.S. and Williams, M.J. (1994) *Fisheries Co-management and Small-scale Fisheries: A Policy Brief*. The Philippines: ICLARM.

Raakjaer-Nielsen, J. (2003) 'An Analytical Framework for Studying: Compliance and Legitimacy in Fisheries Management', *Marine Policy*, 27: 425–32.

Raakjaer-Nielsen, J. and Hara, M. (2006) 'A Review of the Transformation Process in the South African Industrial Fisheries', *Marine Policy*, 30: 43–50.

Raakjaer-Nielsen, J. and Mathiesen, C. (2003) 'Important Factors Influencing Rule Compliance in Fisheries Lessons in Denmark', *Marine Policy*, 27: 409–416.

Roncin, N., Bailly, D. and Raux, P. (2004) 'Determinants of Fishermen's Compliance – Lessons from a Coastal Fishery in Biscay Bay', in Y. Matsuda and T. Yamamoto (eds), 'What are responsible fisheries?', Proceedings of the 12th Biennial Conference.

Silvestre, G.T., Garces, L.R., Stobutzki, I., Ahmed, M., Valmonte-Santos, R.A., Luna, C.Z. and Zhou, W. (2003) 'South and South-east Asian coastal fisheries: their status and directions for improved management: conference synopsis and recommendations', pp. 1–40, in, G. Silvestre, L.R. Garces, I. Stobutzki, M. Ahmed, R.A. Valmonte-Santos, C.Z. Luna, L. Lachica-Alino, P. Munro, V. Christensen and D. Pauly (eds) 'Assessment, Management and Future Directions for Coastal Fisheries in Asian Countries.' WorldFish Center Conference Proceedings 67.

South, N. (1998) 'A Green Field for Criminology?', *Theoretical Criminology*, 2 (2): 211–233.

Squires, D., Omar, I.H., Jeon, Y., Kirkley, J., Kuperan, K. and Susilowati, I. (2003) 'Excess Capacity and Sustainable Development in Java Seas Fisheries', *Environment and Development Economics*, 8: 105–127.

Sunderlin, W.D. and Gorospe, M.G. (1997) 'Fishers' Organizations and Modes of Co-management: The Case of San Miguel Bay, Philippines', *Human Organization*, 56 (3): 333–343.

Sutinen J. and Kuperan, K. (1999) 'A Socio-economic Theory of Regulatory Compliance', *International Journal of Social Economics*, 26 (1/2/3): 174–193.

Sutinen, J.G., Rieser, A. and Gauvin, J.R. (1990) 'Measuring and Explaining Non-compliance in Federally Managed Fisheries', *Ocean Development and International Law*, 21: 335–72.

Sutinen, J. and Andersen, P. (1985) 'The Economics of Fisheries Law Enforcement', *Land Economics*, 61: 387–397.

Tan, A.T.H. and Boutin, J.D.K. (2001) *Non-traditional Security Issues in Southeast Asia*. Singapore: Select Publishing.

Tarr, R.J.Q. (2000) 'The South African Abalone (*Haliotis midae*) Fishery: A Decade of Challenges and Change', in A. Campbell (ed.) Spec. publ. *Fish. Aquat. Sci.* 130: 32–40.

Thakur, R. and Newman, E. (eds) (2004) *Broadening Asia's Security Discourse and Agenda: Political, social and environmental perspectives*. Tokyo: United Nations University Press.

UNDP (United Nations Development Programme) (1994) *Human Development Report 1994*. New York: Oxford University Press.

Van Sittert, L. and Hauck, M. (eds) (2006) Special edition on Fisheries Reform in South Africa, *Marine Policy*, 30: 1–110.

Van Sittert, L., Branch, G.M., Hauck, M. and Sowman, M. (2006) 'Benchmarking the First Decade of Post-apartheid Fisheries Reform in South Africa', *Marine Policy*, 30: 96–110.

White, R. (2003) 'Environmental Issues and the Criminological Imagination', *Theoretical Criminology*, 7 (4): 483–506.

Ziegler, J. (2004) 'The Right to Food', interim report of the Special Rapporteur of the Commission on Human Rights on the Right to Food, in accordance with General Assembly resolution 58/186.

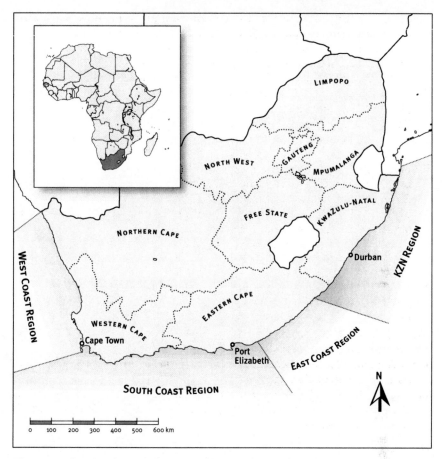

Figure 1 South Africa and its coastal regions

Webliography

Green criminology and the pursuit of social and ecological justice (Chapter 2)

Wilderness Society
www.wilderness.org.au/
A community-based environmental advocacy organisation whose mission is protecting, promoting and restoring wilderness and natural processes across Australia for the survival and ongoing evolution of life on Earth.

The SLAPP Resource Centre
www.slapps.org/
A non-profit organisation that serves as a resource to citizens, legislators, the media, lawyers, and the academic community on Strategic Lawsuits Against Public Participation ('SLAPPs').

European Environment Agency
www.eea.eu.int/
Provides information and reports for improving Europe's environment.

Environmental Justice Foundation
www.ejfoundation.org/
This organisation is dedicated to protecting the natural environment and the people and wildlife that depend upon it by linking environmental security, human rights and social need.

Environmental Bureau of Investigation
www.e-b-i.net/ebi/about_us.html
A Canadian-based community group committed to the investigation
and prosecution of environmental offenders and to the protection
of public resources through the application and enforcement of
environmental laws.

US Environmental Protection Agency
www.epa.gov
Provides detailed reports on environmental crimes and the regulatory
activities of this agency.

University of South Florida
www.cas.usf.edu/criminology/ccjcorpcrime.htm
Provides links to the major agencies in the USA responsible
for corporate behaviour in a number of fields, including the
environment, occupational health and safety, consumer protection,
and food and health.

Corpwatch
www.corpwatch.org
Has links to various reports and documents on corporate crime in
the USA and overseas, including environmental crimes.

Animal rights, animal abuse and green criminology
(Chapter 3)

Society and Animals Forum
www.societyandanimalsforum.org
Provides major resources for the field of human–animal studies,
including two journals (*Society & Animals* and *Journal of Applied Animal
Welfare Science*), and book reviews, bibliography and listserve.

Between the Species
www.cep.unt.edu/between.html
Between the Species is an online journal published by the Schweitzer
Center of the San Francisco Bay Institute/Congress of Cultures.

Animal Legal Defense Fund
www.aldf.org/action

The stated mission of the Animal Legal Defense Fund (ALDF) is to push the US legal system to end the suffering of abused animals. Has a bulletin board and current news.

ASA Section on Animals
www.asanet.org/sectionanimals/
Section on Animals of the American Sociological Association.

Humane Society of the United States
www.hsus.org
Includes descriptions of public-awareness campaigns, programmes, legislation, activist alerts, and educational publications.

Rutgers University School of Law Animal Rights Law Project
www.animal-law.org
Rutgers University School of Law Animal Rights Law Project. Contains law cases and materials, online handbooks, and selected essays.

Ecological and Cultural Change Studies Group
www.ecoculturalgroup.msu.edu/animalbiblio
Homepage of a Michigan State University study group. Links on 'Animals and Cultural Transformations' and 'Animal Studies Bibliographies'.

PETA
www.peta.org
Website of the activist organisation People for the Ethical Treatment of Animals.

Labelling animals. Non-speciesist criminology and techniques to identify other animals (Chapter 4)

Association for the Study of Animal Behaviour
http://asab.nottingham.ac.uk
ASAB provides Guidelines for the Treatment of Animals in Behavioural Research and Teaching.

Association of Veterinarians for Animal Rights
http://avar.org
Contains link to AVAR's 1988 position statement *Toe-clipping of Nonhuman Animals*.

International Society for Applied Animal Ethology
www.applied-ethology.org
Contains ISAE's 2003 *Guidelines for Ethical Treatment of Animals in Applied Animal Behaviour and Welfare Research.*

American Veterinary Medical Association
www.avma.org
Contains AVMA's 2005 *Position Statement on Branding of Animals.*

www.kevinwarwick.com
Homepage of Professor Kevin Warwick at the University of Reading, the first human to have a chip implanted.

American Society of Mammalogists (ASM)
www.mammalsociety.org
Provides access to *Guidelines for the Capture, Handling and Care of Mammals* (1998), prepared by the Animal Use and Care Committee.

www.oie.int/
World Organisation for Animal Health.

Vivisection: the case for abolition (Chapter 5)

www.tomregan-animalrights.com
Contains information about Tom Regan's books, the Culture and Animals Foundation, and The Tom Regan Animals Rights Archive at North Carolina State University.

The Animals' Voice Magazine
www.animalsvoice.com
Magazine containing information, news, campaigns, cases, etc. about violations of animal rights.

National Anti-vivisection Society
www.navs.org
Organisation dedicated to abolishing the exploitation of animals used in research, education and product testing.

American Anti-vivisection Society
www.aavs.org

AAVS's mission is to unequivocally oppose and work to end experimentation on animals and to oppose all other forms of cruelty to animals.

British Union for the Abolition of Vivisection
www.buav.org
BUAV's mission is to use peaceful means to end all animal experimentation. Coordinates with animal rights groups worldwide.

Debating 'animal rights' online: the movement–counter–movement dialectic revisited (Chapter 6)

Henry Salt
www.henrysalt.co.uk/
Introduction to Henry Salt (1851–1939), environmentalist, prison reformer and animal rights advocate.

Friends of Animals
www.friendsofanimals.org
The mission of the US-based Friends of Animals is to cultivate a respectful view of non-human animals, free-living and domestic, and to free animals from cruelty and institutionalised exploitation around the world.

www.lib.ncsu.edu/animalrights
The Tom Regan Animal Rights Archive documents the work of one of the foremost proponents of the rights view on issues such as 'animal experimentation', 'diet ethics', 'farmed animals' and 'animals in the news'. (See also the website entries for Chapter 4 above.)

Center for Animal Liberation Affairs
www.cala-online.org/
CALA publishes the interdisciplinary *Animal Liberation Philosophy and Policy Journal*. Its stated mission is to build up the common activist's knowledge of animal liberation while also appealing to academic specialists to address the important topic of animal liberation.

'At risk': climate change and its bearing on women's vulnerability to male violence (Chapter 7)

Center for Neighborhood Technology 'Travel Matters'
www.travelmatters.org/
A website for those interested in learning more about how travel habits and transportation choices affect global climate change. Offers interactive emissions calculators, online emissions maps, and educational items.

National Science Foundation 'Global Climate Change'
www.exploratorium.edu
A web-based science museum, the Exploratorium contains over 18,000 pages including hundreds covering environmental matters.

Pew Center on Global Climate Change
www.pewclimate.org
The Pew Center aims to provide 'credible information and innovative solutions in the effort to address global climate change'. Offers answers to FAQs and resource links.

Union of Concerned Scientists 'Global Warming'
www.ucsusa.org/global_warming/
A site devoted to climate policy and science with links elsewhere.

Crime, regulation and radioactive waste in the United Kingdom (Chapter 8)

Campaign for Nuclear Disarmament
www.cnduk.org
CND campaigns non-violently to rid the world of nuclear weapons and other weapons of mass destruction and this website provides briefings and contacts.

Committee on Radioactive Waste Management
www.corwm.org.uk
Website of an independent committee appointed by the UK Government to review options for managing UK radioactive wastes currently without an agreed long-term solution. CoRWM has been asked to consult widely.

Greenpeace UK
www.greenpeace.org.uk
Information on environmental campaigns and about opportunities to become actively involved in the work of this organisation.

International Atomic Energy Agency
www.iaea.org
The IAEA was set up as the world´s 'Atoms for Peace' organisation in 1957 under the auspicies of the United Nations family. The Agency works with Member States and partners 'to promote safe, secure and peaceful nuclear technologies'.

United Nations Interregional Crime and Justice Research Institute
www.unicri.it/
UNICRI is a United Nations body established in 1967 to support countries in developing crime prevention and criminal justice systems and this website provides a range of documentation and reports on activities.

Waste Watch UK
www.wastewatch.org.uk
An organisation promoting and encouraging waste reduction, reuse and recycling, working with community organisations and local and national government.

Food crime (Chapter 9)

Food Standards Agency
www.foodstandards.gov.uk
The website of the UK Food Standards Agency contains information about food labelling and other issues of food standards, along with research which it has carried out.

www.defra.gov.uk
The website for the UK Department for Environment, Food and Rural Affairs (DEFRA) contains information about agricultural and food issues and of research commissioned by the government. It also contains some useful statistics.

www.tradingstandards.gov.uk
This is the website of UK Trading Standards Officers, the main

agency dealing with food and drink. The site contains information about food standards and how to make a complaint.

www.which.co.uk
This is the website of the magazine of the British Consumers' Association which carries out regular investigations into a range of food issues.

www.ethicalconsumer.org
Ethical Consumer is a magazine looking at consumer issues, including food, from an ethical viewpoint. They carry out research on supermarkets and food manufacturers, providing scores from an ethical standpoint.

www.foe.co.uk/campaigns/realfood
The site of the British Friends of the Earth (FoE), which has been responsible for the Real Food Campaign directed against the introduction of genetically modified crops into the UK and is concerned about the exploitation of the environment by intensive agriculture.

www.wen.org.uk
The Women's Environmental Network is a campaign group concerned with a range of environmental issues as they affect women. The site contains reference to a range of information about food as well as cosmetics and household products.

www.foodcomm.org.uk
The Food Commission is a campaigning group around a range of food issues. The website contains useful lists of campaigns, publications and links to other relevant organisations.

The 'corporate colonisation of nature': bio-prospecting, bio-piracy and the development of green criminology (Chapter 10)

Amazonlink
www.amazonlink.org/biopiracy/
This site is maintained by an organisation representing rural producers in the Amazon region and aims to alert the public to the serious concerns and injustices that follow from patenting of local resources by outsiders.

Coalition against Biopiracy
www.captainhookawards.org/coalition
An informal group established in 1995, which organises the annual
Captain Hook Awards for Biopiracy.

Friends of the Earth
www.foe.org
Greenpeace
www.greenpeace.org/international/
Websites of two of the leading green activist organisations with
details of campaigns, other news and useful links.

Envirolink
www.envirolink.org/
Established in 1991, the EnviroLink Network is a non-profit
organisation providing access to thousands of online environmental
resources. A clearing house for relevant news and research reports
with discussion forum and section on animal concerns.

Green criminology in the United States (Chapter 11)

Environmental Justice Resource Center at Clark Atlanta University
www.ejrc.cau.edu/
Established in 1994, the Environmental Justice Resource Center
(EJRC) at Clark Atlanta University serves as a research, policy,
and information clearing house on issues related to 'environmental
justice, race and the environment, civil rights, facility siting, land use
planning, brownfields, transportation equity, suburban sprawl, and
Smart Growth'.

Green Action For Health and Environmental Justice
www.greenaction.org/index.shtml
Website of a community action group, Greenaction aims to 'mobilize
community power to win victories that change government and
corporate policies and practices to protect health and to promote
environmental justice'. Site provides reports of campaigns, alternative
energy news and other information.

Pesticide Action Network North American
www.panna.org/

Website of a network campaigning to promote health and protect communities and the environment, drawing attention to the environmental and public health impacts of the food system and pest management and the use of pesticides and genetically engineered crops.

Corporate Crime Reporter
www.corporatecrimereporter.com/

CorpWatch
www.corpwatch.org/

Eco-USA
www.eco-usa.net/
Summaries of chemical effects and toxicity levels, and locations of waste sites by state.

United States Environmental Protection Agency
www.epa.gov

The Association for the Study of Peak Oil and Gas
www.peakoil.net/

Environmental Research Foundation
www.rachel.org/home_eng.htm

Scorecard
www.scorecard.org/
An easy way to map and obtain information on environmental hazards across the US.

The Principles of Environmental Justice
www.toxicspot.com/env_justice/env_principles.html

Non-compliance in small-scale fisheries: a threat to security? (Chapter 12)

Environmental Evaluation Unit, University of Cape Town
www.egs.uct.ac.za/eeu
Provides information on fisheries compliance and fisheries management in South Africa.

The WorldFish Center
www.worldfishcenter.org
Resources related to fisheries conflicts and fisheries management/
co-management.

Institute of Defence and Strategic Studies
www.idss-nts.org/
An information hub for policy makers and researchers on non-
traditional security in Asia.

Institute for Environmental Security
www.envirosecurity.net
Interdisciplinary and international perspectives on environmental
security.

Commission on Human Security
www.humansecurity-chs.org/
United Nations Commission established following the 2000 Millennium
Summit for a world 'free of want' and 'free of fear'. Website provides
links to final report and other works from the Commission.

Index

Note: when added to a page number, 'f' denotes a figure and 't' denotes a table

abalone war 280
'acceptable error margins' 218–19
access rights, South African fisheries 277
act-utilitarianism 68
adulteration of food 57, 207, 213–14, 223, 224, 226
adverse events, FDA definition 121–2
aggression, pesticide exposure 261-2
aggression research 115
agriculture
    climate change and women's work 169
    see also cattle; farming
Altaire 212
American Medical Association (AMA) 144
American Society of Mammologists 96, 97–8
American Sugar Association 225
American Veterinary Medical Association 91
Amnesty International 177
amphibians, labelling 92, 98, 99
anarchist green theorists 22

anecdotal knowledge 241–2
animal abuse
    industries 141–2
    interhuman violence and 59, 62
    terminology 55, 77–8
    webliography 291–2
animal activists, and countermovements 143–6
animal behaviour 58, 94, 95
Animal Care and Use Committees 119
animal ethics 88
animal experimentation 68, 114, 120, 264–5
animal exploitation 74
animal identification 88-100
    consequences of not labelling 106
    dominance and colonisation 104-5
    webliography 292-3
    welfare and suffering 100-4
Animal Identification and Marking Systems, Inc 92
animal liberation 4–5, 73
Animal Liberation 67, 143, 151, 152

animal liberation movement
    14–16, 143
Animal and Plant Health Inspection
    Service (APHIS) 118–19
animal protectionism 143
animal rights
    counterforce to 154
    and green criminology
        55–6, 60–2, 72–8
    implication for vivisection 134
    reasons for having 130–1
    support for 65–72
    webliography 291–2
animal rights debate 140–54
    activists and their
        countermovements 143–6
    egalitarian positions 18
    Singer and 152–4
    social construction of deviance
        141–2
    social movements 140–1
    'terrorism' discourse 148–51
    webliography 294
    welfare and rights on 146–8
animal survival, radio collaring
    95
animal welfare 75
    animal rights debate 146–8
    emphasis on sentience 14
    identification marks
        consequences 92, 97
        suffering 100–4
    regulations 103
Animal Welfare Act (US) 117–18
animals
    as abused signifiers of
        interhuman violence 59–60
    emotional distancing from 71
    labelling see animal identification
    as property 56–8, 63
    as prototypes of criminality in
        humans 58–9
    social attitudes towards 75
    social justice 14–21
    subjective awareness 130–1

    as subjects of rights 68–71
    suffering see suffering
    see also human-animal continuity;
        human-animal interactions;
        human-animal relationships;
        human-animal studies;
        non-human animals
anthropocentrism 61
anthropogenic influences, global
    warming 163
anthropology, Lombrosian
    criminal 58
Anthrozoös 64
APHIS see Animal and Plant Health
    Inspection Service
Arctic ice, thinning of 163
ARD see animal rights debate
ASDA 219
Association for the Study of Animal
    Behaviour 97
Association of Veterinarians for
    Animal Rights 97
atavism 58
atom breakdown 190
Ayahuasca 239

backpack harnesses 94
badgers, radio collars 95
Bahro, Rudolph 7
balance of interests, environmental
    protection 235–6
Basel Convention 188
behaviour
    environmentally destructive
        250
    land ethic 253
    see also animal behaviour;
        criminal behaviour
behavioural training, of dogs 89
benefits argument, vivisection
    see vivisection
Bennett Woolf, Norma 147
Bentham, Jeremy 66–7, 70, 135
Bernard Mathews 219
bestiality 152

Between the Species 64
bio-patenting 237–9
    and bias 239–40
bio-piracy 230, 238–9
    green criminology 243–4
    post-colonial perspective 240–3
    webliography 297–8
bio-prospecting
    critics of 240
    webliography 297–8
biocriminology 58–9
biodiversity, exploitation of 238–9
biomass fuels, climate change
    and women's labour 169–70
biospherical egalitarianism 19–20
biotechnology industries
    230, 237–8
biotic community 22, 35
black fishing 212, 225
The Black Market 57
Blair, Tony 186, 199
body mass, and radio collars 95
Bookchin 22
'born criminal' 58
Bowden, Joseph 211
brain research 115
branding 90–1
brown issues 44, 45t
BSE (bovine spongiform
    encephalopathy) 74, 210, 215
burn research 115
Burns, Robert 256

cadmium 261
capacity to suffer 67, 70
capitalism 7, 9, 10, 11, 42, 58,
    250, 251, 254
'carbohydrate chemist' 213
carbon dioxide, atmospheric
    concentrations 163–4
care-giving, climate change and
    impact on women's 170
Carson, Rachel 259
Cartesian view, animals as moral
    equivalent of machines 66

The Case for Animal Rights 68, 73
casual labour, supermarkets use of
    225–6
'catastrophist' prediction 6–7
cattle
    identification and containment
        89–90, 92, 99–100
    intensive rearing regimes
        75–6
CCER *see* Civil Coordinator for
    Emergency Reconstruction
Chad 176, 177
The Challenge of Animal
    Rights 144
chemical branding 90
Chernobyl 186
Chicago School of Criminology 58
civic tradition, Scottish 66
Civil Coordinator for Emergency
    Reconstruction (CCER) 173
civil liberties, restriction of 8
civil war, Sudan, drought and 176
civilisation, preservation of 7
class, political economy of, and
    pollution exposure 262
class interests, versus planetary
    well-being 43
climate change 161–78
    extreme weather events 163–8
    gender-differentiated impacts
        161–2, 168–71
    and human activity 161
    violence against women after
        natural disasters 171–7
    webliography 295
climate models 165, 167
coastal sea flooding 168
Cohen, Carl 116, 132
commercial confidentiality 49
commercial interests, and
    economic disputes 238
Commission on Human Rights
    (UN, 1990) 48
Commission on Human Security
    271

Common Agricultural Policy (CAP) 210
communitarian views, of justice 3, 11–12, 13, 16
Compliance Classification Scheme 196
confidentiality, environmental planning 49
conflicts
  over logging practices 48
  over rights 44–7
  small-scale fisheries 274–6, 277–8
conflicts of interest, resource exploitation 236-7
consensus, radioactive waste disposal 192
consensus conference, radioactive waste management 198
conservation, green criminology 73
consumers, food poisoning 207
contagious diseases, animal transmission 74
contextual constructionism 141, 142
contingency 44
Convention on Biological Diversity (UN) 239
Copenhagen School 273
corporate colonisation, of nature 237–40
Corporate Crimes Against Animals 141–2
corporate perspective, environmental and health costs 249–50
corporate privateering 241
corporate violence, food crime as 223
CoRWM see House of Lords Science and Technology Committee
countermovements, animal protectionism 143–6
crimes
  against non-human animals 262–6
  see also environmental crime

criminal behaviour 261–2
criminal gangs, meat fraud 215–16
Criminal Justice Policy Review 251
Criminal Man 58
criminalisation
  cruelty to animals 75
  environmental dissent 50
  environmental harm 41
  vivisection 134–6
criminality, animals as prototypes of human 58–9
criminology
  analysis of environmental issues 37
  animals in 56–62
  food crime 222–6
  non-speciesist 87–8
  role, small-scale fisheries 283
  toxic hazards 259–61
  see also green criminology
crop eradication programmes 234
cross-species egalitarianism 18–21, 42
cultural change 13
cultural resources 25

Dade County 172–3
Dalgety Bay 189
dangerous manufacturing processes, inspections of 258–9
Darfur 176, 177
Darwin, Charles 130–1
deaths
  adverse drug reactions 122
  extreme weather 165, 167, 176
  food poisoning 207
  smoking 123
decision-making
  exclusion from, in fisheries 278
  radioactive waste disposal 197
defensive strategy 7
DEFRA 198
deglaciation 192
'delayed gratification' argument 6–7
deliberative democracy 47–50

delinquency 58
denial of rights 243
deprivations, animal harm as 70, 78
deviance, social construction of 141
difference principle 10-11
differential victimisation 37-8
Directive 35, environmental
   liability 193
disease, animal transmission of
   contagious 74
disease control, marking of
   animals 89
disposal, unfit meat and food
   packaging 223-4
disposal options, public opinion,
   radioactive waste 196-8
disposal sites, radioactive waste
   186-7
distancing, from animals 71
distribution
   across generations 13
   norms of just 17
distributional inequalities,
   environmental degradation 9-10
distributive justice 11, 12, 20, 23, 257
division of labour, gender and
   169-70
dogs, identification and training 89
Donoughue, Lord 145-6
The Dreaded Comparison 106-7
drought 166-7, 175-6
drug reactions, deaths due to
   adverse 122
drugs, transnational crime 233-4
Drupsteen, Honourable Justice 193
dumping, of hazardous waste
   188-90

ear tagging 93-4
Earth Community, rights of 40-1
ECC see eco-critical criminology
eco-bio-genocide, as transnational
   crime 233-4
eco-centric perspective 42-4
eco-centric values 21-2, 23-5

eco-crime see environmental crime
eco-critical criminology 251-6
eco-human rights 34
eco-philosophies 34
ecofascism 7
E.coli 216
ecological citizenship 34-5, 41-4, 46,
   47, 51
ecological 'enclosures' 27
ecological justice 38, 39t, 40, 41
ecological 'life support systems' 4
ecological limits 9
ecological rights 46
ecological risks, radioactive
   substances 192
ecological thought, and green
   criminology 33-5
economic globalisation 11-13
economic growth 10-11
economic structures, environmental
   crimes 263-4
ecotopia 5
egalitarianism, justice and 18-21,
   42, 132
El Niño 167
electric shock research 115
electronic monitoring, of offenders
   107
Elite Deviance 57
elite pursuit, environmental
   preservation 26-7
elites, discrimination of small-scale
   fisheries 276
ENERGIA see Global Network on
   Gender and Sustainable Energy
enlightened self-interest 44
Enlightenment 66
Environment Act (1995) 194
Environment Agency in England
   and Wales 194, 196
Environment, Food and Rural
   Affairs (EFRA) Committee 226
environmental crime 249-51
   approaches by governments to
      address 281-2

conceptualisation 35–6
criminological attention 34
economic structures 263–4
mobilisation of opinion 45
radioactive waste 187–90
environmental crisis 43, 265
environmental degradation 9–10,
42, 75, 272
environmental destruction 255, 264
environmental dissent,
criminalisation 50
environmental ethics 73, 88
environmental harm
conceptualisation 36, 39t
conflict over rights 44–7
construction of 40
contestation of 49
criminalisation 41
intensive rearing regimes 75–6
knowledge of 38
paper milling 249
political-economic arrangements
263–4
state responses to 36–7
understanding of 281
Environmental Health Services 207
Environmental Heritage Service
[Industrial Pollution and
Radiochemical Inspectorate]
in Northern Ireland 194
environmental historians 74
environmental issues
criminological work 37, 61
ecological citizenship as starting
point for deliberation 47
types of harm 44–5
environmental justice 37–8,
39–40, 39t
animal rights 76–7
United States 256–9
versus crimes and claims
of powerful 231–2
environmental law 198
environmental liability 193
environmental offenders 260–1

environmental planning 49
environmental policies 192, 251
environmental politics 73–4, 254
environmental pollution 258
environmental preservation 26–7
environmental protection 235–6
environmental racism 190, 256–9, 262
environmental regulations 250–1,
254, 260
environmental rights 35, 39,
231–2, 235
Environmental Rights Convention
– the Convention on Access to
Information, Public Participation
and Decision Making and Access
to Justice in Environmental
Matters 48–9
environmental security 272
environmental value, social
justice 27
environmental victimisation 34, 36,
37–8, 231, 236
environmental victimology 199
environmentalism 7–8, 72–8
environmentalists, division between
workers and 48
environmentally destructive
behaviour 250
EPICA see European Project for Ice
Coring in Antarctica
epizootics, marking of animals 88–9
equal consideration 17, 18, 20, 67–8
equality
challenging human and animal
132–3
of moral concern 15–16, 17, 19
of victims 37
ethic of care 71–2
ethical anti-naturalism 22–3
Ethyl Corporation 254
European Court of Human
Rights 193
European Project for Ice Coring in
Antarctica (EPICA) 163
evolutionary kinship 15

exemption orders, registration, radioactivity practices 195
experimentation
    on humans 114, 134–5
    see also animal experimentation
expertise 47–8
exploitation
    environmental problems 251
    see also animal exploitation; resource exploitation
eye research 115

family violence 59, 62
FARM 225
Farm Animal Welfare Coalition (FAWC) 148–9
Farm Bureau Federation (US) 149
farming, food crime 209–10
Faslane nuclear submarine base 195
FDA *see* Food and Drug Administration
federal enforcement, inadequacy of, vivisection 118–19
federal law, inadequacy of, vivisection 117–18
feminism, animals and ethic of care 71–2
field research, animal identification 91, 92, 93, 94
fisheries
    green criminology 73
    see also small-scale fisheries
fishing, food crime 21–12
fishing quotas 211–12
floods 167–8, 174–5
Flowers Report 191
food
    additives 207, 213, 226
    descriptions 217, 220–1
    fundamental right to 272
    genetically modified 220, 223, 232–3
    government departments covering 207–8
    hygiene 207, 216

labelling 217–21, 223
laundering 215–16
laws 207
poisoning 207, 216
retailers 225
scarcity 167
suppliers 225
Food Agency 106
food chain, offences 207
food crime 206–26
    adulteration 57, 207, 213–14, 223, 224, 226
    amount and variety of 208
    criminological significance 222–6
    food distribution 215–16
    food manufacture 213–14, 225
    food preparation 216–17
    food production 209–12
    misleading packaging 221–2
    offenders 208
    researching 208–9
    selling and marketing 217–21
    webliography 296–7
Food and Drug Administration 121–2
Food Standards Agency 214, 215, 216, 217, 218, 220
foot-and-mouth 210, 211
formal theories
    of justice 3
    see also Rawlsian justice
Foundation for Biomedical Research 144
freeze branding 90, 91
Friends of the Earth 225
FSA *see* Food Standards Agency
fur industry 145

Gaia 7, 8
Gandhi 135–6
gang masters 211, 224
gasoline additives 254–5
GATT 12
gender-differentiated impacts, climate change 161–2, 168–71

genetically modified foods 220, 223, 232–3
glacial retreat 163, 167
glaciation 192
glacier lake outburst floods 167
glasnost 43
global corporations
  and environmental politics 254–5
  political lobbies 225
Global Inventory of Radioactive Wastes in the Marine Environment 189–90
Global Network on Gender and Sustainable Energy (ENERGIA) 178
global positioning system (GPS) 90
global surface temperature 163
global transboundary issues 39t
global warming
  environmental harm 75, 76, 77
  see also climate change
globalisation 11–12, 206, 224, 230–1, 233–4, 255
Gorbachev, President 43
Gorinsky, Dr Conrad 238–9, 240
government departments, covering food 207–8
government strategic action, and public policy 44
Grand Forks flood (1997) 175
Green Belt Movement 178
Green Bible 58
green collar offenders 261
green criminology
  animal rights 55–6, 60–2, 72–8
  bio-prospecting and bio-piracy 243–4
  challenges, achievements, prospects 231–7
  characteristics 230
  and ecological thought 33–5
  expansion of democratic impulse 51
  interdisciplinary, comparative approach 243–4

public accountability 51
radioactive waste 198–9
social justice, webliography 290–1
United States see United States
see also environmental crime
green issues 44, 45t
green movement 4–5, 6–30
green society 5
green utopia 29–30
greenheart nut 238–9
greenhouse gases, rise in levels 163–4, 165
Greenpeace 189
The Greening of Criminology 60
greenwashing 49
Gruen, Lori 153
Guide for the Care and Use of Laboratory Animals (US) 96
Gunns20 case 50

Hammurabi's Code 88
Handling the 20 Toughest Animal Rights Assertions 149
harm(s)
  caused by animal research 115–16
  caused by corporate crimes 142
  to animals 70
  vivisection 119–23
  see also environmental harm
hazardous landfills, US study into 257
hazardous waste, dumping of 188–90
health
  and environmental justice 37
  see also public health
Health and Safety at Work Act (1974) 194
Health and Safety Executive 194
healthy environment, global corporations' contradiction to 254–5
heat waves 164–5
hierarchy of needs or values 6, 7

Himalayas, glacier lake outburst
floods 167
horses, identification of 92
hot dog ingredients 57–8
hot-iron branding 90, 91
House of Lords Science and
Technology Committee
(CoRWM) 192–3, 197
housing construction, environmental
damage 264
human beings 62–3
Human Development Report
(UNDP) 271
human intervention 41–4, 47
human rights
animal rights as devaluation
of 71
basis of 128–9
eco-crime as violation of 187
human vivisection 124–5
relationships between
non-human and 45
see also eco-human rights;
Universal Declaration of
Human Rights
human security 271
human vivisection 124–5
human-animal continuity 4, 15–16,
17–18
human-animal relationships 15, 44,
73–4, 87, 144, 146, 147
human-animal studies 60, 64–5
human-centred notions, rights and
justice 38–9
humane interventions 75
'Humanity Dick' Martin's Act to
Prevent the Cruel and Improper
Treatment of Cattle 75
humans
animals as prototypes of
criminality in 58–9
deaths see deaths
environmental degradation 42
environmental justice 37
experimentation on 114, 134–5

exploitation by see exploitation
harm to, reliance on vivisection
122–3
labelling 106–7
obligation to biotic community 35
hunting ban 145–6
Hurd Deep 189
Hurricane Andrew 172–3, 178
Hurricane Katrina 166
Hurricane Mitch 173–4
hurricanes 165–6, 172–4
husbandry see cattle

'I Care' programme 149
IACUCs see Animal Care and Use
Committees
ice cores, data from 163–4
'illegal', defining 281
illegal fishing 280, 282
illegal immigrants, food crime
211, 224
implant migration 100
In a Different Voice 72
India-Pakistan, sea border conflicts
274–5
indigenous peoples
commercialisation of products
incorporating traditional
knowledge 239–40
environmental victimisation 231
expertise 47–8
women and fellowship with 71–2
see also Inuit
individualism, and animal rights 77
inequality, globalisation and
extensive 255
inflictions, animal harm as 70, 78
institutionalisation, power
relations 12
institutionalised insensitivity, to
right and wrong 232
instrument effect 101, 102
instrumentally rational action 25
intellectual property 237–40
intensive rearing regimes 75–6

Interagency Research Animal Committee (US) 96
interconnectedness, of nature 44
interdependence, human-animal 15
interests
    avoidance of suffering 67
    see also balance of interests; class interests; conflicts of interest, commercial interests; social interests
intergenerational distribution 13
intergenerational responsibility 39
interhuman violence 59–60, 62
International Atomic Energy Agency 189–90
international laws 188, 254
International Society for Applied Ethology 97
international trade agreements 12
Interregional Crime Research Institute (UN) 188
intersubjective sociologising, value judgements 24
Introduction to the Science of Sociology 58
Inuit 76–7
invasive research 119
invisible fence system 89
Ionising Radiations Regulations (2000) 194
Iraq, cities exposed to radiation 190

Janjawid 176
justice
    perfectionist theory of 69
    see also ecological justice; environmental justice; social justice

Kessler, David 122
Krugman, Saul 126–8, 128–9

labelling
    animals 88–100
        webliography 292–3

food 217–21, 223
humans and other animals 106–7
laboratory experimentation see animal experimentation
LACS see League Against Cruel Sports
'land ethic' 253
'land use planning process' 197
language, speciesism and power of 62–4
larval ticks, tagging of mice 93
lawsuits, against tagging 94
lead 261
League Against Cruel Sports (LACS) 145
legal rights 68
legalised adulteration, food 207, 223, 224
legislation
    green criminology 234–7
    labelling 218, 220
    see also food laws; individual acts; international laws; patent law; regulations
legitimacy, fisheries 278–9
'limits to growth' argument 9
litigation, used to silence critics 49–50
local democratic governance 254
logging practices 48
Lombrosian criminal anthropology 58
London Convention on the Prevention of Marine Pollution by Dumping of Wastes and Other Matter (1972) 188
Lovelock, James 7–8

Maathai, Wangari 178
Maggot Pete 215–16
magnesium 255
Malaysia, impact of export-oriented fisheries 275–6
male violence, climate change and women's vulnerability to 162, 171–7

Marine Living Resources Act (1998) 276

marine pollution 189

marketing, food crime 217–21

Marquardt, Kathleen 147

Marx, Karl 19

meaning, focus on, in research 142

meat fraud 207, 214, 215–16, 224

Meat Hygiene Service (MHS) 207, 214

meatpackers, deceptive practices 57–8

Mechanically Recovered Meat (MRM) 213

media, portrayal of women after natural disasters 178

Meeting the Animal Rights Challenge 149

mental life, animals 69

mercury 261

mice, labelling 92, 93

micro-level processes 22

microchip identification 99–100

military research 115

Miller, Loren 239

misleading packaging 217–18, 221–2

misothery 63

Missouri Coalition Against Domestic Violence 174–5

Missouri flood (1993) 174–5

MMT (methylcyclopentadienyl manganese tricarbonyl) 254–5

Moby Dick 75

Monitoring, Control and Surveillance (MCS) 279–80

moral agents 68–9

moral capital, social movements 140

moral claims, eco-centric writers 21–2, 24

moral community 40, 69

moral concern, equality of 15–16, 17, 19

moral egalitarianism 42

moral patients 17, 20–1, 69

moral philosophers 66

moral rights 68

moral rules 40

Morality's Progress 75

movement-countermovement dialectic, ARD 140–54, 294

multinational corporations, weakening, environmental regulations 254

mutilatory identification 97

National Animal Interest Alliance (NAIA) 146–7

National Assembly for Wales 208

National Center for Atmospheric Research (NCAR) 165, 166

natural background radiation 190

natural disasters
  fostered by climate change 164
  violence against women after 171–7

natural environment, humans and 44

natural limits
  ecological-support systems 4
  and social justice 6–14

natural objects, valuation of 24

nature
  corporate colonisation of 237–40
  dynamic concept of 44
  eco-centric's regard for 24–5
  protection of 26–7

NCAR *see* National Center for Atmospheric Research

neo-liberal ideology 10

Nestlé 218

Netherlands
  animal identification 96–7
  food crime 215

New Right 10

New Zealand Royal Commission on Genetic Modification 233

'no proof of concept' 197

non-anthropocentric justice 21–8

non-anthropocentric values 5

non-compliance, fisheries' laws
273, 276, 278
    government response, South
    Africa 279–80
non-human animals
    green criminology 262–5
    in sociology 65
    term 64
    see also animals
non-human rights 45
non-human-centred notions, rights
    and justice 38–9
non-speciesist criminology 87–8
non-therapeutic experimentation
    114, 134–5
non-traditional security 271–2
normative regulation, social life 23
norms, of just distribution 17
North American Free Trade
    Agreement (NAFTA) 12, 254
Not In My Backyard 40
NPPC Handbook 149
nuclear fission power 191
Nuclear Installations Act (1965)
    194
nuclear power plants, exemptions
    from registration 195
nuclear reactors, dumping at sea
    188–9
nuclear weaponry 186

objectification, labelling and 107
ocean surface temperatures 165
offences
    food chain 207
    radioactive waste 195–6
offenders
    electronic monitoring 107
    food crime 208
    sentencing of environmental
    260–1
Official Information Requests 195
oil industry, harms to non-humans
    142
olives, subsidy frauds, Spain 211

oppressed groups, labelling of 106–7
oppression, women's 71
organic embodiment 15
organised criminals
    abalone trade 280
    food crime 224
the 'other' 21, 61, 63, 64, 71

packaging, food crime 217–18, 221–2
pain, infliction of 67, 68
Pakistan-India, sea border conflicts
    274–5
Palmer Drought Severity Index 166
paper manufacturing, green crime
    249–50
Passive Integrated Transponder
    98–100
patent law 240
patenting see bio-patenting
paternalism 18
patriarchal societies 71
People for the Ethical Treatment of
    Animals 147
perestroika 43
perfectionist theory, of justice 69
pesticide exposure, aggression 261–2
pharmaceuticals 242–3
philosophes 66
photographic tricks, food crime 221
pictorial images, food crime 221
planetary well-being, versus class
    interests 43
'platform' of deep ecology 19–20
policing institutions, animal
    cruelty 75
political lobbies, global giants 225
political values, abandonment of
    cherished 8
political-economic arrangements,
    environmental harm 263–4
pollution exposure
    political economy of race and
    class 262
    see also environmental pollution;
    marine pollution

polychlorinated biphenyls 256
poor and minority neighbourhoods, environmental injustice 258–9
Pork Producers' Council 149
post-colonial perspective, bio-piracy 240–3
post-structuralist rebuke, reformist environmentalism 60–1
Potts, Justice 194–5, 199
poverty, women and 170–1
power relations, institutionalisation 12
powerful, environmental justice and rights versus claims of 231–2
precautionary principle 104, 193
predatory-prey relationships 22
Prescription for Disaster: The Hidden Dangers in Your Medicine Cabinet 122
preservatives 213
pressure groups, animal marking 102–3
prisoners, tattooing of 107
pro-animal movement 66, 149
process, focus on, in research 142
profits, extracted by supermarkets 225
progression thesis 59–60
property, animals as 56–8, 63
protection, green criminology 234–7
psychological complexity, animal rights 131
public accountability, green criminology 51
public health, animal experimentation 120
public opinion
    determination of crime or harm 45
    radioactive waste disposal 196–8
public perceptions
    animal rights advocates 143
    vivisection 135

public policy, and government strategic action 44
Putting People First (PPF) 147

R v Secretary of State for the Environment and Others, ex parte *Greenpeace Ltd and another* [1994] 4 All ER 352 194
race *see* environmental racism
radiation research 115
radio collaring 94–6
radio tracking 94
radioactive environmental racism 190
radioactive markers 100–1
radioactive substances, ecological risks 192
Radioactive Substances Act (1993) 194, 195–6
radioactive waste
    disposal areas 186–7
    eco-crime and 187–90
    global implications 199
    green criminology 198–9
    offences and regulation enforcement 195–6
    public opinion and disposal actions 196–8
    risk management 199
    storage 191, 200
    UK *see* United Kingdom
Radioactive Waste Management Advisory Committee 191, 192
radionuclides 190
Rags 153
Ramsay, Gordon 216
rape, in refugee camps 177
Ratner, Gerald 120
Rawlsian justice 3, 10–11, 12–14, 16, 17, 27–8
Reagan administration 233
receptacle view, of value 68–9
redistributive public provision 11
reformist environmentalism 60–1
refugee camps, violence against women 177

Regan, Tom 68–71, 78, 143–5
regulations
    animal welfare 103
    environmental 250–1, 254, 260
    green criminology 234–7
    radioactive, UK 191, 193–8
    see also legislation
'regulatory capture' 236
reptiles, toe amputation 98
rescue and relief initiatives,
    gender-differentiated
    vulnerabilities 178
research
    eco-critical criminology 256
    environmental justice 257
    ideology, vivisection 123
resource depletion 272
resource exploitation 36–7, 230,
    236–7, 238–9
respect, for the 'other' 21
respectability, social movements
    140–1
respectful treatment, animals'
    right to 69
rights
    denial of 243
    of the Earth Community 40–1
    environmental harm and conflict
        over 44–7
    green criminology 234–7
    human and non-human-centred
        notions 38–9
    human security 271
    to food 272
    to a safe environment 193–4
    see also animal rights; human
        rights; non-human rights
risk, discursive modification
    of 232–3
risk management 37
rodents, toe amputation 96–7
Roses, Allen 120–1
Royal Commission on
    Environmental Pollution (1981)
    191, 199

Royal Society for the Prevention of
    Cruelty to Animals 75
Russia, dumping and transportation
    of toxic waste 188–9

safe environment, right to 193–4
Sainsbury's 218
A Sand County Almanac 73
scarcity 23
scientific knowledge, environmental
    policies 191–2
Scotland, black fishing 212
Scottish Environment Protection
    Authority 194
Scottish Executive 208
Scripps Institution of Oceanography
    165
sea, dumping of toxic waste 188–91
sea border conflicts, Pakistan and
    India 274–5
sea-level rise 168
seal hunting 76–7
seals, labelling of 91
securitisation, of fisheries 273, 274,
    282, 283
security
    non-traditional 271–2
    small-scale fisheries 272–4
selection procedures, inadequacy
    of, vivisection 119
self-regulation, radioactive waste
    management 200
self-restraint 20–1
sell-by dates 214
selling, food crime 217–21
sentencing, environmental offenders
    260–1
sentience 14
sexism, speciesism and 63
shock collars 89
silences, environmental planning 49
Silent Spring 259
Singer, Peter 19, 67–8, 71, 151–4
slaves, labelling of 106–7
small-scale fisheries 270–83

conflicts within 274–5
crisis as a security threat 282
impact of export-oriented
    fisheries 275–6
marginalisation by governments
    275
militarisation of 282
security 272–4
South African perspective 276–80
webliography 299–300
social attitudes, towards animals 75
social interests, contestation of
    environmental harm 49
social justice 3, 6–30, 224, 290–1
social life, normative regulation 23
social movements 140
social relationships, marked
    animals 101
social thought, green movement 4–5
social values, abandonment of
    cherished 8
socialism 7
Society & Animals 64, 65
socio-economic characteristics,
    proximity to hazardous waste
    sites 257–8
sociology 58, 65
South Africa, small-scale fisheries
    276–80, 289f
Spain, food crime 207, 211, 212
species egalitarianism 132
speciesism 38, 62–4, 132–3
state
    commitment to protect
        citizens from environmental
        victimization 36, 236
    response to environmental harm
        36–7
state formation, human-animal
    interaction 74
state-sponsored piracy 240–1
Stockholm Declaration on the
    Human Environment 39
Strategic Lawsuits Against Public
    Participation 50

stress research 115
strict/strong program
    constructivism 142
subcutaneous VIP chips 107
subjective awareness, animals 130–1
subjective interests, environmental
    crisis debates 265
subjects-of-a-life 14, 69, 129, 131
subsidies frauds, food production
    210–11
Sudan 1 additive 213, 226
Sudan, impacts of climate change
    176, 177
SUERC nuclear research institute
    195
suffering
    animal identification 97, 100–4
    utilitarianism on 67, 70
supermarkets 210, 225–6
survivalism 6, 7, 9
suspect animals, unmonitored
    animals as 106
sustainability, justice by 9–14

tagging 93–4
tail collars 94–5
tail tattooing 92
take-away sector, food crime 216–17
Tasmania, forest debates 48, 49
tattoo hammers 92–3
tattooing 91–3, 107
temperatures, increases in
    average 164
terns, implementation of
    transponders 99
terrorism
    discourse, animal rights debate
        148–51
    erosion of civil liberties 8
Tesco 214
theriocide 63
Three Mile Island 186
toe amputation 96–8
toe clipping 92
totality, of nature 44

toxic exposures, criminal behaviour
261–2
toxic hazards
criminological perspective
259–61
proximity to low income and
minority communities
257–8
Toxic Substance Control Act 256
toxic waste, dumping at sea
188–90
traceability, of cattle 89
trade agreements 12, 254
Trade Related Aspects of Intellectual
Property Rights (TRIPS) 237, 239
Trading Standards 207, 220
traditional knowledge 242
transnational crime,
eco-bio-genocide as 233–4
transponders, identifying animals
with 98–100
trawler operators, overfishing
conflicts between 275–6
'trickle down' model 10
TRIPS see Trade Related Aspects of
Intellectual Property Rights
tumbling 215

undesirable experiences, FDA
definition 121-2
United Church of Christ 257
United Kingdom
enforcement agencies, food
regulations 207
radioactive waste 190–3
regulations and management
193–8, 200
webliography 295–6
United Kingdom Atomic Energy
Agency 189
United Nations
Commission on Human Rights
(1990) 48
Convention on Biological
Diversity (CBD) 239

Development Programme
(UNDP) 170, 271
Environmental Programme
(UNEP) 167, 190
Interregional Crime Research
Institute 188
United States
environmental degradation and
death of Inuits 76–7
green criminology 248–66
conclusions 266
crimes against non-humans
262–5
a developing idea 249–51
eco-critical criminology 251–6
environmental justice 256–9
neglect by criminologists 248
toxic exposures and criminal
behaviour 261–2
toxic hazards, toxic crimes
259–61
webliography 298–9
radioactive environmental
racism 190
vivisection
inadequacy of federal
enforcement 118–19
inadequacy of federal law
117–18
Universal Declaration of Human
Rights 134
universal human interests 43
universalistic view, of justice 13
upper class, in environmental
research 232
utilitarianism, suffering and equal
consideration 66–8

valuation, of natural objects 24
value, receptacle view of 68–9
value-rational action 25
values
abandonment of cherished 8
construction of environmental
harm 40

eco-centric 21–2, 23–5
  hierarchy of 6, 7
  integration of social justice and
    environmental 27
values war, animal rights debate
  143–4
veganism 142
violence *see* corporate violence;
  interhuman violence; male
  violence
violent conflicts, in fisheries 275–6
VIP chips 107
viral hepatitis experiments 126–7
vivisection 114–36
  benefits argument 116–24
    comparison of benefits and
      harms 119–20
    failure to justify 126
    inadequacy of federal
      enforcement 118–19
    inadequacy of federal law
      117–18
    inadequacy of selection
      procedures 119
    overestimation of benefits
      120–1
    research ideology 123
    summary 123–4
    underestimation of harms
      121–3
  criminalisation 134–6
  defence of 116
  webliography 293–4
  see also human vivisection

Wapishana tribe 238–9
Ward Transformer Company 256
Warren County, EJ movement
  256–7

waste *see* radioactive waste; toxic
  waste
waste industry, corruption in 232
waste management laws 255
water
  adulteration of food 207, 213,
    214, 215
  climate change and women's
    labour 169–70
water voles, decline of female 95
weather, climate change and
  extreme 161–8
Weber, Max 25
webliography 290–300
welfare
  non-traditional security 271–2
  see also animal welfare
welfarism 67
Welsh Food Fraud Co-ordinating
  Unit 208
Which? studies 216, 218, 219,
  220, 221
white issues 44, 45t
white-collar crimes, meat 57
Willowbrook State Hospital 126-8
wolves, Yellowstone Park 105
women
  climate change
    gender-differentiated impacts
      161–2, 168–71
    violence against, after natural
      disasters 171–7, 295
  oppression of 71
workers, and environmentalists,
  division between 48

Yellowstone Park 105

zemiology 187